Soft War

Just war theory focuses primarily on bodily harm, such as killing, maiming, and torture, while other harms are often overlooked. At the same time, contemporary international conflicts increasingly involve the use of unarmed tactics, employing "softer" alternatives or supplements to kinetic power that have not been sufficiently addressed by the ethics of war or international law. Soft war tactics include cyber warfare and economic sanctions, media warfare and propaganda, as well as non-violent resistance as it plays out in civil disobedience, boycotts, and "lawfare." While the just war tradition has much to say about "hard" war – bullets, bombs, and bayonets – it is virtually silent on the subject of "soft" war. *Soft War: The Ethics of Unarmed Conflict* illuminates this neglected aspect of international conflict.

Michael L. Gross is Professor and Head of the School of Political Science at the University of Haifa, Israel. He specializes in applied normative theory, military and medical ethics, asymmetric war, and non-kinetic warfare. He is the author of *Ethics and Activism* (Cambridge University Press, 1997); *Bioethics and Armed Conflict* (2006); *Moral Dilemmas of Modern War* (Cambridge University Press, 2010); *Military Medical Ethics for the 21st Century* (with Don Carrick, 2013); and *The Ethics of Insurgency* (Cambridge University Press, 2015). He has lectured widely on battlefield and military medical ethics at defense centers in Israel, the United States, and Europe.

Tamar Meisels is a political theorist and Associate Professor in the Political Science Department at Tel Aviv University. She earned her D.Phil. in Politics from Oxford University in 2001. Her primary research and teaching interests include liberal nationalism, territorial rights, and the philosophical questions surrounding war and terrorism. She is the author of *Territorial Rights* (2005 and 2009) and *The Trouble with Terror: Liberty, Security, and the Response to Terrorism* (Cambridge University Press, 2008) and Contemporary Just War: Theory and Practice (2017).

Soft War

The Ethics of Unarmed Conflict

Edited by
MICHAEL L. GROSS AND TAMAR MEISELS

Foreword by
MICHAEL WALZER

CAMBRIDGE
UNIVERSITY PRESS

CAMBRIDGE
UNIVERSITY PRESS

University Printing House, Cambridge CB2 8BS, United Kingdom

One Liberty Plaza, 20th Floor, New York, NY 10006, USA

477 Williamstown Road, Port Melbourne, VIC 3207, Australia

4843/24, 2nd Floor, Ansari Road, Daryaganj, Delhi – 110002, India

79 Anson Road, #06–04/06, Singapore 079906

Cambridge University Press is part of the University of Cambridge.

It furthers the University's mission by disseminating knowledge in the pursuit of education, learning, and research at the highest international levels of excellence.

www.cambridge.org
Information on this title: www.cambridge.org/9781107132245
DOI: 10.1017/9781316450802

First published 2017

Printed in the United States of America by Sheridan Books, Inc.

A catalogue record for this publication is available from the British Library.

ISBN 978-1-107-13224-5 Hardback
ISBN 978-1-107-58478-5 Paperback

Contents

List of Contributors — *page* vii
Foreword — xi
Preface — xv

INTRODUCTION

Soft War: The Ethics of Unarmed Conflict — 1
Michael L. Gross and Tamar Meisels

DEFINITIONS AND META VIEWS

1 Defining War — 16
Jessica Wolfendale

2 Coercion, Manipulation, and Harm: Civilian Immunity and Soft War — 33
Valerie Morkevičius

ECONOMIC WARFARE

3 Reconsidering Economic Sanctions — 49
Joy Gordon

4 Conditional Sale — 63
Cécile Fabre

CYBER WARFARE, MEDIA WARFARE, AND LAWFARE

5 State-Sponsored Hacktivism and the Rise of "Soft" War — 77
George Lucas

6 Media Warfare, Propaganda, and the Law of War — 88
Laurie R. Blank

7 The Ethics of Soft War on Today's Mediatized Battlespaces 104
Sebastian Kaempf

8 Abuse of Law on the Twenty-First-Century Battlefield: A Typology of Lawfare 119
Janina Dill

NONVIOLENCE

9 Unarmed Bodyguards to the Rescue? The Ethics of Nonviolent Intervention 134
James Pattison

10 How Subversive Are Human Rights? Civil Subversion and the Ethics of Unarmed Resistance 152
Christopher J. Finlay

11 Bearers of Hope: On the Paradox of Nonviolent Action 166
Cheyney Ryan

HOSTAGE TAKING AND PRISONERS

12 A Cooperative Globalist Approach to the Hostage Dilemma 184
Ariel Colonomos

13 Kidnapping and Extortion as Tactics of Soft War 200
Tamar Meisels

CONCLUSION

14 Proportionate Self-Defense in Unarmed Conflict 217
Michael L. Gross

References 233

Index 258

Contributors

Laurie R. Blank is a clinical professor of law and the Director of the International Humanitarian Law Clinic at Emory University School of Law, where she teaches the law of armed conflict and works directly with students to provide assistance to international tribunals, non-governmental organizations, and law firms around the world on cutting edge issues in humanitarian law and human rights. Professor Blank is the co-author of *International Law and Armed Conflict: Fundamental Principles and Contemporary Challenges in the Law of War*, a casebook on the law of war (with G. Noone, 2013). She is also the co-director of a multi-year project on military training programs in the law of war and the co-author of *Law of War Training: Resources for Military and Civilian Leaders* (with G. Noone, 2013).

Ariel Colonomos is Senior Research Fellow at the National Center for Scientific Research (CNRS – Centre de Recherches Internationales) and Research Professor at Sciences Po in Paris, where he teaches courses on international relations theory and the ethics of war. He has published in the areas of international relations, the ethics of war, and political sociology. His recent books include *Selling the Future – The Perils of Predicting Global Politics* (2016), *Le Pari de la guerre: guerre preventive, guerre juste?* (Denoël, 2009; transl. *The Gamble of War: On Justifying Preventive War*, 2013), and *La Morale dans les relations internationales: Rendre des comptes* (Odile Jacob, 2005; transl. *Moralizing International Relations: Called to Account*, 2008).

Janina Dill is Assistant Professor of Normative International Theory at the Department of International Relations at the London School of Economics and Political Science and a research fellow of the Oxford Institute for Ethics, Law and Armed Conflict (ELAC) at the University of Oxford. She was previously a departmental lecturer at the University of Oxford, where she also served as Associate Director of ELAC and as Deputy Director of the Oxford

Programme on the Changing Character of War (CCW). Janina Dill's research focuses on international law and ethics in international relations, specifically in war. She is interested in how legal and moral imperatives interact with strategic thinking and technological developments to explain conduct in war and the development of conflict more generally. Her latest book is *Legitimate Targets? Social Construction, International Law and US Bombing* (Cambridge University Press, 2015).

Cécile Fabre is a senior research fellow at All Souls College, Oxford, and Professor of Political Philosophy at the University of Oxford. She has written extensively on distributive justice, democracy, and the rights we have over our own body. She has just completed a two-volume project on the ethics of war and peace – *Cosmopolitan War* (2012) and *Cosmopolitan Peace* (2016) – and is currently working on the ethics of economic statecraft.

Christopher J. Finlay completed his Ph.D. at the Department of Modern History, Trinity College Dublin, in 2000 and he is currently Reader in Political Theory at the University of Birmingham, where he works chiefly on philosophical issues arising from political violence and war. His most recent book is *Terrorism and the Right to Resist: A Theory of Just Revolutionary War* (Cambridge University Press, 2015), which was supported by a British Academy Leverhulme Trust Senior Research Fellowship (awarded, 2010), and his work appears in *The Journal of Political Philosophy*, *Political Studies*, *The Review of International Studies*, *History of Political Thought*, *The European Journal of International Relations*, and elsewhere.

Joy Gordon is the Ignacio Ellacuria, S.J. Chair in Social Ethics in the Philosophy Department at Loyola University, Chicago. She has published extensively on the topic of economic sanctions and their humanitarian impact, including *Invisible War: The United States and the Iraq Sanctions* (2010).

Michael L. Gross is Professor and Head of the School of Political Science at the University of Haifa, Israel. He specializes in applied normative theory, military and medical ethics, asymmetric war, and non-kinetic warfare. He is the author of *Ethics and Activism* (Cambridge University Press, 1997); *Bioethics and Armed Conflict* (2006); *Moral Dilemmas of Modern War* (Cambridge University Press, 2010); *Military Medical Ethics for the 21st Century* (with Don Carrick, 2013); and *The Ethics of Insurgency* (Cambridge University Press, 2015). He has lectured widely on battlefield and military medical ethics at defense centers in Israel, the United States, and Europe.

Sebastian Kaempf is a senior lecturer in the School of Political Science and International Studies at the University of Queensland (Australia). His research interests include the ethics and laws of war in contemporary US warfare and the role a transforming global media landscape is playing in contemporary world politics and conflicts. He co-convenes an interactive web platform called www.thevisionmachine.com.

George R. Lucas, Jr. is newly appointed as the VDM James B. Stockdale professor of ethics at the US Naval War College (Newport, RI). He is currently a visiting distinguished research professor at Notre Dame University. His latest book is *Ethics and Cyber Warfare* (2016).

Tamar Meisels is a political theorist and Associate Professor in the Political Science Department at Tel Aviv University. She earned her D.Phil. in Politics from Oxford University in 2001. Her primary research and teaching interests include liberal nationalism, territorial rights, and the philosophical questions surrounding war and terrorism. She is the author of *Territorial Rights* (2005 and 2009), *The Trouble with Terror: Liberty, Security, and the Response to Terrorism* (Cambridge University Press, 2008).

Valerie Morkevičius is an assistant professor of political science at Colgate University. She is the author of several articles on Protestant approaches to the ethics of conflict, including "Changing the Rules of the Game: A Just Peace Critique of Just War Thought" (2011) and "Ethics of War in Protestant Christianity" (2009), as well as articles on the relationship between just war thinking and other political theories, including "Power and Order: The Shared Logics of Realism and Just War Theory" (2015) and "Why We Need a Just Rebellion Theory" (2013).

James Pattison is Professor of Politics at the University of Manchester. His work focuses on the ethical issues surrounding conflict. His first book, *Humanitarian Intervention and the Responsibility to Protect: Who Should Intervene?* (2010), was awarded a "Notable Book Award" in 2011 by the International Studies Association (International Ethics Section). His second book, *The Morality of Private War: The Challenge of Private Military and Security Companies* (2014), considers the ethical problems raised by the privatization of war. He is currently writing a third book, provisionally entitled *Just and Unjust Alternatives to War*. This considers the ethics of the alternatives to direct military intervention, including diplomacy, naming and shaming, economic sanctions, arming rebel groups, and inducements.

Cheyney Ryan is a senior research fellow, and director of human rights programs, for the Institute for Ethics, Law, and Armed Conflict, University of Oxford, where he is also a member of Merton College. He was previously at the University of Oregon, where he founded the peace studies program and co-founded the graduate program in conflict resolution. His current interests include the theory and practice of nonviolent politics, with reference to American traditions and their religious background. He also writes in defense of pacifism and in criticism of the just war tradition.

Jessica Wolfendale is Associate Professor of Philosophy at West Virginia University. She is the author of *Torture and the Military Profession* (2007) and co-editor of *New Wars and New Soldiers: Military Ethics in the Contemporary World* (2011), and has published numerous articles and book chapters on topics including political security, torture, terrorism, and military ethics. Her current research project is a book entitled *War Crimes: Causes, Excuses, and Blame* (co-authored with Matthew Talbert). In addition to her work in political violence, she has a longstanding interest in fashion as it expresses values, sexuality, and identity. She is co-editor of *Fashion: Philosophy for Everyone* (2011), and her most recent article, "Provocative Dress and Sexual Responsibility," was published in the *Georgetown Journal of Gender and the Law*.

Foreword

Michael Walzer

When Clausewitz wrote that war was the extension of politics by other means, he had a very narrow view of those other means: our armed men attacking the armed men of the opposing side. Advances in military technology have expanded the available means to include tanks, airplanes, and missiles without changing the character of Clausewitz's contrast between arguing with intent to persuade (politics) and fighting with intent to kill (war). The argument of this book is that Clausewitz's contrast is too simple. War isn't necessarily lethal, and even when it is, the deaths it causes are not always the result of military combat.

"Soft war" isn't entirely new, as the example of economic sanctions suggests. But some versions of soft war, like cyberwar, are so radically new that we have barely begun to think about them. I have argued for a long time that our actually existing morality (just war theory, for example, but not only that) can guide our response to new tactics and technologies, and I believe that this is true for both hard and soft tactics and technologies. But it is true, so to speak, at too high a level of generality. It doesn't mean that responses in particular cases won't be difficult and contested, as this book demonstrates.

Casuistry, the application of conscience to its cases, is a continuously necessary activity. The activity fell into disrepute years ago because it too often was an apologetic and permissive enterprise. But that's not what it should be or need be. This book is a series of casuistic exercises – in the best sense of that term: careful, nuanced, worried efforts to reach a preliminary understanding of what is allowed and what is prohibited in wars that are fought, so to speak, away from the battles.

We can get some sense of the difficulty of applying old principles to the new world of soft war by looking briefly at the core principle of *jus in bello*: noncombatant immunity. It is an immoral act and a crime to aim your weapons at civilians. The purpose of the prohibition is to minimize the death and injury of innocent men and women. But what if the "weapons" are nonlethal – they don't cause death or injury, at least not directly. The consequences of economic boycotts, for example, range from inconvenience and discomfort to large-scale suffering and avoidable deaths. At what point does noncombatant immunity come into play? And what if the avoidable deaths have more than one cause? The blockade is, so to speak, the initiating cause, but the refusal of the blockaded regime to shift resources from military to civilian needs is another and not insignificant cause. "Smart sanctions" are supposed to be aimed narrowly at the regime and not at its citizens, but, as several of the authors report, these sanctions haven't yet proved smart enough.

In some of the versions of soft war discussed here, it is hard to know who the combatants are and, therefore, who the civilians are. Which groups of men and women are participating in, or complicit in, or necessary to, soft warfare? These people, once they have been identified, are liable to counter-attack – but the counter-attacks presumably have to be as "soft" as the attacks. Or can a lethal response to nonlethal warfare ever be justified? And what if the attack or the counter-attack harms people who are entirely innocent, disengaged from both the hard and soft warriors. What does the principle of proportionality tell us about the harms that extend to them, the soft version of collateral damage?

Sometimes soft war is the continuation of hard war by other means. The discussion of "lawfare" below takes up a key example of this continuation. In asymmetric war, which is very hard, civilians are often used as shields by one side and then killed by the other side. Both sides try to mobilize public opinion against the other, and one way to do that is to appeal to human rights NGOs, UN agencies, and international courts. The appeal most commonly comes from insurgents who put civilians at risk but hold their opponents responsible for their deaths. The opponents may indeed be responsible for not doing enough to protect civilians who are, voluntarily or involuntarily, shielding the insurgents, but they are unlikely to be the only ones responsible. So we need to distinguish good faith moral and legal appeals from bad ones. But this may be a case where the judgments we make about the soft war depend on the judgments we make about the hard war – that is, the asymmetric engagement. We know that there can be crimes in warfare, and we need to argue about what those crimes are and who the criminals are. Can there also be crimes in lawfare – when it is aimed, say, at the wrong people?

Cyberwar is probably the scariest form of soft war because of the growing dependence of contemporary social and economic life on vast systems run by highly sophisticated computers. Hack the computers and the damage can reach very far, breaching the privacy of millions of people, shutting down electrical networks, disrupting financial services, obliterating medical records, intercepting military communications, and breaching the control systems of dangerous weapons. I am not sure that this is soft war; it doesn't seem soft enough; but it also isn't anything like conventional military activity. It belongs in this book because it requires the kind of out-of-the-box thinking that the editors have required of all the contributors.

Many forms of soft war are less frightening than cyberwar is, but they all involve a radically adversarial relationship: "we" are trying to harm enemies who are trying to harm "us." And in this kind of warfare, as in any other, the combatants need to know what harms are permissible and what harms aren't, who can be targeted and who must not be targeted. Anyone who has talked to soldiers fighting in conventional wars will know how important moral guidelines are to them. They want to distinguish what they are doing from mere butchery; they want to feel justified. These feelings may be softer in soft war, but they will take the same form. That's why the arguments of this book are necessary and important.

Preface

Looking at our title, readers will wonder whether the editors are just having fun with oxymorons. Soft War? Unarmed Conflict? What can we have in mind? In a sentence, this book is about the other half of warfare, the half that just war theory and the law of armed conflict do not address and the half that often stymies the superior firepower of state armies.

Hard war is kinetic: bombs, bullets, and missiles; its outcomes are death, injury, and devastation. Hard war is the chief concern of international law and moral philosophy. The big money issues are self-defense, humanitarian intervention, noncombatant immunity, and combatant rights. But this is not the only concern, nor perhaps the most crucial. There is a growing awareness that contemporary warfare plays out on another, parallel battlefield, absent kinetic means and without the force of arms. Soft war is non-kinetic war. Bytes, boycotts, propaganda, nonviolent resistance, and even kidnapping replace bullets and bombs and supplant the predominant role of lethal force that captures our images of war. Unarmed force is not deadly but it is also not passive. It may be soft to the touch but is as coercive as any act of terrorism or targeted killing.

As its name suggests, the law of *armed* conflict neglects unarmed conflict. It pays scant attention to economic warfare and less than that to information operations, nonviolent resistance, lawfare, and public diplomacy. So, too, the academic community, and as we recruited contributors for this volume, we asked each to push beyond his or her comfort zone to think about soft war and its role in contemporary warfare. The result is a collection of original articles, many on subjects the authors had not previously considered closely, but which were dancing at the edge of their thoughts just waiting for the right volume to come along. The result is also a collaborative effort. Apart from the external, anonymous readers who evaluated each chapter (and whom we thank profusely), the contributors also reviewed one another's articles, thereby integrating the sections in a way that is sometimes missing in edited volumes.

This volume came to life in a conference, "The Ethics of the Alternatives to War," graciously hosted by James Pattison at Manchester in March 2015. This was a rich session that allowed us to kick around the idea of soft war, and it was there, over dinner, that we settled on the final title of this volume. As the idea picked up steam, more colleagues joined the project and we thank each for devoting time to write, rewrite, and revise their articles and to carefully read and evaluate other essays in this volume. We are exceptionally grateful to Adam Henschke, Bill Shaw, Chris Brown, Cian O'Driscoll, Danny Statman, David Kretzmer, David Rodin, David Whetham, Gabriella Blum, George Lopez, Henry Shue, Mariarosaria Taddeo, Michael Skerker, and Yitzhak Benbaji for reviewing essays in the volume and to the anonymous reviews we received from Cambridge University Press. External reviewers are the backbone of our profession. Money is too, and the editors also thank the Israel Science Foundation, grant number 156/13 (Michael L. Gross) and grant number 45/12 (Tamar Meisels), for the assistance allowing us to develop and edit this volume.

INTRODUCTION

Soft War: The Ethics of Unarmed Conflict

Michael L. Gross and Tamar Meisels

SOFT WAR

Just war theory focuses primarily on bodily harm such as killing, maiming, and torture. However, the question of other harms is largely overlooked. At the same time, contemporary international conflicts increasingly turn to unarmed tactics, employing "softer" alternatives or supplements to kinetic power that have not been sufficiently addressed by the ethics of war or international law.

What sort of war is "soft war"? Ostensibly an oxymoron, the term "soft war" fuses the more familiar notion of "soft power" (Nye 2004) with coercive tactics that fall short of armed attacks. Soft power, like public diplomacy, does not work by force at all but invites support through persuasion rather than compelling submission with the threat of systems failure or economic ruin. By contrast, soft war is a much broader concept and includes all non-kinetic measures whether persuasive or coercive, including cyber warfare and economic sanctions; media warfare and propaganda, nonviolent resistance and civil disobedience, boycotts and "lawfare" (Gross 2015).

To be sure, many of these tactics will have devastating effects on those who endure them. Here the term "soft war" may strike some readers as objectionable, even offensive, as it embraces crippling tactics such as economic warfare, propaganda and information operations, cyber-attacks, wartime imprisonment, and hostage taking. Admittedly, "softness" in the context of war is only a relative matter. When waged by states, "soft war" is something more than merely espionage, but also something decidedly less than conventional armed conflict, and in obvious contrast to "kinetic" military attacks that characterize conventional or "hard" war. Non-kinetic tactics are "soft warfare" insofar as they fall short of the stuff old-fashioned wars are made of – mass killing fields, wholesale deaths in battle, and aerial bombings.

At the other end of the scale, readers may question whether all tactics in this volume constitute war at all. Can unarmed force – computer attacks, nonviolent resistance, propaganda, and lawsuits – really constitute a war? Jessica Wolfendale addresses these definitional issues, alongside the ethical implications of defining non-kinetic attacks as warfare, in the opening chapter. These new forms of attack fall outside the traditional legal and moral categories of armed conflict and therefore raise questions about when and under what conditions such attacks should be classified as warfare, as well as about the rights and duties triggered by unarmed conflict.

Although the idea of soft war may appear over- and under-inclusive – involving tactics that are hardly soft and others that are hardly war – the concept is conceptually distinct from hard war. In practice, soft war is generally less destructive but no less effective than hard, kinetic warfare. In theory, while the just war tradition has much to say about "hard" war – bullets, bombs, and bayonets – it is virtually silent on the subject of "soft" war. "Soft war" tactics, taken together, illuminate an entirely overlooked aspect of international conflict.

To count as soft war, moreover, non-kinetic tactics need not constitute armed conflict as such. Soft war functions both as an adjunct to hard war and as a stand-alone set of strategies. As an adjunct or prelude to hard war, soft war can go a long way toward fulfilling the last resort criterion of just war. Economic sanctions are a paradigm case. One reason for resorting to economic measures rather than full-scale war is "to provide a first, mild stage in the hostilities, to bring moderate pressure to bear to achieve a settlement, if possible, before the resort to arms becomes necessary" (O'Donovan 2003, 106–107). Another is where direct military action faces logistic impediments (O'Donovan 2003). In both cases, sanctions fulfill an initial, preferably alternative, measure, to be exhausted before reaching the point of last resort.

Similar points obtain with regard to lesser economic measures such as boycotts and conditional sale, as well as to soft power – diplomatic efforts and negotiation. In Conditional Sale, as coined by Cécile Fabre, an international business transaction is made contingent not only on price (as sales always are), but also on a political condition. In these cases, seller requires buyer to enact or desist from a certain policy as a pre-requisite for acquiring goods at a desirable price. These doubly conditional sales (contingent on a politics-condition as well as price) present a further economic measure for addressing grievances or pursuing foreign policy goals more widely, far short of recourse to war. Non-kinetic attacks, such as cyber warfare, may also provide a milder alternative of first resort, or penultimate resort, before hard warfare becomes justifiably necessary, or even advisable from a purely prudential perspective.

As an alternative to hard war, soft war speaks to many of the questions raised by *jus ad vim*, the just use of force short of war, which has received some academic attention in recent years (Brunstetter and Braun 2013, 87–88; Frowe 2016). Like most contemporary just war thinking, the discussion of *jus ad vim* begins with Michael Walzer's *Just and Unjust Wars*, specifically with the preface to its fourth edition. There, Walzer distinguishes traditional *jus ad bellum*, governing the resort to actual war (full-scale attacks, invasions) from the just use of force short of war, dubbed *jus ad vim*. As Walzer explains, the measures governed by *jus ad vim* involve the use (or threat) of force – e.g. embargos or the enforcement of no-fly-zones – and consequently count as acts of war under international law. Nonetheless, "it is common sense to recognize that they are very different from war" (Walzer 2006, xv–xvi). Full-scale conflict always involves grave risks and hazards, unpredictable and all-too -often catastrophic consequences, and the full-fledged "hellishness of war" described throughout *Just and Unjust Wars*. By contrast, *jus ad vim* measures are limited in their scope and intensity, requiring far lesser force and incurring fewer risks to their perpetrators. Morally (not legally) speaking, they fall outside the remit of *jus ad bellum* and require a separate, somewhat more permissive, ethical framework: "We urgently need a theory of just and unjust uses of force" (Walzer 2006, xv–xvi).

Our volume does not neatly fill this gap or supply such a theory. While there is some overlap between forceful measures short of war and the soft war tactics addressed in this collection, the two concepts differ significantly in several respects. Primarily, most soft war tactics do not involve a resort to arms, whereas all tactics covered by *jus ad vim* are, by definition, forceful measures. Consequently, as Walzer notes, *jus ad vim* acts are clearly governed by international laws of war. Many soft war tactics, in contrast, do not count legally as acts of war at all. At the harsher end of the soft war spectrum, some nonlethal tactics discussed toward the end of this book, notably kidnapping and extortion, are often employed as part of an existing state of war, whereas *jus ad vim* acts are (again by definition) necessarily measures *short of war*. *Jus ad vim* is always an *alternative* to war, as its essence is "its advantage in avoiding the unpredictable and widespread destructive consequences of war" (Brunstetter and Braun 2013, 97). Soft war, on the other hand, takes in some of the (relatively) milder measures resorted to in the course of actual war, provided they fall short of killing and maiming. Finally, *jus ad vim* generally refers to the use of kinetic force (such as the use of drones for targeted killings) and here too the concept of soft war (encompassing non-kinetic tactics) adds a crucial and overlooked dimension to the discussion.

SOFT WAR: THE ETHICS OF UNARMED CONFLICT

When traditional armed conflict erupts, it brings into play the full privileges of belligerency, as well as the familiar doctrines of military necessity, the right to self-defense, and the rules of *in bello* distinction and proportionality that supersede ordinary peacetime morality and law. What rules apply to non-kinetic tactics utilized during armed conflict or prior to it? Alternatives, supplements, or precursors to war have remained mostly under the radar of conventional rules of war and international laws of armed conflict. At the same time, they raise concerns analogous to wartime *ad bellum and in bello* principles. Sanctions, restrictions on trade and conditional sale; cyber-attacks, propaganda, and media warfare; lawfare, detention, negotiation, and prisoner exchanges, all raise questions about necessity, last resort, and the chance of success. Once engaged in "soft war," these tactics raise parallel concerns about the appropriate rules of engagement, the distinction between liable and non-liable targets, collateral civilian suffering and proportionality.

The urgency of tackling these new issues from a wartime perspective cannot be overstated, particularly when considering some of the well-publicized cases of unarmed conflict in the past few decades. Between 1990 and 2003, the international community imposed grave and sweeping economic sanctions on Iraq that resulted in widespread malnutrition, epidemics of cholera and typhoid, and the near-collapse of health care and education (Gordon 2010). Less severe were the sanctions imposed on Iran between 1979 and 2015 to deter uranium enrichment and impede Iran's nuclear program. In addition to economic sanctions, Iran suffered one of the more spectacular cyber-attacks as the Stuxnet virus severely crippled its enrichment capabilities (Lucas, this volume).

Like many of the tactics discussed in this volume, cyber and economic warfare are weapons of state and non-state actors alike and may appear side-by side with other soft and hard tactics. They are increasingly salient, if not essential, in conventional war, counterinsurgency operations, guerrilla warfare, and civil war. Israel's problematic disengagement from the Gaza Strip and its subsequent military engagement in Gaza following Hamas' ascent to power saw both sides resorting to armed and unarmed force. Prominent unarmed tactics included economic sanctions and restrictions on trade; propaganda, media warfare, and lawfare; and restrictions of liberty, detention, imprisonment, kidnapping, and hostage taking negotiations. Hostage taking does not aim to impair military capabilities through death and destruction but to coerce an enemy to exchange hostages for prisoners held by the other side. In many cases, negotiating the terms of release can advance political and military goals without resorting to force of arms. In Hezbollah's and Hamas' confrontations with Israel, for example, hostage taking caused relatively few deaths and injuries and proved more successful and cost efficient than kinetic warfare (Meisels, this volume).

"Lawfare" is also an exceptionally effective coercive but non-kinetic tactic. "Lawfare," writes Jessica Wolfendale, "refers to a belligerent's use or abuse of International Humanitarian Law (IHL) to hamper their opponent's military strategies or undermine their opponent's perceived legitimacy by leveling accusations of war crimes against them" (Wolfendale, also Blank and Dill this volume). Fleshing this out, George Lucas describes how a terrorist group like Hamas could use civilian volunteers as "human shields" and then invoke the law to condemn Israel for causing disproportionate civilian casualties. And, indeed, the Palestinian Authority has filed lawsuits against Israel in the International Court of Justice (ICJ) in The Hague for alleged war crimes throughout the Gaza conflicts. Lawfare reaches also beyond the ICJ or ICC. In October 2015, 20,000 Israelis filed a class action suit against Facebook claiming that social network posts have inspired many recent terrorist attacks.

The following sections place each of the contributor's chapters in the context of soft war and unarmed conflict. Although just war theory occupies center stage in the political theory of international relations, non-forceful instruments of foreign policy are often more effective and less destructive than resorting to widespread carnage. Each chapter examines options for attaining the ends of war that fall short of deadly force.

SOFT WAR: THEORY AND PRACTICE

Definitions

Hostile measures do not always involve lethal force but do they constitute a state of war? In "Defining War," Jessica Wolfendale leads with this foundational question: Are soft war and unarmed conflict war? In international law and just war theory, war is normatively and legally unique. In the context of international law, war's special status gives rise to a specific set of belligerent rights and duties and to a complex set of laws related to civilians, prisoners of war, trade and economic relationships, and humanitarian aid. The task of defining war requires not just identifying the empirical features that are characteristic of wars but also explaining and justifying war's special legal and moral status. This task is particularly important in light of the questions raised by the new forms of conflict discussed throughout.

In the first chapter, Wolfendale proposes a definition of war and explains when and how some forms of unarmed conflict could count as wars. To count as war, Wolfendale stipulates three conditions:

(1) There are two or more organized groups;
(2) These groups are engaged in intense hostilities;
(3) No party to the conflict and no other third party has the authority and ability to effectively adjudicate between the opposing sides, punish them, and otherwise maintain effective control in the arena of the conflict.

Wolfendale argues that this definition can account for war's unique legal status, is consistent with the purposes of the legal framework governing war, and permits a deeper understanding of the nature of contemporary conflicts. She then applies her definition to three case studies: lawfare, economic sanctions, and cyber warfare, suggesting that these forms of unarmed conflict meet the definition of war.

The possibility that soft war tactics constitute war raises hard questions about how the traditional categories of combatants and civilians apply to unarmed conflicts. This opening chapter offers some suggestions to interpret these concepts in the context of unarmed conflicts. In particular, Wolfendale (and Gross in the conclusion) argue that the concept of "combatant" should expand to incorporate a view of liability based on an agent's contribution to unarmed conflict rather than on their formal affiliation with military organizations.

Valerie Morkevičius compliments this discussion by considering civilian immunity. Historically, the just war tradition holds that civilians are not liable to direct lethal harm because they do not pose a direct lethal threat to others. Soft war tactics challenge this logic as well. Soft tactics – economic warfare, cyber warfare, and information warfare – are not necessarily lethal. If the alternative is causing the deaths of civilians indirectly and unintentionally through conventional means (such as bombing military targets), would targeting civilians directly using nonlethal measures be permissible? Drawing on the just war tradition (as developed by Augustine, Aquinas, and de Vitoria), Morkevičius argues that direct nonlethal attacks on civilians are sometimes justifiable and then delineates the circumstances under which such attacks could be morally permissible.

In keeping with just war principles associated with *jus ad bellum*, Morkevičius suggests that direct nonlethal attacks on civilian property must *aim at peace*. That is, they may not undermine the possibility of post-conflict reconciliation. Consequently, nonlethal tactics that lead to overwhelming social disorder or humanitarian crisis are impermissible. Nonlethal attacks must also be necessary and proportionate to the good they hope to achieve, and they must stand a reasonable probability of success. Pointing out that some tactics of soft war, e.g. economic and information warfare, are not always effective, Morkevičius concludes that while direct, nonlethal attacks on civilians may be theoretically permissible, they are not always useful in practice.

Economic Warfare

Morkevičius' discussion of civilian liability to nonlethal harm paves the way toward a careful consideration of economic warfare and its potentially devastating effect on civilians and their communities. Economic sanctions are, perhaps, the paradigm of non-kinetic warfare, but at their worst are the harshest of soft tactics. They can be severe and, in extreme cases, approach full-scale war. Although a penultimate strategy, sanctions may at times be worse than war, as is well illustrated by the sanctions that preceded the 1991 Gulf War.

Joy Gordon sets off an important and diverse discussion in Part II. Economic sanctions, Gordon reminds us, are often seen as a "middle route": less forceful than military measures but more robust than diplomacy. However, that changed with the UN Security Council sanctions imposed on Iraq. These sanctions prevented Iraq from rebuilding in the aftermath of the bombing campaign of the first Gulf War, resulting in the ongoing collapse of Iraq's infrastructure for over a decade. In response, scholars and practitioners developed targeted sanctions, "smart sanctions," which would bring direct pressure against the leaders of target countries while sparing the civilian population. Nevertheless, smart sanctions have disappointed. They are not always effective, raise concerns about due process, and often inflict unjustifiable harm on noncombatants.

Comprehensive sanctions, for their part, share many of the problematic features described by Walzer with regard to old-fashioned sieges. From a just war perspective, sieges pose a puzzling exception to the rule prohibiting deliberate assault on civilians (Walzer 1977, 162; 171–172). Civilians are not legitimate wartime targets and must not be targeted directly. When states resort to economic warfare, however, civilians are at the forefront and often the first to suffer. This discrepancy between civilian immunity and their direct vulnerability under economic warfare formed part of Morkevičius' argument about the limited legitimacy of direct nonlethal attacks on civilians, as well as Gordon's critique of comprehensive sanctions. Nevertheless, despite grave consequences for civilians, economic sanctions, even outright sieges, remain part of the legal arsenal of states.

In the second paper on economic warfare, Cécile Fabre focuses on *conditional sale*. Conditional sale is a nonviolent economic tactic states may utilize to enforce human rights and prevent abuse without wide-scale military action. To illustrate, Fabre postulates the following scenario: Suppose that some political actor – call it Affluenza – possesses goods, *G*, which some other actor – call it Barrenia – badly needs or wants. Suppose further that Affluenza wants something from Barrenia, though is not willing, able, or justified, to go to war for it. Instead, it threatens to raise the price of G to a level that Barrenia can ill afford, unless Barrenia gives in to its demands. If Barrenia does give in, Affluenza will lower the price of *G*. Affluenza, in other words, makes its willingness to sell at an affordable price conditional on Barrenia's bending to its will.

When, if ever, is *Conditional Sale* morally justified? Assuming that Affluenza has full control over *G* and trades directly with Barrenia's regime, Fabre argues that a *conditional sale* is permitted to redress a justified grievance against Barrenia, or to pursue foreign policy goals more widely. Clearly, in the real world, this assumption does not always pertain. Relaxing it toward the end of the chapter, Fabre highlights some of the difficulties raised by *Conditional Sale* for private economic actors in both the buyer and seller communities.

Nonviolent Resistance

Resort to economic sanctions, as discussed by Gordon, raises hard definitional questions about liable targets and civilian immunity set out by Wolfendale in her opening chapter. However, as demonstrated by Fabre's conditional sale, resort to soft warfare will not always involve a clear distinction between combatants and civilians on any definition, either by affiliation as members of military organizations or based on their actual contribution to the conflict. When injustices are opposed by entirely nonviolent methods that avoid direct confrontation, there are no combatants and everyone is a civilian.

In the first of our chapters on nonviolence, James Pattison looks at "civilian peacekeeping," an underappreciated means of preventing government oppression. Most notable among civilian peacekeepers is "international protective accompaniment" by such groups as Peace Brigades International and Nonviolent Peaceforce. Civilian peacekeeping comprises unarmed bodyguards protecting threatened groups or individuals by deterring abuses, or if abuses occur, reporting them. Pattison offers a detailed defense of this strategy as a morally desirable part of a preventive and reactive toolkit for tackling human rights abuses and mass atrocities.

Civilian peacekeeping avoids many of the pitfalls of armed humanitarian intervention and "military peacekeeping" (e.g. many current UN missions). Consequently, Pattison supports this nonviolent option under a fleshed-out account of last resort in Just War Theory. At the same time, and as opposed to other advocates of peacekeeping tactics, Pattison recognizes that civilian peacekeeping is not necessarily an alternative to armed peacekeeping or humanitarian intervention, but often supplements these military operations in a joint effort to maintain human rights.

Can human rights themselves be subversive and, if so, how subversive are human rights? Christopher Finlay poses this question about civil subversion within the ethics of unarmed resistance.

Human rights violations challenge the authority and legitimacy of oppressive regimes. In contrast, Finlay examines how human rights might also afford the *means* to resist political authority, arguing that various forms of protest, political mobilization, and obstruction might effectively be legitimated and protected by human rights. Freedoms of association, speech, and assembly, for example, might enable a secessionist movement to erect a rival source of political authority within a state. If this rival drew support away from the existing state, then it might be possible for secessionists to undermine its ability to rule in the disputed territory and pressure a state to relinquish control.

If this is possible in circumstances of political oppression, Finlay argues, it might also, more surprisingly, be true even in circumstances where a state respects human rights. By protecting a group's ability to construct parallel institutions of government, law enforcement, education, and welfare, respect for human rights can enable a group to subvert the authorities they oppose. Secessionists, in effect, leverage human rights to gain territorial rights. And as long as the secessionists do so nonviolently and pose no threat to human rights themselves, they make it very difficult for states to respond effectively without resorting to violence and oppression. By viewing human rights from the perspective of tactical nonviolence, Finlay shows how human rights have a hidden potential for political subversion.

Cheyney Ryan closes this section by focusing on the role that provoking violence plays in nonviolent politics and the (dangerous) use of children within a nonviolent struggle. Nonviolent action sometimes seeks to provoke a *violent* response in an effort to stoke moral outrage and increase sympathy for a cause. While this may be common practice among violent guerrilla fighters, the provocation of violence is particularly vexing when it is employed by political movements that pride themselves on nonviolence (Gross 2015; Ryan, this volume). Ryan dubs this "the paradox of nonviolent action" and one of its most dramatic examples was the 1963 protests in Birmingham, Alabama, led by Dr. Martin Luther King, Jr. These protests were very successful, but also deeply controversial because they mobilized children to march into violent situations. As he describes the Birmingham protests, Ryan argues that nonviolent provocations of violence were not paradoxical so long as the "provocations" are themselves legal and legitimate. In the Birmingham case, in particular, he reminds us that the actions of demonstrators were not only *legal*, but were also the sort of actions that in other circumstances would be innocuous, or certainly no cause for alarm – people eating at a lunch counter, shopping at a clothing store, or registering to vote. This clearly sets nonviolent provocation apart from violent and illegal provocation as was the result of rock throwing in the first Intifada (1987–1990), for example.

What of engaging children in such protests? The mobilization of children raises important ethical issues about the use of minors in soft war. Mobilizing young children to fight hard wars is morally problematic as well as internationally illegal, though one can easily imagine desperate struggles for liberation in which such practices might be justified or excusable. What about mobilizing "child soldiers" in soft war? Here, Ryan reflects ambivalently on the use of young children in the Birmingham protests and critically considers the arguments for and against this soft war tactic.

Cyber Warfare, Media Warfare, and Lawfare

An entirely different set of nonviolent measures involves computers, the media, and the law, raising further questions for contemporary just war theorists. George Lucas leads off this section with his discussion of State-Sponsored Hacktivism and the Rise of "Soft" War. Lucas points out that the apparent state sponsorship of what are criminal and vigilante actions now offers a new chapter in inter-state conflict. The alleged North Korean attack on Sony Pictures in 2013 and theft by Chinese cyber "warriors" of some 22 million personnel files of US civil servants in 2014 are recent chapters in this new form of warfare where states employ tactics once limited to non-state organizations and individuals. Instead of individuals and non-state organizations acquiring and using sophisticated cyber weapons that confer upon them the military prowess of states, we have instead witnessed an evolution in the opposite direction: state agents and agencies are behaving more and more like individual hackers.

Lucas examines the ethical challenges posed by disruptive malevolent cyber activity. Soft war, he tells us, now includes vandalism, extortion, and theft of property in the cyber domain carried out by states (rather than criminal or terrorist organizations) alongside the theft or exposure of sensitive or classified information. The massive cyber-attacks on US financial institutions by the "Cyber Warriors of Izz ad-din Al-Qassam" in the Fall of 2012, for example, were (like an earlier attack on Saudi Aramco by the "Sword of Justice") most probably coordinated acts of Iranian government cyber warriors in retaliation for the Stuxnet/Flame/Olympic Games cyber-attacks by the United States and Israel in 2010. The relentless theft of industrial and defense secrets, and vandalism by the PLA's "Shanghai Unit 61398" constitute an obvious case in point, as do other attacks (labeled "Aurora," "Red October," "Dark Hotel," and "Regin," respectively) that were presumably launched by Britain and the United States.

In cyber conflict, many activities constitute crimes within the domestic jurisdiction where they occur, and are governed by the European Convention concerning Cybercrime (Bucharest 2001). However, many involved nations (China, North Korea, Iran, and Russia, for example) are not signatories to this agreement. Furthermore, unlike Stuxnet (a state-sponsored act of sabotage), these activities cannot be readily subsumed under existing international law (notwithstanding attempts to do so by the *Tallinn Manual* [Schmitt 2013]). The jurisdictional limbo and ambiguity of "state-sponsored hacktivism" thus invites closer, more careful ethical analysis to better understand the phenomenon and to formulate appropriate defensive responses

Lucas also reminds us that "the weapons and tactics of 'soft war' are not limited to the cyber domain. They involve state use of conventional and cyber social media to disseminate propaganda and sow confusion, obfuscation, and disinformation" (Lucas, this volume).

In "Media Warfare, Propaganda, and the Law of War," Laurie Blank addresses some of the issues raised by Lucas in the previous chapter and by Kaempf in the following chapter. In today's 24/7 media and internet culture, airstrikes, artillery barrages, and infantry maneuvers are accompanied by equally intense debates in the media about the legality and legitimacy of military action. With the involvement of international, regional and national courts, commissions of inquiry, and, perhaps most important of all, the court of world opinion – the battle of words is as important as military capabilities. Numerous factors form, sway, and cement public opinion. These include the efforts of militaries and armed groups to control information flows and of journalists, advocacy groups, fact-finding missions, and ordinary civilians to seek, publicize, and comment on information. This complex mix leads to a combustible arena of media warfare that significantly affects the legal framework that governs conflicts.

Most notably, Blank's chapter explores how propaganda and media warfare intersect with international law and explains how information operations and media coverage affect perceptions of legal compliance. As Blank explains, the information battle-space actually affects the application and interpretation of the law of armed conflict. Although media coverage is essential to protect persons and enforce legal and moral norms, media coverage equally affects the interpretation and development of the law of armed conflict itself.

In the following chapter, "Today's Mediatized Battlespaces," Sebastian Kaempf describes how, in our highly mediatized world, warfare is not confined to the kinetic arena. Rather, state and non-state actors now wage their wars in and through global media platforms. Media technology, in other words, has become a soft war weapon in its own right.

Kaempf examines the media strategies of the United States and ISIS and investigates the strategic importance that state and non-state actors attach to the mediatization of their wars. Both actors have actively mediatized their war so that it is impossible to understand their physical combat practices without accounting for their virtual dimensions. Kaempf then examines the ethical dimensions of American and ISIS media strategies. The United States uses the media to sanitize war and mask its killing, thereby (and paradoxically) obscuring the military's high level of compliance with core just war principles (e.g. discrimination, necessity, and proportionality). In contrast, ISIS uses the media to graphically depict indiscriminate and disproportionate violence. Pointing to these diverging practices, Kaempf shows how media is neither a peripheral nor a neutral element in combat, but a central element of warfare.

Arguing that the mediascape is inseparable from the modern battlefield, Kaempf asks whether scholars need to apply just war principles to the media dimensions of today's wars. Addressing this question, Kaempf argues that our traditional principles are out of sync with and need to be adjusted to contemporary war's mediatized reality. A set of difficult and complex questions follow: How do scholars apply just war principles to the mediatized reality of today's wars? Can we separate the ethical elements of committing atrocities from mediatizing them? Do different moral principles govern each? Is there anything wrong about truthfully reporting atrocity (as is currently the case with ISIS)? Alternatively, is it better to refrain from publicizing collateral harm even when lawful and morally permissible (as does the United States, claims Kaempf)?

Janina Dill focuses on lawfare in the next chapter. Beyond the media, the law can achieve strategic advantages in wartime because a violation of the laws of war is strategically costly in the twenty-first century. Belligerents may use the law to lodge complaints and publicize grievances about war crimes, or they may abuse the law by provoking an enemy to violate the law by using human shields or resorting to perfidy.

Dill helpfully distinguishes the legitimate recourse to the law from its abuse, reserving the derogative term "lawfare" solely for the latter. Because it is not always easy to identify bad faith arguments and non-compliance on the battlefield, Dill suggests that at least one necessary condition for abuse should be a use of law against its own object and purpose. The purpose of law is to successfully regulate conduct during armed conflict. It is entirely legitimate, even desirable, to invoke the law to this end. Abuse, on the other hand, is to use the law in bad faith.

Abuse occurs in several circumstances. One turns on indeterminacy, i.e. exploiting the flexibility of the law to "make a legal argument contrary to the object and purpose of the law" to facilitate a violation of law. An example is American interpretations of its interrogation protocols to preclude charges of torture and ill-treatment. Another abuse of law is perfidy, an act exploiting the adversary's compliance with law so as to benefit strategically from behavior that in itself amounts to a breach of law. Feigning civilian status while launching an attack is an all too common example of this type of lawfare.

In the remainder of her chapter, Dill explores two further types of lawfare, which are often difficult to distinguish from legitimate uses of law. Both involve the reputational costs and benefits attached to the use of law in war, and Dill dubs these types of lawfare "reputation-destroying" and "reputation-preserving" lawfare, respectively. The first of these brings us back to human shields and similar abuses of civilian immunity (e.g. placing military sites near civilian population centers), which serve the purpose of provoking an attack that will harm civilians that then allows the defender to fling charges of war crimes against the attacker. In Chapter 9, James Pattison explores such reputation-destroying lawfare when he demonstrates how foreign volunteers protect noncombatants or combatants and dare their enemy to violate the law.

In each case, Dill calls our attention to abuses of law that, as Blank and Kaempf point out, lean heavily on the media and information operations to publicize allegations of war crimes and compel an attacker to desist and halt his attack. As the term "lawfare" evokes the equivalence of recourse to law and warfare, Dill suggests that we avoid using it simply to refer to the use of law in war. The astonishing subjection of warfare to international law over the last decades is due to, and its continuation depends on, IHL being a true alternative and more than a mere substitute for armed force in international relations.

Hostage Taking and Prisoners

The final section pushes the concept of non-kinetic warfare to its outer limits and considers restrictions of liberty during conflict. When combatants engage in warfare, they not only attack and kill one another, but also capture and incarcerate opponents, soldiers, and civilians. Nonetheless, long-term deprivation of freedom has not received the attention it deserves within contemporary just war theory.

As International Humanitarian Law codified combatant status, it included the legal requirements for attaining prisoner of war rights when captured. International law also supplies a list of complex legal privileges and immunities that requires captors to treat POWs, as well as any detainee regardless of his legal status, in a humane manner. Following 9/11, legal and philosophical debates about wartime prisoners shifted to the practice of administrative detention and to the status and rights of irregular combatants arrested and detained by states. Much attention focused on the detainees held by the US military in Guantanamo Bay. The last section of the book pursues the crucial issue of loss of liberty in contemporary armed conflict and raises questions about the ethics of hostage negotiations and the capture and imprisonment of state soldiers by non-state insurgent organizations.

As these last two chapters end our volume, it is important to explain how they fit within the general theme of soft war. Seizing and holding prisoners quite clearly involves the use, or threat, of force. Undeniably, wartime seizure and detention may result in death, as may cyber-attacks and economic sanctions. The costs of prisoner exchanges in an age of terrorism, discussed in Ariel Colonomos' chapter, alongside the agony and anguish endured by prisoners and their families, has led some observers, most notably in Israel, to regard wartime capture as a fate worse than death. This makes hostages particularly valuable bargaining chips.

Notwithstanding the armed force necessary to seize prisoners, hostage taking remains a non-kinetic means of war-fighting that falls short of deadly violence. Wartime capture and detention is a temporary incapacitating measure often employed in lieu of taking a life to disable enemy forces. Prisoner negotiation and their rate of exchange, moreover, do not involve armed force at all. Negotiating the terms of repatriation is an alternative means of advancing political goals that do not require force of arms.

In Chapter 12, Ariel Colonomos addresses dilemmas of hostage negotiations. Nations confronted with ransom demands to free captured nationals face hard practical and normative choices that range from refusing to negotiate, to compliance, to freeing hostages by force. Drawing our attention to the universal scope of this hostage dilemma, Colonomos argues that such cases demand multilateral solutions, rather than state-instigated military action or unilateral ad hoc capitulation to captors.

Hostage taking is a grave concern for many Western, Middle Eastern, and African states. Nevertheless, it is more than a state matter. Hostage taking threatens universal human rights, while responses to hostage taking have implications that reach beyond the citizens of the state concerned. Consequently, Colonomos suggests, solving hostage crises is not the prerogative or responsibility of individual states. Instead, we need an internationally coordinated approach toward freeing hostages and globally agreed standards of negotiation that reflect a unified rate of exchange for their release. Rather than remaining a state monopoly, negotiations ought to be a multi-national endeavor involving new international institutions, carried out in a uniform manner and on the basis of an internationally agreed upon set of standards.

Colonomos' discussion of hostage negotiations touches on wider national and international concerns regarding wartime detention. Foremost among them are the appropriate legal arrangements for wartime capture and incarceration in an age of terrorism. Meisels takes up this final challenge in the closing chapter of this section. Kidnappings and hostage taking within contemporary armed conflicts do not fall neatly into our existing prisoner of war regime. Like Colonomos, Meisels considers the differences between contemporary wartime hostages and conventional prisoners of war and explains how hostage taking violates human rights and international law. Meisels defends traditional distinctions between uniformed combatants – permitted to kill and capture during wartime – and irregular combatants who lack this privileged status. Ultimately, she argues, the rights of clandestine irregulars ought not to be extended in any way that would legitimize their hybrid identities as civilian-combatants or effectively legalize their hostage taking or kidnapping activities.

Conclusion

In the final chapter, Michael Gross turns to the question of self-defense. While the previous chapters discuss an offensive aspect of soft war – economic sanctions, nonviolent resistance, lawfare, media warfare, propaganda, and hostage taking – the final chapter asks how states and non-states may defend themselves against unarmed force.

The UN Charter grants the right of self-defense to those facing an armed attack but the offensive measures outlined throughout this volume rarely rise to that level. Instead, Gross turns to the legal doctrine of countermeasures to provide a framework for unarmed self-defense. Countermeasures are "self-help" measures and at the heart of reprisal. Nowadays, they often arise in the context of trade disputes and allow an aggrieved state to respond to an unlawful act with an equivalent unlawful act of its own. The defining criterion is equivalence: countermeasures exact a measure of harm equal to that which the victim suffers with the goal of restoring the status quo. In soft war, however, acts of aggression may be lawful (propaganda, sanctions) or unlawful (cyber-attacks). At the same time, the goal of unarmed conflict is not to restore any status quo but to disable or defeat an enemy. With these caveats in mind, Gross examines proportionate self-defense in response to cyber warfare, economic warfare, and lawfare.

As in hard war, soft war defense must be effective, strive to disable rather than punish an adversary, admit of no alternative that is less destructive and similarly effective, and respect the fundamental rights of the participants. And while fundamental rights protect noncombatants from disproportionate collateral harm and devastating direct harm, they do not necessarily protect noncombatants from direct attack during unarmed conflict. As a result, adversaries will conduct cyber, media, and economic operations against noncombatants directly. But not all noncombatants are fair game. Soft war recognizes the principle of participatory liability, which confers liability on noncombatants who supply war-sustaining aid (who Gross calls "participating civilians") but modulates permissible force accordingly. If combatants are liable to lethal harm because they pose a lethal threat, then participating civilians who pose a less-than-lethal threat are only liable to nonlethal harm: material loss from economic sanctions or cyber warfare, reputational harm from lawfare or information operations, or deprivations of liberty from incarceration. Participating civilians do not have blanket noncombatant immunity during soft war. Nevertheless, participating civilians retain their immunity from excessive force. This caveat protects them from cyber-attacks that may cause injury or loss of life, economic sanctions that bring mass casualties or penury, or lawfare that offers legal cover for terrorism or ethnic cleansing. As such, the scope of noncombatant immunity shrinks in soft war, permitting a range of self-defensive responses that fall short of lethal force and which often prove exceptionally effective.

Gross's discussion of self-defense in response to unarmed tactics underlies all the soft war issues discussed throughout, tying them together and concluding our volume on a note similar to its beginning. Thinking about "soft-war" is in its infancy, as are its tactics and permissible defensive measures. Many soft war issues have not received the attention they deserve within just war theory, and some that have (e.g. economic sanctions) have not been carefully addressed in connection with the timely events and concepts discussed in this book. No existing volume on just war theory encompasses this range of topics or tackles this aspect of the changing practice of modern warfare. The following collection of essays meets recent challenges to just war theory posed by soft war and unarmed conflict.

DEFINITIONS AND META VIEWS

1

Defining War

Jessica Wolfendale

In international law and just war theory, war is treated as normatively and legally unique. In the context of international law, war's special status gives rise to a specific set of belligerent rights and duties, as well as a complex set of laws related to, among other things, the status of civilians, prisoners of war, trade and economic relationships, and humanitarian aid. In particular, belligerents are permitted to derogate from certain human rights obligations and to use lethal force in a far more permissive manner than is the case in other kinds of conflicts and in domestic law enforcement operations. Given war's unique status, the task of defining war requires not just identifying the empirical features that are characteristic of war but explaining and justifying war's special legal and moral status.

In this chapter, I propose a definition of war that captures war's unique features and can offer insights into when and how some forms of unarmed conflict could count as wars. The definition I will defend is as follows:

A war exists when all the following conditions are met:

(1) There are two or more organized groups.
(2) These groups are engaged in intense hostilities.
(3) No party to the conflict and no other third party has the authority and ability to effectively adjudicate between the opposing sides, punish them, and otherwise maintain effective control in the arena of the conflict.

I will argue that this definition can account for war's unique legal status, is consistent with the purposes of the legal framework governing war, and permits a deeper understanding of the nature of contemporary conflicts. My definition will not include any claims regarding *jus ad bellum* and *jus in bello* criteria, except in so far as these categories are only taken to apply to conflicts that are classified as war.

In Section 1, I discuss the normative and legal significance of defining war. In Section 2, I defend my definition of war, and in Section 3, I apply my definition to three case studies discussed in this volume: lawfare, economic sanctions, and cyber war. I argue that it is possible for these forms of unarmed conflict to meet my definition of war. This possibility raises hard questions about how traditional categories, such as the categories of combatants and civilians, can be applied to unarmed conflicts, and I offer some suggestions for how such concepts could be interpreted in the context of unarmed conflicts.

DEFINING WAR

The Legal and Normative Implications of Defining War

The complex legal framework governing war (including international humanitarian law (IHL), of which the Geneva Conventions are part) governs a wide range of issues, including the status of civilians and refugees in war, asylum laws, treaty obligations, as well as the legal rights and obligations of belligerents in a conflict (International Legal Association (ILA) 2010, 4). For example, regardless of the justness of their cause, belligerents on both sides have the right to kill enemy forces without warning and the right to detain prisoners of war without trial for the duration of the conflict (ILA 2010, 2). In addition, it is legally permissible for belligerents to cause some harm to civilians if doing so is a side effect of a necessary military operation, and the harm is not directly intended and is not disproportionate to the importance of the military objectives of the operation (Luban 2002, 9).[1]

The laws of armed conflict also restrict how enemy forces may be treated. Since "fighting back is a legitimate response of the enemy" (Luban 2002, 9), enemy combatants may not be tried or punished for their participation in a conflict (even if their cause is unjust), they may not be tortured or mistreated if they are captured (International Committee of the Red Cross (ICRC) 2010), and if captured they must be released upon the cessation of hostilities.[2]

The legal freedoms and constraints imposed on belligerents reflect distinct features of armed conflicts. First, armed conflicts typically occur in circumstances in which a state's domestic authority and law enforcement either do not apply to the conflicting parties (as in conflicts between states, or between states and foreign non-state groups) or cannot apply (as in cases of severe civil unrest where domestic authority has broken down). Thus in a typical war there is either no authority that has jurisdiction over the parties involved (as in inter-state wars), or there is no authority that is capable of enforcing its jurisdiction over the conflicting parties (as in a civil war or insurgency).

This feature of war gives rise to practical and political reasons in favor of maintaining the current legal framework of armed conflict, even if one believes that, morally speaking, some belligerents do not have a right to fight back and some combatants should be punished for fighting for unjust causes. For example, while Jeff McMahan (2006; 2009) has criticized the view that combatants on both sides of a conflict are morally equal, he defends the legal equality of combatants:

> The law must of course permit just combatants to kill enemy combatants. . . . And it would be wholly inefficacious to forbid unjust combatants to do the same; therefore the law must at present permit all combatants to kill their enemy counterparts. (McMahan 2009, 109)

An additional practical reason in favor of the current legal status of belligerents is that it may be impossible to resolve such conflicts without the freedoms that belligerent status involves. For example, it would be impossible to apply the high evidentiary standards characteristic of law enforcement operations to a war situation. Likewise, it may be impossible for military forces operating in a combat zone to gain sufficient intelligence to enable them to restrict the use of force only to military targets, and so it may be impossible to avoid inflicting some harm to civilians and civilian infrastructure. The urgency of ending a conflict might also rule out the use of law enforcement operations such as long-running infiltration of enemy groups, and surveillance operations.

Thus, even though the laws of armed conflict are more permissive both in terms of the evidentiary standards that are required to be met before enemy forces may be attacked and in terms of permissible collateral damage, these laws aim to minimize the overall destruction caused by an armed conflict.

Definitions of War

Given war's unique status, a plausible definition of war should meet a number of basic criteria. It should be able to account for war's unique status, and distinguish war from other forms of political and nonpolitical violence. Arguably, it should also be consistent with everyday usage. However, it need not be *identical* with common usage given the frequent use of "war" to describe many different kinds of battles, such as the "war against drugs." Finally, the plausibility of a given definition must be assessed in light of the purpose for which the definition is created.

A definition of war can serve a number of purposes: It can be designed for use in a particular legal context to enable the ready identification of situations to which a specific body of laws apply; it can be intended to describe the conditions under which war is morally permissible; or it might be intended to help identify certain kinds of conflicts for the purposes of political or sociological analysis.

Taking these factors into account, we can distill the following rough taxonomy of definitions of war. The following categories are not intended to be exhaustive[3] or exclusive – a definition of war could include normative, political, and sociological elements.

Just War Definitions

Just war definitions identify the conditions under which waging war is morally permitted rather than the conditions that define war as such. This conception of war is part of the just war tradition associated with thinkers such as Augustine, who was concerned with whether waging war is consistent with Christian principles (Reichberg et al. 2006, 72) and Thomas Aquinas, who developed and elaborated many of the *jus ad bellum* criteria, including just cause, legitimate authority, and rightful intention (Reichberg et al. 2006, 176–177). Just war conceptions of war were further developed by thinkers including Francisco de Vitoria (2003) and, in the twentieth century, Michael Walzer (2000).

Juridical Definitions

Juridical definitions of war emerged in the seventeenth century in the context of the developing international law of war, and aim to identify the conditions under which the laws of war apply, rather than determining when war is just.[4] For example, Hugo Grotius in *The Rights of War and Peace* (1625) defines war simply as "the state of contending parties, considered as such," and argues that a definition of war should not include the criteria of a just war "because it is the Design of this Treatise [*The Rights of War and Peace*] to examine, whether any War be just, and what War may be so called. But we must distinguish that which is in Question, from that concerning which the Question is proposed" (Tuck 2005, 136).

A good example of a contemporary legal definition, and one that I will discuss later, is that proposed by the International Law Association (ILA) at The Hague in 2010. The ILA defines armed conflict as occurring when there is "the existence of organized armed groups" who are "engaged in fighting of some intensity" (ILA 2010, 2). The ILA's definition is intended to be consistent with the development of jurisprudence on the laws of armed conflict during the twentieth century, and to allow the identification of conflicts to which IHL would apply.

Political and Sociological Definitions

Broadly speaking, political definitions focus on the aims that characterize the use of war and sociological definitions describe a set of specific material facts about a conflict, such as the duration, number of casualties, and the nature of the belligerents. A classic example of a political definition is Carl von Clausewitz's definition of war as "an act of violence intended to compel our opponents to fulfill our will" (von Clausewitz 2008, 92).

An example of a sociological definition is the following definition proposed by Singer and Small (1972) and Deutsch and Senghaas (1971), who define war as any series of events that meets the following three criteria:

(1) Size: war results in at least 1000 battle deaths (not counting, therefore, the indirect victims through famine, lack of shelter, and disease)
(2) Preparation: war has been prepared in advance, and/or is being maintained, by large-scale social organizations through such means as the recruitment, training, and deployment of troops; the acquisition, storage, and distribution of arms and ammunition; the making of specific war plans and the like; and
(3) Legitimation: war is legitimized by an established governmental or quasi-governmental organization, so that large-scale killing is viewed not as a crime but as a duty.

This definition (and other sociological definitions) aims to allow identification of a particular *kind* of war for the purposes of answering specific questions about, for example, the duration of certain kinds of conflicts.

A NEW DEFINITION OF WAR

In this section, I defend the following definition of war:

A war exists when all the following conditions are met:

(1) There are two or more organized groups.
(2) These groups are engaged in intense hostilities.
(3) No party to the conflict and no third party has the authority and ability to effectively adjudicate between the opposing sides, punish them, and otherwise maintain effective control in the arena of the conflict.

In relation to the taxonomy of definitions described above, this definition fits most naturally in the category of sociological definitions. The definition is not normative or political, since it makes no reference to the aims of the parties involved or the conditions of a just war. Rather, it is intended to pick out the material facts that can explain and justify war's unique legal status. Thus, while it is not a legal definition, it is a definition that can serve the purposes of international law by identifying the characteristics of war that warrant the application of the laws of armed conflict.

Elements of the Definition

There Are Two or More Organized Groups

In their report, the ILA stated that the existence of "organized armed groups" is determined by, among other things, the presence of a command structure, "training, recruiting ability, communications, and logistical capacity" (ILA 2010, 2). I concur with this characterization of organized groups, with the exception that I think unarmed groups could be belligerents. As I shall argue in Section 3, I believe that a state of war can exist in which at least one party does not use military weapons or direct physical violence.

I agree with the ILA that the wearing of uniforms is not required for the status of "organized groups" to be met, since such a requirement is arbitrarily narrow and, after 1977, is no longer listed as a criterion of combatant status under the Geneva Conventions, replaced instead by "carrying arms openly" (1977 Additional Protocol (I) to the Geneva Conventions, Art. 44).[5] To give just one example, ISIS fighters do not wear any kind of conventional uniform, yet I would argue that the conflict against ISIS counts as a war under most plausible definitions of war, and that ISIS counts as an organized group in the relevant sense.

Intensity of Hostilities

Intensity is a concept that cannot be defined precisely. While the ILA does not define intensity, they reject definitions of intensity that include a specific number of casualties or that require a conflict to continue for a specific duration, stating that while "the requirement of intensity will normally have a temporal aspect... a lesser level of duration may satisfy the criterion if the intensity level is high" (ILA 2010, 30).

The ILA is correct to reject definitions of intensity that include a fixed number of casualties. In Singer and Small's (1972) definition, one criterion of war was "at least 1000 battle deaths" (van der Dennen 1980, 6). The problem with this condition (and with any definition that includes a set number of casualties) is that the line between war and lesser conflicts becomes arbitrary. Under Singer and Small's definition, a conflict that meets the criteria of preparation and legitimation, but that only causes 995 battle casualties would not count as a war. Yet it is difficult to see why an additional five casualties could explain or justify the significant change in status signaled by calling a conflict a war. It is important that a definition of war explain when and why a conflict becomes a war, but appealing to a fixed number of causalities is not a plausible way of marking that distinction.

For that reason, I propose that intensity should be measured by the level of disruption caused by a conflict to those living in the arena of conflict (combatants and civilians), including the impact on their physical safety; access to basic goods such as food, water, warmth, and shelter; and the functioning of basic civilian infrastructure. In essence, a conflict meets the criterion of intensity when it becomes so disruptive that the ability of civilians to meet their basic needs is seriously threatened, and the local authorities are unable to effectively control the conflict and protect civilians and civilian infrastructure from harm. However, the intensity requirement does not require that each party to a conflict experience the same degree of disruption. Thus, this criterion could be met in cases where neither party to a conflict experiences significant disruption, as when a conflict between two states takes place primarily outside the geographic boundaries of both states.

This means that intensity can't be measured simply by the numbers of people killed or wounded in a conflict, but requires looking more broadly at the impact of a conflict on civilians' ability to meet their basic needs, as well as the impact on the functioning of basic civilian infrastructure such as the electricity and water supply. In addition, the intensity of a conflict will also depend on preexisting facts about the stability of the local government in the arena of conflict, the effectiveness of local law enforcement and emergency services, and the ability of local infrastructure and resources to withstand attacks. So a conflict in a weak state with few resources might meet the criterion of intensity far sooner than an equivalent conflict within a strong state with effective law enforcement and emergency services.

In relation to the concept of "hostilities," I argue that the concept of hostilities should incorporate ways of inflicting harm that do not involve the infliction of physical violence. This would allow my proposed definition to be applied to conflicts that do not use military force, and would capture how such conflicts could still cause sufficient disruption and destruction to justify the imposition of the legal framework of war. Thus, I define "hostilities" as the intentional infliction of substantial damage (which need not be limited to physical damage) to the lives and welfare of individuals (including their access to basic goods, as well as their physical and psychological health), and to the infrastructure, environment, and basic functioning of states and communities.

No Adjudicating Authority

> No party to the conflict and no other third party has the authority and ability to effectively adjudicate between the opposing sides, punish them, and otherwise maintain effective control in the arena of the conflict.

This criterion is necessary in order to distinguish war from other forms of inter- and intra-state violence. One problem with competing definitions such as the ILA's is a failure to clearly distinguish war from conflicts involving belligerents who fall under the legal jurisdiction of a third party that is able to enforce its authority. Fighting between two criminal gangs in a state, for example, should not be treated as a war if the state is able to maintain effective authority over its jurisdiction, since both groups are legally subject to the state even if neither group acknowledges that fact.

This criterion applies to both inter- and intra-state conflicts. The criterion may be most easily met in the case of international conflicts, given that as yet there is no organization that has effective authority over conflicting states, since effective authority does not just mean legal authority or jurisdiction. Arguably, the UN has at least some legal authority over member states, but it does not as yet have enforceable authority over them.

In cases of non-international armed conflicts such as civil wars, one party to a conflict may have political authority over the other, but if the conflict reaches a degree of intensity such that one party can no longer effectively *enforce* its authority over the other, then the third criterion would be met. However, we may wonder when this point is reached. In my view, the third criterion would be met when one party's authority is so weakened that they lose effective control over a sufficient number of areas in their jurisdiction such that they are unable to protect civilians in those areas or enforce their political and legal authority.

The Aims of Belligerents

Even if one accepts the above defense of the elements of my definition, one might argue that my definition is inadequate because it makes no reference to the aims of belligerents. This omission may seem troubling, since it suggests that conflicts involving non-political groups such as criminal gangs and corporations could count as wars. I argue that this omission can be defended.

As it stands, my definition does not distinguish traditional war from certain extreme forms of criminal violence. For example, the ongoing conflict between Mexican drug cartels and the Mexican government is conducted by organized groups – drug cartels are highly structured, with chains of command and supply lines – and clearly meets the criterion of intense hostilities (there have been over 60,000 casualties in the last ten years (Bender 2014)). So it appears that this conflict meets my definition of war. Interestingly, while the ILA's definition does not include any reference to the aims of belligerents, the ILA states that, in relation to the Mexican conflict: "If the criminal gangs decided to *challenge civil authorities for the right to govern, as opposed to fighting to prevent the break-up of their criminal activities*, Mexico could become the scene of a non-international armed conflict" (ILA 2010, 28. Emphasis added). This suggests that the ILA doesn't consider the conflict in Mexico to be an armed conflict because the drug cartels are fighting to maintain control over their criminal activities, rather than seeking political power. While this view accords with many traditional understandings of war, I believe it is flawed.

Can a Criminal Organization Wage War?

If the conflict between the drug cartels and the Mexican government were characterized as a war, the drug cartels would have at least some of the legal privileges of belligerents. While they would not count as lawful belligerents unless they carried their arms openly, and belonged to an organization that was able to apply military discipline and abide by the laws of armed conflict (1977 Additional Protocol (I) to the Geneva Conventions, Art. 44), cartel soldiers would have the right to target Mexican government soldiers, attack military targets, and expose civilians to a degree of harm in the course of the armed conflict, proportionate to the importance of their military objectives. Likewise, the Mexican government would have expanded powers permitting the use of force that endangers civilians to some degree. Such consequences are disturbing and seem, on the face of it, to offer strong reasons why this conflict and others like it should not be defined as wars.

But this is too quick. If a conflict meets the criteria of intensity, organization, and lack of effective authority, why shouldn't it be called a war? Since, as I have argued, the legal status of war is justified in part by practical and political considerations regarding how to mitigate the destruction caused by wars, perhaps it should not matter if one of the belligerents is a criminal organization.

There are two main objections to this view. First, while cartel foot soldiers would be legally accountable for violations of the laws of armed conflict and for their criminal activities, it is highly counterintuitive to suggest that criminals could be legally permitted to kill Government soldiers and endanger civilians in pursuit of a criminal aim. In addition, unlike ordinary combatants, members of drug cartels cannot plausibly be given any "benefit of the doubt" regarding the legality or morality of their cause. It is implausible to suppose that members of drug cartels don't realize that they are engaged in highly illegal activities.

The argument described above has some force. However, if the reason why cartel soldiers shouldn't have *any* of the legal rights granted to belligerents is because they are fighting for a clearly illegal cause, then this claim can't be limited only to soldiers fighting for criminal organizations. Soldiers fighting for Milosevic in the former Yugoslavia (Hartmann 2011), for example, could hardly be unaware that they were involved in a genocidal campaign.

In addition, some of the reasons traditionally given for excusing combatants fighting for an unjust cause (such as forcible conscription and exposure to propaganda) apply to cartel soldiers. For example, a number of drug cartels use child soldiers, many of whom are poor, uneducated, and are "enticed or manipulated" into working for the cartels (Beckhusen 2013).[6] If there is any force to the idea that the laws of war should apply equally to both sides regardless of the morality of their cause, then one cannot draw a non-arbitrary distinction between cartel soldiers and (say) combatants fighting for genocidal regimes. If the latter shouldn't be prosecuted for fighting, there are reasons for excusing the former as well.

The second reason for denying belligerent status to drug cartels is that the cartels' primary aim is to further their criminal enterprises. While drug cartels and other criminal organizations might aim to *influence* political decision-making (for example, by bribery) and may challenge state authority in some areas and even become *de facto* leaders in those areas, this is typically in pursuit of their criminal goals and not in pursuit of political power *per se*.

This argument relies on two problematic premises. First, this argument assumes that it is possible to draw a sufficiently clear distinction between political and criminal aims to enable the ready identification of the aims of groups involved in conflicts. While there are wars in which the aims of both parties are clearly political (however "political" is defined, which is itself an important question), there are many wars where the distinction is far from clear, such as in wars of conquest and wars of plunder.

Second, this argument assumes that political (but not criminal or non-political) aims play a central role in justifying war's unique status. It is true that early just war theorists such as Aquinas and Augustine often distinguished war from private violence on the grounds that war was characterized by the pursuit of public welfare. For example, Aquinas argued that an individual could not declare war because it was not his duty "to summon together the people, which has to be done in wartime" (Reichberg et al. 2006, 177). However, the fact that political aims may play a role in *justifying* war does not mean political aims are essential to *defining* war, particularly since some political aims (such as genocidal campaigns and forcible occupation of a foreign country) are criminal according to international law, and arguably morally worse than the aims of some non-political groups who are involved in conflicts.

In addition, as I argued above, my definition is not a normative or political definition. Instead, it is intended to identify the conditions that must be present in order to justify the application of the laws of armed conflict. While the aims for which a war is fought are important for the purposes of sociological and normative analysis, they are not relevant to the question of whether a conflict should count as a war in the first place. Thus, my view echoes Grotius' claim that "We do not include Justice in the Definition of War" (Tuck 2005, 136). In Grotius' account, war is not defined as involving the pursuit of public or political aims. Rather, public wars are simply one "species" of the "genus" of war and the term can also be applied to other forms of conflict, such as that between private individuals (Tuck 2005, 136).

Furthermore, limiting the term "war" to conflicts fought for public rather than private aims arbitrarily restricts the use of the term. If two conflicts are identical in every respect (intensity, organization, and so forth) except that one is in pursuit of private aims and one is in pursuit of political aims, it strikes me as implausible to say that only one of these conflicts is a war even though the material facts in each case are identical.

UNARMED CONFLICTS

The chapters in this volume discuss many different forms of unarmed conflict. Several chapters discuss the use of non-kinetic or nonviolent tactics within the context of an existing war, such as kidnapping and extortion (Meisels, this volume). Here, I want to consider whether the use of unarmed force *by itself* could constitute a war as I have defined it. As we shall see, the possibility that unarmed force could amount to war raises hard questions about the scope and possibilities of "fighting back" against unarmed force, how to apply categories such as "combatant" and "civilian," and how to understand the distinction between civilian and military targets. If unarmed conflicts can count as wars, it may be the case that some of the central concepts in the laws of armed conflict would need to be reformulated to accommodate this possibility.

Lawfare

The term "lawfare" typically refers to the use or abuse of IHL by belligerents in order to (for example) hamper their opponent's military strategies, or undermine their opponent's perceived legitimacy by leveling accusations of war crimes against them (Blank, this volume; Dill, this volume; Dunlap 2010). Thus "the most common understanding of lawfare is not State A's use of law to get State B to do its bidding against B's will, but A's abuse of law to that end" (Dill, this volume, 3). However, the question of whether lawfare itself could be a form of war has not been seriously considered. It is difficult to see how even bad faith appeals to IHL could, in themselves, cause sufficient harm to ever count as a form of war.

That said, I think it is possible that the use of legal resources by one group against another could meet my definition of war. To illustrate this possibility, I will modify a real-life example, that of the actions of the Texaco oil company in Ecuador. The Texaco oil company was accused of causing massive environmental damage "leading to devastating impacts on plants and wildlife, human health, and local cultural practices" (Joseph 2012, 71) in Ecuador's Amazonian rainforests from 1967 to 1990. The indigenous people from that region have spent many years seeking compensation through US courts from Texaco and its merged successor company ChevronTexaco (now known as Chevron), and the company has been accused of using "new, recycled and even contradictory legal arguments ... to thwart its adversaries" (Joseph 2012, 70).

For the sake of argument (I am not claiming that this is in fact the case) let us suppose that Chevron did cause the degree of devastation to the environment, local culture, and health of the indigenous people that it has been accused of, and did so intentionally or at least in full knowledge of the destructive effects of its operations. Would Chevron's subsequent use of the legal system to avoid compensating the indigenous people and paying for environmental cleanup operations amount to a war against the indigenous people? This is a separate question from whether the original oil operation itself was as an act of war, an issue that I cannot explore in this chapter.[7] Rather, the question is whether Chevron's use of legal tactics to avoid environmental clean-up constitutes a form of war because of the foreseeable effects of such legal tactics on the continued risks posed to the indigenous people and their community by Chevron's failure to address the environmental damage.

I suggest that the answer might be "yes" *if* it can be shown that the legal obstacles used by Chevron continued and even worsened the environmental damage and health impacts of the original oil operations. If this is the case, then arguably the criterion of "intense hostilities" would be met, since Chevron's activities would amount to a serious and ongoing attack on the basic welfare and needs of the indigenous people. Chevron's actions constitute an attack because the ongoing harm to the indigenous people would be the result of the environmental effects of the oil operations *and* Chevron's abuse of the law – an abuse that worsened and continued the original harm. This would thus be a case of "lawfare" because the abuse of the law is a central means by which serious harm is inflicted.

In addition, Chevron counts as an "organized group" as I have defined it, and if (as has been claimed) the Ecuadorian government was unable (and unwilling) to conduct effective cleanup operations (Joseph 2012, 72) there is no effective authority to "adjudicate between the opposing sides, punish them, and otherwise maintain effective control in the arena of the conflict." While the US court system has a degree of legal authority over the parties involved, the court system does not possess effective authority over the arena of combat – in this case, the affected area in Ecuador.

If this is correct, and Chevron is committing an act of war against the indigenous Ecuadorians, then who are the combatants, and what rights and privileges do they have? Would the indigenous Ecuadorians have the right to use lethal force against the leaders of Chevron and the lawyers involved in the case? Or even against the Ecuadorian government for its failure to protect them? If so, could they expose innocent civilians to risks in the use of such force?

My tentative answer is that, yes, the indigenous Ecuadorians would have the right to use lethal force against those most responsible for the destruction of their home. However, we first need to clarify what "most responsible" means in the context of an unarmed conflict.

Since Chevron is not a military organization, we can't use traditional methods of distinguishing combatants from noncombatants and military from non-military targets. There must be an alternative method of determining combatant status. While I cannot offer a detailed solution here, one possibility is to construe combatant status in unarmed conflicts in terms of an individual's normative relationship to the relevant harms rather than in terms of whether they wear a uniform or carry arms openly. This idea is similar to Michael Gross' idea of "participatory liability" (this volume, 397; 2015, 68–72), but differs in one important aspect. In Gross' view, a civilian may be subject to some form of defensive force depending on the degree of their "contribution to a war effort" (this volume, 397). Gross doesn't clarify whether this contribution is to be understood in causal terms (i.e. determined by whether and to what degree a civilian's actions make a causal difference to the war effort), but it is reasonable to interpret his account in this way. In my view, in contrast, an individual's relationship to the harms in question need not be causal in order to warrant ascriptions of responsibility, particularly given the notorious difficulty of establishing individual causal responsibility for harms that are the result of collective actions (Kutz 2000). Instead, the relationship between an individual and her actions can be explained in terms of the centrality of an individual's role to the achievement of the collective aims (Kutz 2000, 159). In this view,

Chevron's senior management and the lawyers involved in the case would bear significant responsibility for the harm inflicted on the indigenous people, since their actions and their roles reveal a normative commitment to intentionally furthering ends that foreseeably cause continued harm, regardless of each person's individual causal contribution to that harm.

But while this account may allow the identification of combatants in unarmed wars, it is less clear how to identify the equivalent of legitimate institutional targets such as military headquarters. If Chevron's leaders are combatants, would this mean that the headquarters of Chevron are a legitimate target? Not necessarily. In a conventional war, military headquarters and base camps are legitimate targets at least partly because the main function of those institutions is to assist in prosecuting the war. But the headquarters of a corporation like Chevron are involved in many different operations and functions. The pursuit of the legal war against the indigenous people would be only one small aspect of their operations. So, while some of Chevron's leaders are arguably responsible for the harm inflicted on the indigenous people, the company *as an institution* is not geared toward that end. Thus, while I think a case can be made for the use of lethal force against individual members of the corporation on the grounds outlined above, it is far more difficult to make the case that Chevron headquarters would be a legitimate target.

This has implications for the issue of collateral damage. If I am right that, at least in this example, there is no clear equivalent to legitimate targets such as military headquarters, this suggests that there might be a much lower tolerance of collateral damage in the prosecution of unarmed wars. If we can identify responsible individuals (but not large-scale targets), then perhaps the most appropriate normative framework to adopt in these cases is that of targeted killings or assassinations. While both of these tactics are controversial (Finkelstein et al. 2012), they provide the best way of encompassing the possibility of unarmed conflicts and permitting the use of force against responsible parties without significantly endangering civilians.

Economic Sanctions

According to Joy Gordon (this volume), economic sanctions "typically involve the withdrawal of trade, although they may also include terminating foreign aid, blocking the use of currency, denying access to international financial institutions, and blocking access to humanitarian aid." Gordon notes that over the last century economic sanctions have been used for a range of political purposes, from being viewed initially as a "form of warfare, serving the military interests of the parties to a conflict" to being used "to express disapproval, or to exert influence or create pressure, by causing inconvenience or imposing additional costs on the economy of the target nation," as, for example, when the UN Security Council imposed economic sanctions against South Africa for apartheid (this volume, 58–59).

But because economic sanctions typically do not involve kinetic force and were framed by the League of Nations and the United Nations as "peaceful pressure" (Gordon, this volume, 63), "sanctions have eluded both the scrutiny and the criticism which would have been forthcoming if the same acts were seen as a form of warfare" (Gordon, this volume, 61). Yet the idea that just war principles can be applied to economic sanctions is not particularly controversial (Meisels 2011; Pierce 1996). In addition, if we accept the claim that wars need not involve the use of military force, as I argued in an earlier section, one of the reasons against applying a just war framework to economic sanctions falls away.

It is relatively easy to show that the use of economic sanctions could meet the criteria of war as I have defined it. This would be the case if sanctions are imposed by an organized group, cause severe foreseeable harm to the civilians, infrastructure, and environment of the state or community targeted by the sanctions, and there is no effective authority with jurisdiction over the parties involved. There is at least one real-life case where the use of economic sanctions plausibly meets these criteria: the use of economic sanctions against Iraq authorized by the UN Security Council, and implemented primarily by the United States (with support from the British) after the 1991 Gulf war. There is evidence that the sanctions caused severe suffering to the civilian population, and hindered the repair of essential civilian infrastructure. For example, the imposition of the sanctions has been linked to the deaths of 237,000 children under the age of five (Gordon 2014–2015, 2), and contributed to severe cholera and typhoid epidemics in 1994 by denying Iraq access to resources that would have enabled the rebuilding of sewage and water treatment plants that had been damaged in the first Gulf War (Gordon 2004; 2010).

If these claims are accurate, then it is clear that the use of sanctions in this case fits my definition of war. This does not mean that the use of sanctions against Iraq was therefore wrong, but it does mean that Iraq would have been justified in viewing themselves as belligerents in a war with the United States[8] during the time the sanctions were imposed, and that Iraq had a right to fight back against the sanctions.

As with the lawfare example, however, clearly identifying the legitimate targets against which Iraq could use defensive force is difficult and a full discussion of this question is beyond the scope of this chapter. The sanctions were authorized by the UN Security Council, and were carried out with the assistance of thousands of individuals and organizations, many of whom would not count as legitimate targets in a conventional war. However, the method of assigning responsibility that I discussed earlier can offer a useful first step in thinking about this case. The policy makers and officials most responsible for formulating and executing the policy bear significant responsibility for the harm caused by the sanctions, so a case can be made for considering them legitimate targets. In addition, other individuals who played an integral role in enforcing the sanctions (for example, inspectors whose role involved ensuring that sanctioned goods were not permitted to enter Iraq) may also be legitimate targets depending on how central their role is to the enforcement of the sanctions. Other possible legitimate targets could include buildings (not necessarily in Iraq itself) such as warehouses that were used to store goods banned by the sanctions. In those cases, if those structures played a central role in the enforcement of the sanctions, they would count as legitimate targets also.

Cyber Warfare

In his contribution to this volume, George Lucas outlines the history of cyber-attacks, from early pranks and "cyber vandalism" (Lucas this volume, 86) to sophisticated attacks involving "vigilantes" targeting government and commercial service sites as a form of political protest, or in order to expose perceived wrong-doing (Lucas this volume, 87). None of these attacks would, in my view, constitute war. As with economic sanctions, cyber-attacks meet my definition of war only if an organized group orchestrates such attacks and inflicts intense hostilities in a context in which there is no third party authority able to enforce its jurisdiction. As yet, no cyber-attacks fit this description.

However, this may change. As Lucas notes, "many states are resorting to massive cyber attacks" instead of using more traditional channels (such as diplomacy or trade negotiations) to "pursue political objectives against other states" (Lucas this volume, 88). Examples of such supposedly state-sponsored attacks include the attack on Sony Pictures (attributed to North Korea), and the attack on US financial institutions by an organization calling itself "Cyber Fighters of Izz ad-Din al-Qassam," a group linked to Iran (Lucas this volume, 89). If cases like these are in fact state-sponsored cyber-attacks orchestrated by organized groups, this raises the possibility that such attacks could increase in frequency and intensity. However, while cyber-attacks such as those described above could be launched by organized groups in a context where there is no effective third-party authority, could such attacks cause sufficient harm to meet the criterion of intense hostilities?

Lucas notes that cyber-attacks rarely if ever cause physical damage to people and property. Instead, "the [cyber] conflict results in loss of information, loss of access to information processing, and an inability to carry out essential activities (such as banking, mining, medical care, trade, and commerce) that rely largely upon information processing". Thus, although there has been no "cyber Armageddon" involving massive disruptions of essential services, the cyber-attacks that have occurred are "quite destructive and malevolent ... capable of causing massive social upheaval, or bringing about a 'death by 1,000 cuts' through pilfering of industrial or state secrets, or by interference with trade, commerce, finance, medical care, and transportation" (Lucas this volume, 91–92).

Given that cyber-attacks could seriously interfere with essential services such as medical care and transportation, it is possible that cyber-attacks could inflict intense hostilities, even if little physical damage is done. Since I define hostilities to include acts that inflict "substantial and ongoing damage to the lives and welfare of individuals, and the infrastructure, environment, and basic functioning of states and communities," cyber-attacks that seriously affect medical, transportation, and financial systems could cause this level of damage to the welfare of civilians and the functioning of the state. In such cases, the "combatants" would not be soldiers but the computer experts responsible for carrying out the attacks, and those in charge of authorizing and coordinating the attacks. However, because of the likelihood that cyber-combatants might be operating from primarily civilian locales, as with the lawfare case, I would argue that defensive force would have to be limited to attacks on individuals as much as possible. Of course, if cyber-attacks were launched from military installations, then such installations could be considered legitimate targets.

While the above examples refer to state-sponsored attacks, it is possible that non-state groups could also wage war through cyber-attacks, if such groups did not fall under the jurisdiction of an effective authority. However, it is much less likely (although not impossible) that an individual could wage war in this manner. This is not because an individual couldn't cause extreme harm through cyber-attacks, but because in most cases there would be an effective authority with jurisdiction over that individual, and thus the breakdown of effective authority that is characteristic of war would not be present.

CONCLUSION

In this chapter, I have argued in favor of a definition of war that I believe captures the nature of war and accounts for war's distinct legal and normative status. Given that one of the important roles played by the law of armed conflict is to minimize the destruction caused by war, my definition would restrict use of the term "war" to conflicts that exist in a context in which authority has broken down, and where the welfare of all those affected is seriously threatened.

In applying my definition to three examples of unarmed conflicts, I have shown that it is possible that the use of non-kinetic methods could, in rare cases, meet the criteria of war. Through expanding the idea of "hostilities" to include ways of harming that do not rely on physical violence, and through exploring how categories such as combatant and civilian might apply in unarmed conflicts, my definition allows a better understanding of the legal and normative implications of the use of unarmed force.

NOTES

I would like to thank Michael Gross, Tami Meisels, Valerie Morkevičius, and an anonymous referee for their helpful feedback on this chapter.

1. This is in stark contrast to law enforcement operations. Police officers are strictly prohibited from causing harm to innocent people in their pursuit of criminals, and criminals have no legal right to fight back against law enforcement.

2. Article 118, Convention III relative to the Treatment of Prisoners of War (Geneva Conventin III, 1949).
3. See van der Dennen (1980) and Eagleton (1932–1933) for detailed surveys of definitions of war.
4. I thank Valerie Morkevičius for pointing out this helpful distinction.
5. The 1977 Additional Protocol (I), Art. 44 replaced Geneva Convention III, Art. 4. The United States, however, has refused to ratify Protocol I. I thank an anonymous reviewer at Cambridge University Press for directing my attention to this fact.
6. Thus a reason in favor of giving cartels belligerent status is that doing so might protect vulnerable cartel soldiers from prosecution. I thank Valerie Morkevičius for this suggestion.
7. However, given my conception of "hostilities," it is plausible that the infliction of extreme environmental damage could fit my definition of war if the other conditions were met.
8. And perhaps Britain, although "the United States clearly held the leadership position" (Gordon 2010, 32) in relation to central decisions regarding the sanctions.

2

Coercion, Manipulation, and Harm: Civilian Immunity and Soft War

Valerie Morkevičius

For canonical just war thinkers, war was a scourge. War destroyed lives and communities, and warped the souls of its participants. But war was not humankind's only affliction, and some of these other injustices – especially the breakdown of civil order – were deemed much worse. When, on the balance of things, the use of coercive force could lead ameliorate injustice, thinkers within the historical just war tradition permitted the recourse to war as a corrective measure. But they were no idealists. They did not believe war could be eliminated. Instead, canonical just war thinkers shared with realists a profoundly pessimistic view of the human condition and moral progress (Gilpin 1981; Syse 2007). They did hope, nevertheless, to define limits on when coercive force could be used (what we now call *ad bellum* principles), as well as some limits on how such force could be used (what are now termed *in bello* principles).

I, too, doubt that war can be outlawed or completely tamed. War is a fact of life in an international system lacking both an effective mechanism for resolving inter-state conflicts and an efficient means for reining in rogue states (Augustine 1984; Hobbes 1996; Morgenthau 1946). Faced with war's inevitability, my primary concern is how its most pernicious effects on noncombatants can be reduced. For this reason, in the case of soft war, I am willing to permit nonlethal coercion of civilians, by targeting their property, *if the alternative is the use of lethal tactics*. While civilians' lives and bodies should never be attacked directly and intentionally, nonlethal attacks may be permissible within a tradition that has historically not treated coercion as *mala in se*.

In what follows, I develop an argument in favor of permitting limited, nonlethal attacks on civilian property. To do so, I adopt a canonical just war framework, following in the footsteps of Augustine and Aquinas, to think through some tough moral questions that soft war tactics pose for civilian immunity. I believe that the moral nature of war is essentially unchanged across time – and that if we tell ourselves that war today is more civilized and restrained than it was at some time in the past, it is only because we have learned "more effective ways of using force than the crude expression of instinct" (von Clausewitz 1984, 76). Arguments similar to the one I build in this chapter could be developed within other just war traditions – the Islamic and Hindu traditions, for example. In this chapter, however, I've chosen to work within the historical Western just war tradition. This approach reflects my realist roots. The Western just war tradition is the language of the great powers (Sjoberg 2014, 153). It is also the language of international law (Walzer 2002, 927). This is especially true of the military interpretation of the laws of armed conflict, which takes military necessity – rather than civilians' human rights – as its starting point (Luban 2013). The historical just war tradition, likewise, was interested in mitigating the horrors of war, while keeping the rules simple and practical enough to be feasibly applied on the battlefield. Thus, an *ad fontes* approach is not so much a way of looking back, as a way of looking forward by bringing a more realistic portrayal of the dilemmas of warfare back in. As I see it, the choice is not between no war and war, nor between a completely bloodless war and total annihilation. Certain kinds of injustices will continue to make war an unfortunate necessity for the foreseeable future. As the means of warfare change, however, we must continuously think about whether our current *in bello* norms will permit us to resolve such conflicts quickly, and with the least possible loss of life, especially for civilians. Certain soft war tactics seem to offer new ways of doing just that, even though they may not be deemed acceptable in a humanitarian reading of international law, or from a revisionist just war perspective.

Although I argue that certain types of coercion and manipulation using soft war tactics may indeed be morally permissible, I also assert that the use of such coercion must be strictly limited. Coercion that relies on the threat of deadly harm is impermissible. So too is coercion that leads inexorably (albeit slowly) to civilian injury and death. For this reason, coercion that seriously undermines civil order is also impermissible. Lastly, coercion – like any other war tactic – must only be used with the end of peace in mind. Thus, coercion that would make post-war reconciliation significantly more difficult should be eschewed.

To develop the case for permitting limited nonlethal attacks on civilian property, I proceed in five steps. First, I briefly define what I mean by soft war. Second, I defend the basic underlying claim of canonical just war thinking: that coercion is permissible to achieve order. Third, I demonstrate that the traditional view of noncombatant immunity was far narrower than it is today. Fourth, I suggest that three broad just war principles – necessity, order, and proportionality – can do a lot of work for us as we try to reason through what sorts of soft war tactics may be allowable. Lastly, I conclude by thinking through several scenarios in which soft war attacks affecting civilians may be impermissible, possibly permissible, or likely permissible.

SOFT WAR

The term soft war is used in two distinct ways. Sometimes, it refers to a category of political action that falls somewhere between "normal" state relations and all-out war. As such, it can include such diverse practices as coercive diplomacy, sanctions, and isolated cyber-attacks. Alternately, soft war can refer to a set of tactics. In this sense, it describes non-kinetic, or sometimes simply nonlethal, means. Such tactics include cyber warfare and information warfare. The phrase is reminiscent of Nye's "soft power," which refers to "the ability to shape the preferences of others through attraction, rather than force," and some soft war tactics do just that (Nye 2004, 5). Propaganda, rumors, control over the media's storyline – all forms of information warfare – can be used to attract segments of the enemy's population to our side. Other means of soft war, though non-kinetic, nonetheless aim at hurt. The use of sanctions to cripple the enemy's economy, for example, or the use of cyber-attacks to shut down the enemy's power grid do not strive to attract the other to our position, but rather to *coerce* him. The potential for soft war to cause real harm means that *in bello* limits matter, just as they do in conventional war.

In this chapter, I will take soft war to be a form of warfare, even though some of the tactics in question – sanctions, for example – are not contemporarily treated under the law of war. Although the demarcation line between war and peace is of great importance in Walzerian just war thinking and international law, this division has historically not been of particular concern. After all, within the canonical tradition, the permissibility of coercion on both the domestic and international levels relied on the same general principles. While revisionist just war thinkers also blur the line between policing and war, their approach differs from the canonical just war framework I am using here. For revisionists, the desire to consistently protect individual human rights motivates a concerted effort to establish a single set of ethical principles for the use of force and coercion across all contexts from the bottom up. By contrast, within the historical just war tradition, policing and war run parallel because both deal with the leader's obligation to maintain order both at home and abroad in a disorderly world.

ORDER AND COERCION

Within the canonical just war tradition, coercion is a permissible tool of statecraft when it is used for the purpose of maintaining or restoring a just order. For Augustine, order – a kind of earthly peace predicated on balancing the wills of many within the commonwealth – was a "gift of God" (Augustine 1984, 600, 877). We focus so much on justice these days – especially those of us in academia – that we tend to forget the value of order. But if we think about the misery generated by the collapse of order in places like Iraq and Syria today, we can get some idea of why early just war theorists held a deep fear of disorder.

After all, we cannot pursue any sort of good life without a fundamental basis of order.

The problem is that order is hard to come by in a world full of centrifugal forces. Sounding like a classical realist, Augustine argues that "all men desire to be at peace with their own people, while wishing to impose their will upon those people's lives. For even when they wage war on others, their wish is to make those opponents their own people" (Augustine 1984, 867). The corrupted nature of mankind after the fall means that everyone seeks domination (Augustine 1984, 604).

And so, polities work to achieve order, through the work of judges and executioners, statesmen and soldiers. Such work is essential: "the duty of anyone who would be blameless includes not only doing no harm to anyone but also restraining a man from sin or punishing his sin, so that either the man who is chastised may be corrected by his experience, or others may be deterred by his example" (Augustine 1984, 876). Order requires some degree of justice, albeit only of a very thin sort, as evidenced by just war thinkers' tendency to encourage people to endure tyranny rather than revolt (Aquinas 2002, 18; Augustine 1984, 599, 870; Morkevičius 2013, 401).

But order also requires some degree of coercion. Augustine thus explains that even those professions that seem the most heartless – the torturer and the executioner – can actually be motivated by love (Augustine 1984, 860). Love operating in the realm of necessity judges and tortures and punishes in order to find out the truth and restore a just order. Just as a state has the right (and the duty) to maintain order domestically, it also has the right to do so in its relationships with other states (Anscombe 1961, 47). Aquinas makes it clear that the same logic is operating in both contexts, declaring that the prince must use force both "in defense of the commonwealth against those who trouble it from within" and "against enemies from without" (Aquinas 2002, 240). Ultimately, for both Augustine and Aquinas, it is "the injustice of the opposing side that lays on the wise man the duty of waging wars" (Aquinas 2002, 240; Augustine 1984, 862). Thus war, like policing, is a coercive tool used by a state in the pursuit of order.

The international order is considerably thinner than the one we aim for domestically. Nonetheless, states seek an Augustinian order in international society, in which "life will be in some measure secure against violence resulting in death," where "promises, once made, will be kept," and where "the possession of things will remain stable to some degree" (Bull 1995, 4). Domestically, the strength of social and political institutions encourages individuals to govern themselves (Foucault 1995, 202–203). Internationally, however, institutions are considerably weaker. Thus, Morgenthau argues that when states do abide by the rules of international law, they do so not because they believe they "ought to," but rather because they share common interests "backed by power as a last resort" or because the balance of power deters states from upsetting the order of the system (Morgenthau 1958, 226). Put differently, international order relies on the rewards and punishments accorded to those who do – or don't – live by the rules (Gilpin 1981, 9).

ON INNOCENCE

The logic of the just war tradition is that the use of force is warranted only in response to a specific wrong committed by the other. Consequently, force can only intentionally be used against those committing the wrong. The tradition thus clearly distinguishes between those liable to harm *because they are participating in the harm*, and those not liable because they are non-harming. The Latin term *innocent*, in this case, does not refer to a moral category, but instead means *non noceres*, or not harming or not injuring (Slim 2003, 499).[1]

Interestingly, for Augustine and Aquinas killing the innocent does not come up when discussing the problem of war. Augustine reports that sometimes judges unintentionally torture and even condemn the innocent, but because such tragedies arise out of a lack of information rather than a desire to harm, he does not find the judges to be culpable. Aquinas does spend a chapter in the *Summa theologiae* discussing the problem of killing the innocent – but it is his chapter on homicide, and not the chapter on war. (Indeed, it is in this context that he develops the famous principle of double effect.) The idea that innocents caught up in war must be protected arose from the Peace of God movement in the early Middle Ages, and was already canon law by Aquinas' time. Thus, his decision to deal with innocents only in his homicide chapter is significant – it squarely associates the killing of innocents with murder.

De Vitoria, writing some two hundred years later, specifically melds Aquinas' concept of double effect with the principle of noncombatant immunity. Like his predecessors, de Vitoria rules the killing of innocents unlawful. Again, his discussion blurs the line between law enforcement and war: "within the commonwealth it is not permissible to punish the innocent for the crimes of the evil, and therefore it is not permissible to kill innocent members of the enemy population for the injury done by the wicked among them" (de Vitoria 2003, 315). De Vitoria carefully identifies the innocent as individuals who are outside the sphere of political or military influence, including children, women (unless they are otherwise implicated), travelers, clergy, and monks "unless there is evidence to the contrary or they are found actually fighting in the war" (de Vitoria 2003, 315). This view of innocence is not far from Walzer's, which creates a class of "nonparticipating civilians," who are not only not soldiers, but also do not "make what soldiers need to fight" (Walzer 2000, 30, 146). It is, however, rather distant from the revisionist view, which is concerned with individuals who make themselves liable to violence by posing a threat to others.

On Killing and Other Harms

Civilian immunity in the classical just war tradition is expressed by the *in bello* principle of discrimination, which demands that civilians never be the direct targets of harm. But what exactly is harm? Clearly, not all harms are deadly, as the contemporary literature is replete with injunctions to choose the least harmful course of action (Kamm 2004, 659; Lazar 2014, 57; McMahan 2011, 152). Harm frequently describes property and economic damage, and even the risk of psychological harm. Arquilla finds that deliberately targeting "civilian economic or other assets" violates noncombatant immunity (Arquilla 1999, 395). Gross takes harm to include "not only death and injury directly caused by military action, but also indirect effects of war: destitution, disease, lawlessness, and insecurity"; at the broadest extent this includes "using [civilians] without their consent or against their will to procure one's ends" (Gross 2005/2006, 561–562). And when Walzer asserts that "it is wrong to threaten what it would be wrong to do," he adds psychological threats to the list of impermissible harms (Walzer 2004, 48). Put simply, contemporary just war thinking, in both its Walzerian and revisionist strands, has inherited a view of harm rooted in the individual human rights tradition, and reflective of contemporary international humanitarian law. This perspective prohibits harm against innocent noncombatants.

The historical just war tradition was also very specific about what harm entailed, namely, unjustly taking the life of another. Because *harm* was historically understood as the use (or threatened use) of lethal force, the tradition did not forbid other forms of coercion and manipulation. Thus, although the tradition was concerned with limiting the use of lethal force against non-combatants, it was relatively sanguine about other sorts of harm that could befall them. Augustine and Aquinas say nothing at all about property damage in war. De Vitoria does – but not in the way we might expect. Instead, he justifies the destruction of homes and farms and the seizure of personal property as appropriate means of war (de Vitoria 2003, 317). Arguing that the goods produced by the common people are necessary for the enemy's war effort, de Vitoria declares that destroying or confiscating them may be a vital part of weakening the enemy's forces.

Thus, the tradition suggests that it may be morally permissible to target civilian property. This is clearly in contravention of international humanitarian law, particularly Additional Protocol I. I think there is something to the moral intuition that undergirds humanitarian law (and contemporary just war thinking) that forbids directly targeting civilian property in war. It is far too easy to imagine how a more permissive approach to civilian property could lead to disaster. This is especially true if we imagine the fire bombings of World War II, and the logic that such massive destruction was necessary in order to shut down the militarized economy of Germany and Japan. Indeed, the claim to be aiming at "economic targets" belied a more inconvenient truth – the deliberate targeting of the innocent in the hopes of undermining morale (Anscombe 1961, 59).

But carpet bombing may not be the best analogy for targeting civilian property using soft war tactics. After all, many soft war tactics do not cause physical destruction of property. Many do not cause immediate physical harm to persons, either. If war is inevitable, and if we aim to reduce the suffering of noncombatants, we must seriously consider the possibility that targeting civilian property may be a less evil way to go about the business of maintaining and restoring order.

WITHIN THE LIMITS: NECESSITY, ORDER, AND PROPORTIONALITY

Drawing on the idea that, historically, immunity meant that nonparticipating noncombatants could not be *directly targeted with lethal force*, I argue that while deliberate and permanent destruction of civilian property is morally impermissible, soft war tactics that passively use or even temporarily disable civilian infrastructures may be permissible. Other forms of coercion, such as putting pressure on civilians by limiting access to certain goods, may also be permissible, so long as the denial of such resources will not lead to lethal consequences.

However, the possibility of directly targeting civilian property in this way must be limited by three other principles: necessity, order, and proportionality. Necessity and order are not usually explicitly mentioned in accounts of *in bello* principles, but they undergird the tradition's deeper logics. Both necessity and order limit our actions so that our tactics do not undermine the war's ultimate aim, which must always be to secure peace. Proportionality, the most familiar of the three, figures prominently on most lists of *in bello* just war principles. Here I use it slightly differently, to apply to *direct* attacks, and not only to collateral damage.

Necessity

If wars are fought with peace in mind, force and coercion should be employed only to the extent necessary. The reason is quite simple – excessive use of force renders peacemaking more challenging. When innocents are threatened, at least some of them are likely to fight back (either as individuals, or by joining military or paramilitary forces), and they may even be justified in doing so. Although Augustine and Aquinas denied individuals the right to self-defense, de Vitoria did recognize it in the context of resisting a private (i.e. criminal) attacker. Later, Martin Luther made use of the concept to justify limited resistance to unjust authorities – namely, by defending one's person, family, and property (Luther 1974, 136, 139). Even if we don't accept their armed resistance as justified, the transformation of innocents to combatants under duress expands the scope of the conflict. After all, the deaths of innocents – even when unintentional and indirect – harden hearts and make reconciliation more difficult.

Thus, to prevent war-fighting from rendering peace impossible, the principle of necessity limits the use of force to militarily significant targets. More than this, it requires that any specific target be necessary in itself for the war effort: successfully prosecuting the war effort would be frustrated without it. This particular view of necessity is reflected in international law, which limits attacks to military objects whose "destruction, capture, or neutralization" would offer a "definite military advantage" (AP I, 52(2)). As Walzer explains, we may even consider attacks on civilian industries that directly contribute to the war effort – if their production cannot "be stopped, or their products seized or destroyed, in some other way without significant risk" (Walzer 2000, 144).

Necessity is frequently used this way in the canonical tradition. Aquinas argues that even in cases of personal self-defense, it is "unlawful" to use "more violence ... than is necessary" (Aquinas 2002, 264). Similarly, de Vitoria only permits the recourse to double effect in war as an exculpatory principle if the attack "advances a just war that cannot be won in any other way" (de Vitoria 2003, 315). Likewise, Vitoria cautions "if the war can be satisfactorily waged without plundering farmers or other non-combatants, *it is not lawful to plunder them*" (de Vitoria 2003, 317). So even if we open the door to the possibility of soft attacks on civilian property, we can only go through it if such an attack is truly necessary to our war effort.

Order

The overarching principle of order also limits the targeting of civilian goods. If war is fought for the aim of peace, attacks that seriously disrupt order in certain ways are morally impermissible. First, attacks that would make peace more difficult to restore *post bellum* – by violating trust, for example – should be eschewed. This includes tactics that make the attacker appear to be an untrustworthy negotiator, such as false flag attacks or faked surrender. Second, attacks that induce chaos within the opposing state violate this principle. Chaos is not mere disorder, but rather total disorder that constitutes a humanitarian disaster. The UN office for the Coordination of Humanitarian Affairs defines such humanitarian crises as "complex emergencies" that lead to "total or considerable breakdown of authority" (UN OCHA 2015, 11). Such chaos can either be political, as when a strategy generates a power vacuum that leads to the complete breakdown of law and order, or economic, when it completely cripples the systems of production or trade. In the first case, widespread violence ensues; in the latter, widespread malnutrition and starvation. Both scenarios are likely to displace large numbers of people. The nature of an attack that would generate such a humanitarian crisis will vary according to the target's resilience and vulnerability. States with strong state capacity will be better able to absorb and mitigate the effects of attacks on civilian property, but weak states may find themselves utterly unable to do so.

Proportionality

Necessity and order work together to tell us what may be targeted in a general sort of way, but proportionality helps us to figure out if a particular target may be attacked using a particular tactic. Quite simply, the *in bello* proportionality criteria ask us to weigh the harms of a necessary attack against the goods it is expected to achieve. Traditionally, proportionality modifies the amount of *indirect* harm we may permissibly cause civilians when we directly attack a military target (but unintentionally harm civilians at the same time). But if the aim of war is peace, then it makes sense we should wish to account for proportionality even in direct attacks, especially since it is civilian property we are considering harming.

Weighing the proportionality and necessity criteria together leads naturally to a consideration of alternatives. How else could a particular objective be accomplished? Could it be done in a way that harms fewer people, particularly fewer noncombatants? In the case of soft war, this is particularly interesting. The possibility of exercising coercive power without the use of kinetic force (and possibly with less deadly results) affects the outcome of the proportionality calculus in important ways, as the following section will explain.

PRACTICAL LIMITS: CYBER WARFARE, INFORMATION WARFARE, AND SANCTIONS

In this final section, I work through what the traditional concept of innocence – as mediated by necessity, order, and proportionality – might mean for determining what sorts of targets are morally permissible using various sorts of soft war tactics.

Off Limits

As we have seen, the traditional concept of innocence focuses on protecting people, not property. Nonetheless, the prohibition on targeting innocents with deadly force logically implies that any civilian property that is essential for human survival cannot be directly targeted, for any reason. Such attacks are not only indiscriminate, but are also disproportionate, because no amount of wrong suffered can morally justify directly targeting noncombatants' lives. Thus, food supplies, crops and livestock in the field, markets, and housing are never legitimate targets. De Vitoria is simply wrong to suggest that goods and infrastructure may be targeted because they are also used by the military. His view leaves no space for civilian life. Indeed, contemporary international law makes this clear, prohibiting attacks on objects "indispensable to the survival of the civilian population" (AP I, 54(2)).

Here, Walzer's distinction between the production of goods soldiers need as persons and goods soldiers need as soldiers is useful (Walzer 2000, 146). Food and medicine sustain soldiers' bodies, but those bodies are fundamentally human. Such vital necessities cannot be targeted. But guns and tanks and warplanes sustain warfare, and hence can be targeted, even at the site of their production. Of course, this distinction is fuzzier in practice than it is in theory (Fabre 2009). Despite the interconnectedness of modern systems of industrial production, preserving this somewhat forced distinction is worthwhile. While those seeking to blur this division today intend to protect civilians by complicating our understanding of the divide between civilian and military spheres (raising the specter that modern war may never be morally permissible), in practice this line of thinking is apt to backfire. As long as military planners believe attacking the enemy's war-making capabilities is an efficient way to win wars, industrial production will come under attack. If we accept – whether as realists or traditional just war thinkers – that war is tragically inevitable, we must aim to elucidate *in bello* principles that are realistically practicable.

Targeting essential goods (or the means of their production) directly is to target civilian lives. And so the line must be drawn here. In the soft war context, this means that sanctions may not restrict civilian access to necessary imports of food and medicine. Energy supplies may be interrupted, to drive up costs, but cutting them off entirely would be impermissible in most cases, as modern societies are dependent on oil, gas, and electricity for heating, for refrigerating food and medicine, and for purifying water supplies. While the deaths that result from such sanctions may not be as quick as the deaths caused by an exploding bomb, they are equally direct (Gordon 2010). Certainly, a responsible state could try to ration goods to be sure that the most vulnerable do not suffer more than anyone else, but increasing globalization has left few states in a position of being self-sufficient in terms of agriculture and energy. Sanctions imposed gradually over a significant length of time do give states a chance to reorganize their domestic production, but such sanctions are significantly less likely to be effective, and hence are unlikely to meet the necessity test (Haass 2002, 99). But the crux of the matter is this: Even if we could imagine a scenario in which we could impose sanctions on essential goods for a short time, stopping before a humanitarian crisis emerges, it would still be unjust to target such goods. In doing so, we are threatening civilians with death – even though *we* know we don't intend to carry through with it – and this is impermissible (Shue 2016, 73–74).

Likewise, infrastructures necessary for sustaining civilian life may not be targeted in cyber warfare. Cyber or electromagnetic pulse attacks that would shut off the electrical grid are impermissible due to their effects on medical and sanitation systems. Cyber-attacks that disable the electrical grid are potentially reversible, but nonetheless should be eschewed as the consequences to civilians (especially over the medium to long term) of disrupting the flow of power can be quite grave (Shue 2016, 302). Similarly, cyber-attacks that would lead nuclear plants to meltdown or dams to overflow would be tantamount to targeting civilian lives, even if their deaths were (technically) only incidental to the initial attack.

Furthermore, any cyber-attack that would destroy medical equipment or medical information storage is impermissible. More subtly, cyber-attacks that would delete medical information from local servers, holding it for ransom, are similarly impermissible. Holding vital medical data hostage is akin to holding civilians hostage, by hindering the ability of their doctors to provide them necessary health care. Although these sorts of attacks ostensibly target property, not persons, the humanitarian effects are so widespread and devastating as to render them impermissible. Furthermore, such attacks are unlikely to meet the necessity criterion. Just as broad-based sanctions (or for that matter, carpet bombing) are unlikely to effectively coerce a state into changing its behavior, electrical grid attacks are unlikely to be effective, as most militaries have backup power sources (Bayles 2001, 52). Similarly, military computer systems are more likely to be secured – or to have backup systems – than civilian ones.

If medical and sanitation facilities are vital to civilians' physical lives, historical archives and online libraries are essential to their cultural lives. Just as The Hague Convention and Additional Protocol I protect cultural property in armed conflict, we should eschew targeting cultural objects on the internet. Some of this content is "born-digital," existing only in digital form – such as digital photographs and recordings, as well as documents and archives stored only electronically (Dinniss 2012, 232). Digital reproductions of physical works, as well as libraries and archives that exist both in physical and digital forms, are also important to protect, as they may become the only record of important objects of cultural heritage if the original is ever destroyed. Such valuable cultural resources play an important part in people's stories about who they are, and as such, should never be permanently erased.

Many of the tactics of information warfare are also likely to be impermissible from within the traditional just war framework. Lying is impermissible, although failing to disclose information or selectively disclosing information is not. Lies make trust impossible, and thus hinder the possibility of reaching a negotiated peace. As Bonhoeffer put it, "'falsehood' is the destruction of, and hostility to, reality" (Bonhoeffer 1997, 163). We cannot come to agreement when we share no common foundational truths. Indeed, it can be argued that the Versailles peace process failed partly because of its inability to produce "a truthful accounting of the war's causes and consequences, nor the affirmation of moral truths by victors of vanquished" (Lu 2002, 21). The recognition of the importance of truth to peacemaking has led to the development of numerous truth and reconciliation commissions in post-conflict societies worldwide. Reconciliation cannot happen without truth telling, but truth telling is more costly the more lies one has to confess. To put it another way, the problem with lying is that it fundamentally undermines order in the present, and creates conditions that make the restoration of order in the future even more difficult.

The importance of dealing straightforwardly with the enemy is made clear in Augustine's counsel to Boniface: "when fidelity is promised, it must be kept, even to an enemy against whom war is being waged" (Augustine 1994, 220). Yet Augustine also declared that "[s]uch things [as ambushes] are legitimate for those who are engaged in a just war . . . it does not matter at all, as far as justice is concerned, whether he wins victory in open combat or through ruses" (Augustine 2006, 83). The reason is that ambushes, unlike lying, involve withholding information rather than providing false information. As Aquinas explains, certain types of ambushes do not actually constitute violations of the truth-telling principle. "There are two ways in which someone may be deceived," Aquinas explains, either "by being told something false, or by not having a promise kept" or alternatively "because we do not reveal our thoughts or intentions to him" (Aquinas 2002, 246). The first type of deception is always wrong in Aquinas' view, because it involves a breaking of faith with the other. The latter is not inherently wrong, because there is no requirement for us to reveal all our plans to everyone.

Lying in the context of information warfare can take several forms. The media can be used to broadcast factually incorrect descriptions of events, including misrepresenting the agents behind attacks, grossly exaggerating the number and scale of attacks, or even simply inventing attacks. More subtly, social media can be used to spread patently untrue rumors for the sake of disrupting support for a particular regime, for discrediting the regime's opponents, or fomenting disorder by encouraging various social groups to view each other as threats. Even worse, such information attacks could be carried out in a doubly dishonest way. Beyond the disingenuous content, the sources of the information could also be misrepresented – enemy government agents could pose as friendly co-citizens on social media, for example.

These sorts of disinformation campaigns, however, are unlikely to meet the just war criteria laid out in this chapter. The tradition's concern with ordinary life and the civil order – as expressed in the requirement to aim at peace – explains why information warfare that spreads deliberately false information to the civilian population is impermissible. This is particularly the case when a state launches the informational equivalent of a false flag information attack. A case in point would be Russia's alleged involvement in generating false news reports during the summer of 2014. Russian news media picked up stories reportedly covered by local Ukrainian Russians, in which individuals claiming to be Ukrainian Russians described horrific acts of violence against civilians allegedly committed by ethnic Ukrainians. Such wide-scale information warfare "[reinvented] reality, creating mass hallucinations that then translate into political action" (Pomerantsev 2014). When consumed by local Ukrainian Russians, this news coverage only inflamed tensions, making peaceful reconciliation more difficult. Because civil society is based on trust, lying to or otherwise manipulating the public is highly disruptive of domestic order. For this reason, even if it were very limited effects in terms of fatalities –

as in the Crimea, for example – it is morally impermissible. Put differently, if indiscriminate sanctions or cyber-attacks destroy the physical infrastructure civilians need to survive, lies and false flag attacks devastate the social infrastructure on which civilians depend. These types of attack sow such wide-reaching disorder that they are almost certainly disproportionate in all cases.

Possibly Permissible

It is clear enough that directly targeting goods or infrastructure essential to civilian life is morally wrong. But what of cases where there is an intervening variable? Targeted sanctions pose just such a case. Targeted sanctions, or "smart" sanctions, aim to coerce the opponent directly, by blocking arms sales, freezing the assets of key leaders, and by limiting access to dual-use items. The latter are goods that are normally used by civilians, but which have military applications. In principle, by targeting dual-use goods, noncombatant suffering can be minimized or avoided. In practice, however, restricting access even to dual-use goods may lead to noncombatant suffering on a broad scale, as Joy Gordon makes clear in her contribution to this volume. One key example is chlorine, which can be used for chemical weapons production, but is also an essential part of many sanitation systems. The inability to procure chlorine in sufficient amounts increased the prevalence of various infectious diseases in Iraq under the sanctions regime imposed in 1991 (Arya and Zurbrigg 2003, 10). The permissibility of such sanctions hinges on the proportionality of the harm suffered by non-combatants. This, in turn, depends partially on the capacity (and willingness) of the target state to adapt in ways that safeguard its civilians.

The intent of the sanctions-imposing state also matters, because it is never permissible to intentionally target civilians' lives. If this civilian suffering is not the *intent* of the sanctions-imposing state, it is not inherently morally culpable, under the logic of double effect. Caution must be exercised here, due to the problem of double intent. Restricting access to dual-use goods is meant to constrict a state's military prowess, but those who impose sanctions often also hope that economic pressures will coerce the population of their opponent into resisting – and perhaps overthrowing – their regime. However, sanctions that threaten civilians with death may be not imposed to coerce them into revolting against their government.

However, if the intent does not involve this type of threat, but simply aims at restricting a state's access to militarily sensitive items, the use of sanctions may be permissible. Proportionality then becomes the relevant consideration. It is possible for states to adjust to sanctions regimes in ways that leave the economy largely intact and thus spare the civilian population from the brunt of the effects. Regimes that fail to do this are failing in their responsibility to protect their population. If the regime is *incapable* of responding in this way – if it is a failed or failing state, which lacks the relevant state capacities – then the imposer of the sanctions may bear even more responsibility. The fact that there is an intervening variable between the actor imposing the sanctions and the outcome of the sanctions does not in itself affect the proportionality calculus. If the targeted state can reliably be predicted to fail to deflect the costs of the sanctions from its own civilians, or if after their imposition it becomes apparent that the sanctions regime will lead to widespread negative health effects, then the attack should be deemed disproportionate.

The logic of sanctioning dual-use goods applies metaphorically to the cyber world, as well. It may be permissible to use cyber warfare to target traditional telephone services and voice-over-internet protocols. On the one hand, such attacks are necessary if civilian and military communications run over the same lines. However, disabling communications infrastructure could lead to civilian harm, if, for example, individuals are no longer able to call an ambulance for help or to summon a fire engine. Practical matters, such as the density of the population and its distance from emergency response centers, must be taken into account. In some cases, such negative effects may be proportionate – after all, there are other (admittedly less efficient) ways of transporting injured individuals to hospital or getting the attention of the fire brigade. But the permanent destruction of communications infrastructure is less likely to be proportional. Short-term increases in emergency response time may be tolerable, but over the long term the civilian costs will mount. Thus, it may be permissible to temporarily shut down communications – perhaps as part of a broader, kinetic attack – but proportionality concerns suggest that the target state's infrastructure should not be so damaged that it cannot repair it in good time. Permanent destruction of communications infrastructure would also be contrary to the aim of peace, as ultimately the inability to communicate effectively over the entire polity would undermine order considerably.

Likely Permissible

Nonetheless, it would seem other kinds of civilian property, which are not essential to survival, could morally be restricted, commandeered, damaged, or destroyed for military purposes. Sanctions on non-essential goods, for example, are likely to be proportionate. While banning the export of toys, chocolate, and wine to an enemy state may make life less pleasurable, the inability to obtain such items is not a risk either to survival or to social order. The same would seem to apply to music and films, sporting equipment, passenger cars, and the like. Such luxury sanctions are aimed at hurting the target state's elite, and at hindering the regime's "ability to offer supporters rent-seeking opportunities" (Drezner 2011, 100). Of course, such sanctions also affect ordinary civilians directly, but not with a threat to life and limb. Proportionality would not seem to be at stake, given the rather trivial nature of these goods. The more intractable question, however, would be whether such sanctions can possibly be effective. Unfortunately, the track record for targeted sanctions generating the desired policy outcomes has been disappointing at best (Drezner 2011, 102).

Some aspects of cyber warfare, however, are rather more parallel to conventional war than to sanctions regimes. For example, in conventional warfare, military vehicles are permitted on civilian roads. By analogy, cyber-attacks that transmit themselves (harmlessly) through civilian devices to target military ones – operating like the Stuxnet virus – are permissible. True, civilians may find in such cases that their goods are used to ends that are not their own. But it is hard to see how such coercion *in itself* disrupts the civil order to an unacceptable degree since the target is a military one. Proportionately, the disruption would seem to be less than if kinetic force were used. Thus, necessity is the most significant principle for evaluating this sort of passive use of civilian infrastructure. Presuming the chosen target is relevant to success in the war, this type of passive use of civilian infrastructure seems permissible.

In a similar way, conventional militaries are permitted to occupy civilian airports and other transportation infrastructure. Public halls can be taken over to house soldiers and store goods. Armaments factories can be disabled or destroyed. Accomplishing the same using cyber war tactics also seems to be legitimate. The possibility of accomplishing such aims without employing lethal force – and in some cases, without even permanently destroying the infrastructure – makes cyber warfare tactics used for these ends seem preferable to conventional means, particularly in terms of proportionality.

What about attacks on specifically civilian cyber infrastructure? If we accept that coercion, per se, is not what is forbidden by the tradition, then it would seem to be the case that civilian property can also be targeted. (Presuming, of course, that the attacks are nonlethal.) Social media networks used to communicate and organize civilians can presumably be shut down. In a similar manner, radio and television signals could be jammed, and internet news portals could be closed. Such attacks could meet the necessity criterion, if the enemy state is using the media to communicate with its supporters, to encourage resistance, or even simply to mislead its population.

Civilian banking could also be targeted, to coerce government and military officials whose funds also lie in civilian banks. Civilians, of course, do need access to their finances in order to live. The tradition's concern with order means that an attack on the communications or financial sectors would predictably lead to the breakdown of domestic law and order, particularly if such a breakdown itself led to significant injury or death among the civilian population. (And it would be immoral to continue such an attack if the negative side effects became too widespread.) For this reason, it would seem to be impermissible to permanently wipe out civilians' banking information – the effects would be too far-reaching. To shut down the banking system for several days, however, while deeply inconvenient, might be permissible. It would certainly have a coercive effect, but all things considered, would be less damaging to the civilian population then a conventional attack, the likely alternative.

CONCLUSION

Historically, the canonical just war tradition's concern with sparing the innocent was limited to sparing their lives from direct attack. Reflecting our increased appreciation for individual human rights, contemporary just war thinking tends to embrace a broader view of non-combatant immunity that forbids many kinds of nonlethal coercion, including destruction of civilians' property.

In contemporary liberal democracies, thick social bonds and robust institutions have created societies in which the state's coercive aspects are less obvious for some of us. But international society lags far behind. Tragically, war remains inevitable. The alternative to soft war is thus not peace, but hot war. When engaged in a conflict that meets the *ad bellum* requirements of just war, it may be morally permissible – and perhaps, all things considered, morally better – to coerce enemy governments by directly commandeering, threatening, or even destroying civilian property, rather than killing civilians indirectly (and unintentionally) by engaging in conventional warfare.

Above all, it is important to remember that the means of soft war are nothing more than tactics. The fact that some soft war tactics may be justifiably used *in bello* if they respect the limits of necessity, order, and proportionality, does not mean that wars employing soft war tactics are necessarily more just than conventional ones. We must still ask – and perhaps even more persistently, given the seductiveness of nonlethal means of war-fighting – whether the wars we engage in are fought for just causes, and whether we have really tried to find peaceful ways to resolve our differences. Although the availability of less destructive means does affect the *ad bellum* proportionality calculus, we must be careful not to treat soft war tactics as a free pass, legitimizing any and all uses of coercive force. Put simply: the means cannot justify the ends.

NOTE

1. Another familiar phrase using the same verb is "primum non nocere," or "first, do no harm" from the Hippocratic Oath.

3

Reconsidering Economic Sanctions

Joy Gordon

It seems that hardly a week goes by without an announcement that economic sanctions are to be imposed, or strengthened, in the context of either foreign policy or global governance. This is due at least in part to the sense that targeted sanctions ("smart sanctions") have addressed many of the central objections that have been raised over the last two decades: that trade sanctions are overbroad, that sanctions may cause humanitarian damage, and that sanctions are often unsuccessful at getting the target state to comply with the demands made of it. But, I would argue, targeted sanctions have been disappointing in many regards; and many sanctions regimes do not even purport to be "smart."

Economic sanctions typically involve the withdrawal of trade, although they may also include terminating foreign aid, blocking the use of currency, denying access to international financial institutions, and blocking access to humanitarian aid. While there may also be measures imposed as penalties or retaliation in the context of trade, this article concerns the use of economic sanctions only in political contexts.

In the twentieth century, both the concept and the application of economic sanctions have undergone such radical transformations that analyzing either their enduring features or their ethical implications is quite elusive – surprisingly so, since sanctions are a much-used and much-discussed tool of statecraft. At the end of World War I, economic sanctions underwent a conceptual transformation from being simply a form of warfare, serving the military interests of the parties to the conflict; to being a mechanism of peacekeeping, on behalf of the universal interests of the international community as a whole. During the Cold War, economic sanctions were heavily used, primarily by the superpowers, to express disapproval, or to exert influence or create pressure, by causing inconvenience or imposing additional costs on the economy of the target nation. Although moral claims were sometimes made – for example, to protest military aggression or undemocratic practices – they were invoked for the most part by individual countries acting on their own behalf, and in pursuit of their own policies. As a tool of international governance, economic sanctions effectively disappeared between World War II and the collapse of the Soviet Union, with two significant exceptions: The UN Security Council's imposition of sanctions on Rhodesia and South Africa, both for the practice of apartheid, and for Rhodesia's unilateral declaration of independence. The sanctions against South Africa were quite extraordinary in many ways: They genuinely represented a moral claim that transcended the competing interests and ideologies of the superpowers; they were imposed with the consent and encouragement of many leaders in the black community, which was affected by the sanctions; and the imposition of sanctions involved not only policies of state actors, but a broad-based grass roots movement in the West. They concluded with the dramatic end of apartheid, and the election of Nelson Mandela to the presidency.

By the late 1980s, economic sanctions were seen as an attractive tool for political pressure by widely diverse groups. For the State Department and the US administrations, sanctions seemed an ideal "middle route": They provided a means of doing something that seemed more substantial than mere diplomatic protests and persuasion, but without the political costs of military intervention. Among political scientists there was a resurgence of interest and support, and a widely held belief that sanctions, if used correctly, could indeed be effective. The sanctions against South Africa had wide support from religious leaders and peace activists as a nonviolent method of achieving political change.

In the wake of Iraq's invasion of Kuwait in 1990, all of these groups supported the use of sanctions as a nonviolent means of pressuring Iraq to withdraw from Kuwait. But it quickly became clear that the sanctions imposed on Iraq were of a different sort than had ever been seen before. The range of economic activities prohibited by the Security Council was the most extensive ever, outside of the context of siege warfare. The UN Charter required all member states to enforce the Council's measures, and, consequently, the participation of the international community was nearly universal. Because the sanctions were extreme and comprehensive, they triggered a massive humanitarian crisis, bringing into question the ethical legitimacy of sanctions in general. Religious leaders, including Pope John Paul II, condemned the sanctions as inhumane. Anti-sanctions activist groups sprang up, accusing the Security Council of perpetrating human rights violations.

At the same time, with the Cold War over, the Security Council entered a period of much greater activism. Sanctions quickly became a significant tool in situations where the Council was responding to aggression, breaches of the peace, and threats to peace. In the 1990s, the Council imposed sanctions in another dozen situations, and continues to do so with some frequency.

In a sense, economic sanctions are problematic because, both conceptually and in concrete application, they are so variable. Economic sanctions are sometimes a trivial interference with business, causing little more than inconvenience. In other circumstances, the effects of sanctions are indistinguishable from those of siege warfare. Yet, while warfare is (at least in theory) subject to ethical limits, such as those articulated in Just War doctrine and international law, actions that are seen as nonviolent are not ordinarily viewed as something whose damage must be limited and monitored. Thus, to some extent, sanctions have eluded both the scrutiny and the criticism that would have been forthcoming if the same acts were seen as a form of warfare.

It is worth looking closely at the various transformations that economic sanctions have undergone over the last century, in regard to their legitimacy and uses, as well as the risks they present and the contradictions contained in the notion of economic sanctions.

THE HISTORY OF SANCTIONS

Although sanctions have long played a role in international disputes (often in the form of economic warfare accompanying military conflict), in the twentieth century they have come to be framed, at least by the major powers, as a peaceful means of exercising international coercion, offering an attractive alternative to the bloodshed of warfare. After World War I, in the Pact of Paris, the sixty-three signatory nations agreed to "condemn recourse to war for the solution of international controversies, and renounce it as an instrument of national policy" (Kellogg-Briand Pact of 1928, Art. 1), and provided that all disputes shall be settled by "pacific means" (Kellogg-Briand Pact of 1928, Art. 2). There was a sense that war itself was on the verge of becoming obsolete.

In the post-World War I climate, economic sanctions were re-framed in terms of inconvenience and embarrassment, as an option that presented no ethical difficulties, especially by comparison to war.

> The economic weapon, conceived not as an instrument of war but as a means of peaceful pressure, is the great discovery and the most precious possession of the League. Properly organised, it means the substitution of economic pressure for actual war . . . In League of Nations so far as they can be applied, this means that for the blowing up of men to pieces with high explosives, the suffocating of civilian populations with poison gas, the dropping of bombs on crowded cities, the blinding, the mutilation, the brutalisation of myriads of men, we should be substituting merely a temporary dislocation and paralysis of trade, a rise in prices, some restriction of comforts and luxuries, the rationing of necessities, the ignominy of being exhibited as a moral outlaw. (Bertram 1931, 169)

There was at the same time an insistence that economic sanctions would be an effective response to military aggression, and that they would accomplish their goals quickly as well. Woodrow Wilson, in arguing that the United States should join the League of Nations, maintained that such a boycott was "more tremendous than war": "Apply this economic, peaceful, silent deadly remedy and there will be no need for force. The boycott is what is substituted for war" (Foley 1923, 71–72).

The belief that war itself might become obsolete evaporated with World War II; and the hope that economic sanctions could stop aggression went with it, when the League of Nations' attempt to impose sanctions on Mussolini failed to so much as give him pause in the annexation of Ethiopia. Nevertheless, when the Charter of the United Nations was drafted, economic sanctions were incorporated as an option available to the Security Council in addressing threats to the peace, breaches of the peace, and acts of aggression. Article 41 provides that

> The Security Council may decide what measures not involving the use of armed force are to be employed to give effect to its decisions ... These may include complete or partial interruption of economic relations and of rail, sea, air, postal, telegraphic, radio, and other means of communication, and the severance of diplomatic relations.

Article 42 provides that where the Security Council finds these measures inadequate, it may use force to maintain or restore international peace and security. Thus, in the systems of international security envisioned by the League of Nations and the United Nations, economic sanctions were re-framed as "peaceful pressure," in contrast to their historical role as the economic component of war. Nevertheless, they were considered "peaceful" not because economic sanctions are purported to do no material or human damage, but because sanctions are placed in comparison with "actual war." From their origins as a curious combination of the "peaceful" and the "deadly," economic sanctions have come to be seen as a middle route, something more substantial than mere protest or denunciation, yet not violent, in contrast to military intervention.

As a response to the two world wars, it is easy to see the humanitarian and pacifist motivation underlying the theory and institutionalization of economic sanctions. Yet even in those contexts, economic sanctions are described in odd, paradoxical terms: They are "peaceful" yet "deadly," they are "potent" yet involve no force. They are civilized and humane, yet devastating and intolerable.

SANCTIONS AFTER WORLD WAR II

Although economic sanctions were available to the Security Council from the inception of the United Nations, for the most part, Cold War interests made it impossible for the Security Council to utilize the measures available to it under Articles 41 and 42. The veto power of the five permanent members of the Council effectively provided them with immunity, and at the same time, the risk of vetoes by the Soviets and the West largely paralyzed the Council.

But while the Security Council was almost completely inactive on this score, other nations, especially the United States, were not reluctant to use sanctions either unilaterally or in alliance with other nations. The United States was the "most prominent practitioner of peace time restrictions on trade and other economic transactions" since World War II (Leyton-Brown 1987, 225). Of 104 sanctions episodes between World War II and the end of the Cold War, "the United States was a key player in two-thirds. In 80 percent of U.S. – imposed sanctions, the policy was pursued with no more than minor cooperation from its allies or international organizations" (Elliott 1995, 51).

The "sanctions decade"[1] began as the Cold War came to an end, while political scientists wrote about the efficacy of sanctions with renewed confidence, and human rights activists embraced sanctions as a peaceful alternative to military intervention. The sanctions imposed on Iraq proved to look very much like the boycott that was originally envisioned in the days of the League of Nations. They were an immediate response, on behalf of virtually the entire international community, which would have a devastating effect on the aggressor nation, even without military action.

The fact that the sanctions originated in the Security Council, rather than in an independent alliance of nations, meant that, under Article 25 of the Charter, the member states of the United Nations were bound to comply, and this broad international participation, in turn, meant that the sanctions would be far less porous than any sanctions imposed during the Cold War. Indeed, they were nearly comprehensive. Regardless of whether they succeeded in achieving their stated political objectives, the sanctions would in fact succeed dramatically at strangling the Iraqi economy. In doing so, they would generate a massive humanitarian crisis. A few months after the sanctions were first imposed, the bombing campaign of the Persian Gulf War destroyed nearly all of Iraq's infrastructure: roads, bridges, factories, oil refineries, the electrical grid, telecommunications, and water and sewage treatment plants. The sanctions then prevented Iraq from rebuilding. The result was extensive malnutrition throughout the population; increased child mortality; and the collapse of the ability of the education and medical systems to meet the needs of the population (cf. Gordon 2010).

New criticisms of sanctions began to emerge, this time questioning not only their efficacy, but their ethical legitimacy. Where the literature of the 1980s sought to formulate criteria for the effective use of sanctions in achieving political goals,[2] the 1990s saw the emergence of extensive discussions about how sanctions could be ethically employed, often adapting the framework of Just War doctrine, such as the principles of discrimination and proportionality.[3]

SMART SANCTIONS

Targeted sanctions –"smart sanctions" – began in large measure as a response to the UN sanctions imposed on Iraq. In the wake of this humanitarian crisis, there were efforts in many venues to think about designing sanctions that would not have the humanitarian impact of broad trade sanctions, would impact the leadership rather than the population as a whole, and as a result would be more politically effective. These targeted sanctions included arms embargoes, financial sanctions on the assets of individuals and companies, travel restrictions on the leaders of a sanctioned nation, and trade sanctions on particular goods. Many viewed targeted sanctions as an especially promising tool for foreign policy and international governance: They do not entail the risks and costs of military intervention; nor do they raise the same ethical problems as broad trade sanctions. Many still see targeted sanctions as the best solution to a broad array of difficult situations.

Since the mid-1990s, UN sanctions have not, on their face, imposed broad measures prohibiting the target country from engaging in ordinary trade or prohibiting target countries from importing goods necessary for their industry or infrastructure. But it would be a mistake to think that targeted sanctions are used so consistently, and implemented so well, that sanctions overall no longer raise ethical concerns. While UN sanctions may now be "smarter," sanctions imposed by nations against other nations can be explicitly indiscriminate, with broad prohibitions affecting shipping, banking transactions, the target state's energy sector, imports in general, and exports of critical commodities. Recently, this has been true, for example, of Australia's sanctions on Syria's energy sector, Canada's sanctions on Syria and North Korea, the EU's sanctions on Iran, and the US sanctions on Cuba, North Korea, Burma, Sudan, and Iran.[4]

In addition, to the extent that states or institutions do use targeted measures, there continue to be considerable difficulties with each type, with regard to implementation, effectiveness, or humanitarian impact. Some of these are difficulties that may be resolved as these measures continue to be refined. Others are rooted in fundamental conflicts between competing interests, or intractable logistical challenges, which are likely to persist

Finally, it will be important to look closely at the legal issues raised by the listing of individuals or companies whose assets are frozen or seized, which are considered the most narrowly targeted measures in use. Although the lists do not directly affect large numbers of individuals, the arbitrariness of the Security Council sanctions committees has come to be seen by critics[5] and by the European courts[6] as so deeply problematic that the practice of blacklisting has brought into question the scope and even the legality of the Council's powers under Chapter VII.

NATION-TO-NATION SANCTIONS THAT ARE NOT SMART: THE US SANCTIONS AGAINST IRAN

While the United States has been extreme in its unilateral measures against Iran, US officials have often claimed that the sanctions are narrowly targeted to affect only the political and military leadership, and that their intent is not to harm the Iranian people. At a press briefing in 2010, a State Department official said that the United States is seeking to "target specific entities within the Iranian Government but not punish the Iranian people" (National Iranian American

Council 2010). Secretary of State Hillary Clinton said "our efforts to apply pressure on Iran are not meant to punish the Iranian people, they are meant to change the approach that the Iranian Government has taken toward its nuclear program" (National Iranian American Council 2010). A senior US official said "We have never been attracted to the idea of trying to get the whole world to cordon off their economy" (National Iranian American Council 2010).

However, it is clear that the US sanctions are designed to interfere broadly in Iran's trade, its energy sector, its banking system, and the state's ability to function in any regard; and they have been very successful at this. As a result, the sanctions have done considerable harm to the population as a whole, in particular the political opposition to the regime, as well as women and other vulnerable groups. The sanctions measures imposed in 2012 were especially damaging, because they were comprehensive, targeting all sectors of Iran's economy, in particular its oil sector (International Campaign for Human Rights in Iran 2013, 11). Bankruptcies, payoffs, and plant closures increased dramatically (International Campaign for Human Rights in Iran 2013, 13). Because Iraq was highly dependent on imports for its pharmaceutical industry, the healthcare system was severely affected (International Campaign for Human Rights in Iran 2013). There were significant increases in poverty, hunger, and malnutrition (International Campaign for Human Rights in Iran 2013, 14).

While these trends affect the population as a whole, they specifically increase the hardship on women:

> Women are often the most victimized by sanctions because, as a group, they are the most economically vulnerable. Women have a harder time finding jobs, are among the first to get laid off, and have fewer workplace protections. As those primarily responsible for running their households, women face increased loads of stress trying to feed their families, obtain needed medication, and buy necessary goods amidst skyrocketing levels of inflation. A forty-five-year old housewife in Tehran reports, "In the last few months, I have bought very little protein such as meat and poultry and have also refrained from buying any clothes for the children." At the micro-level of household economies, women bear the larger burden for managing their families' survival. In Iran, as in all societies, increased militarism and violence at the global and national levels exacerbates inequalities between men and women. As societies become more militarized, so do the very citizens living within them; as fear, anxiety, and stress rise in the lives of ordinary people, so do patriarchal and violent responses to conflict and hardship in intimate life. (International Campaign for Human Rights in Iran 2013)

The sanctions also triggered greater oppression by the regime, reducing the space for dissent and democratic opposition. The Iranian government had already engaged in repression in the face of the protests regarding the 2009 election, following further repression and human rights abuses in the face of the Green Movement. However, the sanctions gave the state additional justification. The International Civil Society Action Network noted that "the sanctions and threat of war allow the state to invoke 'a state of emergency' and in so doing suppress critics and voices of dissent" (International Civil Society Action Network 2012). One consequence of the banking sanctions is that Iranian students are in effect denied access to British and other universities, because there is no legal way to make financial transfers to pay their school fees (International Civil Society Action Network 2012).

Rather than starving the Revolutionary Guard (IRGC) and the Iranian regime, the criminalization of normal international commerce meant that much of the economy was tied to the black market or gray market. For a private company to import equipment and materials for production requires ties to the IRGC or bribes to the regime, with the result that the IRGC and the regime hold far greater control over the economy, and, as systemic corruption becomes the norm for commerce, gain far greater profits. The banking sanctions forced a growing reliance on a cash-based economy, where Iranians have had to use black marketeers to pay for medical or educational costs (International Civil Society Action Network 2012).

Thus, the sanctions on Iran were not just indiscriminate, but have in fact been counter-discriminate: They have given the state and military the opportunity to consolidate their control, while those who are the most vulnerable, and who have the least input into state policies, are affected most severely.

TARGETED SANCTIONS: CONTINUING DIFFICULTIES

Where those imposing sanctions have in fact tried to craft them narrowly to target specific goods or individuals, the track record of sanctions in regard to effectiveness has been quite mixed. In 2002, Tostensen and Bull surveyed the difficulties with effectiveness and implementation of the various types of targeted sanctions. They attributed some of the problems to lack of experience in implementation, or underdevelopment of the political or administrative systems involved. As I shall now argue, more than a decade later many of these problems remain unresolved.

Arms Embargoes

Arms embargoes can seek to block the flow of arms to an entire country, to particular groups or areas within a country, or to particular individuals or groups, wherever they are (Fruchart et al. 2007). From the inception of the UN until 1990, the Security Council imposed arms embargoes only twice: against South Africa and Rhodesia. In the decade that followed, the Council imposed arms embargoes a dozen more times.

An arms embargo seems like an ideal example of a targeted sanction, in that it is intended to interrupt the flow of precisely the goods that could escalate a conflict or facilitate a human rights abuse. In situations where the UN imposes an arms embargo as a form of conflict management, to achieve a peaceful political resolution of an armed conflict, UN peacekeepers are often present, and the embargo is more effective as a result of UN monitoring and enforcement (Fruchart et al. 2007).

But while there has been considerable refinement in the use of arms embargoes, there continue to be substantial practical problems in implementation. They do little to actually reduce the flow of weapons. On the contrary, the prohibition creates a black market for weapons, accompanied by opportunities for higher profits than in the legal arms trade. There are systematic ways to circumvent the prohibitions, such as the use of "flags of convenience" to disguise an aircraft's country of origin; cargo planes filing false air routes; and the forgery of end-user certificates (Wenzel and Faltas 2009, 115). There is often collusion of multiple state actors. For example, in the case of arms trafficking to Liberia, numerous Eastern European countries exported the illicit arms, while several West African states facilitated illegal shipments (Wenzel and Faltas 2009, 111).

The sheer quantity of weapons available globally makes it difficult to significantly reduce the flow of arms. Multiple studies have found that arms embargoes may not significantly reduce the flow of arms (Wallensteen et al. 2003, 105). An arms embargo may just make weapons more expensive; and "the higher the cost of the arms, the more attractive the deal to illegal arms dealers" (Brzoska 2002, 128). One commentator notes that "The world is literally awash in arms" (Cortright and Lopez 2002, 14). There is greater success in restricting the sale of major weapons systems, since those are more likely to be produced by state enterprises and subject to stricter controls (Brzoska 2002, 12). However, light weapons can more easily be manufactured and sold by private companies. Embargoes have the least effect on their availability, and light weapons are the ones most commonly used in current armed conflicts (Brzoska 2001, 10). Some have suggested that illegal arms sales establish criminal networks for shipments and financing that then lend themselves as well to human trafficking and drug trafficking. In this case, it might be argued that arms embargoes do more harm than good. However, it seems that, at the least, arms embargoes have been disappointing as a means of blocking access to weapons.

Visa Bans

Although visa bans are not economic sanctions, they are often included in the list of targeted sanctions. Visa bans can designate individual political leaders or wrong-doers by name, and the restrictions affecting them would not affect anyone else. But there are problems with implementation, as well as a serious question as to their effectiveness. Often there are no clear procedures providing guidance for states that encounter banned individuals in their territory, or attempting to enter it. It is not difficult for individuals to hold passports in multiple nationalities, or to use fraudulent passports (Wallensteen et al. 2003, 115). One sanctions expert noted that, in the case of North Korea, the corruption and illicit movement of persons via a system of aliases was at least as extensive as the illicit movement of goods (Lopez 2013).

While there may be symbolic value in imposing visa bans, there is little evidence that it is so costly to political or military leaders as to cause them to reconsider a policy or state practice, or that restricting travel affects such individuals in any way that goes beyond inconvenience (DeVries 2002, 99).

Aviation Bans

Aviation bans sometimes include trade measures, such as prohibitions on selling parts for repairs and maintenance, and sometimes involve non-economic measures, such as flight bans. As with arms embargoes, there are many ways that flight bans can be circumvented. Planes can be registered under different names, and the pilots can file false flight plans (Wallensteen et al. 2003, 119). Restrictions on passenger flights are implemented relatively well, compared to cargo flights; since commercial passenger airlines are generally well-regulated, while the air cargo industry is not, aviation bans on cargo flights are quite porous (Conroy 2002, 162). The illegal flights, in turn, often contribute to the black market in the sanctioned country. The flight ban imposed on UNITA in Angola was violated continuously, with tons of goods being flown in daily on illegal but highly profitable flights, benefiting those who could afford to buy black market goods (Conroy 2002).

There are also humanitarian impacts that are not widely acknowledged. The lack of regular commercial flights can significantly impact the population as a whole. The flight ban imposed on commercial flights to and from Haiti was seen as a way of denying the wealthy the opportunity to shop for luxuries abroad. But another consequence was that hundreds of Haitians hoping to receive asylum in the United States or elsewhere had no way to leave the country (Conroy 2002). In the case of the Security Council sanctions on Libya, the aviation ban meant that travel presented a much greater hardship for the population as a whole; for example, a flight from Tripoli to Alexandria, Egypt, is 90 minutes, whereas driving takes 15 hours (Conroy 2002).

Targeted Trade Sanctions

Targeted trade sanctions seek to interrupt the flow of particular commodities, such as timber, diamonds, or oil, on the grounds that they benefit political or military leaders responsible for human rights abuses or aggression. For example, since Liberia used timber taxes to purchase arms, the Security Council prohibited the import of Liberian lumber (UN Security Council, Resolution 1378, 2003). Liberia, which held a democratic election in 2005 after years of governance under a brutal regime, is often cited as an instance of the successful use of sanctions. But the sanctions targeted two of the country's three most significant exports – diamonds and timber – further compromising

Liberia's struggling economy. In addition, the implementation of the sanctions regime required some 15,000 UN peacekeepers, as well as the near-complete control of the state (Carisch and Rickard-Martin 2013, 5). It is not clear that there would be sufficient political support to implement such labor-intensive measures on a regular basis.

To the extent that the export of a particular commodity can be undermined, if it is a significant part of the target state's economy – and it almost always is – there can also be the problem of overbreadth that characterized the Iraq sanctions: Compromising a significant export may interrupt the cash flow of the leadership, but also damages a sector of the economy; legitimate business can be affected; and by undermining the state's source of funding, it will also deprive the state of the funds needed to perform legitimate governmental functions.

As with the other types of targeted sanctions, there are logistical difficulties with their implementation. Commodities are often fungible, and it may be impossible to identify whether a particular shipment of timber or oil came from the sanctioned state. Even if there are certification procedures, they are often not standardized, or lend themselves to forgery. As with arms embargoes, interrupting the flow of a commodity may simply result in new transport routes to circumvent monitors (Wallensteen et al. 2003, 124). In the case of mineral sanctions on the Democratic Republic of Congo (DRC), for example, gold is much harder to track than other minerals, and can easily be transferred abroad without detection (Carisch and Rickard-Martin 2013, 7).

THE FUTURE OF TARGETED SANCTIONS

There was considerable optimism in the 1990s about the possibilities of smart sanctions. Many expected them to provide an elegant and powerful solution to the failings of broad economic sanctions. They seemed like the perfect fix: measures that are hard-hitting, impacting those responsible for terrorism or international law violations, without the ethical and humanitarian problems that come from crippling an entire economy. Certainly, enormous efforts have gone into refining targeted sanctions, of every sort, to improve their effectiveness, and to resolve the human rights problems that have also emerged.

On one hand, it seems that it has become politically imperative to frame the imposition of economic sanctions as "smart," by using terms like "narrowly targeted," or by using lists of individual persons or companies that create an impression of punishing specific wrong-doers.

But while targeted sanctions are more politically palatable than broad sanctions, they continue to be problematic on many levels. Some, such as arms embargoes, have problems with implementation that appear to be unresolvable, after more than a decade of efforts by practitioners, consultants, and academics.

But more significantly, the availability of targeted sanctions did not bring an end to the humanitarian damage or the ethical issues presented by broad sanctions, at least not in the way they were expected to. This is partly because sanctions that are described as "targeted," such as aviation bans or commodity sanctions, in fact may still do structural harm to the economy or infrastructure. At the same time, the pervasive rhetoric of targeted sanctions seems to have had, so to speak, a certain collateral damage: It has short-circuited the public discussion of humanitarian impact. Where the 1990s witnessed growing demands for humanitarian monitoring and prior assessment of humanitarian impact, this has largely ceased. It seems that the universal belief is that since sanctions are now "smart," we no longer have to worry about harming the innocent. But that is not true at all. At best, there are inconsistencies and difficulties with targeted sanctions that to some extent compromise their political effectiveness, and incidentally affect those with no responsibility for the target state's policies. These are disappointments of the sort we would see in the implementation of any public policy. But additionally, there also continue to be sanctions regimes that are indiscriminate by design, and do extensive damage to the population as a whole. This is true, for example, of the sanctions imposed on Iran by the United States, EU, and others, targeting its major banks as well as the major shipping lines, compromising Iran's financial sector and its imports and exports.

Most significantly, as the case of Iran demonstrates, neither the Security Council resolutions nor international norms can be counted on to ensure that a sanctions regime does not do indiscriminate harm. To the contrary, the language of "targeting" or of listing individual wrong-doers seems to obviate the need for scrutiny. This is the case even if there is a humanitarian crisis brought on in large measure by the sanctions.

CONCLUSION

How we view economic sanctions, their possibilities, and their limitations, has undergone considerable transformation. Initially seen as a powerful yet humane tool for global governance, there were always doubts about the effectiveness of sanctions, and by the 1990s there was growing concern about whether it was even ethical to use them at all, given the humanitarian damage they could do. It seemed that with the advent of targeted sanctions, both the ethical and the strategic concerns might be put to rest. But, we might say, rumors of their demise have been a bit premature.

NOTES

1. This phrase is taken from Cortright and Lopez (2000).
2. Hufbauer, Schott, and Elliott, for example, conclude their analysis in the second edition of *Economic Sanctions Reconsidered* with a list of "do's and don'ts" for effective sanctions (Hufbauer, Schott, and Elliot 1991).

3. For example, Damrosch proposed three criteria for determining whether sanctions are appropriate:

   (1) Civilian impact: A program of economic sanctions should not diminish the standard of living of a significant segment of society below the subsistence level;
   (2) Wrong-doer impact: Economic sanctions should target those in whom a change in behavior is sought, and should either diminish their capacity to continue wrongful behavior or penalize them so that they are induced to desist from the wrongful behavior;
   (3) Wrong-doer/civilian impact: To the maximum feasible extent, sanctions should be designed to avoid enriching the perpetrator of wrong-doing at the expense of their victims. (Damrosch 1993, 281–283)

   Haass argued that economic sanctions are a "serious instrument," which warrant as rigorous a justification as military force. Like Damrosch, he suggested that sanctions should focus as far as possible on those responsible for the offending behavior, and limiting penalties to the area of dispute. They should also cause less collateral damage to innocents. Furthermore, humanitarian exceptions should be part of any comprehensive sanctions regime, partly on the moral grounds that innocents should not be made to suffer. However, he added, sanctions should not necessarily be suspended if humanitarian harm is the direct result of a cynical government policy that creates shortages among the general population in order to garner international sympathy (Haass 1997, 82).

   Himes argued for criteria drawn from just war theory. He identified seven: (1) because sanctions cause suffering to innocent people, they should not be employed without good reason such as aggression or repression by the offending nation; (2) Less harmful means should be employed first; (3) the goal should be clearly stated; (4) the sanctions should be selective and should be aimed primarily at those responsible for the crisis – sanctions that pressure a nation's elite are to be preferred to those that undermine the well-being of the average citizen; (5) there should be monitoring systems in place to assess the consequences of the sanctions; (6) where sanctions are imposed for humanitarian or human rights purposes, as in South Africa, there should be support among those who are the victims of a regime's injustice; and (7) arguments for sanctions should be persuasive enough for widespread support of the policy, even if it is carried out unilaterally (Himes 1997, 13).

   Christiansen and Powers, also drawing on Just War doctrine, argued that economic sanctions may be legitimate where (1) they are a response to a grave evil; (2) they are part of a concerted diplomatic effort to avoid war; (3) they are implemented in such a way as to avoid irreversible grave harm to civilians; (4) less coercive means were pursued first; (5) the harm is proportional to the good ends likely to be achieved; (6) they are imposed by a multilateral entity (Christiansen and Powers 1995, 98).
4. Even though the nuclear sanctions have now been lifted, the US sanctions concerning human rights in Iran remain in place, interfering in Iran's access to international investment and financial transactions. See, e.g. "As sanctions on Iran are lifted, many U.S. business restrictions remain" (*National Public Radio*, January 26, 2016). In the case of Cuba, while the Obama administration eased some of the sanctions against

Cuba, the core components of the embargo are contained in federal legislation, and those measures can only be lifted by Congress.

5. See, for example, Fassbender's (2006) report, "Targeted Sanctions and Due Process," criticizing the lack of due process in the 1267 sanctions regime.
6. The most significant case in this regard was *Kadi II*, in which the European Court of Justice invalidated European laws implementing Security Council resolutions (*Kadi vs. European Commission*, ruling of the Grand Chamber, July 18, 2013).

4

Conditional Sale

Cécile Fabre

INTRODUCTION

Although just war theory occupies center stage in the political theory of international relations, non-forceful instruments of foreign policy are often both more effective and less destructive than wide-scale military action. In this paper, I focus on a particular kind of economic sanctions, which (to my knowledge) has not been given separate treatment in the relevant political-theoretical literature, and which I call *Conditional Sale*. To illustrate, suppose that some political actor – call it Affluenza – has in its possession commodities or goods, *G*, which some other actor – call it Barrenia – badly needs or wants. Suppose further that Affluenza wants something from Barrenia, though is not willing, able, or justified to go to war for it. Instead, it threatens to raise the price of *G* to a level – *p100* – that Barrenia can ill afford, unless Barrenia gives in to its demands. If Barrenia does give in, Affluenza will lower the price of *G* to *p1*. Affluenza, in other words, makes its willingness to sell at an affordable price conditional on Barrenia's bending to its will. On what grounds and under what conditions may it so act? The best-known political actor that makes regular use of this particular instrument is Russia, whose vast natural resources (notably oil, gas, and coal) are key to its foreign policy, and which grants highly subsidized prices to its favored neighbors such as Belarus and Moldova while hiking prices as a restortive measure against others such as Ukraine (Lough 2011).

A sale is conditional by definition: when I offer to sell you *G* at a given price *p*, I offer to transfer to you my property rights over *G* on condition that you pay me *p* for it. Call this the price-condition. My concern here is with cases where Affluenza is willing to have Barrenia acquire property rights over *G* on condition that Barrenia should meet both its price-condition and what I shall call its politics-condition. In other words, sales, in this paper, are doubly conditional. In the next section, I bring the question into sharper focus by highlighting differences between conditional sale, economic sanctions, and conditional aid. All three are forms of economic statecraft (Baldwin 1985), but they differ in morally salient ways. In the sections entitled "Conditional Sale as a Response to a Justified Grievance" and "Conditional Sale in the Absence of a Justified Grievance," I make a first pass at the question, on the assumption that Affluenza has full control over *G* and trades directly with Barrenia's regime. I argue that *Conditional Sale* is permitted under strict conditions, as a means to redress a justified grievance against Barrenia, or to pursue foreign policy goals more widely. In the section that follows these, "Complicating the Picture: Conditional Sales and the Problem of Private Businesses," I relax that simplifying assumption and briefly highlight some of the difficulties raised by *Conditional Sale* for private economic actors in both communities.

There are six preliminary *caveats*. First, similar conclusions can be reached about conditional purchases: thus, Seller might have a natural resource *G* and might badly need to increase its foreign currency reserves; Purchaser might then be tempted to make its purchase of *G* at Seller's asking price *p100* conditional upon Seller meeting its politics-condition, failing which it will only buy *G* at *p1*. I focus on conditional sales rather than purchases for ease of exposition.

Second, I posit that Affluenza seeks to get from Barrenia political-cum geostrategic goods such as access to territory, the destruction of weapons stocks, and political changes, rather than economic goods such as the status of a privileged trade partner.

Third, I make no assumption as to whether or not the price Affluenza sets for *G* – be it the high *p100* or the comparatively low *p1* – is above or below market price. One might think that if *p100* is below market price anyway, Barrenia *clearly* has no complaint; conversely, one might think that if *p1* is above market price, Barrenia *clearly* has a complaint. To hold those claims presupposes that the market price is a fair price. Yet, it is not clear that it always is. And even if it is, Barrenia might *not* have a complaint for being asked to pay *p1* – even if *p1* is above market price – on condition that it changes its policy, if its policy is unjust. Conversely, Barrenia might well have a complaint about being made to pay *p100* as the price to pay for conducting its just foreign policy – even if *p100* is below market price – if it can ill afford to pay it. Or so I shall aim to show.

Fourth, and relatedly, I assume (again, to simplify) that Affluenza and Barrenia seek to trade over *G* for the first time. If they have already traded over *G*, conditionality can take two different forms. Affluenza can either threaten to raise the price at which *G* is normally sold unless Barrenia complies with its demands (in which case the price would remain the same) or it can offer to lower the normal price if Barrenia complies (failing which the price would remain the same). A full account of conditionality in economic statecraft – which space prevents me from offering here – must be sensitive to this particular issue.

Fifth, a moral assessment of conditional sales presupposes a background theory of distributive justice. I take the following points for granted. Namely, individuals have private property rights over the resources they need to lead a flourishing life, and, in so far as they form sovereign and territorially bounded political associations, they have joint ownership rights over some of the resources that those associations need to shape their collective destiny. Yet, subject to a no-undue sacrifice proviso, they are under duties of assistance to distant strangers. The content of those duties in turn depends on what one takes the requirements of global justice to be. Following Henry Shue, I distinguish basic human rights – what we need in order to lead a life worth living – from non-basic human rights – what we need in order to live a flourishing life (Shue 1980). I submit that justice does not require merely that the affluent secure the basic human rights of the distant poor; it also requires, more demandingly, that if distant strangers would lead a less than flourishing life as a result of lacking a particular resource, those who have surpluses of that resources are under a duty to help them get hold of it. Taken together, those claims support the right freely to engage in international trade (that is, to sell to and buy from other agents under mutually agreed-upon terms), conditional upon meeting the demands of justice.

Finally, there are strong arguments in support of the view that any political or moral restrictions on global trade should be set by international organizations such as the WTO. That view is analogous to the claim that, save in cases of self-defense against an imminent attack, a political community may not go to war against another without authorization from the United Nations. It finds support in the deeper and largely empirical two-pronged claim that unilateral sanctions, of which unilateral conditional sales is an example, can lead to destructive trade wars, and that politically unrestricted global trade has brought prosperity to millions. I do not take a stand on this here. But *if* those points are sound, then the conclusion that *Conditional Sale* is morally permitted is subject to the *caveat*, which I shall take as given throughout, that the destructive impact of such a policy must not outweigh the goods it might bring about.

ECONOMIC SANCTIONS, CONDITIONAL SALE, AND CONDITIONAL AID

Economic sanctions consist in restricting or raising the costs of their target (T)'s ability to engage in trade and financial activities with the sanctioning party (S) and/or with third parties. S may decide to freeze the financial assets of key members of T's regime or key businesses within T, to ban the purchase by its own citizens or residents of T's valuable export commodities such as oil, diamonds, and other natural resources, or to forbid the sale and exports of certain goods to T. Economic sanctions are imposed for various ends: restricting nuclear proliferation, supplementing counter-terrorism measures, giving T inducements to comply with the laws of war, etc. When applied unilaterally by a sovereign state, they usually apply to individuals and businesses who are residents of, and/or trade from, that state. Likewise, *mutatis mutandis*, when sanctions are applied by associations of states (Baldwin 1985, Barber 1979, Ellis 2015, Hufbauer, Schott, and Elliott 1991, Wallensteen 1968).

Conditional sales are a form of economic sanctions. But, whereas sanctions typically prohibit the sale of certain goods altogether as a means to get their target to comply, in conditional sales the seller is willing to sell but at a higher price than it would accept were the target to do what it wants. Thus, Affluenza says to Barrenia not "we will only sell you *G* if you stop doing *x*/ do *y*," but, rather, "we will sell you *g* at price p_1 only if you stop doing *x*/ do *y*; otherwise, we will only sell at price p_{100}." As long as Barrenia is willing to pay the higher price, it can carry on not doing what Affluenza wants. Should Barrenia still want to transact, it faces a choice between paying a high price and not doing what Affluenza wants on the one hand, and paying a lower, more affordable price and acceding to Affluenza's wishes on the other hand. Affluenza's offer is more interesting than a straightforward offer to sell *tout court* subject to a politics-condition, for should Barrenia refuse to meet the politics-condition on the straightforward offer, Affluenza gets nothing at all. Here, it will at least get significant financial revenues, and it pays to ask whether it may so profit from Barrenia's decision.

Now consider conditional aid. Typically, the aid provider offers a package of economic and financial assistance to a beneficiary party, on the condition that the latter should embark on various political and economic reforms – in practice, market liberalization, the democratization of its institutions, and so on. The beneficiary thus has a choice between getting the aid and doing the provider's bidding on the one hand, and getting nothing while retaining their independence from the provider on the other hand.

Contrastingly, in conditional sale, the issue is whether Affluenza is morally permitted to set whatever price-condition it wishes, at whatever politics-conditions it wishes. The cost for Barrenia of sticking to its policy, contra Affluenza's wishes, is either a considerable monetary loss, or not transacting at all and thereby not getting the resources it badly needs or wants. By contrast, in conditional aid as in standard economic sanctions, the cost of sticking to its policy is simply not getting something that it badly needs or wants.

My question, then, is this: On what grounds and under what conditions is Affluenza morally permitted to resort to *Conditional Sale*? The latter policy is justified, I argue, only if:

(a) Affluenza is morally permitted to make *G* available to Barrenia in the first instance (failing which, withholding access to *G* altogether whatever Barrenia does, or economic sanctions, are the only justified option of economic statecraft) and:

(b) Affluenza is not under an independently justified unconditional duty to give *G* to Barrenia (contra *Conditional Aid*).

As we shall see, whether those conditions are met depends on what kind of good *G* is, on whether Barrenia's policy is morally wrong, and on the kind of control that Affluenza has over *G*.

CONDITIONAL SALE AS A RESPONSE TO A JUSTIFIED GRIEVANCE

Suppose that Affluenza owns *G* and controls its production and sale – via state-owned companies. Barrenia conducts a policy, *P*, which Affluenza would like to see it rescind. By assumption, Affluenza's regime has a direct say on G's availability to its friends and foes on the world stage.

In contrast to standard economic sanctions, *Conditional Sale* gives Barrenia the option of holding on to *P* while procuring *G* – though at a premium price. It also provides Affluenza with a source of revenue – quite an important one in fact if Barrenia is willing to meet its higher-price-condition. Taken together, and in the light of a general presumption in favor of international free trade, those two considerations suggest that Affluenza is morally permitted to adopt this policy in preference to standard economic sanctions. *Vis-à-vis* Barrenia, it seems that it is morally permitted to make *G* available to the latter at a higher price for failing to rescind *P*, and at a lower price in exchange for rescinding *P; vis-à-vis* their fellow citizens, it seems that Affluenza's leaders are morally permitted subject to proper internal authorization procedure to run the risk either that Barrenia will not transact at all or that Barrenia will be willing to meet the higher-price condition but not the politics-condition.

Upon closer inspection, however, we need to distinguish between cases where *P* is wrongful, and thus generates a justified grievance on Affluenza's (and/or other actors') part, and cases where Barrenia acts within its rights by pursuing *P*.

Let us assume that *P* is wrongful. We must draw a further distinction, between cases where *P* wrongs Affluenza and cases where it wrongs a third party on whose behalf Affluenza acts. In the former case, it is up to Affluenza to decide whether to impose standard economic sanctions or to go for *Conditional Sale* – in other words, to sell *G* at *p1* if Barrenia rescinds *P*, or to sell *G* at *p100* if Barrenia refuses to desist. Granted, it might seem odd for Affluenza to agree to Barrenia's wrongful policy in exchange for increased revenues. However, Affluenza might take the view that those ongoing rights-violations are an acceptable price to pay for the chance of pursuing other just and more urgent ends thanks to those extra revenues.

Now suppose that Barrenia systematically violates the rights of one of its own minorities. In this case, *Conditional Sale* is not justified. Recall that at the bar of justice, those who are in a position to help the less fortunate lead a flourishing life are under a duty to do so. By implication, they are under a duty to help prevent Barrenia's systematic violations of its minority's rights. But by going for *Conditional Sale*, Affluenza gives Barrenia the option of acquiring *G* and continuing its rights-violating policy, while itself making a profit from Barrenia's decision. Clearly, it may not do that. This is so irrespective of the kind of good that *G* is. Most clearly, if *G* is the kind of good that Barrenia uses to conduct the unjust policy, Affluenza is not morally justified in making it available in the first place unless Barrenia desists. For example, Affluenza may not offer Barrenia a choice between buying the weapons at *p1* in exchange for not using them to kill its minorities, and buying weapons at *p100* if it persists in using them to such ends. To repeat, it may only offer to make the weapons available – *at whatever price* – conditional upon Barrenia's wholly abandoning its wrongful policy.

Perhaps surprisingly, similar considerations apply if *G* is particularly prized by Barrenia's leaders, or (more likely) if it is the kind of good without which Barrenia's population cannot lead a flourishing life. In all those cases, Affluenza may not give Barrenia the option of carrying on with its unjust policies, and derive a profit from it. Instead – and depending on the kind of good that *G* is – it must do either or some of the following: withholding *G* altogether until such time as Barrenia changes its policy, giving *G* unconditionally, giving *G* conditionally, or selling *G* subject to Barrenia changing its policy.

If *G* is the kind of good without which Barrenia's members cannot lead a flourishing life, then (at the bar of justice) Affluenza may not withhold it altogether. The question is whether it may sell it, or whether it must give it. Suppose that Barrenia cannot pay for *G*, at whatever price Affluenza is willing to offer, without further undermining overall its members' prospects for a flourishing life. In this case, Affluenza must opt for giving *G*. Whether it may do so conditionally or not in turn depends on whether *G* is a basic necessity (in other words, whether Barrenia's members have a *basic* right to it) or whether it is a non-basic good (though still protected as a matter of (non-basic) human right. I believe (though will not defend that claim here) that justice mandates unconditional aid for basic necessities and permits conditionality for non-basic goods. Of course, this creates a perverse incentive for Barrenia to violate the rights of some of its members as a means to place Affluenza under an obligation to give *G* (albeit conditional upon its rescinding its policy). If the evidence suggests that Barrenia would not commit such rights-violations but for the fact that it would be able to get Affluenza to give *G*, Affluenza would be under a duty not to give in to Barrenia's blackmail. But if Barrenia's rationale for adopting *P* has nothing to do with putting Affluenza under that kind of pressure, then Affluenza is under the aforementioned duties.[1]

Suppose now that Barrenia *can* afford to pay for *G*, but that its leaders are unwilling to do so, at whatever price Affluenza sets. In this case, Affluenza is under the same duties as yielded by Barrenia's inability (as distinct from unwillingness) to pay.

Finally, suppose that Barrenia can afford to pay for *G* at a lower price than Affluenza is hoping to get, that it can do so without further undermining in other respects its population's prospects for a flourishing life, *and* that it is willing to pay that price for the sake of its population (perhaps sensing that improving living conditions is the only way to avert a revolution). Affluenza is not under a duty to give *G*, since Barrenia can pay without cost to justice, but in so far as Barrenia's population need *G*, and so long as it cannot procure it elsewhere, Affluenza is under a duty to sell at a price that Barrenia can afford. More generally, there sometimes is a duty to sell – a point which, incidentally, the literature on global distributive justice tends to overlook, focused as it is on the provision of aid.

So far, I have assumed that Barrenia's residents need *G* to lead a flourishing life, such that denying them access to *G* is unjust. But suppose that *G* is a dual-use resource: It is a constituent of, or is needed for, a flourishing life, *and* is needed above and beyond that threshold. Such is the case with more or less all natural resources, including oil and water. In such cases, Affluenza may withhold *G* from Barrenia above and beyond that threshold; if it chooses to make *G* available above and beyond that threshold, it must do so subject to the politics-condition.

My suggestion, thus, is that aid, whether conditional or not, is morally preferable to selling (and *a fortiori* to withholding) when *G* is needed by Barrenia's civilian population and when Barrenia is guilty of human rights violations. In the next section, we will consider cases where Barrenia's policy is not wrongful. Beforehand, however, we should deal with a putative objection to my argument against *Conditional Sale*. I argued above that when Barrenia is guilty of human rights violations, *Conditional Sale* is morally problematic precisely because it offers Barrenia a choice between buying *G* at price *p1* subject to rescinding P, and continuing with *P* at the cost of paying price *p100* for G. Of course, Barrenia might decide not to transact at all, in which case its population will suffer the considerable hardship of not getting G. Equally, Barrenia might also decide to pay *p100*, in which case its victims will continue to suffer. Affluenza, I argued, ought not to give Barrenia that option. Granted, Barrenia might be willing to rescind *P* as a means to get *G* for the low price; but if its leaders direct the revenues it thereby keeps (in the form of the difference between *p1* and *p100*) to their private coffers, at the expense of the population, this further strengthens the case in favor of *Conditional Aid* and against *Conditional Sale*.

Why should any of this be a concern of Affluenza's, some may object? After all, *ex hypothesi, G* is not needed as a matter of survival by Barrenia's population (for if it were, as we saw above, Affluenza would be under an obligation to give it, and the objection would not arise). Moreover, whether or not Barrenia's citizens suffer as a result of their regime's decision is that regime's responsibility, and no one else's. In the legal-philosophical literature, this question is known as the question of intervening agency. On some views, an agent is not morally responsible for what comes about as a result of other agents' wrongfully adding at *t2* to what he did at *t1*. On other views, both the initial and the intervening agent are morally responsible for the final outcomes.

The latter view strikes me as plausible. If I negligently throw a lit cigarette in a bush at time *t1*, and if you pour petrol on the bucket at *t2*, I am at least in part responsible, not just for having thrown my cigarette butt but also for the ensuing forest fire that develops at *t3*. The fact that you intervened at *t2* does not wholly exempt me (Hart and Honoré 1959; Zimmerman 1985).

Does this support the claim that Affluenza is somewhat responsible for the predicament of Barrenia's population under *Conditional Sale*? At first sight, one might think not. For by opting for *Conditional Sale*, Affluenza expands the range of options available to Barrenia, and it might seem unclear how that alone could render them responsible for (some of) the consequences of the latter's decision. However, by making *G* available to Barrenia at a higher price, it predictably contributes to exposing that population to worsening conditions – worsening, that is, to the point where their human rights would be violated. Given that there is an alternative in the form of *Conditional Aid*, Affluenza is partly responsible for the predicament of Barrenia's victims, and thus is accountable to them for its decision to sell rather than give.

To recapitulate, Affluenza is permitted to go for Conditional Sale as a response to Barrenia's rights-violating policy *only* when it is itself a victim of that policy. But if the policy is directed against Barrenia's own population, Affluenza may not opt for *Conditional Sale*: It may not, that is, give Barrenia the option of procuring the good it needs or wants without having to rescind its policy.

CONDITIONAL SALE IN THE ABSENCE OF A JUSTIFIED GRIEVANCE

So far, I have assumed that policy *P* is wrongful. Suppose now that neither Affluenza nor third parties have a claim against Barrenia that the latter should not carry out P: Barrenia acts within its rights when pursuing *P*. However, *P* is not in Affluenza's interest: Affluenza wants Barrenia to pursue policy *Q*. Is *Conditional Sale* justified in this case?

If Barrenia merely *wants* G, it seems, at first sight, that Affluenza may make its willingness to sell it at a price that Barrenia can afford conditional upon pursuing *Q*, so long (obviously) as *Q* is not itself morally wrong and provided that Barrenia does not have a prior right to *G*. It also seems, more obviously still, that Affluenza may give Barrenia the option of continuing with its rightful policy. This after all is the give and take of negotiation in foreign policy: Barrenia can always go to another supplier, or go without *G*.

If Barrenia *needs* G, however, we might worry about Affluenza's negotiating stance – even if (let us suppose) Affluenza is not under a duty to *give* G to Barrenia. Consider, by analogy, Joel Feinberg's well-known case of the lecherous millionaire who offers the mother of a desperately ill child the money needed for one last ditch life-saving operation, so long as she has sex with him (Feinberg 1986, 227–230). Suppose that the millionaire is not under a duty to give her the money. Even so, if he does decide to give it, he may not do so subject to this, or relevantly similar, condition. On one view, this is because in so doing he would coerce the woman into accepting: even though his offer enhances her set of options, he is structuring her choice situation in such a way that she can only choose between two evils. On other views, the woman is not coerced, precisely because she has more choice than she would have had, had the offer not been made; the millionaire, however, exploits her desperate situation, and therein lies his wrong-doing. On other views still, the millionaire's offer is wrongfully coercive precisely because it is wrongfully exploitative (Feinberg 1986, ch. 24; Feinberg 1988, chs. 31–32; Wertheimer 1987, 1996).

I doubt that the lecherous millionaire's offer is coercive, precisely because it increases the mother's options. But it is nevertheless a wrongfully exploitative offer. Standardly, a transaction between two parties A and B elicits this criticism only if it meets the following conditions (Reeve 1987; Wertheimer 1996):

(a) A benefits from the transaction;
(b) A gets B to agree to the transaction by seizing on a feature of B's or of her situation such that B would not agree otherwise;
(c) The outcome of the transaction is harmful or (if the transaction is mutually advantageous) unfair to B.

The lecherous millionaire benefits from the transaction; he clearly takes advantage of the mother's desperate wish for her son to live. It is unfair that, although she too benefits (for her son does live), she should *avoidably* be placed in a situation where she has to choose between her son's survival at the cost of surrendering sexually to a man she does not want, and protecting her sexual integrity at the cost of her son's life – in other words between two extremely bad states of affairs. I emphasize *avoidably*, for therein lies the particular wrong-doing that the lecherous millionaire commits against her: after all, he could give her the money without asking for anything in return. Even if one holds (which many would not) that the woman can nevertheless be deemed validly to have consented, and thus that he does not rape her, he nevertheless wrongs her, by taking advantage of, or using, her vulnerability to get her to agree to relinquish control over the terms under which she will do things for him.

Strictly speaking, it is possible wrongfully to exploit another person even if the offer is meant as an inducement to get that person to do that which they are under a duty to do anyway and which they *could* do without the inducement. If this is correct, then the case against wrongful exploitation when the exploitee acts within her rights is all the more robust. Suppose that B culpably subjects A to a lethal threat without just cause and is seriously wounded in the ensuing shootout. Unless A calls emergency services within the hour, B will die. If she calls them now, B will make a full recovery. If she calls them in half an hour, B will survive but with lifelong injuries that will dramatically impair his quality of life. B still holds his gun, and would be able to inflict a minor wound on A with it: A has run out of ammunition and dares not try and disarm him herself. So she offers to call 999 in half an hour so long as B drops his gun now – failing which, she will not make the call. B would not agree to this but for the fact that he will die otherwise; and were A to dial 999 now, B would agree to drop his gun without qualms. Does it make sense to say that A wrongfully exploits B? Clearly, B ought to drop his gun here and now. At the same time, A could call 999 now, thereby enabling B wholly to recover. Relative to this baseline, the outcome of the transaction is harmful to B. It is a harm, moreover, which A needlessly inflicts on him, for B *would* drop the gun if A called 999 now. It seems that A wrongfully takes advantage of B's admittedly self-inflicted vulnerability to get something (causing B to live with the lifelong effects of serious injuries) to which she does not have a right.

If we have reasons to worry about exploitation in cases such as these, where B is under a duty to do what A demands, *a fortiori* we also have reasons to worry when B is not under a duty so to act – in the present context, when Affluenza merely seeks to pursue its own ends by getting Barrenia to rescind policy *P*, even if those ends are not in and of themselves wrongful. Incidentally, note that in some cases, the transaction can be deemed wrongful merely in virtue of the fact that Affluenza itself is responsible for Barrenia's predicament. If, for example, Affluenza has wrongfully made it impossible for Barrenia to find other suppliers or become independent from Affluenza's *G*-holdings, or if it has wrongfully failed to transfer to Barrenia aid to which the latter was entitled (as a result of which it is broke), *Conditional Sale* is unquestionably wrongful. At the bar of the theory of justice that underpins my argument in this paper, given that the rich have been and continue to be consistently derelict in their obligations to the poor, the overwhelming majority of conditional sales are wrongful.

My concern, though, is with wrongful *exploitation* – and so with conditional sales that are wrongfully exploitative. Assume for the sake of argument that Affluenza is not responsible for Barrenia's weak bargaining situation. Under this policy a transaction (T) involves the following: Affluenza will sell *G* to Barrenia at price *p1* only if B adopts policy *Q* (T1), or will sell *G* to Barrenia at price *p100* were Barrenia to continue with policy *P* (T2). To illustrate, in 2010 Russia cut down the price of her gas exports to Ukraine by 30% over a period of ten years, in exchange for an extension of the lease of the naval base at Sebastopol.

Conditional Sale clearly meets the first exploitation condition: under either T1 or T2, Affluenza gets revenues. It meets the second condition in either one of two ways: under T1, when Barrenia is dependent on Affluenza's resources and when it is in such financial straits that it cannot afford to pay *p100*; under T2, when B can pay the higher price but is wholly dependent on Affluenza's resources.

That said, a transaction that meets both the first and the second condition is wrongfully exploitative only if, in addition, its outcome is harmful or unfair to Barrenia and its population. *Ex hypothesi*, Affluenza is not under a duty to give *G* to *Barrenia* – for example, because giving *G* away without a price-condition would be too much of a sacrifice at the bar of justice. The question is whether Affluenza is permitted to sell *G* under either the politics-condition or premium-price-condition without falling foul of the general requirement not to wrongfully exploit someone in need.

Suppose that under T2 Barrenia's financial resources would become so depleted within five years that its population would suffer a dramatic decline in their standard of living, to the point that most of them would no longer lead a flourishing life. Under those circumstances, T2 would be harmful to those citizens, even though, in the very short term, they would be better off for having access to *G*. In this case, T2 is wrongfully exploitative.

Under T1, Barrenia's financial resources would not be depleted to the same extent. But having to adopt policy *Q* might in fact be harmful to its population overall in the medium term. If so, T1 is harmful to them too, and (in so far as it also meets both the first and second exploitation conditions) wrongfully exploitative.

In cases such as these, given that both possible transactions, T1 and T2, are wrongfully exploitative, *Conditional Sale* is wrong. If Affluenza is willing to make *G* available to Barrenia, it should either give it away or sell it at a price that Barrenia can afford. Returning to Ukraine's case, on a plausible reading of Russo-Ukrainian negotiations, Russia's leadership took advantage of Ukrainian citizens' dependence on Russian gas to get those citizens' leaders to agree to a policy inimical to their compatriots' interests – as was clearly shown in 2014 when President Putin used the presence of the Russian Fleet in Sebastopol as both a reason for, and a means to enforce, the annexation of Crimea.

By implication, however, there may well be cases where only T2 or only T1 is harmful to Barrenia. If so, at first sight, Affluenza ought to make the other offer, if it is to make an offer at all. Furthermore, and again by implication and at first sight, if Barrenia merely wants *G*, and does not need it, then Affluenza can impose whatever conditions it wishes, for Barrenia to accept or reject as it wishes.

I say "at first sight," because the outcome of a transaction that is not harmful to Barrenia might nevertheless be unfair to them. When might that happen? When A benefits more than B from the transaction – or so one might think. If so, not all offers of conditional sale would be unfair in this sense (though some might be): it might be more important to Barrenia that it get *G* than to Affluenza to get either the premium price or the lower price combined with policy *Q*.

In any event, even if Affluenza were to benefit more than Barrenia, the charge of unfairness would hold only if it is grounded in a plausible account of when and why inequalities are unfair. On my account of global justice, so long as all individuals wherever they are in the world have prospects for a flourishing life, inequalities are not unjust. Affluenza, thus, would not *wrongfully* exploit Barrenia (though it might be exploiting it *tout court*) by offering a choice between T1 and T2, since Barrenia's citizens would still enjoy prospects for a flourishing life under either transaction.[2]

To recapitulate, I have argued that *Conditional Sale* is wrongfully exploitative only if (a) Affluenza benefits from the transaction and (b) gets Barrenia to agree to the transaction by seizing on a feature of Barrenia's or of its situation such that Barrenia would not agree otherwise; and (c) if the outcome of the transaction is harmful or unfair to Barrenia and its population. As we also saw, even if only conditions (a) and (b) are met, *Conditional Sale* is wrongful so long as Affluenza's policies are responsible for Barrenia's poor bargaining situation. In all other cases, *Conditional Sale* is a legitimate means to get Barrenia to abandon its rightful policy.

COMPLICATING THE PICTURE: CONDITIONAL SALES AND THE PROBLEM OF PRIVATE BUSINESSES

So far, I have assumed that Affluenza owns *G*, and that its government controls its production and sale. Matters are rarely so simple, however. More often than not, privately owned businesses produce, own, and sell export products. By resorting to *Conditional Sale* as a foreign policy tool, Affluenza in effect says to the relevant businesses: "you must sell at *p1* if Barrenia complies with our demands; you can only sell at *p100* if it does not desist." Is that morally problematic?

Perhaps. If Barrenia decides not to transact at all, those businesses will bear the costs and so, ultimately, will (some) of its citizens. Alternatively, if Barrenia agrees to transact at the low price and to do Affluenza's bidding, those businesses will lose revenues that they might have been able to get had Affluenza not adopted the policy.

Whether Affluenza's regime may so act depends *inter alia* on whether the ends it pursues through *Conditional Sale* are just ends, and if so whether those ends are in the interest of Affluenza's citizens themselves or whether they benefit third parties. On the first count, if the ends are unjust, *Conditional Sale* is unjust – though not because it controls the prices at which private businesses can transact with Barrenia but, rather, because one simply may not act unjustly. In such cases, in other words, there is no difference between the simple picture painted in the previous two sections and the complex picture outlined here.

Suppose now that Affluenza's ends are just, in the sense that the policy that is pursued by Barrenia wrongs Affluenza's citizens. It might be tempting to think that Affluenza's regime may opt for *Conditional Sale*, thereby exposing private businesses and those economically dependent on those businesses to the possibly harmful consequences of income losses, only if it is suitably representative of its citizenry. As I argue elsewhere, although democratic authorization is not required for justly resisting grievous rights-violations, the less serious the wrong-doings at issue, the greater the moral importance of such authorization (Fabre 2012, 150–156). In the present context, thus, *Conditional Sale* does not require democratic authorization if it is a means for the redress of basic rights-violations (in those cases, for example, where there is a just cause for war but where resorting to war would be unjust for breaching the requirement of proportionality); it does require it when the stakes are not as high, and in particular when the policy is considered as a means to pursue mere foreign policy goals.

The same considerations apply if the ends pursued by Affluenza are just in the sense that they benefit third parties – for example, a minority within Barrenia that is oppressed by policy *P*. If Affluenza is not, in this case, under a duty to restrict freedom of trade with Barrenia for the sake of this minority, it may so act only with the authorization of its own citizens, for similar reasons just adduced in the self-defensive case.

But suppose now that Affluenza *is* under a duty to victims of that policy to thwart Barrenia. If so, whether or not *Conditional Sale* is morally justified as a means to do so, notwithstanding the costs accruing to those businesses, does not depend on whether Affluenza's regime is authorized so to act by its citizens. If those costs are within the range of what may be justifiably asked of individuals for the sake of justice, it is appropriate to ask of those businesses that they should shoulder some of the burdens attendant on fighting injustice. If a war of intervention were mandatory in such cases, they (and tax payers generally) would be under a duty to carry the relevant financial burdens through higher taxes, loss of state-provided services, or a combination of both. If so, carrying the burdens of soft humanitarian measures such as *Conditional Sale* via loss of revenues is not in principle unfair – so long as those businesses are appropriately compensated for their losses out of fairly designed general taxation. (For in this way, the overall burden of the policy is spread fairly among all members of Affluenza.) Note that my point does not rely on the assumption that those businesses are owned and managed by citizens of Affluenza. In fact, it extends to all businesses operating from Affluenza, irrespective of nationality – in just the same way as all taxpayers within a given country, irrespective of nationality, have to contribute to the financing of domestic and foreign policy.

So much, then, for Affluenza's private economic actors. But what about Barrenia's private businesses, who are in effect told by Affluenza's regime that they will only be able to purchase *G* if their regime does Affluenza's bidding? Do they have a grievance? If it were the case that Affluenza does not owe those agents anything at all, either on the grounds that its duties do not extend beyond its borders, and/or that its freedom to trade as it wishes outweighs any considerations other than the wellbeing of its own members, then Barrenia's private economic actors would not have a grievance. However, on my account of global justice, Affluenza, and its members, do have duties to distant strangers not to deprive the latter of the opportunities for a minimally flourishing life. Granted, Barrenia's private economic actors do have to incur the costs of their regime's refusal to accede to Affluenza's wishes when those costs are morally acceptable. But in just the same way as Affluenza's decision to opt for *Conditional Sale* is constrained by the impact of the policy on Barrenia's civilians under the simplifying assumptions of the previous two sections, so is its decision constrained in this more complex picture.

CONCLUSION

In this chapter, I scrutinized a very specific kind of economic statecraft, which consists in an offer to sell subject to satisfaction of both a price-condition and a politics-condition. In its dual conditionality, it is a more complex instrument of foreign policy than either standard economic sanctions or conditional aid. I argued that, depending on the ends pursued by the seller and the nature of the goods under scrutiny, *Conditional Sale* is sometimes morally permissible but also, sometimes, morally preferable to those other forms of economic statecraft.

NOTES

I am extremely grateful to Elizabeth Ellis, Joy Gordon, Michael Gross, Tamar Meisels, and David Rodin for their comments on an earlier draft of this paper.

1. I am grateful to Elizabeth Ellis and David Rodin for pressing me on this.
2. My point here implies that the super-rich cannot wrongfully exploit the medium-rich (at least so long as the inequalities between them are not the product of an injustice). This may seem counter-intuitive, yet I do think that this is correct.

CYBER WARFARE, MEDIA WARFARE, AND LAWFARE

5

State-Sponsored Hacktivism and the Rise of "Soft" War

George Lucas

INTRODUCTION

The focus of this chapter is an important new tactic of "soft" war. In cyber space this concept offers an obvious comparison with a concept now well-established in international relations: namely, "soft power" (Nye 2004), according to which diplomacy, trade agreements, and other policy instruments may also be used, alongside or in lieu of threats of military force or other "hard-power" (kinetic or forceful) measures, in order to persuade adversary nations to cooperate more readily with any given state's strategic goals.

"Soft war" (or "unarmed conflict"), by analogy, is a comparatively new term designating actual warfare tactics that rely on measures other than kinetic force or conventional armed conflict to achieve the political goals and national interests or aspirations for which wars (according to Clausewitz [1830] 1976) are always fought. Importantly, I will argue that "soft war" is fully equivalent to what Chinese military policy strategists earlier deemed "unrestricted" warfare: i.e. "warfare" carried out within domains in which conventional wars are not usually fought, employing measures not previously associated with the conduct of war (Liang and Xianangsui 1999; Lo 2012). Cyber conflict of one type should be included within the purview of "soft" or "unrestricted" warfare, but the particular kind I describe here is *not* "effects-based" conflict like Stuxnet, nor the kind of "cyber Armageddon" long predicted by analysts like Richard Clarke (Brenner 2011; Clarke 2010). Instead, it is a distinctive type of conflict that has evolved to dominance in their place: a phenomenon I label "state-sponsored hacktivism." To clarify this claim, I begin with a background review of malevolent activities in cyberspace itself.

A BRIEF HISTORY OF CYBER CONFLICT (OR MALEVOLENT ACTIVITIES IN THE CYBER DOMAIN)

Not so long ago, cyber "activism" (on the internet, at least) was limited to pranks, practical jokes, and random acts of vandalism carried out by individuals or perhaps small groups or "gangs." Pranksters attached software "viruses" to emails that, when mistakenly opened, quickly spread through an organization's internal network, posting goofy messages and perhaps even erasing valuable data or software stored on hard drives. Cyber vandals posted offensive messages or unwanted photos, or otherwise defaced an organization's website for no apparent reason. About the only crimes committed in those early days were trespassing (technically, by "invading" a private company network or an individual's computer itself) and destruction of property. Apart from mean-spiritedness or a perverted sense of humor, however, about the only reasons given for such malicious activities were a collective grousing by disaffected programmers and computer "geeks" about the monopolistic practices and mediocre software distributed by Microsoft Corporation (Greenberg 2012).

Malicious behavior in the cyber domain, however, quickly evolved into a variety of more serious and sinister activities. On the one hand, it was not long before sophisticated individuals and criminal gangs exploited the very same software vulnerabilities as did the pranksters, but did so in order to steal bank deposits, credit card numbers, or even one's personal identity. On the other hand, cyber "activism" itself likewise evolved into ever more sophisticated acts of political sabotage: defacing or even temporarily shutting down government or commercial web sites with so-called "DDoS" attacks (distributed denial of service), dispatching software "worms" that traveled from computer to computer, penetrating each machine's firewall and virus protection software in order to gain control over the PCs or laptops themselves, transforming each into a "bot" (from "robot") or "zombie" (indicating the transfer of control and agency from the original owner/operator to a remote hacker). These individual machines were then remotely networked with others into a massive "botnet" controlled by political dissidents or criminal organizations, who, in turn, used them to launch DDoS attacks on banks and financial institutions and divert their funds to secret accounts.

"Hacktivism" is a term that came into somewhat indiscriminate use to classify all these distinctive and diverse acts of malevolence and mischief in the cyber domain, ranging from straightforward crime and vandalism to many forms of political protest carried out on the internet. Technically, the "hacktivist" is one who engages in vandalism and even in criminal activities in pursuit of political goals or objectives, rather than simply for personal satisfaction or financial gain. Early on, the term solely referred to the internet activities of individuals and dissident groups (and was not applied to the activities of nations like China or North Korea, or terrorist groups like Hamas). Well-known individuals (like Julian Assange of WikiLeaks) and loosely organized groups like Anonymous, LulzSec, and "Cyberwarriors for Freedom" resorted to internet malevolence to publicize their concerns, or otherwise further their political aims. These concerns ranged from personal privacy, liberty, and freedom of expression to opposition to political regimes like Syria or Egypt.

There are many ways of carrying out "hacktivism." I find it useful to focus upon the political goals of the "hacktivist" (as opposed to the financial interests of the conventional criminal). These political goals can be categorized as transparency, whistle-blowing, and vigilantism. WikiLeaks purports, for example, to provide greater *transparency* regarding the otherwise covert activities of governments and large corporate organizations. The actions of *whistle-blowers* (like US Army Private Bradley (Chelsea) Manning, and NSA Contractor Edward Snowden), somewhat in contrast, aimed specifically to expose what each individual took to be grave acts of wrong-doing or injustice on the part of the US government or military (in these specific cases).

The *internet vigilantes* like "Anonymous," for their part, are a bit harder to pin down, since the loosely organized federation's individual members espouse a wide variety of disparate causes. The organization's behavior in response to each chosen cause, however, clearly involves taking the law (or, in its absence, morality) into the group's hands unilaterally. That is, based upon their shared judgments regarding immoral or illegal behavior by individuals, organizations, or governments to whom the group objects, the group launches attacks against selected targets ranging from the Syrian government of Bashir al Assad (for engaging in massive human rights violations) to organizations and individuals who might be engaged in perfectly legitimate security and defense operations to which members of Anonymous nevertheless object (Knappenberger 2012).

This is vigilantism. And, as its name suggests, the members of Anonymous cannot easily be traced or held accountable for their actions. As in all instances of conventional vigilantism, the vigilante's judgment as to what or who constitutes a moral offense is deeply subjective, and often wildly inconsistent or otherwise open to serious question.

Importantly, in all cases involving transparency, whistle-blowing, and vigilantism, the *burden of proof* is on those who deliberately violate fiduciary duties and contractual (legal) agreements into which they may have entered, or who disobey or flout the law itself, in order to expose or protest against activities they deem to be even more egregious than their own actions. Such actions constitute important forms of democratic moral discourse in what Jürgen Habermas termed "the public sphere" (Calhoun 1992; Habermas 1991). This comparative judgment on the part of the protestor or whistle-blower, for example, is technically known as "the Principle of Proportionality." It demands of them that the degree of harm brought about through their own actions be *demonstrably less* than the harm already done by others to which they seek to call attention, or bring to a stop. The problem is that this comparative judgment is notoriously difficult to make. Vigilantes often exaggerate or misrepresent the harm against which they protest, and seriously underestimate the effects of their own activities on public welfare.

Otherwise, the remaining difficulty with such actions is that there is no independent or adversarial review of these decisions. According to what is likewise termed the "Principle of Publicity" or the Principle of Legitimate Authority, the final authority to evaluate the legitimacy of the protestor's or dissident's actions rests not with that individual or dissident organization, but with the wider general public, in whose collective interest the individual purports to act. So, in all these cases, it must be possible in principle to bring the individual dissident's actions and intentions before an impartial "Court of Public Opinion" for independent review (de Oliviera 2000; O'Neill 1986). The last criterion is the one most frequently ignored, and most often failed by both vigilantes and would-be whistle-blowers. They are prone to suffer from an abundance of self-righteousness.

THE ADVENT OF STATE-SPONSORED INTERNET ACTIVISM

Having established this context for the discussion of cyber hacktivism generally, what now are we to make of its most recent evolution: namely, the rise of state-sponsored or government "hacktivism"? Nations and governments are entering the cyber fray alongside private groups, either attempting to combat or shut down other hacktivists and stifle dissent within their own borders, or, instead, to pursue political objectives against other states that were traditionally resolved through diplomacy, economic sanctions, and finally, a resort to kinetic force. *Many states at present appear to be resorting to massive cyber-attacks instead.* Such nations are thought to include pro-government groups or organizations in China (e.g. PLA Shanghai Unit 61384), the Russian Federation, and especially North Korea.

A recent high-visibility example of such state behavior was the apparent attack by North Korean operatives on Sony Pictures over the pending release of the movie comedy, "The Interview." Never (it was frequently remarked) had such a bad movie received such first-class publicity (e.g. see: Burr 2014; Kelner 2014; Neumaier 2014). The entire affair seemed itself almost comedic, save for the important principles at stake: interference in the internal affairs of another nation, freedom of expression, violations of personal privacy for foreign state purposes. The kind of extortion and blackmail involved, and its impact on corporate and individual behavior in a sovereign land, might not have seemed so funny in alternative circumstances. The United States thus treated this instance of massive, state-sponsored hacktivism as a serious act of international conflict.

In other, earlier instances: the "Russian Business Network," a branch of organized crime in the Russian Federation, is believed to have cooperated with the government in launching a preemptive cyber-attack on government organizations and military sites in the Republic of Georgia in 2008, prior to a conventional Russian military incursion into the breakaway Georgian province of Ossetia (Harris 2014). The United States indicted five members of the PLA Shanghai unit by name in the spring of 2014, for having been responsible for massive thefts of patents and trade secrets from US-based aerospace and defense industries (DOJ 2014). The indictments were not expected to result in actual arrest and prosecution, but were intended instead to send a message to the Chinese government that its disavowal or denial of state accountability for these crimes under international law was no longer plausible.

One of the most interesting of these earlier developments was the work of "Cyber Fighters of Izz ad-Din al-Qassam," an organization that takes its name from a prominent early twentieth-century Muslim cleric and anti-colonialist. In 2012, on the anniversary of the 9/11 terrorist attacks in the United States, this group allegedly carried out a massive DDoS attack on US financial institutions. The attack was described in a Twitter post by the group as having been launched in retaliation for the continued presence on YouTube of the American-made film, "The Innocence of Muslims," which portrays Islam and the prophet Mohammed in a very scandalous and unflattering light. The group vowed to continue the attacks until the offending film itself was removed from the internet.

Two things stood out regarding the resulting very serious disruptions of American financial institutions. First, despite its claim of independence, the group's attack was not indiscriminate. The institutions targeted were primarily those that had complied with the terms of the ongoing US economic sanctions against Iran. In particular, the group's demand that a film be censored on account of its political or religious content seemed hollow: Their leaders had to know that this was a demand that was beyond the power of a democratic government anywhere to grant, even were they willing in principle to comply with this demand.

The second oddity was that the anonymous Twitter site from which this group issued its September 2012 proclamation turned out to be the same account from which messages had flowed a few weeks earlier (allegedly from another vigilante group entirely) in the aftermath of a massive cyber-attack on the internal computer network of ARAMCO, the Saudi Arabian oil giant. Those attacks, on August 15, 2012, allegedly carried out by an organization calling itself the "Cutting Sword of Justice," erased data on all affected computer drives, and inserted in their place the image of a burning American flag. US security officials seemed quite certain that the first of these attacks was an act of retaliation by Iranian agents in response to the damage done to their own nuclear and oil infrastructure by Stuxnet and Flame, respectively, both weapons attributed to (but never acknowledged by) the US and Israeli governments.

Suppose all these allegations and counter allegations are true: In particular, suppose that the two attacks in close sequence in 2012 (and others since) were not carried out by distinct and independent organizations, but instead represent the coordinated actions of a state government (Iran) retaliating for similar attacks upon its cyber infrastructure by other states (Israel and the United States). Add to these the known and ongoing, state-sponsored, malevolent cyber activities of the People's Liberation Army in China, the "Russian Business Network," and North Korean operatives. The conclusion is that states, as well as individuals and dissident groups, are now directly and deeply involved in hostile activities that increasingly transcend the boundaries of traditional espionage, covert action, and the "dirty tricks" of the past. Rather, this ongoing, high-stakes, but low-intensity conflict carried out by states against one another has evolved into what a number of experts (e.g. Gross 2015) are coming to call "soft war."

CYBER HACKTIVISM AND "SOFT WAR"

By analogy with the concept of "soft power," soft war is a mode of warfare or conflict that is intentionally non-kinetic: i.e. it does not entail the use of conventional weapons, or the destruction that accompanies conventional armed attacks. But it is a disruptive new innovation in international conflict, and *it is still a very grave matter*. As the cases cited above demonstrate, "soft war" cyber-attacks – state-sponsored hactivism – can do real damage, and inflict genuine harm, although rarely (in contrast to the case of Stuxnet) does this involve causing real physical harm to physical objects. Rather, the conflict results in loss of information, loss of access to information processing, and an inability to carry out essential activities (such as banking, mining, medical care, trade, and commerce) that rely largely upon information processing. Why bother to pursue the risky and wantonly destructive traditional strategic objectives of conventional warfare that Clausewitz describes as "destroying the enemy's army, occupying his cities, and breaking his will to resist" when the strategic objectives can be met instead by rendering the enemy's armies inoperable and non-functional, bringing his cities' commercial and civil activities to a standstill, and forcing his military leaders to commit suicide when they are "doxed," or "outed" to their families and the wider public on Ashley Madison?[1] The harms inflicted through "state-sponsored hacktivism" may be far more precise and less genuinely destructive than their conventional counterparts, even those inflicted through "effects-based" cyber warfare. But they are every bit as effective, destructive to those whose lives and careers they destroy, and are far easier for adversaries and rogue states to master and utilize than the sophisticated techniques of "effects-based" cyber warfare (Lucas 2016).

Unlike the highly publicized concept of a "cyber war," however, *the weapons and tactics of "soft war" are not limited to the cyber domain*. They can involve state use of the media, including cyber social media as well as conventional media, for purposes of propaganda, confusion, obfuscation, and disinformation. Soft war could involve the use of nonlethal (or "less-lethal") weapons in conventional attacks. For terrorist "pseudo-state" groups like Hamas, soft war could involve forms of what has elsewhere been called "lawfare," for example, using civilian volunteers as "human shields" to deter conventional attacks on physical infrastructure or military installations by adversaries, one among a range of nonviolent tactics to be so termed (Dunlap 2011): e.g. using the law itself (in this instance, the Law of Armed Conflict) to thwart an adversary. Cyber tactics are only some of a range of options employed in the deliberate waging of so-called soft war.

The evolution of cyber conflict itself toward the "soft war" model of hacktivism, specifically, is quite different than the full-scale, effects-based equivalent of cyber "warfare" predicted by many pundits (such as Clarke and Kanke 2010 and Brenner 2011) during the last decade. The much-touted "cyber Armageddon" or "cyber Pearl Harbor" was to be a massive disruption and destruction of conventional systems, like air traffic control and electrical grids, resulting in widespread death and destruction on parallel with a massive conventional war. But state-sponsored vigilantism and hacktivism appear to signal something quite distinct from this familiar, but often highly exaggerated and implausible, scenario. This state-sponsored conflict is virtual, not physical; nonviolent, rather than kinetic, but nevertheless quite destructive and malevolent in other respects, equally capable of causing massive social upheaval, or bringing about a "death by 1,000 cuts" through pilfering of industrial and state secrets, or by interference in trade, commerce, finance, medical care, and transportation.

And, just as with increased reliance on the exercise of "soft power" (diplomacy, sanctions, media relations, and the like), the advent of "soft war" has distinct advantages for those nations that engage in it. Essentially, *this kind of warfare proposes to substitute cleverness and ingenuity for brute strength*. It is less costly to wage, less destructive of property, of lives, and of national treasure (as well as international prestige). Yet it is quite capable of achieving the same political goals, when properly utilized, as "hard" kinetic war, as well as capable of undermining or fending off an adversary that relies solely upon "hard" war tactics. It is, in short, the equivalent of bringing Asian martial arts that rely on balance, timing, and tactical sophistication to bear upon an enormous, powerful, but wholly conventional bully. The martial arts expert can hold his or her own, and even prevail, even though smaller, lighter, and perhaps less physically strong than the bully.

This comparison is apt, since "soft" war is directly attributable to two Chinese military strategists, reflecting on the future of military conflict in the aftermath of the lopsided victory of US-led coalition forces in the 1991 Gulf War against the conventional forces of Iraqi President Saddam Hussein. In a landmark essay in 1999 cited earlier, entitled "Unrestricted Warfare," two senior colonels in the People's Liberation Army, Qiao Liang and Wang Xiangsui, argued that the United States had become an international bully, physically too strong and too reliant on extensive war-fighting technology to resist by conventional means. Instead, they proposed, new forms of conflict needed to be devised, more indebted to subtleness and cleverness than to brute force, in the spirit of Sun-Tzu, in order to effectively oppose the brute physical power of the American "hegemon."

There is no explicit regime under international law that specifically governs this kind of conflict. Ought there to be? Or is it sufficient to rely on state interests, and the norms emergent from accepted state practice, to serve as a guide to when, and how, to engage in "soft war"? Ought the same or similar guidelines applicable to kinetic war also guide entry into and conduct during this "soft" mode of warfare as well? Or ought it to remain, as its original formulators speculated, "unrestricted" or "without bounds"?

In the accounts of conventional hacktivism above, I used terms like "proportionality," "publicity," and "legitimate authority" advisedly to describe ways in which vigilante groups like Anonymous, or whistle-blowers like Manning and Snowden, might be determined to have gone astray in their otherwise well-intentioned cyber activities. In a manner similar to earlier discussions of *jus ad vim*, the morally justified use of force generally (e.g. Brunstetter and Braun 2013; Ford 2013), might we now reasonably require that states only engage in such conflict when presented with irreconcilable differences sufficiently grave to justify conventional use of force (as, admittedly, happened on both sides of the Iran/United States-Israel dispute over Iran's nuclear weapons program)? And ought we to demand or reasonably expect that, when faced with the alternative of resorting to "soft" or kinetic warfare to resolve such disputes (consistent with a Principle of Last Resort), not only should all viable and reasonable alternatives short of war be attempted, but that the "soft war" alternative should always be chosen in lieu of the conventional resort to the use of kinetic force? Perhaps most importantly, might we demand, or reasonably expect, that nations engaging in such conflict with one another should do their utmost to avoid deliberate targeting of purely civilian, non-combatant individuals and their property, as is legally required in conventional war? Or, as in the example of using volunteer civilians as human shields, should attacks on financial institutions or civil infrastructure that merely involve a denial of access or service be subject to a more tolerant regime in which the combatant–noncombatant distinction is less viable, and perhaps less significant?

"SOFT WAR" AND "SOFT" LAW (ETHICS)

The foregoing are chief among the questions waiting to be addressed and clarified in the wake of the advent of "soft war" generally, and specifically in the aftermath of the increased resort by state-sponsored agents to the kinds of tactics once limited to dissident individuals or non-state groups. While the lion's share of such normative work has occurred within the context of existing international law (most notably, the *Tallinn Manual* [Schmitt 2013]), that legal framework will simply not suffice to provide reliable guidance in this new domain of conflict. There are a number of reasons for this skepticism (see Lucas 2016, ch. 3).

Contributors to the *Tallinn Manual* (Schmitt 2013), for example, including some of the most eminent legal minds in the world today, brilliantly attempted to interpret and extrapolate existing international law (the regimes pertaining to armed conflict and humanitarian treatment of war's victims, and those pertaining to criminal activity in particular) so as to bring existing legislation to bear upon conflict in the cyber domain. But as demonstrated in this essay, *"soft war" is not "war,"* strictly speaking, and so not subject to the jurisdiction of international legal regimes pertaining to armed conflict. Neither is it simply crime (although it sometimes involves the commission of otherwise-criminal actions by state agents). Nor can it be easily dismissed as merely the routine crimes committed by covert agents in the midst of conventional espionage operations (Lucas 2016, chs. 1–2; Rid 2013).

Finally, as noted above, "soft war" *includes, but is not limited to* the cyber domain. "Media war" is not "war," and it is also not limited to cyber conflict. Use of nonlethal weapons, or tactics of "lawfare" (including human shields) not only occur outside the cyber domain (and so are obviously not addressed within the *Tallinn Manual* [Schmitt 2013]), but (in the latter instance) are also designed precisely to frustrate the bright-line statutes of existing international law, turning the letter of the law against its underlying regulatory purpose. The same seems to be true, as Gross argues, of kidnappings and hostage taking, when undertaken for political motives (Gross 2015).

Even within the cyber domain alone, "soft war" tactics are more akin to espionage than to war or crime, and thus, once again, not explicitly addressed in international law, nor are state parties to existing legal arrangements eager to see such matters addressed there. In fact, this is the chief obstacle to pursuing normative guidance through the medium of law: Those who are party to the law, and whose consent would be required to extend or amend it, are deeply opposed in principle to any further intrusion upon their respective interests and activities through treaty or additional legislation. Insofar as international law rests fundamentally upon what states themselves do, or tolerate being done, this opposition to further legislation (the one issue in the cyber domain on which the United States, Russia, and China seem to agree) seems a formidable obstacle to pursing governance and guidance through legal means.

This is not as unpromising as it might seem, however, when one recognizes the historical fact that the principle bodies of international law pertaining to conflict of any sort largely codify, after the fact, norms of certain kinds of practice that emerge from public reflection by the practitioners themselves upon the better and worse features of that practice, and upon the ends or goals ultimately served by these practices. Law and regulations give the appearance (at least) of being stipulative, and are thought to be imposed externally, often upon unwilling subjects or agents. Best practices, by contrast, *emerge* from the shared practices of the interested parties, and reflect their shared experience and shared objectives.

International law, seen in this light, is more properly understood as grounded in common accord, consensus, and voluntary compliance. Its inherently cosmopolitan character (often overlooked by politically appointed "Committees of Eminent Persons," eager to impose their terms of behavior on others) instead reflects Immanuel Kant's conception of standards of regulative order that moral agents themselves have both formulated and voluntarily imposed upon themselves, in order to guide and regulate their shared pursuits. Their compliance with principles that they themselves have formulated is thus more feasible and readily attainable.

This is a somewhat prolix manner of expressing a doctrine known in international relations as "emergent norms." This concept is encountered more broadly in moral philosophy as a kind of "trial and error," experiential groping toward order and equilibrium, a process that Aristotle (its chief theorist) described generally as the methodology of the "imperfect" sciences. The moral philosopher Alasdair MacIntyre should be chiefly credited with having resurrected this methodology in the modern era, from whence we can discern it already at work in the cyber domain, as well as in the field of military robotics (e.g. Lucas 2014, 2015). Legal scholars, for their part, have dubbed this sort of informal and voluntary regulatory institution (as occurs in the Codes of Conduct of professional organizations, or the deliberations and recommendations of practitioners in the aftermath of a profound moral crisis) as constituting "soft" law.

What seems urgently required at the moment is a coherent and discernable body of "soft" law for "soft war": that is, the relevant stakeholders in the community of practice – in this case, frankly, adversaries engaged in the kind of low-intensity conflict that I have described under the heading of "soft" war – to formulate and publicize the principles that they have evolved to govern their practice. In earlier eras, like the Cold War, for example, espionage agents from adversarial nations evolved a sophisticated set of norms to govern their interaction and competition, designed largely to minimize unnecessary destruction, loss of lives in their respective clandestine services, mutual treatment of adversaries in captivity and prisoner exchanges, and other tactics designed to reduce the risk of accidental or unnecessary escalation of conflict (especially conflict that might cross the threshold of kinetic war in the nuclear era). All of these informal normative arrangements intended to facilitate, rather than inhibit, the principle aim or goal of espionage itself: reliable knowledge of the intentions and capabilities of the adversary. In the nature of things, there were no "councils" or "summit meetings," and no published or publicized "codes of conduct." Rather, these norms of prudent governance and guidance came to be "understood" and largely accepted (and complied with) by the members of this interesting community of practice.

What the broad outlines of the content of this "soft law" for "soft war" might be are already outlined above, utilizing somewhat more familiar "just war" terminology, which serves well for this purpose (Lucas 2016). Adversaries and stakeholders pursuing "soft war" have an interest, for example, in seeing that it does not accidentally "go kinetic," or involve needless and unnecessary "collateral damage" to vital civilian infrastructure, especially of the sort that might lead to widespread physical destruction and loss of life. They share a common interest in proportionate response, and the dictates of military necessity, of the kind exhibited in the conflicts (allegedly) between the cyber warriors of Iran, the United States, and Israel described above. And adversaries like the United States, China, and the Russian Federation, still locked into a preliminary mode of "unrestricted" or limitless warfare, need to consult more directly and frankly than has been possible to date on where common interests lie in imposing boundaries and regulative order on their "soft" conflicts, before the incessant damage being done on an ongoing basis to all parties to these conflicts forces an escalation into something far more serious and irreparable.

I have deliberately confined myself to only one very prominent tactic in the arsenal of soft war more generally, in an effort to illustrate how cyber conflict itself is being assimilated less as a new and distinctive form of conflict, as a valuable tactic in a new form of warfare generally. I conclude on a positive note, by observing that this increased resort to "soft war" tactics, including (but not limited to) cyber conflict, holds promise that the very real conflicts and disagreements that have often led nations to make war upon one another may themselves evolve into a mode of authentic opposition and conflict resolution that nonetheless ends up resulting in dramatically reduced bodily harm and loss of life, while doing less damage – and more easily reversible or repairable damage – to the property of adversaries and innocents than was heretofore conceivable in conventional conflict.

NOTE

1. This infamous "dating" website actually promoted and facilitated adultery, including among highly-positioned MPs in the United Kingdom, Belgium, France, as well as members of Congress and the military in the United States. The "hacking" of its discrete and highly confidential clientele database was featured in the *Times* of London and the *New York Times*, not to mention Rupert Murdoc's tabloids during the summer of 2015. See, for example: Dino Grandoni, "Ashley Madison, a Dating Website, Says Hackers May Have Data on Millions," *The New York Times* (July 21, 2015): B3. Posted 20 July 2015: http://www.nytimes.com/2015/07/21/technology/hacker-attack-reported-on-ashley-madison-a-dating-service.html [accessed June 27, 2016].

6

Media Warfare, Propaganda, and the Law of War

Laurie R. Blank

In today's 24/7 media and internet culture, warfare does not take place only in the kinetic arena of the battlespace. Airstrikes, artillery barrages, and infantry maneuvers are accompanied by equally intense debates and discourse in the media about the legality and legitimacy of military action, with allegations of war crimes and justifications for attacks flying as quickly as drone strikes. With the involvement of international, regional and national courts, commissions of inquiry, other judicial and quasi-judicial entities—and, perhaps most of all, the court of world opinion—this battle of words can often seem to be as important as military capabilities.

Information-based operations and exchanges can take many forms during conflict, such as information operations, psychological operations, and propaganda, to name a few. Independent media coverage and social media add to the mix. Indeed, "winning modern wars is as much dependent on carrying domestic and international public opinion as it is on defeating the enemy on the battlefield" (Payne 2005). Numerous factors form, sway, and cement that public opinion, including the efforts of militaries and armed groups to control information flows and attempts by journalists, advocacy groups, fact-finding missions, and ordinary civilians to seek, publicize, and comment on information. This complex mix leads to a combustible arena of media warfare that has significant consequences not only for the way wars are fought and won, but for the legal framework that governs conflicts. This chapter will explore how propaganda and media warfare intersect with the international law framework governing conflict, focusing on how information operations and media coverage link back to legal compliance – specifically claims of law violations or compliance – and legitimacy. In essence, the information battlespace has a significant effect on the application and interpretation of the law of armed conflict, including the very definitions that form the heart of the legal framework.

INFORMATION OPERATIONS AND PROPAGANDA

The US Department of Defense (DoD) defines information warfare as "actions taken to use information and information systems to access or affect foreign information and information systems and defend one's own information and information systems" (Hanseman 1997). The goal of information warfare is, like all forms of warfare, to achieve or promote specific objectives with regard to a specific adversary. As a US Air Force report explains, "[i]nformation is no longer a staff function but an operational one. It is deadly as well as useful" (*Air Force 2025* 1996, 12).

Psychological operations, often called PSYOPS, are "[p]lanned operations to convey selected information and indicators to foreign audiences to influence their emotions, motives, objective reasoning, and ultimately the behavior of foreign governments, organizations, groups, and individuals" (US DoD 2012, 9–10). Such operations can be used as part of offensive military operations, or defensively to counter enemy propaganda and misinformation.

Finally, propaganda is the spreading of ideas, facts, or allegations, sometimes false or exaggerated, to promote a cause, government, or leader. The US military defines propaganda as "any form of communication in support of national objectives designed to influence the opinions, emotions, attitudes, or behavior of any group in order to benefit the sponsor, either directly or indirectly" (US DoD 2010). The use of propaganda in wartime, in the lead up to war, and in the aftermath of war is pervasive and timeless. States, like earlier sovereign entities before the rise of the modern nation-state system, use propaganda to rally support for military operations against other states or non-state forces. However, the growth of technology and instant media coverage of events around the world has provided new and extensive opportunities for propaganda for many other groups as well. For example, the nature of modern media provides "terrorists [with] a low cost yet powerful means to spread their propaganda – often disinformation – to millions of people worldwide" (Cilluffo and Gergely 1997, 88). On the broadest level, terrorist attacks have certain primary objectives: to get attention; to gain recognition of the group and its goals or demands; and to obtain a certain degree of respect and legitimacy (Nacos 1994, 16). To that end, "terrorists look to attack those places that given their location or their significance will attract the attention of the media" and thus give them the "opportunity to be a member of the 'triangle of political communication'" (Torres Soriano 2008, 2–3).

As the means and opportunities for propaganda continue to expand with technological advances, so do the targets and goals of that propaganda. Claims of wrong-doing and atrocities have always played a role in war propaganda. In recent conflicts, however, the asymmetry in capability between state forces and terrorist groups or other non-state armed groups has been matched by a steadily growing reliance by such groups on propaganda aimed at the legal compliance and legitimacy state forces rely on in carrying out military operations. This form of information operations – relying on the internet and the intensive and instantaneous media coverage of attacks, drone strikes, and other aspects of the conflict – often proves to be more effective than kinetic operations in achieving goals of delegitimizing the enemy or causing them to change or halt their operations. Thus, "given sufficient force and duration, information operations that exploit an adversary's killing of civilians may force an enemy to do what shells and rockets cannot: desist and stand down at little or no cost to guerrillas" (Gross 2015, 223). The discussion in this chapter explores how this form of media warfare affects the implementation and development of, and advocacy about, the law of armed conflict.

AN INTRODUCTION TO INTERNATIONAL LAW AND ARMED CONFLICT

Law has regulated the use of force, military operations, and conflict throughout history. Also known as international humanitarian law or the law of war, the law of armed conflict (LOAC) governs the conduct of states, individuals, and non-state actors during armed conflict and provides the overarching parameters for the conduct of hostilities and the protection of persons and objects. LOAC applies during all situations of armed conflict, with the full panoply of the Geneva Conventions and customary law applicable in international armed conflict and a more limited body of conventional and customary law applicable during non-international armed conflict. The central LOAC principles of distinction, proportionality, and precautions determine the lawfulness of targeting individuals and objects during armed conflict. The principle of distinction mandates that all parties to a conflict distinguish between those who are fighting and those who are not and that parties only target those who are fighting (API 1977, art. 48). In addition, soldiers and all other fighters must distinguish themselves from civilians. The principle of proportionality states that parties must refrain from attacks in which the expected civilian casualties will be excessive in relation to the anticipated military advantage (API 1977, art. 51(b)(5)). All parties must take precautions when launching attacks to ensure that the objects of attack are legitimate targets and that all feasible measures are taken to minimize harm to civilians and the civilian population (API 1977, arts. 57–58).

LOAC authorizes the use of lethal force as first resort against enemy persons and objects that are legitimate targets within the parameters of the armed conflict (Corn 2009) and also provides, based on treaty provisions and the fundamental principle of military necessity, for the detention of enemy fighters and of civilians posing imperative security risks (Geneva Convention III 1949, art. 4; Geneva Convention IV 1949, arts. 42, 78). Along with these authorities, however, come obligations – such as the obligation to use force in accordance with the principles of distinction and proportionality, the obligation to protect civilians and those no longer fighting from the ravages of war to the extent possible, and the obligation to treat all persons humanely.

Similarly, the just war tradition – legal and moral parameters for resorting to war – is centuries old (Brownlie 1963, 4–5). Modern *jus ad bellum*, the international law governing when a state may lawfully use force on the territory of another state, has its roots in early twentieth-century treaty law and is encapsulated in the United Nations Charter framework. In particular, the United Nations Charter prohibits the use of force by one state against another in Article 2(4): "All members shall refrain in their international relations from the threat or use of force against the territorial integrity or political independence of any state, or in any other manner inconsistent with the Purposes of the United Nations" (UN 1945, art. 2(4)). In addition to the customary exception that force may be used with the consent of the territorial state, the Charter provides for two exceptions to the prohibition on the use of force: the multinational use of force authorized by the Security Council under Chapter VII in Article 42, and the inherent right of self-defense in response to an armed attack under Article 51. When a state uses force in self-defense, the force used must be necessary and proportionate to the goal of repelling the attack or ending the grievance (ICJ 1996, 246; ICJ 1986). Thus, the law focuses on whether the defensive act is appropriate in relation to the ends sought. The requirement of proportionality in *jus ad bellum* measures the extent of the use of force against the overall military goals, such as fending off an attack or subordinating the enemy (Schmitt 2006, 282). The requirement of necessity addresses whether there are adequate non-forceful options to deter or defeat the attack. To this end, "acts done in self-defense must not exceed in manner or aim the necessity provoking them" (Schachter 1986, 132). A third criterion is immediacy, which addresses the temporal constraints on the use of force either before or in response to an armed attack.

THE RELATIONSHIP BETWEEN LEGITIMACY AND LOAC

Legitimacy has always been an essential component of military operations – particularly with regard to public support for the launch of operations and the continuation of those operations. When public support for an operation wanes, political leaders face significant challenges in continuing the mission in the face of diminished legitimacy. In counterinsurgency operations, legitimacy is the dominant and ultimate goal that enables mission success. As the Counterinsurgency Field Manual proclaims, "Lose Moral Legitimacy, Lose the War" (Dep't of the Army 2006, 7–9). Although

> [m]ilitary legitimacy is about might and right ..., in operations ... such as stability operations and counterinsurgency operations (COIN), might must be right to achieve mission success. That is because mission objectives in COIN are more political than

military, and legitimacy is the center of gravity in achieving those political objectives. (Barnes 2009)

Until recently, the justification for the use of force and the extent of force used – *jus ad bellum* concepts – were key components of legitimacy. Compliance with LOAC is now central to the perception of strategic legitimacy. The United States and other states seek to – and must – leverage the international legitimacy that flows from compliance with international law when they use force to achieve strategic goals. As Brigadier General Mark Martins, then Commander of the Rule of Law Field Force in Afghanistan, stated in 2011:

> The question [of rule of law in military operations] urges inquiry into how law has constrained, enabled and informed our own military operations since September 11th, 2001, even as it also causes us to mull whether and how an abstract concept we all approach with a multitude of assumptions arising from our own experiences can possibly help oppose ruthless and diverse insurgent groups halfway across the globe. The case I will briefly sketch today is this: your armed forces heed and will continue to heed the law, take it seriously and in fact respect it for the legitimacy it bestows on their often violent and lethal – necessarily violent and lethal – actions in the field. (Martins 2011)

Understanding LOAC and *jus ad bellum* – and the nature of their interactions – is therefore essential to any discussion of legitimacy. This understanding then builds the foundation for analyzing the impact of propaganda and media warfare on the application, interpretation, and development of LOAC.

MEDIA WARFARE AND PROPAGANDA: THE IMPACT ON LOAC AND LEGITIMACY

Information, whether through media coverage, propaganda, or other avenues, has become a dominant force in the question of legitimacy, as many recent conflict situations demonstrate. In counterinsurgencies and other contemporary military operations, for example, protection of civilians is a, if not *the*, primary mission objective because counterinsurgency success rests on winning the support of the local population. Civilian deaths, injuries, and destruction, even if they are lawful and the unintended consequence of successful operations against the insurgents, can severely undermine both legitimacy and chances for success. As a result, LOAC compliance lies at the heart of legitimacy in such scenarios and the perception of crimes against civilians can unravel hard-fought successes quickly.

Similarly, in certain conflicts, the interplay between LOAC and the *jus ad bellum* plays a significant role with respect to legitimacy. The perceived justification for the use of force impacts the legitimacy of any operation, as it has historically, but we now see extensive manipulation of information about LOAC compliance in the conduct of hostilities as a tool for debates about the lawfulness of using force in the first place. In Kosovo, an operation driven by moral legitimacy claims rather than classical (UN Charter-based) international law justifications for the use of force, the conduct of the NATO operations against the Milosevic regime dominated the media and advocacy community's presentation of the conflict. As a result, in NATO countries, "collateral damage, rather than ethnic cleansing and the refugee crisis, threatened to become the central issue of the Kosovo conflict, undermining the moral credibility of, and hence public support for, the campaign" (Porch 2002, 101). Similarly, the use of allegations of LOAC violations to dispute the lawfulness of Israel's use of force in self-defense and to undermine the legitimacy of Israel's military operations has marked each of the conflicts between Israel and Hamas in Gaza over the past seven years (Blank 2011).

In any mission where civilian protection is the central goal – whether counterinsurgency or humanitarian intervention or many types of stability operations – harm to civilians or perceived harm to civilians has multiple negative consequences. First, in the most direct form, civilian harm impedes mission accomplishment in the short term if the mission is protection of civilians. Second, civilian harm bolsters the opposition forces (whether insurgents or a state repressing its own population) and serves as an effective recruiting and public relations tool. Third, regardless of the actual legality of the acts that led to the civilian harm, the mere perception that the military is causing the deaths of civilians can be sufficient to engender claims of war crimes and other LOAC violations. The fourth negative consequence, the loss of legitimacy, stems directly from the second and third described above. When insurgents appear to be the better protectors of the civilian population, the counterinsurgent loses legitimacy, the ultimate objective in counterinsurgency. When state forces engaged in counterinsurgency or humanitarian intervention appear to be committing war crimes, they lose legitimacy at home, eroding valuable public support for the mission. These considerations lay the foundation for an insurgent group's effective use of the media and propaganda to undermine the legitimacy of state forces by maintaining a steady flow of information about civilian casualties and other forms of violence and destruction, framed in a way to allege directly, or merely create a perception of, violations of LOAC.

For example, recent conflicts highlight how news coverage of civilian casualties can immediately impugn – even to the extent of delegitimization – law-compliant militaries, even when there is no evidence that the civilian casualties were the result of unlawful conduct. These consequences happen at a variety of levels, from the simple effects of dramatic and tragic information conveyed through the media to the more sinister manipulation and exploitation of the media and technology to achieve a strategic advantage. First, the very nature of civilian casualties produces assumptions about misconduct, and the general public has an inherent tendency to believe the truthfulness of television and other news coverage, "without taking into account the context and a group of other circumstances that 'surround' these images" (Torres Soriano 2008, 4).

Media coverage of conflict, and of the harmful consequences to and suffering of civilians, is absolutely essential. Only through the provision of information and access to varied reporting can the public stay informed and therefore capable of understanding, analyzing, and even advocating about the conflict. At the same time, however, it is important to recognize the power of media coverage in inadvertently producing or supporting conclusions about the conflict that go far beyond the coverage.

Second, insurgent groups and terrorist groups have become quite adept at manipulating the media coverage and technology to advance their form of information operations. One technique, called morphing, allows for the fabrication of evidence on video by changing one image or shape into another and has been used on many occasions to suggest the commission of atrocities, even as far back as the First Gulf War, when Iraq dismantled the dome of a mosque to give the appearance that the United States had attacked and destroyed the mosque (Leventhal 1999). Similarly, "video images of [one] state's forces committing atrocities on their own people [can] be altered to change their uniforms to those of the enemy state" (Brown 2006, 206). Both Hezbollah and Hamas have used falsified photographs and videos, even fabricating "ambulance drive-bys" for the international press (Frum 2008).

The immediate contrast between the nature of media coverage and the methodology of how LOAC works to maximize lawful action during conflict sets the stage for the use of media information and propaganda in this manner. Media coverage and internet or cell-phone videos tell the world what appears to have happened in a particular attack or firefight. Even today's nearly instantaneous real-time dissemination is therefore retrospective – the audience learns about the event based on the results. LOAC, in contrast, rests on a prospective analysis. Questions of civilian harm implicate the principle of proportionality, introduced briefly above, which requires parties to refrain from any attack in which the expected civilian casualties are likely to be excessive in light of the military advantage gained from the attack (API 1977, art. 51(5)(b)). Thus, proportionality operates to minimize incidental civilian harm, or collateral damage. At the same time, not all civilian deaths are violations of the law. The law has always tolerated "[t]he incidence of some civilian casualties ... as a consequence of military action" (Gardam 1999, 283–284).

Although it may seem straightforward to prohibit attacks when the loss of innocent life will be excessive relative to any military benefit, in practice applying proportionality is rarely clear-cut because it compares civilian harm and military advantage, two dissimilar factors. As one commentator glibly explained, military commanders are not issued a "proportionometer" to help them make such calculations (Holland 2004, 48). Comparing the destruction of a munitions factory or a storage facility for rockets, for example, to the number of civilian deaths or serious injuries is difficult, perhaps impossible. Even though "balance" or "weighing" are the most common terms used when discussing proportionality, the actual test requires an examination of "excessiveness," as stressed in Additional Protocol I. Therefore, that "proportionometer" cannot help determine precisely when one additional civilian death will "tip the scale" and make an otherwise lawful attack disproportionate. Instead, "focusing on excessiveness avoids the legal fiction that collateral damage, incidental injury, and military advantage can be precisely measured" (Schmitt 2006, 293). Rather than a mathematical concept, therefore, proportionality is a guideline to help ensure that military commanders weigh the consequences of a particular attack and refrain from launching attacks that will cause excessive civilian deaths.

Critically, as the very language of Additional Protocol I shows, referring to "anticipated" military advantage and "expected" civilian casualties, proportionality must be viewed prospectively, not in hindsight. Instead, the information available and the circumstances at the time of the military operation in question must govern any assessment of the balance between military advantage and civilian casualties. Combat, even a minor firefight, involves confusion and uncertainty – the "fog of war" – so these "decisions cannot be judged on the basis of information which has subsequently come to light" (Canada, Reservations and Stmts. of Understanding [1990] 2005, 332). The law does not judge commanders based on the outcome alone, nor does it require commanders to be right in all circumstances. However, although the law is clear that proportionality is a prospective analysis that looks only at the expected civilian casualties and the anticipated military advantage, current conflicts evince a steady erosion toward a retrospective analysis driven by media coverage of civilian casualties and propaganda that easily exploits that coverage.

A second concern with a retrospective approach stems from the vastly different nature of military advantage and civilian casualties. The former is abstract, has little or no emotional impact, and is difficult to convey in pictures, while civilian casualties are dramatic and emotional and "lend themselves to powerful pictures and strong reactions" (Holland 2004, 47). Observers will often find it difficult to assess fairly whether collateral damage is excessive in practice because the military advantage from an attack may not be immediately apparent. It may seem simpler to merely add up the resulting civilian casualties and injuries after an attack and assess the actual value gained from a military operation, because "the results of an attack are often tangible and measurable, whereas expectations are not" (Schmitt 2006, 294). However, doing so fails to do justice to the complexities inherent in combat; the proportionality of any attack must thus be viewed from the perspective of the military commander on the ground, taking into account the information he or she had at the time.

Media Coverage and LOAC: Reconciling Different Perspectives

With regard to most media coverage of conflict, the focus on results and effects is simply a natural consequence of reporting on events as they happen and the lack of information about the moment of decision rather than the moment of impact. As highlighted above, media coverage of conflict is essential. Such reporting and analysis helps to guide policy makers and the public and to inform the public discourse. Most importantly, media coverage gives the victims of conflict a voice – sometimes their only voice. In the case of atrocities, this impact cannot be overestimated, as the reporting on the concentration camps in Bosnia demonstrated all too clearly (Gutman, 1992). The discussion here in no way suggests that media coverage of conflict – or civilian casualties in general – be curtailed, restricted, or even critiqued for a focus on civilian casualties and suffering, on the destruction that war brings, or on military operations in general. Rather, with regard to general media coverage, the instant discussion seeks to highlight the need for awareness about how results-focused media reports can impact the interpretation, application, and presentation of LOAC in the general public discourse. Understanding how LOAC works and how media coverage can unintentionally drive changes in the law – and the detrimental effects of those changes – is essential to both protect and preserve the critical role of the media and of LOAC in protecting civilians during conflict.

Perception and LOAC

Beyond the need to explore the general relationship between and consequences of media coverage and LOAC application, a more problematic arena involves the exploitation of media coverage and this natural effects-based approach, where factual results substitute almost automatically for legal conclusions. The ease with which today's media and internet discourse effectively merges perception with legal analysis in the area of collateral damage offers fertile ground for propaganda and the use of media coverage to delegitimize an enemy by painting it with the brush of war crimes. For LOAC-compliant militaries and groups, these challenges are magnified by the difficulty of "advance[ing] cold legal arguments in the face of media attention focused on images of dead and maimed civilians" (Bellflower 2010, 114). The way in which instantaneous distribution of video and reporting on drone strikes, close air support for patrols, and other attacks suggests that LOAC violations have been committed enables the use and exploitation of media warfare in several ways, including negative effects on mission accomplishment and coalition cohesion, and the opportunities for insurgent groups (and sometimes other states) to manipulate media coverage and the law for their own advantage. More important, however, are the long-term consequences for LOAC itself and, therefore, for the protection of civilians during conflict.

First, when civilian protection is at the heart of the mission – as in most current operations – "superfluous civilian injury or destruction of civilian property is, in the short term, nearly always at odds with mission accomplishment" (Whitaker 1996, 8), offering opportunities to undermine an enemy's mission. What matters more, in the end, is that the *perception* of such civilian harm has the same effect. Indeed, one author has presciently noted that "perception management could be the battlefield of the future" (Smyczek 2005, 240). Coalition operations similarly can suffer fissures as a result of the legitimacy deficit that civilian harm – or the perception thereof – causes. "Recent conflicts have continued to demonstrate to U.S. military and political leaders how allies and coalitions can be highly sensitive to perceived law-of-war and human rights violations and how such violations can undermine legitimacy, adversely affecting the 'soft power' on which the leadership of many international cooperative activities depends" (Beard 2009, 422).

In the counterinsurgency conflict in Afghanistan, minimizing civilian casualties became a key feature of US strategy in its effort to win "the hearts and minds" of the local population. As General Stanley McChrystal, former ISAF Commander in Afghanistan, stated in testimony before Congress, "I would emphasize that how we conduct operations is vital to success .... This is a struggle for the support of the Afghan people. Our willingness to operate in ways that minimize casualties or damage, even when doing so makes our task more difficult, is essential to our credibility" (McChrystal 2009). The connection between the civilian casualties and US and NATO legitimacy in Afghanistan was direct and immediate. News coverage of civilian casualties from airstrikes led some Afghan officials to claim that the civilian deaths were intentional. For example, over 130 people were killed, including at least ninety civilians, in the September 2009 NATO bombing of two tankers in Kunduz, Afghanistan, on the orders of the commander of the nearby German army base. The immediate reaction was that the attack must have been a LOAC violation because of the number of civilian deaths, notwithstanding uncertainty about how many dead were insurgents and how many civilians. In fact, President Hamid Karzai of Afghanistan even suggested that the attack had actually targeted innocent civilians, issuing a statement that "targeting civilian men and women is not acceptable" (Farrell and Oppel 2009). LOAC is clear that any analysis of the lawfulness of an attack must be based on the perspective of the commander at the time of the attack, not on the after-the-fact results of the attack. Without knowing more about the information that the commander had and the decision-making process, it would be difficult, if not impossible, to reach any legal conclusions in the immediate aftermath of the attack. However, such an approach offers little benefit or appeal in the world of media coverage, where instant conclusions and graphic pictures are the key to success. Lengthy investigations into the commander's perspective at the time of the attack, what he knew or should have known, and his expectations regarding civilian casualties and military advantage simply do not fit into today's media cycle. But the easy math of the retrospective analysis – multiple civilian casualties, and therefore LOAC violation – does. The leap from collateral damage to deliberate targeting was swift and demonstrated how quickly perception becomes reality.

The legitimacy consequences – weakening support for the war and driving a wedge between coalition members – were immediate as well: public support for the German mission in Afghanistan wavered substantially and Germany's Minister of Defense, Deputy Minister of Defense and Army Chief of Staff all resigned over the incident. One year later, the federal prosecutor investigating the German commander for violations of both law and procedures dropped the case, concluding that he had violated no rules in ordering the airstrike – based on the information he had at the time of the strike. However, the investigation, using a prospective approach to proportionality and targeting, was no match in the propaganda world for immediate claims of civilian casualties and disproportionate attacks in the media. In essence, US and NATO operations in Afghanistan, as well as other recent conflicts, were conducted amidst the added complexity of what some have termed "broadcast via broadband," which involves "an unimaginable convergence of hi-tech gadgetry and populist journalism, enriched by millions of bloggers ... offering their opinions, ... questioning decisions by officials, ... in a nutshell, scrambling opinion with fact and affecting the course and conduct of a war" (Kalb and Saivetz 2007, 21). The Taliban used this environment to its advantage, regularly manipulating the scene of attacks to create the impression of greater civilian casualties and, according to some reports, killing civilians themselves and depositing the bodies at the site of coalition airstrikes to raise the casualty count (CNN 2009). When public opinion and coalition problems diminish support for military operations, a group using the media to its advantage in this way can often be far more effective than kinetic attacks in stalling or even ending the operations.

Exploiting Media Coverage and the Effect of Civilian Casualties

In a much more insidious challenge, media coverage of civilian casualties has become a major strategic and tactical tool of insurgents and terrorist groups seeking to win the upper hand in the battle for legitimacy and local support. Unfortunately, notwithstanding LOAC's primary focus on the protection of civilians, civilians are not only often in greater danger from military operations now than in the past, but civilian casualties have become a tool in and of themselves. "News coverage is dominated by ... the newest trend, civilian deaths, leaving coalition commanders to engage in an endless cycle of public apologies" (Richarz 2010). While significant media attention on innocent civilian deaths is not only appropriate, but also essential, during wartime, the way in which that coverage is manipulated and encouraged for strategic purposes raises serious concerns. Media reports on civilian casualties caused by state forces, whether in Gaza, Iraq, Pakistan, Lebanon, or Afghanistan, generally produce an immediate outcry and claims of criminal liability. Insurgents then take advantage of this attention, "employ[ing] 'grey propaganda,' a judicious mix of truths and untruths that exploit the uncontested fact that noncombatants often die in military attacks, however necessary and permissible this may be in the view of international law ... [because] no nation is going to find it easy to defend any civilian casualties with the sophistry of proportionality" (Gross 2015, 224).

Insurgents quickly see the strategic and tactical benefits of greater media attention to civilian casualties and the quick-time reaction to such casualties. With international law compliance in the spotlight, "such groups and [rogue states] use new informational technologies to exploit images of dead civilians and other evidence of alleged law-of-war violations" (Beard 2009, 424) to attack law-compliant militaries where it matters: legitimacy. Furthermore, these propaganda successes provide great motivation to use tactics that deliberately place civilians in greater danger, such as human shields, launching attacks from civilian buildings and areas, and co-opting ambulances for transport of fighters, because of the guaranteed media attention and victory they offer. The resulting civilian casualties are caused by the unlawful behavior of the insurgents, but the public views them as the result of the attack, fostering the perception of LOAC violations.

Once it finds itself in or creates an environment in which civilian casualties are immediately and directly linked to LOAC violations and thus the legitimacy of the military operation overall, the insurgent group has significant incentives to create situations leading to greater and greater civilian casualties – and thus more strategic power. In effect, "winning the 'war of perception' may be as important as success on the battlefield" (Popescu 2010). Here lies the true danger for civilians: one party to a conflict benefits greatly – on a strategic and a tactical level – from civilian casualties and therefore creates an environment in which civilians are at greater risk for loss of life and property. Militants use civilian deaths to their advantage on a strategic level to undermine support for the military campaign both domestically and internationally. In pursuing their goal of gaining "political leverage by portraying U.S. forces as insensitive to LOAC and human rights ..., opponents unconstrained by humanitarian ethics now take the strategy to the next level, that of orchestrating situations that deliberately endanger noncombatants" (Dunlap 2001). Civilians thus become pawns at the strategic level as well, because they are used not only for tactical advantage (e.g. shelter) in specific situations, but for broader strategic and political advantage as well (Blank 2012).

THE CONSEQUENCES FOR INTERNATIONAL LAW: DEFINITIONS AND APPLICATION

Media warfare – whether by design or by simply taking advantage of the effects of real-time media coverage – combined with effective propaganda to maximize those effects not only has immediate consequences for the legitimacy and execution of military operations, but poses long-term risks for the role of international law in regulating the use of force and the conduct of hostilities.

Eroding the Principle of Military Necessity and the Concept of Military Objective

A first area in which the explosion of media warfare – in conjunction with the increasing linkage between LOAC and legitimacy – has significant consequences for the development and implementation of international law is the foundational principle of military necessity and the concept of military objective. The principle of military necessity states that parties to an armed conflict can use all force necessary to achieve the complete submission of the enemy as quickly as possible, as long as such force is not prohibited by international law (Lieber Code, art. 14). This principle lies at the heart of the difference between peacetime and wartime, most notably the authority under LOAC to use force as a first resort against enemy personnel and to detain enemy personnel without charge for the duration of the conflict. As media warfare and propaganda using war crimes allegations to delegitimize military operations increases, however, we see a steady shift toward a law enforcement paradigm for analyzing conflict situations. In effect, the default position in much of the public discourse becomes a presumption that any use of force is illegal, that any civilian deaths are war crimes, and that military forces are only entitled to use force in self-defense – rather than in the pursuit of lawful military objectives.

The consequences for LOAC are significant, as these changing presumptions lead to fundamental shifts in how basic authorities are interpreted. For example, LOAC does not include an obligation to attempt to capture belligerents before using lethal force, or to use the least harmful means possible against such belligerents (Corn et al. 2013) – but in recent years, there is a growing refrain to that effect (Goodman 2013). Although LOAC mandates that hospitals, houses of worship, and other cultural facilities enjoy special protection from attack, it also provides for exceptions to that protection when such objects are used for military purposes, therefore becoming legitimate targets (Geneva Convention IV 1949, arts. 18–19). Consider the impact of media coverage and exploitation of that coverage, however. The footage of an attack on a hospital does not show the military use of that hospital beforehand; rather, it shows the damage, destruction, and casualties that result from the attack. Indeed, even when such military use is reported, the power and effect of the images of destruction far outweigh any possibility of careful legal arguments overriding the instinctive emotional response. The effect is not only to incentivize groups to use such objects for military purposes, but also to erode the balance on which the protection – and removal of protection – for such objects rests.

Precautions

The principle of precautions is an essential element of LOAC's central purpose of protecting civilians from the hazards of war. In many ways, precautions are the very heart of the methodology of LOAC (Corn 2015), which mandates that parties to a conflict take steps to limit the effects of combat to those who are fighting. Most of the discourse about precautions focuses on the obligations of attacking parties to take precautions, as set forth in Article 57 of Additional Protocol I. Indeed, these precautions, and the methodology for targeting that the obligations produce, help to create the regulatory web of LOAC that seeks to minimize harm to civilians during war. However, the principle of precautions is not limited to attacking parties, but extends equally to the obligations of defending parties as well.

Here is where the steady refrain of media coverage and media warfare surrounding civilian casualties has a detrimental effect on LOAC. Although LOAC mandates that defending parties take precautions to protect civilians during conflict – including not locating military objectives in densely populated areas and removing the civilian population from combat areas where feasible (AP I, art. 58) – the general public discourse about the law of war and the obligations of warring parties wholly ignores these obligations. For example, before the most recent conflict in 2014, few commentaries about the conflicts between Israel and Hamas in the Gaza Strip condemned Hamas for using protected objects for military purposes and using the civilian population as human shields, notwithstanding extensive evidence of Hamas using such tactics deliberately.

The extensive co-mingling of civilian and military objects we see in recent conflicts poses a grave danger to civilians. The fact that objects are co-mingled and civilians are present in and near military objectives in no way absolves an attacking party of any legal and moral obligations. At such times, the role of law in military operations is of heightened importance, requiring that parties scrupulously adhere to LOAC's principles so as to maximize protection for civilians and minimize incidental harm. However, the almost exclusive focus on the attacking party's obligations in recent years creates perverse incentives for the defender to use the civilian population as a shield. When parties face no legal consequences, and a potential operational advantage, for co-mingling civilian and military objects, every apartment will be a command center as militaries and armed groups embed themselves in cities to use the civilian population as a shield. Beyond the tactical advantage, the broader strategic purpose is more problematic. This latter goal, which is significantly more insidious, is to use resulting civilian deaths as a broader strategic tool to accuse the attacking party of war crimes, diminish support for the war effort in that country, or otherwise change the course of the conflict. Both the tactical and strategic goals are only realized at the direct expense of the civilian population and run directly afoul of LOAC's central purposes and fundamental principles. Unfortunately, the ability to use media warfare and propaganda to great success in highlighting what appears to be the attacking party's failure to observe the rules has an equally damaging effect on LOAC by burying the issue of defending party's precautions in the avalanche of media coverage and propaganda.

Misconceptions and Exploitations of the Principle of Proportionality

As explained above, immediate claims of criminality after an attack that causes civilian deaths fail to adhere to the basic parameters of LOAC's principle of proportionality, by eschewing the necessary prospective approach and finding violations based solely on an after-the-fact totaling of death and destruction. In effect, such a retrospective approach is akin to "assess[ing] incidental civilian losses for which the attacker is responsible by simply conducting a body count. Such an oversimplification is as superficial assessing the quality of a hospital by only counting the bodies in its morgue" (Holland 2004, 47).

But the consequences go beyond the analysis of a particular attack. The potential erosion of the prospective nature of the proportionality analysis has significant detrimental impacts on the implementation of LOAC and the fulfillment of LOAC's goals overall. Judgments based solely on effects become akin to a theory of strict liability, where civilian deaths automatically equal war crimes. In addition, the retrospective approach does not provide either clarity or predictability for commanders planning and executing future military operations. A commander who is to be judged based on post-attack effects has no way to know, at the time of the attack, how to determine the parameters of lawful conduct. Here, it is important to emphasize that proportionality is more than just a principle; it is a methodology for assessing lawfulness in advance through careful consideration of both the value of the military advantage and the likelihood of civilian casualties.

In the absence of the correct application of LOAC and that methodology, efforts to avoid the problematic public relations consequences of any civilian casualties from strikes targeting specific leadership targets could lead commanders to instead simply adopt the tactic of large-scale attacks on enlisted personnel on the assumption that such attacks engage no complicated and amorphous proportionality judgments. Whereas carefully targeted strikes can have substantial efficacy in reducing the enemy's ability and will to fight while causing only minimal casualties, the alternative would lead to extensive casualties and prolonged conflicts, certainly an unappealing result from the perspective of military leaders, political leaders, or the public. More troubling, an effects-based analysis will ultimately lead militaries to either reject the law altogether as unworkable and unrealistic, or refrain from any military operations because it proves too difficult to use force within the rules. Either option poses grave danger to the very civilians the law seeks to protect. Media warfare relies on the power of effects and results – often to the great detriment of the law itself.

CONCLUSION

Media coverage sheds light on one of the darkest and bleakest activities of mankind: war. It tells the story of victims, soldiers, insurgents and more, and helps the public and policy makers understand what is happening and the consequences of military action for people and states. In this way, media coverage is an essential tool for the protection of persons and the enforcement of legal and moral norms.

At the same time, the interplay between media coverage and LOAC raises concerns partly due to the vastly different perspectives and methodologies of the two arenas. In order to preserve LOAC's principles and processes, it is helpful to understand how the two interrelate and, in particular, how media coverage's impact on public discourse can have significant and problematic consequences for the interpretation and development of LOAC. Finally, the gravest concern stems from the exploitation of today's ubiquitous media and internet coverage combined with the impact of perception and retrospective analysis on LOAC and legitimacy: the use of civilian casualties and civilians as pawns in an insidious strategic game of creating ever greater numbers of civilian casualties to undermine the legitimacy and efficacy of military operations. In the end, this exploitation undoes the very goal that LOAC and media coverage often share: protection of civilians.

7

The Ethics of Soft War on Today's Mediatized Battlespaces

Sebastian Kaempf

INTRODUCTION

In today's transformed heteropolar media landscape, state and non-state military actors alike are waging their wars in and through global media platforms. In this virtual war of spectacles, media technology has become a medium of war, a soft power weapon in its own right. Given the ubiquity, simultaneity, and instantaneity of these soft power weapons and given the strategic importance military actors attach to the mediatization[1] of their war efforts, this chapter identifies a number of pertinent questions with direct implications for just war thinking. To what extent does the mediatized reality generated by this soft power weapon pose a challenge to our moral judgment about conflict? And how can the just war tradition provide guidelines for evaluating the morality of today's mediatized battlespaces?

To examine these questions, the chapter first demonstrates how the emergence of today's heteropolar global Mediascape has generated a level playing-field for state and non-state actors alike to mediatize their war efforts on a global scale. It then focuses on the ethical dimensions of the strategic use of this soft power weapon by looking at two prominent military actors who have been recognized as operating with a highly professional and innovative media strategy: The Islamic State of Iraq and the Levant (ISIS) and the United States. Finally, the chapter examines how their strategic use of these soft power weapons raises important moral questions that just war thinkers need to take seriously.

TODAY'S HETEROPOLAR MEDIASCAPE AS A LEVEL PLAYING-FIELD

The importance attached to the mediatization of war has long been acknowledged. From Alexander the Great's effective use of spreading propaganda and T.E. Lawrence's view of "the printing press as one of the most important weapons in a commander's arsenal" to today's embedded journalism programs or terrorists' public beheading videos, military actors throughout history have recognized – and used – the media platforms of their time as a form of soft power weapon (Carruthers 2011; Virilio 1989).

And yet, until the emergence of digital new media technology (such as web2.0, twitter, Facebook, Flickr, and YouTube) in 2002, most state of the art media technology had tended at first to predominantly favor empires and states, not non-state military actors. For example, the invention of the telegraph in 1794, radio airwaves after World War I, television after World War II, or the first version of the internet, web1.0, constituted media platforms that – because of their infrastructural nature, costs, maintenance, and need for large numbers of highly specialized professionals – could, at the time of their inception, only be afforded by a small number of rich and politically powerful actors such as empires, states, and media conglomerates (Kaempf 2013; Rid and Hecker 2009). Non-state actors simply lacked the capacities to build, let alone maintain and operate, such vast and costly media platforms. On occasion and only with a significant delay, trickle down effects would make some of these media technologies affordable to non-state actors. This meant that with each new media platform innovation between the nineteenth and twentieth centuries, state actors have tended to sustain an asymmetric structural advantage over non-state actors regarding their capability to mass-mediatize their wars. The innovations in media technology have thereby tended to retain if not even widen the corridor of action for states more than they did for irregular forces or rebels (Rid and Hecker 2009, 125–141).

This meant furthermore, as Thomas Rid and Marc Hecker have shown (Rid and Hecker 2009, 1–13), that non-state actors for most of the nineteenth century perceived the empire's and state's communication facilities as a military target that could be physically attacked to weaken the armies of states and empires (for instance, by cutting down telegraph masts). Alternatively, following World War II, irregulars slowly but successfully began using and manipulating state-owned or – controlled mass media outlets as a weapon to attack the moral support and cohesion of opposing political entities (for instance, the way in which the North Vietnamese managed to use US media against the US government). Therefore, prior to the digital media revolution, irregulars tended to use traditional mass communication platforms as either military targets or weapons – an indication of the extent to which the structural form and trajectory of the various information revolutions spanning the last two centuries had benefitted the armies of states and empires rather than irregular forces (Kaempf 2013).

The emergence of the latest information revolution, web2.0, however, has reversed this historical trend. The different structural nature of digital new media platforms, combined with its low costs and commoditized applications, constitutes the first media revolution that has benefitted non-state and irregular groups far more than it has governments and counter-insurgents (Gillmor 2010,

1–13). For irregulars, this new information technology constitutes neither a target nor a weapon, but has come to serve as an extended strategic operating platform.

In other words, old ways of war and communication are not necessarily coming apart but are being augmented by the coming about of a new, self-organizing, networked Mediascape (Owen 2015). In this process, the technological asymmetries of the past regarding the global Mediascape have been rebalanced as digital new media technology has increased the options for irregulars more than for governments and their armies. In this sense, the complex, decentralized, and bottom-up nature of today's digital media technology is rocking the traditional hierarchies, upending traditional players, changing the global media environment, and thereby the mediatization of war (Owen 2015).

Digital media technology thereby has fundamentally transformed the old multipolar global media landscape through the double process of multiplication and diversification (Kaempf 2013). Alongside traditional media platforms (such as radio, newspapers, or television), entirely new yet structurally different digital media platforms have emerged. Through this transformation from a multipolar to a heteropolar media landscape, states and non-state actors alike now possess the technological capacity to wage their wars in and through global media platforms (Der Derian 2001; Owen 2015). As a result, today's wars are not only fought interactively on the ground in the streets of Baghdad or in the valleys of the Hindu Kush mountains, but also and increasingly through today's newly emerging heteropolar Mediascape. In this visual war of spectacles, media technology has become a medium of war, a soft-power weapon in its own right (Stahl 2010, 31–35).

Given the strategic importance that today's military actors attach to the use of media as a soft-power weapon (i.e., a weapon that while it does not kill, is still seen and used as a powerful tool in the actor's arsenals and seen as an integral part of their overall war-fighting strategy), and given the ubiquity, simultaneity, and instantaneity of these soft-power weapons, raises important moral questions. What are the strategic rationales behind the ways in which state and non-state military actors mediatize their wars? To what extent do the realities deliberately produced by this soft-power weapon pose a challenge to our moral judgment about conflict? And how can the just war tradition provide guidelines for evaluating the morality of today's mediatized battlespaces?

To examine this, the next two sections of this chapter investigate the media strategy of two prominent contemporary military actors: the United States and ISIS. Both military actors sit at opposite ends of the strategic spectrum, one being the most powerful military state actor, the other being a non-state armed group. Based on these two examinations, the final section of this chapter identifies the moral questions these practices of mediatizing war raise and offers some preliminary direction on how we might start thinking about the moral implications for the just war tradition.

THE SOFT WAR BATTLEGROUND ETHICS OF THE UNITED STATES

In February 2006, then US Secretary of Defense Donald Rumsfeld gave a remarkable speech at the Council on Foreign Relations. It was the Bush Administration's first public statement about the challenges that states in general, but US warfare in particular, were facing in a transformed heteropolar media landscape. Today, Rumsfeld stated,

> We are engaged in the first war in history – unconventional and irregular as it may be – in an era of emails, blogs, cell phones, Blackberries, instant messaging, digital cameras, a global internet with no inhibitions, hand-held video cameras, talk radio, 24-hour news broadcasts, satellite television. There's never been a war fought in this environment before. (Rumsfeld 2006)

In contrast to its adversaries in the "Global War on Terror," who have adapted quickly and skillfully to this new media environment, Rumsfeld continued, the US military "is operating like a five and dime store in an eBay world" (Rumsfeld 2006). He was both right and wrong in this assessment.

He was right in the sense that the global media landscape has changed fundamentally and that the US wars in Iraq and Afghanistan were among the first major conflicts waged in this new media environment. He was also right in suggesting that al Qaeda, the Taliban, and Iraqi insurgents had been much quicker to adjust to the possibilities offered by the emergence of digital media technologies than the US military. And he was right in his suspicion that digital media devices in general constituted a technological innovation that benefitted non-state military actors more than state actors such as the United States.

However, he was wrong in his claim that in the current environment, the US military was operating like a "five and dime store in an eBay world." While the US military was indeed slow to adjust its media strategy to the digital media revolution, the Pentagon already had been operating one of the world's most sophisticated and innovative media strategies for decades. These strategies are the outgrowth of what James Der Derian calls the American "military-industrial-media-entertainment complex" that had originated as a result of the Vietnam War (Der Derian 2001). Here, the conclusion drawn by key decision-makers was that the war in Indochina was not lost militarily in the jungles of South East Asia but politically at home in Congress and on the streets of Washington and Saigon due to the alleged bias with which an uncontrolled US media had been allowed to report on the war in Vietnam (Carruthers 2011, 96–106). The media, in their eyes, came to be seen as an enemy within whose ability to report on US wars needed to be curtailed and controlled (Louw 2010, 148–150). As a consequence, the Pentagon set up structures that limit journalists' access to the battlefield and information in order to regain the capacity to shape and control how the media reports its wars (Carruthers 2011, 96–141). Both popular support at home and winning hearts and minds abroad were seen as hinging on the capacity to cover and visualize war in real-time and instantaneously without showing war's horrors. War needed to become a media spectacle that was digestible to the home front by taking bloodletting out of war itself, i.e., by visually sanitizing the conduct of US warfare.

At the same time, the capacity to mediatize war as a spectacle was in synch with the principle logic driving the idea of the Revolution in Military Affairs (RMA) and netcentric warfare. Its two main architects, Charles Cebrowski and John Garstka, assumed that the information advantage of this new networked mode of warfare would generate battlefield superiority so overwhelmingly in favor of the US military that enemy forces – overwhelmed through superior weapons and their mediatization – would have no choice but to drop their weapons. Netcentric warfare would break the enemy's will to resist and would enable the United States to take Clausewitz out of war (Der Derian 2001; Garstka 2004). Mediatizing US warfare therefore was aimed at multiple audiences: maintaining popular support at home, winning hearts and minds abroad, and shocking and awing adversaries into a state of panic and strategic paralysis (Buley 2008).

This capacity to regain control over the mediatization of its own wars developed over time, from the Panama invasion in 1988 via the 1991 Gulf War all the way to the post-9/11 wars in Afghanistan and Iraq. For reasons beyond the scale and scope of this chapter, the US media has largely become complicit in this system (Carruthers 2011; Kaempf 2013; Louw 2010, 150–165). The result is a mediatization of American wars that is real-time and instantaneous but which fails to convey the horrors of war itself: No American body bags are shown, the sight of collateral damage is regularly omitted, and the wider context of the war is no longer questioned. American wars now appear live on US media as surgical, clean, and humane (Stahl 2010, 25–28). Furthermore, netcentric warfare and its mediatization as a spectacle are predicated on physically and visually overwhelming enemy forces.

To illustrate this, here are two examples. First, during the 1991 Gulf War, the media, unable to freely roam the battlefields in Iraq, was focusing its coverage instead on the military marvels such as precision-guided weapons (Carruthers 2011, 130–139; Louw 2010, 153–156). Regular footage of the bombs-eye view of these weapons descending accurately on their predesigned targets created the vision of a high-precision bombing campaign at a time when only 8 percent of the weapons dropped by US aircraft were actually precision-guided (Conetta 2004). Second, during the 2003 Iraq war, reporters for the first time were embedded with front line troops, providing unprecedented live television footage of the war. And yet, as detailed research has shown, 70 percent of this footage focused on the lives of individual US soldiers (creating an emotional bond for the home front with "our" soldiers), 20 percent of the overall coverage focused on the personal experience of the embedded journalist him/herself (who, dressed half-civilian, half soldier, served as a bridge between the home and battlefront), and only the remaining 10 percent of the reporting was on the actual war-fighting (which – because it was shown from the perspective of

US forces – painted US soldiers not as aggressors but as beleaguered victims) (Carruthers 2011). This was the result of the Pentagon's "soda-straw-view" media strategy, devised before the beginning of OIF and deliberately aimed at providing audiences with a personal connection to US troops and reporters but limiting the footage of the war itself to a very narrow, tactical level, which obscured the overall operational, let alone strategic, dimensions of how the war was unfolding (Carruthers 2011, 225–234).

These two examples are far from comprehensive. Yet, they provide a glimpse not only into the strategic importance the Pentagon attaches to the media as a soft power weapon but also into the level of sophistication with which these media strategies are implemented. US warfare has become mediatized to such an extent that – as Hoskins and O'Loughlin show – practices of warfare as a whole can no longer be fully fathomed unless one accounts for the role of media within it (Hoskins and O'Loughlin 2010, 3–19). In other words, Rumsfeld's speech in February 2006 obscured the scale and scope of the Pentagon's media strategy that had already been in place for several decades. Thus, instead of the suggested "five and dime store," the US military was operating more like Wal-Mart in an eBay world.

Given the Pentagon's ability to shape the mediatization of its own wars through US and international media outlets, to what extent is the mediatized virtual reality generated by this soft power weapon in line with the moral reality of the US military's physical conduct of war?

The Discrepancy between the Ethical Reality on the Ground and in the Mediatization of US Wars

The Vietnam War not only changed the Pentagon's view of the media, it also triggered groundbreaking changes in the US conduct of war. One such consequence has been that US warfare has largely fallen in line with International Humanitarian Law (IHL) (Thomas 2001; Zehfuss 2010, 543–566). Through extensive teachings of IHL to its soldiers, through the placement of military lawyers into each layer of the US war machine, and through the increasing use of more sophisticated and more precise military technology, US warfare over the decades since Vietnam has incorporated the norm of civilian immunity into its military operations (Kaempf 2009). For today's US military, the laws of armed conflict, Michael Ignatieff writes, have become "the casuists bible," largely prescribing and proscribing how US military might can be deployed (Ignatieff 2000, 199). This sea change in the actual conduct of war neither means that violations of IHL do not occur (though they have become significantly less frequent in comparison with previous US wars), nor that precision-guided weapons are as precise as they are oftentimes claimed to be, nor that no civilians get killed (which, under certain circumstances, is permissible under IHL) (Crawford 2013; Dill 2015a; Thomas 2001; Zehfuss 2010). But overall, the conduct of US warfare has come to display a level of respect for the principle of non-combatant immunity that is historically unprecedented and evidenced in the relatively low number of enemy civilians killed directly and intentionally in US wars today (Crawford 2013; Kaempf 2013).

Another such normative transformation in US warfare occurred with regards to US casualties. As a result of the "body-bag syndrome" triggered by the Vietnam War, US warfare has been transformed to make it less risky for US soldiers themselves. US warfare today has become post-heroic and risk-averse, oftentimes waged through a technology that distances its soldiers from the risks of the battlefield (Coker 2002; Van Creveld 1996). This does not imply that no American soldiers die in today's combat zones (or that a much larger percentage gets wounded – and survives – rather than killed), but that the actual number of US soldiers killed in action (KIA) has dropped to historically unprecedented levels (Kaempf 2014). For instance, between the 1991 Gulf War and the May 2003 overthrow of Saddam Hussein's regime, US casualty figures in all conflicts were not only extremely low (both in terms of absolute numbers as well as by historical comparison, ranging in the tens and hundreds rather than in the tens of thousands), but also the majority of US fatalities in most of these conflicts were not caused by the enemy but friendly fire and accidents (Kaempf 2014).

Both normative changes regarding civilian immunity and the combat risks faced by US soldiers mean that US warfare today has largely complied with the principle of non-combatant immunity while also becoming significantly less life-threatening to US forces themselves.

Paradoxically, however, this new battleground reality has not been reflected in the mediatization strategies of the Pentagon. The virtual reality of US operations conveys a grammar of killing that is bloodless: Images of dead US soldiers and body bags are not permitted to be shown and images of dead enemy civilians rarely feature in American media (Stahl 2010, 20–29). This is the result of a deliberate media strategy by the Pentagon that is aimed at creating, but also sustaining, the popular notions of "costless wars" (Ignatieff 2000, 199). It is a form of "virtual cleansing," a process of sanitizing violence that has aimed at "overpowering the mortification of the human body" (Der Derian 2001, 120). Carefully selected images conveyed by US military operations have made the dead disappear, and thereby have produced a visual "grammar of killing" that avoids the spilling of blood (Coker 2001; Stahl 2010). For the Pentagon, the ability to frame the representation of its military operations via the media as humane, surgical, and clean is seen as essential to creating and sustaining the legitimacy of warfare in the eyes of the public (Der Derian 2001, 9–17). By enlisting publics in virtual and virtuous ways, this form of mediatization by the Pentagon has not only altered the physical experience of conflict through the means of technology, but has also sought to obscure the fact that waging war is still about being killed and killing others.

In other words, the paradox in the Pentagon's media strategy lies in the discrepancy between the physical and virtual realities of US warfare. This might not be too surprising to some – but it is still striking. US warfare has largely upheld IHL and the collateral damage inflicted has been historically low in numbers and did not – with exceptions – violate IHL. And yet, though the indirect and unintentional killing of civilians is legally permissive, the Pentagon's media strategy seeks to visually blend out such incidences. Similarly, even though US military casualties are historically low, they are equally omitted from the US media. Given the levels of legal compliance and historically unprecedented restraint with which this post-heroic form of war is being waged, why does the Pentagon not feel comfortable to convey US warfare for what it is and to instead convey its wars as sanitized of any bloodletting?

The answer is a complex one and probably points to a mix of reasons. First, IHL's permissiveness regarding collateral damage and the risk-transfer from US soldiers to enemy civilians tends to be controversial (Shaw 2005) and is oftentimes hard to explain to a public that increasingly demands that more needs to be done to protect the innocent from the devastation of war (Kaempf 2009). Second, the Pentagon remains haunted until today by the images of dead civilians and US soldiers that occurred in Vietnam and remains hyper-sensitive toward the potential blowback that these images could generate (Carruthers 2011; Stahl 2010). Third, the instantaneous nature of media coverage is seen as requiring careful management of journalists and their war coverage as public support for US wars is seen as depending on the ability to frame the latter as bloodless (Kaempf 2013; Stahl 2010). Finally, the changed attitudes toward casualties among enemy civilians and US military personnel suggest – in the eyes of American decision-makers – that the sustainability of US warfare depends on its ability to act as what Ignatieff calls "Empire Light": the ability to deploy global military might without the costs to US lives and enemy civilians (Ignatieff 2003).

The end result is the strategic use of media as a soft-power weapon that deliberately distorts the moral reality of war at a time when the physical reality of US warfare has come to comply with IHL.

THE SOFT WAR BATTLEGROUND ETHICS OF ISIS

It is in this regard but also for additional reasons that the contrast between the US military and the Islamic State of Iraq and the Levant (ISIS) could hardly be starker. For the last twenty-five years, the US military has been the biggest and most powerful military state actor with a global reach. For even longer, its physical war-fighting has been fully integrated into a highly sophisticated virtual strategy that employed media as a soft-power weapon. By contrast, ISIS emerged as a local non-state military actor out of the merger between Syrian and Iraqi extremist jihadist rebel groups on June 29, 2014. And yet, despite the unbridgeable material differences,

ISIS attaches a similar strategic importance to the mediatization of its military operations as the United States. And it provides for the most recent example of how non-state armed groups/terror organizations have benefitted from the digital new media revolution far more than state actors have. ISIS thereby illustrates how the technological and structural asymmetries of the past regarding the global Mediascape have been rebalanced, enabling non-state armed groups to generate a level playing field in today's heteropolar global media landscape.

Admittedly, ISIS is not the first non-state military actor to have used media as a soft-power weapon, but it needs to be credited with taking its use to an entirely new and historically unprecedented level, and in the process it has both professionalized and revolutionized such practices. ISIS therefore provides an important case of the emancipatory potential of the digital new media revolution for irregulars and rebels.

Given the level of professional human resources, the level of finances and technical equipment made available provides a strong indication that – as Marwan Shehade argues – "the Islamic State believes that media warfare is equal in importance to its military operations" (Hashem 2014). ISIS operates one central media committee that consists of several professional sub-divisions, such as "Al-Furqan" and "Al-Itisam," that produce and disseminate online media material. Each division is responsible for its own visual material and news production, but concentrates on different target groups and themes, from recruitment, social welfare, rule of law, and religious activities, all the way to conveying military warfare (Hashem 2014). These sub-divisions are largely staffed with professional web and graphic designers, filmmakers, and PR specialists. Beyond these centralized committees, ISIS also generates large amount of media content through its military forces on the ground and through sympathizers across the globe (Channel 4 2014). These are predominantly young "digital natives" rather than "digital migrants," i.e. a generation of young, tech-savvy journalists, programmers, and fighters who have come of age during, and therefore are immersed in, a digitized environment.

It is partly for this reason and partly because of the technological opportunities afforded by digital new media that ISIS has predominantly focused on utilizing the latest social media tools available as part of its mediatization strategy. Its principle media outlets have been media platforms such as YouTube, Vimeo, Instagram, Tumblr, Twitter, and Snapchat. It operates a number of jihadist websites that are mirrored across different platforms. But besides using customer-built media platforms, ISIS also produces high-quality feature-length films, designs custom-made apps for android phones, and uses innovative swarming strategies in an attempt to snowball its messages through the virtual Mediascape. Analysts believe that the quality and scope of its online engagement makes ISIS stand out from the crowd of other non-state military groups, past and present (Bonzio 2014).

Currently, ISIS is using social media far more extensively – some would even argue more effectively – than any other non-state armed group.

To give a few examples: Thousands of ISIS Twitter followers installed a custom-built android app, called "Dawn of Glad Tidings," which allows ISIS to enter and use their accounts and address books to send out centrally written updates. Released simultaneously, these messages swamp social media through a snowballing effect and thereby allow ISIS a far larger online reach than their own accounts would otherwise permit. Similar swarming techniques have been used by creating virtual armies of Twitter-bots designed to boost the propaganda efforts remotely. Their function is to post the same content several times accompanied with the most popular hashtags (e.g. #worldcup2014), in order to reach the broadest public possible (Berger 2014). Hundreds of Twitter accounts have been hijacked as part of a campaign that allows for the voice of a dozen to be heard by hundreds of thousands across the globe, thereby generating the impression of a burgeoning, large, and extremely popular movement (Bonzio 2014; Kathib 2015).

Recently, its designers have produced an ISIS-themed first-person shooter video game. Ripped off from the highly popular "Grand Theft Auto" franchise, the video game is downloadable and tasks players with shooting police and blowing up military convoys (Crompton 2014). Its feature length films, produced by the media sub-division "Al-Furqan," are of cinematic quality, complete with graphics, animations, slow-motion, echoing jihadist hymns in the background and replete with Arab and English subtitles. They have devised strategies that prevent their emails from being filtered out into spam folders, have produced media manuals for young jihadists, and offer an electronic customer service center that offers help, tech support, and advice (Sueddeutsche Zeitung 2014).

Again, these examples are far from comprehensive but they serve to illustrate the tech-savviness, professionalism, and expert knowledge that ISIS is willing to invest. And they are strong indicators of the strategic importance the ISIS leadership is attaching to digital media platforms as an integral part of its war-fighting. In other words, ISIS's battlefield operations are mediatized at such a scale and scope that its combat practices – in the eyes of the ISIS leadership – can no longer be fathomed unless one takes the media dimension into account. The strategic purpose behind this mediatization is multiple and different channels and platforms are being used to address and reach different audiences (Bonzio 2014; Kathib 2015). Much of its propaganda (shown in the Western media) is frightening because it directly conveys systematic and deliberate violations of IHL: In one of their propaganda videos, "Swords IV," ISIS's captives are shown digging their own graves before being executed. Another such video showed the intentional destruction of ancient cultural artifacts including entire temples and museums; another showed the burning alive of the captured Jordanian pilot or the public beheading of Western journalists, while on Twitter ISIS has posted images of a cold-blooded massacre of Iraqi soldiers in Tikrit (Kathib 2015; Stern and Berger 2015).

But other ISIS messaging (less conveyed through Western media) focuses on its social activity – photos of supporters bringing in the harvest, delivering food shipments, or the security provided by ISIS members in occupied towns. Members recently distributed an earnest English-language newsletter documenting the often dull details of their community work. One series of video clips called "Mujatweets," released by ISIS's media arm on YouTube, portrays a number of ISIS militants as they engage in noble activities such as visiting an injured fighter at the hospital or distributing candies to children (Stern and Berger 2015). This means that ISIS's overall media output is not all barbaric.

Thus, even though the most gruesome footage of atrocities has gained most traction in Western media, ISIS's media contents are far more diverse and are systematically shaped according to the target they are designed to reach. When speaking to the Western public, for instance, tactics such as organized hashtag campaigns (e.g. #AllEyesOnISIS) or hijacking of trending hashtags (e.g. #worldcup2014) are frequently used to increase the visibility of the group (Berger 2014). Yet the message differs, according to whether the goal is to intimidate or to inspire. In the former case, material is generally limited to photos of mutilated bodies and videos of hostage executions. In the latter, potential recruits are also presented with a more humane side of the jihadists.

The media content changes once more as the target shifts from an international audience to the local population. English is replaced by Arabic, with graphic pictures being integrated with images showing administrative services being efficiently run under the Islamic State – a clear warning to ISIS's opponents but also a promise of a peaceful life for those who remain faithful.

Such a systematic process of media customization is arguably unique in the jihadist universe, as is the dimension and the level of professionalism characterizing ISIS's propaganda campaign. There is nothing new in the early adoption of new technology by violent, extremist groups. Even the purposes for which social media are being exploited have largely remained the same as in the past. What has hardly any precedent is the breadth of the communication strategy implemented by ISIS, covering the type of content to be released as well as the way in which material is produced and disseminated (Bonzio 2014; Kathib 2015).

And yet, at least with regard to ISIS's actual war-fighting media strategy, the question arises over the extent to which this soft power weapon is reflective of the moral reality underpinning ISIS's battleground behavior.

Representing the Unethical Reality of War through ISIS Media

ISIS's war-fighting on the battleground is in direct, deliberate, and oftentimes systemic violation of core just war principles such as discrimination, civilian immunity, proportionality, and respect for Prisoner of War (POW) status. The brutal and indiscriminate violence, torture, sexual exploitation, and enslavement directed against religious minorities such as the Yazidis (which the UN High Commissioner for Human Rights now argues constitutes attempted genocide) certainly stand out (Tagesschau 2015). But so do the public beheading or burning of foreigners, the extensive use of child soldiers, the enforced conversion to Islam, the destruction of cultural artifacts such as temples, historic sites, and sculptures in museums. Anyone or anything that does not belong to ISIS's version of sharia-based Islam is – in the eyes of the perpetrators – a legitimate target. In other words, there is a level of discrimination present in ISIS's violence, but it is based on old jihadist notions of inside and outside of the law, rather than existing just war principles.

With perhaps a few exceptions, these violations are deliberate and systematic. They are part of the strategic calculus of ISIS and serve the purpose to frighten and paralyze ISIS's local enemies, to forewarn those in ISIS-controlled territory, and to send shock waves across a wider global (Arab and Western) audience. The level of angst and panic, for instance, that has been generated by these horrific and deliberate violations (and the mediatization thereof), while triggering the formation of a Western-Arab military coalition, has lead local forces to oftentimes abandon the fight against approaching ISIS forces out of fear of what consequences would await them (Kilcullen 2015). Furthermore, the public execution of the Jordanian pilot resulted in Saudi Arabia suspending its part in the anti-ISIS air campaign. In other words, the level of horrific and indiscriminate violence used – while reflective of the jihadist radicalism espoused by ISIS – serves the purpose to shock, frighten, and discipline.

The systematic and deliberate level of atrocity is deeply disturbing and has rightly been condemned for its illegal and immoral practices. And yet, what is fascinating in that regard is how this inherently immoral battleground behavior is actually reflected in and through ISIS's media strategy. Far from trying to hide, let alone publically deny, such acts, ISIS covers them directly in their own media outlets and distributes them through its social media strategy. The horrific and indiscriminate violence used gets staged and celebrated in front of running cameras and disseminated through twitter feeds (Spens 2014). It is a virtual celebration of atrocity, aesthetically animated and shot in HD quality. Here, the public execution videos are quite instructive: These are horrific, yet deliberately staged and mediatized events (Kathib 2015; Spens 2014). If the intention and purpose were just to kill a captured enemy fighter or a journalist, then this could be accomplished much faster and in a more sanitized and "less" painful way (for instance, by shooting someone). But to kill someone in the ways shown (through a sword or through burning them alive) is using them as a media weapon. This is of particular significance given that ISIS – due to its access to oil revenues by the end of 2014 – was no longer reliant upon ransom for income. The mediatization of public beheading therefore became a tool of war, aimed at provoking and scaring its adversaries (Kathib 2015; Spens 2014). It is the moment when the terrorist becomes auteur and media producer in one – and the aim is to celebrate the shedding of blood in order to direct this violence virtually to the outside world.

What this serves to show is that ISIS's media strategy deliberately places its indiscriminate war-fighting practices and atrocities center stage. There is not much discrepancy between ISIS's physical and virtual war-fighting strategies. Far from hiding or denying violations to existing moral principles, it virtually demonstrates its defiance of the latter.

VIRTUALLY OBSCURING BATTLEFIELD COMPLIANCE OR TRUTHFULLY REPRESENTING ATROCITY: CONCLUDING THOUGHTS ON WHAT THIS MEANS FOR JUST WAR THEORY

This chapter demonstrated the strategic importance that state and non-state actors attach to the mediatization of their wars and the integral role media plays in the strategic thinking of both US and ISIS war-fighting. The level of professionalism and innovation that these very different actors have invested into the media dimensions of their respective wars is striking. Both actively mediatize their wars to such an extent that the reality of their physical combat practices has become unfathomable without accounting for its virtual dimensions.

And yet, the contrast between the US and ISIS media strategies could not be starker. The Pentagon's media strategy deliberately sanitizes the battlefield compliance of its forces to obscure that war is still about killing – even if such killing conforms to the just war principles of discrimination, proportionality, and double effect. This discrepancy between the physical and virtual battlefields does not exist for ISIS, however. ISIS's media strategy not only shows how war is about killing, but also places center stage the inherently indiscriminate and disproportionate violence that is the hallmark of its fighting. The discrepancy between visually obscuring legal battlefield compliance (in the case of the US) and truthfully reporting battlefield atrocity (in the case of ISIS) demonstrates that neither actor views the media as peripheral but rather as central to their respective modes of combat.

This centrality of war's mediatization for both actors raises important and more general questions over the need to examine the morality of media strategies in war. Traditionally, just war principles have not been applied in this manner, focusing their moral analyses instead on the physical battlefield practices of military actors. And one might plausibly argue that this is all Just War Theory can and should do. But what does retaining this traditional focus on morally evaluating the physical dimension of combat mean for the ability of Just War Theory to morally evaluate the justice in war when diverse military actors themselves, like the US and ISIS, no longer separate between physical and virtual battlefields? When military actors not only see them as two parts of the same coin but organize their war-fighting strategies accordingly? It seems as if we should at least start debating whether just war's traditional focus is out of synch with and possibly needs to be adjusted to contemporary war's mediatized reality.

The remainder of this chapter seeks to suggest first inroads by engaging these pertinent questions. It is beyond the scope of this chapter, however, to provide definite, fully-developed answers to the complex nature of these questions. The aim, therefore, is merely an initial attempt to outline possible ways in which Just War Theory might be able to start thinking about these issues.

The moral purpose of Just War Theory is to (1) limit the physical suffering and bodily harm caused by war and to (2) allocate clear responsibility or culpability for military action which causes such harm. And such physical harm, one might argue, is caused not by bytes and bandwidths but by bullets and IEDs, not in cyberspace but on the physical battlespace. From this perspective, even if the reality of the conduct of war has taken on a virtual dimension, the reality of how harm is actually inflicted means that any moral judgment of the media dimensions of US warfare does not fall into the remit of Just War Theory. For, as long as the physical conduct of war is compliant with existing moral and legal standards, then a media strategy that sanitizes – and thereby obscures – the representation of such compliant battlefield behavior does not generate any physical suffering or bodily harm. Distorting the media representation of one's own wars is undoubtedly controversial (both politically and from a perspective of journalistic ethics), but arguably is of no concern from a just war perspective as long as physical conduct of war is compliant with existing values. If no physical atrocity occurs, a media strategy that obscures the physical reality of compliant warfare is not problematic from a just war perspective.

The situation, however, is entirely different when atrocities occur and when the media strategy of a military becomes complicit in the production of such atrocities. And this, arguably, is the case with ISIS's mediatization strategy that has become highly implicated in the atrocities themselves.

Take, for instance, the public execution video of the captured Jordanian pilot: His execution (being burnt alive in an iron cage) was staged on an elevated platform, with fans (to produce more dramatic imagery) and filmed by three cameras (for better editing). The release of the video, some four months after the actual execution, was deliberately timed to achieve its biggest impact on ISIS's enemies. Similar to public beheading videos, the intention was not primarily to execute the prisoner but to brutally display and turn the atrocity itself into a virtual weapon to discipline, scare, frighten, and terrorize. Here, the media production of a soft power weapon is paramount to the physical atrocity being committed. In other words, at some level, it is difficult to differentiate between the physical act of execution and the mediatization of the atrocity itself. The media dimension is integral to generating harm (both to the executed prisoner and to the target audience) in ways that Just War Theory arguably needs to examine. And it raises a complex set of questions about harm, agency, and responsibility of all those implicated in the physical and virtual aspects of this atrocity. For instance, what is the level of responsibility here? Clearly, those giving the orders and those following orders to conduct the atrocity by physically executing the pilot are culpable. But what about those producing the media dimension of this act? Can we separate the ethical elements of committing atrocities and mediatizing them? Given the intentionality of the atrocity to be staged in order to then be used as a soft-power weapon, those producing the video (and those ordering them to do so) also bear some form of responsibility in ways that ordinary journalists probably would not. But at what level? Here, committing the physical atrocity weighs more heavily than deliberately capturing the act itself. Those responsible for the media element do not engage in the killing itself. And yet, they should not be blameless as their involvement is not aimed at merely capturing "the reality of war" as an ordinary journalist would claim. Instead, their involvement impacted on the particular staging of the atrocity and was aimed at turning a single atrocity committed against one human being into a terrorizing weapon aimed at others. Furthermore, while those responsible for the production of the soft power weapon were not involved in causing harm to the captured pilot, their objective was to create emotional harm to those on the receiving end of ISIS's propaganda machinery. They were – in a different way – complicit in how the execution was staged and in converting the harm caused into a virtual weapon in war. Committing atrocities and deliberately mediatizing them – as illustrated in this example – point to different levels of harm caused as well as different levels of moral culpability. But this difference does not mean that Just War Theory can morally sanction one and ignore the other. Both acts – executed by ISIS as part of their military conduct – need to be judged from a moral point of view.

What are the implications for the just war tradition? As this chapter has shown, the just war tradition needs to be concerned with the morality underpinning the media strategy of military actors in the context of atrocity. If there are no atrocities and the conduct of war is in compliance with legal and moral standards, then even a highly sanitized media strategy like the one offered by the Pentagon is of no real concern for just war thinking – the political controversies and questions over journalistic ethics that such practices raise notwithstanding. However, if atrocities do occur and if a military actor's media strategy is complicit in the production of such atrocity, then this falls into the remit of just war thinking. Blaming only those who physically commit the atrocity falls short of the nature and intention that lead to the atrocity in the first place. Here, those in charge of the mediatization are not blameless precisely because they have been complicit in the production of the atrocity in the first place.

NOTE

1. Mediatization refers to the integral part media plays in the actual planning and conduct of war. In contrast to the term "mediation," it denotes an understanding of the extent to which media technologies have become such a central part of the practices of warfare that the latter cannot be fathomed unless one accounts for the role of media within it. For a detailed account of the "mediatisation" of war, see Hoskins and O'Loughlin (2010, 3–19).

8

Abuse of Law on the Twenty-First-Century Battlefield: A Typology of Lawfare

Janina Dill

WARFARE, LAW, AND LAWFARE

Is international law (IL) a substitute for armed force in international relations? Put differently, can IL be state A's means of getting state B to do its bidding against B's will? Ideally, that is exactly what law is: a means of coercion that pre-empts the use of force. In the face of competing claims, divergent perceptions, or conflicting interests, law tells us who or which side is in the right, saving us the trouble of a physical confrontation. Of course, we rely on law to be effective in this task because it is typically backed by a threat of enforcement. Those who break a law tend to incur a penalty. In the archetypal understanding of enforcement that penalty is force or violence. Law is hence at best a temporary substitute for force. When push comes to shove the coercive power of law depends on violence.

To the extent that this is still the dominant way in which we think about law, international lawyers have to engage in what Thomas Franck aptly called "defensive ontology" (Franck 1995, 6). If association with the coercive power of the state is what renders a rule a law, then IL cannot really be law. After all, international relations are anarchical in the sense that states are not subject to a superior authority with a monopoly on the use of force that could enforce this "law." States comply with it either because that is how they want to behave anyway or because a rule of IL is backed by the material power of another state (for this view see Goldsmith and Posner 2005; Grieco 1988; Krasner 1999; Nardin 2008; Thompson 2012). As enforcement accounts for the coercive power of law, the answer to the initial question – can IL be a substitute for armed force in international relations – must be no. It cannot even be relied on to be the temporary substitute that domestic law is. As Eric Posner puts it: "[l] aws do not enforce themselves. If a weak country cannot coerce a more powerful country through force of arms, then it cannot coerce the other country with law either" (Posner 2011).

The term "lawfare" expresses the observation that this story, which is associated with the realist tradition of International Relations (IR) scholarship, no longer holds true. Since John Austin offered the definition of law as a command laid down by a sovereign and backed by a threat of sanctions (Austin 1832, lecture I; also Austin/Campbell 1879/2002), a wealth of alternative theories of law have emerged. They criticize that a credible threat of sanctions is neither what characterizes most laws, nor the dominant reason why laws are obeyed (Cotterell 2003). By the same token, IR scholarship has shown that IL can have effects on state behavior that are not reducible to an underlying threat of force (Brunnée and Toope 2010; Dill 2015a, 50ff). Like domestic law, IL often relies for its compliance pull on actors' desire to be deemed legitimate (Dill 2015b). The coercive power of IL then stems from the association of legality with legitimacy and the reputational costs that states in defiance of IL incur as a result. Moreover, compliance with IL is connected to many contemporary societies' identities. That means a number of states obey IL habitually and even beyond what is instrumentally rational. IL is thus a means not just of coercion, but also of persuasion. Far from IL's originally dominant characterization as an epiphenomenon of material power (Carr 1946, 170; Morgenthau 1948, 249; Waltz 1979, 88), it is now widely recognized as exerting influence on state behavior even when it is not backed by force.

While sometimes used to refer to the strategic use of IL in general, lawfare has most often been the banner under which scholars discuss the observation that this coercive and persuasive capacity of IL does not disappear with the outbreak of armed conflict. Quite the contrary; in the twenty-first century, legitimacy in war, like in peace, is predominantly measured in terms of legality (Dill 2015a, 154ff, 239ff; Kennedy 2006 and 2012, 160). Since the use of force is prima facie illegitimate, state belligerents clamor for the legitimacy afforded by international humanitarian law (IHL). Specifically when the world is watching, most states go to considerable length to avoid the appearance of non-compliance, the usually high stakes in war notwithstanding. As a result, evoking IL can serve as "a substitute for traditional military means" to shape the behavior of states at war (Dunlap 2009, 54).

Not surprisingly, this is particularly true for states whose societies' identities are connected to the rule of law, such as the United States and Israel. The Israel Defense Forces (IDF) as well as the US Armed Forces have institutionalized legal argument in the conduct of hostilities through IHL training, the presence of lawyers in or alongside the chain of command, and legal review of military practices (Attorney General's 2015; US Department of Defense 1974). They vociferously defy allegations of non-compliance (State of Israel 2015) and consider those that are substantiated a strategic defeat. Of course, both states have considerable material power and they have largely kept their soldiers beyond the jurisdictional reach of international adjudication and thus enforcement of IHL. The exercise of the coercive and persuasive power of law in war even against such belligerents then signals the emancipation of the laws of war from material power. "Lawfare" denotes IL's ability to serve as a substitute for armed force in international relations even, as it were, when push comes to shove.

But why did we need the semantic fusion of law with warfare to grasp this phenomenon? An alternative, admittedly less catchy, way of describing what is going on would be "law operates like law, even in war." Two prescriptive projects, which are in tension with each other, explain the popularity of the term lawfare. One strives to draw attention to the role and also the usefulness of IL. Despite the mounting empirical evidence for IL's impact, in IR scholarship IL's acceptance as a variable in its own right is only partial. The equivalence of legal argument and the use of force suggested by one neat compound noun may convince the realist scholar that IL is a worthwhile object of inquiry. After all, no one ever doubted the crucial role of war in international relations. Even more importantly, the term lawfare may help convince the military practitioner that the maxims "*inter arma silent leges*" or "*Kriegsraison geht vor Kriegsmanier*" belong in the past. A "bumper sticker to help military personnel understand why the law needs to be incorporated into their thinking and planning," (Dunlap 2010, 126) is what General Charles Dunlap, who popularized the term, meant it to be (Dunlap 2008 and 2011).

The second prescriptive project responds to the demand for a delineation of legitimate uses of IL as a means of coercion from illegitimate ones. This demand has risen in lock-step with the proliferation of legal arguments about and in war. In recent years, a myriad of articles have probed the term "lawfare," some mapping how the term is usually used (Ansah 2010; Luban 2010; Werner 2010), others arguing how it should be used (Noone, 2010; Tiefenbrun 2010). The most common understanding of lawfare is not state A's use of law to get state B to do its bidding against B's will, but A's *abuse* of law to that end (Blank 2010; Horton 2007; Horton 2010; Jensen 2007; Lebowitz 2010; Posner 2011; Rivkin, Casey, and Delaquil 2004; Rivkin and Casey 2005; Samson 2009; Schmitt 2010; Williams 2010). This "lawfare critique" seeks to draw attention to the misuse of the coercive and persuasive power of law in war.

Calling *all* recourse to law in the context of war lawfare should indeed be rejected. It might help convince realist skeptics of the importance of IL, but the price of suggesting equivalence between legal argument and violence would be a considerable discreditation of the former. IL asks for a "duel ... with words rather than Swords" (Carlson and Yeomans 1975). It is therefore not a weapon of war like an F-16 jet or an M24 rifle, which can cause immediate physical harm. It is not a strategy of war like effects-based targeting or shock and awe either. Neither is an evocation of law a tactic akin to an ambush or the use of white phosphorous to obscure the battlespace. The success of the latter is determined by physical strength, chance, and possibly cleverness. In contrast, who wins a legal argument is determined, or so we hope, by who has the better claim to being in the right. An additional difference is, of course, that a resort to legal argument can amount to coercion (if it is backed by a threat of violence, reputational or economic costs), but it can also be genuinely persuasive. I doubt that an air strike has ever truly convinced anyone that they were in the wrong.

If abuse of law robs law of what distinguishes it from a firefight, we may then want to reserve the term lawfare as a synonym only for abuse of law (I will use the terms interchangeably in the following). But what distinguishes the use of IL in war from its abuse? The experts participating in an influential symposium on lawfare in 2010 correspondingly "agreed that the legitimate application of international law against participants in an armed conflict should not be labelled 'lawfare.'" Yet they were unable to agree on a definition of "legitimate application" (Scharf and Andersen 2010–2011, 20f), or so the record of the meeting relates. Before giving a positive answer to the question by proposing a definition and a typology of lawfare, I will discuss several closely related ways of delineating the use from the abuse of IHL, which we encounter in the literature that denounces lawfare as the wrong way to use law. They all ultimately determine whether law is used or abused not based on the merit of the legal argument, but with regard to the perceived merit of the belligerent for or against whom the law is invoked.

A CRITIQUE OF THE LAWFARE CRITIQUE

The most straightforward of these delineations simply asserts that certain actors use the laws of war legitimately while others do not. Posner (2011) provides the most striking example of this approach when he defines lawfare as "both the efforts of enemy nations, terrorist organizations and their supporters to counter American military superiority by threatening US policy makers and soldiers with prosecution and civil litigation, and the pressure brought to bear by NGOs who take to the media marketplace insisting that IL places sharp limits on military action." Glenn Sulmasy and John Yoo (2007, 1836) famously lamented that "our commitment to adhere to the law of armed conflict, [has] been a catalyst for our opponents to use legal rules and processes as part of their operations, what military observers term 'lawfare'." The US Department of Defense in 2005 echoed the notion that "lawfare is what others do" by suggesting that recourse to IL, much like terrorism, is for the weak and generally in defiance of US interests: "Our strength as a nation will be continued to be challenged by those who employ a strategy of the weak, using international fora, judicial processes and terrorism."

Few scholars would endorse the stark simplification that the laws of war are properly used in the furtherance of US interests, and lawfare is chiefly defined by its potential to constrain US freedom of action in the realm of national security. However, the notion that we can recognize lawfare by asking against whom IL is invoked is surprisingly common. In this view "[l]awfare tends to be used as a weapon against countries where the rule of law is strong" (Tiefenbrun 2010, 52). The charge of "lawfare" is then routinely leveled against legal challenges aimed at liberal state belligerents that are generally thought to be committed to

IL, but fight non-compliant non-state actors in so-called asymmetric wars (Blank 2010; Dunlap 2014a; Dunlap 2014b; Samson 2009; Schmitt 2010). The contention is that legal criticism of these belligerents, namely Israel and the United States, gives their militarily weak adversaries an unexpected and, most maintain unfair, advantage. Such "lawfare" hampers the militarily superior belligerent's victory on the battlefield and/or undermines it in the "court" of public opinion. In this view, evoking legal argument to challenge states that are (1) at war, (2) presumed to be law-abiding, and (3) facing a non-compliant adversary is an abuse of the law or lawfare.

Of course, nothing guarantees that a belligerent that generally upholds the law and incorporates legal considerations into the conduct of hostilities does never circumvent or violate IHL. Legal compliance is also not measured in relative terms, meaning in comparison to how well or badly one's enemy does. Finally, the often implicit demand that the threat these countries face should be taken into account when their practices are scrutinized before the law (for instance, Schmitt and Merriman 2015) would be questioning the very idea that war can be subject to legal rules. Before every war at least one belligerent is threatened and once in war, as a matter of logic, all sides are. If an existential threat impedes the force of law in war, all we have in war is law thus impeded. Yet, this line of argument very rarely culminates in the explicit conclusion that a redrafting or rejection of the laws of war is necessary (for exceptions, see Ricks 2002; Sulmasy and Yoo 2007). After all, the defended belligerents benefit from the legitimacy afforded by the notion that war can be waged legally.

This delineation of use from abuse of IL according to a belligerent's records of legal compliance is seemingly more convincing when it turns on the belligerent who makes the legal argument, rather than the belligerent against whom law is invoked. Elizabeth Samson concedes that in principle any actor is capable of "lawfare," "but presently Lawfare is being pursued largely by Islamic ideologues, their supporters, and their financiers who sympathize with the actions of Islamic militants" (Samson 2009, 61). Can Hamas, which violates IHL by firing rockets indiscriminately at Israel's population centers (UN Human Rights Council 2015, 29ff), demand that Israel use force proportionately when attacking targets in the Gaza Strip? Or is that an abuse of IHL? By breaking the law I lose certain rights, but I do not lose the right to evoke any and all law or to avail myself of legal protections in the future. Of course, continued violation of a law will tarnish my appeals to that very law with hypocrisy. But to dismiss a legal argument purely on the basis of the speaker's attitude to IL in general is to confuse its logos, the substantive merit of an argument, with its ethos, the credibility or merit of the speaker (Aristotle/Ross 2010, 7–1356a; for a similar argument about the "lawfare critique" in general, see Luban 2010, 460). The legal argument of a hypocrite may be as valid as that of a saint.

Of course, third parties may call on a belligerent to comply with the law vis-a-vis a population whose belligerents defy that law even without the stain of hypocrisy. A civilian population does not lose any protections under IHL because their fighting forces violate it (Article 51(8) Protocol Additional to the Geneva Conventions of 12 August 1949, Relating to the Protection of Victims of International Armed Conflicts Adopted 1977, herein API). It is uncontested that non-compliance of one belligerent does not release another from their legal obligations. The age of legally privileged reprisals against civilian populations is long over. Demanding the protection of a population whose military forces violate the law is therefore by no means an abuse of IHL. Just as we cannot simply recognize abuse of law by asking who the law is used against, we cannot recognize "lawfare" or an abuse of law by asking who appeals to the law or on whose behalf the law is invoked.

A more sophisticated approach to the distinction between use and abuse does not hinge on who makes the argument, but on how and why it is made. General Dunlap says in his defense of lawfare that "a weapon can be used for good or bad purposes, depending upon the mind-set of those who wield it. Much the same can be said about the law" (Dunlap 2010, 122). While related, the mindset behind and the purpose of a legal argument are not quite the same. We can think of the purpose as the substantive goal or end to which law is invoked. Why does a belligerent appeal to IHL: to halt the use of a specific weapon or tactic, to shame the adversary, to gain the attention of the ICC Prosecutor's office etc. I will return to the question of law's "proper purpose" below. The mindset could refer to an actor's general attitude toward law, which I dismissed as the appropriate criterion for defining abuse or lawfare above. Alternatively, mindset could denote the "how" of a legal argument, something that might be better grasped with a term like state or frame of mind in which the argument is made or law is used in a particular instance. This is what commentators who express "concern that the credibility and independence of legal arguments is undermined by their strategic use" worry about (Werner 2010, 68).

I venture that the way in which law is invoked in war is almost always strategic or instrumental. The state of mind of a belligerent resorting to legal argument can be expected to be self-interested. Belligerents may comply with law habitually or sometimes because they think it is the right thing to do, hence in a non-instrumental way. But when a belligerent at war alleges an IHL violation by their adversary or asks for the legal opinion from a third party, it is not because being aware of the errors of their ways might do the adversary some good. As David Luban puts it, "[a]nyone who voluntarily has recourse to the institutions of the law has ulterior motives: nobody ever files a lawsuit out of disinterested curiosity in the answer to a legal question" (Luban 2010). If in peace time we do not consider the strategic use of law reprehensible or a threat to the law, why should it be considered abusive in war? War is the ideal type of a zero-sum game, in which the stakes are so high that the survival of the participants may be threatened. We should not expect "disinterested curiosity" from the rational belligerent.

Denouncing the strategic use of law as abuse is a red herring all too often connected to one of the delineations of abuse and allegations of lawfare discussed above, which really hinge on who is using law against whom. The proliferation of this kind of argument has a straightforward explanation. When law meets war, it creates two specific temptations to allege abuse disconnected from the legal argument's validity. First, if law never ruled out courses of action that are militarily expedient or even necessary, we would hardly need it. It is hence extremely likely that at one point or another every belligerent in war will be confronted with a legal argument that is highly inconvenient. At least for one side the constraints of IHL will regularly be prohibitive of victory. The allegation of abuse seems a ready means to dismiss such inconvenient arguments, which are the very linchpin of IHL's restraining capacity. Second, IHL affords the same permissions to and imposes the same constraints on the belligerent that is the aggressor as on the belligerent that acts in legitimate self-defense. This is as necessary for IL to elicit compliance as it is counterintuitive, even somewhat distasteful. There is a temptation to satisfy our desire to express the moral and legal asymmetry we (sometimes correctly) perceive between belligerents by accepting the defender's resort to law as appropriate use, while denouncing the aggressor availing herself of legal justifications or protections as abuse. The notion that invoking law to help an unjust aggressor achieve victory must be a use of the law for an improper purpose may be intuitively compelling, but it is mistaken.

The second temptation brings into sharp relief why it is nowhere more important than in war to abstract from the credibility of the speaker when determining the validity of resort to law or when alleging abuse of law. The descent of divergent perceptions or conflicting interests into war tends to signal that two sides no longer consider each other valid interlocutors. IL ideally affords a language in which we can nonetheless formulate, make intelligible, and adjudicate competing claims. The grounding of the definition of the proper use of law in the merit of the invoker robs IL of this capacity as legal argument becomes nothing more than a reproduction of the state of enmity that defines war. This, in turn, challenges the association of legality with legitimacy, on which, I argued above, law depends for its coercive and persuasive capacity much more than on actual enforcement. It is not per se a threat to the law if speakers use IHL in ways that assist the side they hope will prevail in a military confrontation. It is a threat to the law if they refuse to engage with and denounce as abusive and thus invalid this strategic use of law every time it assists the other side. That is an abuse of the abuse charge.

USE AND ABUSE OF LAW

In the following, I will propose a definition of abuse of IHL or lawfare properly so-called, with two closely related aims. The first aim is to ground the delineation of use from abuse in what IL has to say about the state of mind in, and purpose for, which it should properly be invoked. This supports the second aim of coming to an understanding of abuse of IL that hinges on the visibility of an improper state of mind and faulty purpose in the use of law itself. Of course, no definition of abuse or lawfare is abuse-proof, which is why I will highlight the difference between what counts as abuse of IHL in theory and what an invocation of IHL looks like that we can call out as such without risking the delegitimization of IL. I will use the terms abuse of law and lawfare synonymously.

General Dunlap's reference to the mindset in which law is used strikes us as compelling because the law itself seemingly asks for a specific state of mind when it demands that it be used in good faith. The Declaration on Principles of IL Concerning Friendly Relations and Cooperation among States, like the United Nations Charter, enjoins states to fulfill their legal obligations in good faith. Article 31(1) of the Vienna Convention on the Law of Treaties insists that treaties are interpreted in good faith. The importance of good faith for IL is as obvious (see Farnsworth 1995; Zoller 1977) as its meaning is obscure. It is not itself "a source of an obligation where none would otherwise exist" (ICJ 1988, 105). Nor is good faith an interpretive approach that reveals parts of an otherwise obscured meaning of law (Ipsen 2004, 11). One way to understand it is as "a phrase which has no general meaning or meanings of its own, but which serves to exclude many heterogeneous forms of bad faith" (Summers 1968). Bad faith denotes dishonesty, duplicity, or deception. Examples of using law in bad faith include negotiating without any intention to settle or adopting a legal argument one knows to be false.

The requirement of good faith might at first appear like interference with the ideal that legal arguments are judged on their own merit rather than on the honesty of the speaker. Crucially, we do not say someone "is" or "has" bad faith, like someone is dishonest or has a duplicitous character, but someone acts or reasons in bad faith. It is never "taken into consideration by law in the abstract, as a purely psychological disposition" (Virally 1983). A dishonest state of mind becomes bad faith when it is invested in a specific legal argument or action and can thus (in theory) be diagnosed as an attribute of that argument or action rather than just of the speaker. It is precisely because the specific mode of persuasion associated with law centers on the argument, asking us not to take into account what we know about the speaker that law needs to draw a line at the deliberate misrepresentation of rule or fact. So the difference between a mere instrumentalization of law and the instrumentalization of law in bad faith is that in the latter case I know the facts or the reasoning I use to further my own ends to be wrong.

Making a legal argument in bad faith is failing to use law in the way law itself prescribes. With a view to the integrity of the law we might therefore be tempted to call the "mere" use of law in bad faith abuse. It certainly is a misuse. For instance, publicly alleging war crimes and demanding an investigation, while I do not myself think war crimes were committed, is a use of law in bad faith that is neither trivial nor easily excused. But the subjection of war to law is not an end in itself and neither is the law's integrity. More important than showing respect for the law in the resort to law is using law to further compliance, i.e. that practices in warfare meet the standard set by IHL. I therefore propose to reserve the term abuse for the use of law in bad faith in order to facilitate or cover up a violation of the law. Lawfare is then the coincidence of two necessary conditions: the use of law in bad faith and an actual breach of law.

Does this definition really serve the purpose of minimizing spurious claims of abuse, the aim of making abuse discernible? The legal ideal notwithstanding, bad faith alone, even though it is invested into a legal argument, is extremely hard to diagnose in an argument that could in principle be valid. Who knows whether I really believe that war crimes have been committed when I call for the ICC to step in or whether I merely want to cast aspersions. This difficulty is compounded in the context of war. The declared antagonism makes us prone to diverging perceptions of reality. Is there enough preliminary evidence for a reasonable person to call for an investigation or is the claim so outlandish that it must be in bad faith? As mentioned above, enmity tends to carry the attribution of bad faith in its wake, which accounts for the not unusual confusion in the literature and political commentary of the strategic use of law and the use of law in bad faith. The former looks like the latter if who is speaking is on the other side of an M24. An allegation of bad faith regarding an argument that could in theory be made in good faith is therefore, without further evidence, even if it is connected to a breach of law, likely ad hominem. To safely call it abuse the argument needs to not only strike me as being made in bad faith, but should ideally be beyond the possibility of good faith.

To illuminate what it means for a legal argument to be "beyond good faith" for the outside observer we need to connect the way in which law is used (the state of mind) to the purposes for which it is used. Again we should not expect that belligerents evoke law for purposes other than their own. But, like the way in which arguments are made, the law itself limits the ends to which it should be used. The object and purpose of a rule is a guide to which practices or what kind of behavior a law seeks to forbid. Article 31(1) of the Vienna Convention demands that a treaty be interpreted "in light of its object and purpose." Legal doctrine teaches that when a legal argument is made to endorse practices against the object and purpose of that law we know the interpretation to be invalid (Holmes 1998). Law proscribes its use for the purpose of undermining its own regulative goal.

Both elements of lawfare, the breach of law and the use of law in bad faith, can, but do not have to, amount to a use of law in defiance of its object and purpose. While many breaches of law will also defy the violated law's regulative goal, not all do. I could violate the law simply by falling short of the prescribed standard. By the same token, I could conceivably use the law in bad faith and still further its object and purpose: for instance, when I deliberately misrepresent the facts to induce compliance in a belligerent. However, some uses of law in bad faith also amount to a defiance of the law's object and purpose, such as the use of a duplicitous legal argument to facilitate a breach of law. Neither a mere breach nor a mere use of the law in bad faith is negligible, but each tends to be less contestable when amounting to a defiance of the law's object and purpose.

In the remaining space of this chapter I discuss four types of abuse that we may encounter on the twenty-first-century battlefield corresponding with four different ways in which bad faith, a violation, and a defiance of the law's object and purpose can coincide (for an overview see Table 8.1).

A TYPOLOGY OF LAWFARE

I call "indeterminacy-based lawfare" a deliberate exploitation of the open-endedness of all language and hence the contestability of a law's meaning to justify breaches of the rule that defy its own object and purpose. If I make a legal argument to justify my behavior, which I know is contrary to the object and purpose of the law I am invoking, I am not only making an argument in bad faith in that I knowingly misrepresent reality, I am also using law against itself to enable the violation in the sense of limiting its reputational costs. One actor who knowingly uses law to justify another actor's practices contrary to the object and purpose of law, does not violate a substantive obligation, but still abuses the law as her use of law in bad faith facilitates a practice in violation and indeed defiance of the law. This type of abuse has been alleged against the United States in the context of the war on terror. A body of literature documents how the contestability of the definition of torture was used in order to legitimize the notorious treatment of detainees at Guantanamo Bay (Luban 2005a; Luban 2007; Waldron 2010a, chapter 9).

While the interrogation techniques in question clearly amounted to a breach of the prohibition on torture under IL, whether the authors of the so-called torture memos were aware of this, i.e. used law in bad faith, is controversial (for the gamut of views, see Clark and Mertens 2004; Luban 2005b; Posner and Vermule 2004; Wedgwood and Woosley 2004). In this case, the recourse to legal argument was made by lawyers acting in an official capacity so that the line between strategic use and abuse in bad faith is drawn by the applicable code of professional ethics, here the Rules of the American Bar Association. In the "court" of public opinion, the seriousness of the justified breach is a crucial ingredient for the validity of the allegation of bad faith. Conceptually, knowingly justifying mere non-compliance is an abuse of law. After all, it involves both the use of law in bad faith and against itself. However, even in good faith different interpretations of a legal text are possible and an actor may well in good faith deem herself or the belligerent she defends in compliance with a law while that is not the case. It is because violations that defy the object and purpose of the law tend to be more obvious and in principle incontestably violations that we can more readily assume that someone who justifies them does so knowingly, hence in bad faith.

TABLE 8.1 *Lawfare typology*

	The relationship between the two elements: use in bad faith and the breach of IHL	**The connection of the two elements to the threshold of gravity: the defiance of IHL's object and purpose**	**The same law is breached and used in bad faith**	**The use in bad faith is a speech act**
Indeterminacy-based lawfare	The use in bad faith is meant to enable (make less costly) the breach	The use in bad faith defies the law's object and purpose – "ideally" so does the breach	Yes	Yes
Perfidy-based lawfare	The breach is meant to enable the use in bad faith	The breach contains the defiance of the law's object and purpose and also reveals bad faith	Yes	No
Reputation-destroying lawfare	The breach is meant to enable the use in bad faith	The breach and use both defy the law's object and purpose	No	Yes
Reputation-preserving lawfare	The use in bad faith is meant to enable (make less costly) the breach	The use in bad faith defies the object and purpose – "ideally" so does the breach	No	No

Of course, even what the object and purpose of a treaty or provision are and whether or not a practice defies them, are by no means always beyond contestation (Buffard and Zemanek 1998; Jonas and Saunders 2010, 566). While the prohibition on torture has one overriding goal, which practices such as waterboarding clearly defy (for a dismissal of a purposive interpretation even of the prohibition on torture, see Waldron 2010a), identifying practices against the object and purpose of IHL is often more difficult. IHL has a split regulative purpose (Dill 2015a, 83). It neither seeks to simply render war humane, nor does it just bow to military necessity. It strives for a compromise between these often directly contradictory goals. That means that a legal argument justifying the harming of civilians is not necessarily invalid. At the same time, it is very well possible that an argument justifying a militarily necessary practice is. That is the military price for the mantle of legitimacy afforded by IL. It may be contestable when exactly an interpretation has tilted too far toward either humanitarianism or military pragmatism, defying the law's purpose of striking a balance. Specifically for IHL, the qualification of the breach as defying the object and purpose of the law to demonstrate bad faith is hence crucial. In addition, for this type of indeterminacy-based lawfare bad faith should ideally be demonstrated separately before we cry foul.

An abuse of law does not have to be a speech act. Breaches of law that rely on the compliance with law of the other side to generate an advantage on the battlefield also amount to an abuse. The most straightforward example of this is perfidy. In the case of what I want to call "perfidy-based lawfare," the belligerent acts in a way that invites the adversary's trust grounded in a legal rule: for instance, the trust not to be threatened by a civilian. Many non-state belligerents in contemporary wars have a track record of failure to distinguish themselves, which is under most circumstances a violation of IHL (Article 44(3) API). If the failure to distinguish takes the form of feigning civilian status (Article 37(1)c API), it engages the commitment of the other side to the principle of distinction (Article 48 API) and its corollary civilian immunity. For instance, in the recent military confrontation between Israel and Hamas, allegedly booby-trapped persons in civilian clothes relied on the IDF's upholding distinction in order to get close to troops before detonating their explosives (Breaking the Silence 2015, 47). Using the rule of distinction in order to gain a military advantage from a breach of distinction counts as a use of the rule against its own object and purpose. The strategic success of the violation of distinction arises from the violator knowing that the other side does not expect the practice because it is a violation. Bad faith is hence manifest in the violation itself.

Of course, not every breach that defies a law's object and purpose is perfidy-based lawfare, hence an abuse of law. Abuse suggests purposeful engagement. Non-compliance, however serious, might stem from ignorance of law or a prioritization of other imperatives, hence from a failure to engage with the law. Is it abuse of IL if my non-compliance is due to my hope that it will give me a military advantage vis-a-vis an enemy that is committed to IHL? Well, I may hope that my own lack of casualty aversion gives me a leg-up over an enemy who is very risk averse, but unless I actively engage that risk aversion to maximize the strategic benefit accruing from this difference, I am not using the enemy's casualty aversion, let alone abusing it. Abuse requires use. Given the difference between non-compliance and abusive breaches of law, we cannot simply refer to a belligerent's general compliance record as a proxy for abuse and thus as grounds for alleging perfidy-based lawfare.

Both indeterminacy- and perfidy-based lawfare use in bad faith the legal principle or rule that is also violated (in the examples, the prohibition on torture and the principle of distinction respectively). They differ in that in the case of indeterminacy-based lawfare the use of law in bad faith and against itself is a speech act, which though connected, is an act separate from the violation. In the case of perfidy-based lawfare, an act on the battlefield is a material breach that is both a use of law against its own object and purpose and a use of law in bad faith. Indeterminacy-based lawfare is associated with belligerents beholden to the law, whose temptation is to weaken the law's constraining force while not incurring the reputational costs of being found violating IL. Perfidy-based lawfare capitalizes on an asymmetry of commitment to IL for the achievement of an advantage on the battlefield. This is the specific temptation of non-state actors who are less (some not at all) susceptible to the imposition of reputational costs and thus the constraints of IHL than their adversaries.

According to the definition of abuse proposed here, there are two additional types of potential lawfare, which are less obvious because they are a combination of the use in bad faith of one rule and the breach of another. What I call reputation-destroying lawfare, like perfidy, violates law in order to use it in bad faith to gain an advantage. What I call reputation-preserving lawfare, like indeterminacy-based lawfare, uses law in bad faith for the purpose of a successful violation. Reputation-destroying lawfare, like indeterminacy-based lawfare, relies on speech acts. To the contrary, in the case of reputation-preserving and perfidy-based lawfare, both the violation and the use of law in bad faith are acts on the battlefield. The following examples discuss potential cases of reputation-destroying and – preserving lawfare and highlight the respective challenges in establishing that the elements of abuse – the use of law in bad faith and a violation – are actually present and that the threshold of gravity of a defiance of the law's object and purpose is met.

It is a fairly recent phenomenon that non-state belligerents engage in legal arguments. In line with the definition proposed, it is not an abuse of law when the Taliban alleges a violation of IL by coalition forces (see Islamic Emirate of Afghanistan 2015) even if the collateral damage that is denounced as disproportionate is not manifestly so and the argument may well be made in bad faith. That is true even if the proximity of military equipment to civilians contributed to the civilian death toll. However, comingling can amount to a breach of the defender's duty to take precautions in attack (Article 58 API). Moreover, the deliberate use of civilians to protect military equipment falls foul of the prohibition on using human shields (Article 51(7) API). If such a breach is meant to enable the claim that the adversary broke the principle of proportionality, it is a breach defying the law's object and purpose. The allegation against the other side to have caused disproportionate collateral damage is then a use of Article 51(5)b API in bad faith. If the allegation is made by the belligerent that "created" the civilian casualties, the speech act betrays that the belligerent knows the practice to be a violation. It hence reveals bad faith. In the case of reputation-destroying lawfare, the challenge is to prove the breach and its purpose. If the allegation is made by an actor other than the one who violated the law, it may in addition be difficult to prove bad faith.

Reputation-preserving lawfare seeks to ward off the reputational costs of an IHL violation, which reputation-destroying lawfare seeks to impose. In both the 2009 and 2014 military campaigns in Gaza, the IDF issued warnings on an unprecedented scale to motivate the civilian population to leave areas to be attacked (Schmitt and Merriman 2015; State of Israel 2015, 170ff). According to the accounts of returning soldiers, individuals remaining in warned neighborhoods were presumed to be open to attack, amounting to a breach of the principle of distinction. "[T]he directive [was] 'Whoever you identify is an enemy' ... the justification that's behind it is that the IDF distributed hundreds of thousands of flyers warning the residents to evacuate" (Breaking the Silence 2015, 159, similar 37, 58f, 88, 106, 137, 144, 170, 180; see also UN Human Rights Council 2015, 68; Human Rights Watch 2014; for a denial of this claim see State of Israel 2015, 177, para. 306f). While by no means all rules of IL for the conduct of hostilities have an overriding humanitarian purpose, Article 57(2)c API, the duty to warn civilians if possible, does. An interpretation of the provision that seeks to justify the weakening of civilian protection, indeed a breach of distinction, defies its object and purpose. While considerable evidence points to the violation of distinction and the connection to the warnings, proving bad faith, i.e. the use of warnings to cloak in legitimacy a practice the IDF *knows* violates the law, would require separate evidence.

CONCLUSION

Lawfare, or the abuse of IL in war, is testimony to its coercive and persuasive power. You can only effectively abuse law if you can in principle effectively use it. That effectiveness largely depends on IL's association with legitimacy. What threatens this association of legality with legitimacy is not the strategic, self-interested use of law in war. Even abuse as defined here does not necessarily destroy the legitimacy of the legal regulation of war, though it of course can. It may not always be evident or easy to establish, but the use of law in bad faith to facilitate a violation that is severe enough to amount to a use of law against its own object and purpose tends to ultimately discredit the abuser more than it discredits the law. What risks giving legal argument the dynamic of a firefight rather than an attempt at persuasion is rooting proper use in the merit of the belligerent that it assists and dismissing as abusive recourse to law because it furthers the aims of the belligerent "on the other side." Maybe it is not even abuse of law as defined here that should be called lawfare then, but the abuse of the abuse charge, which robs law of its capacity to be a true alternative and more than a mere substitute for armed force in international relations. This capacity is the driving force of the astonishing subjection of warfare to IL over the last decades. The continued relevance of law in war crucially depends on it.

NONVIOLENCE

9

Unarmed Bodyguards to the Rescue? The Ethics of Nonviolent Intervention

James Pattison

INTRODUCTION

In this chapter, I will consider an underappreciated means of preventing and tackling conflict, human rights abuses, and government oppression. This is "civilian peacekeeping," the most notable method of which is "international protective accompaniment" by groups such as Peace Brigades International and Nonviolent Peaceforce. This comprises unarmed bodyguards protecting potentially threatened groups or individuals by deterring abuses, or if abuses occur, reporting them.

My aim in this chapter is straightforward: to defend civilian peacekeeping as a morally desirable part of a preventive and reactive toolkit for tackling human rights abuses, including mass atrocities. This is, in large part, because it avoids many of the real and alleged pitfalls of humanitarian intervention and "military peacekeeping" – that is, peacekeeping that uses armed soldiers (e.g. many current UN missions). To that extent, I will argue that civilian peacekeeping is a desirable option under a fleshed-out account of last resort in Just War Theory. Notwithstanding, the chapter also argues that civilian peacekeeping should not always be undertaken at the expense of military peacekeeping or humanitarian intervention, but rather sometimes used in addition to these methods and potentially alongside them. To that extent, in contrast to some of the defenders of civilian peacekeeping who are overly critical of military peacekeeping or humanitarian intervention (e.g. Carriere 2010), I will defend the need for military peacekeeping and humanitarian intervention *as well*. To that extent, I will suggest that Just War conditions such as Presumptive Last Resort should not be seen as always requiring *one* particular means; a combination of means may be required.

The chapter will proceed as follows. In the next section, To that extent, I will outline in more detail what civilian peacekeeping involves. I will then present the prima facie case for civilian peacekeeping by first delineating ten (real and alleged) frequently noted problems faced by military peacekeeping and humanitarian intervention, as well as eight related advantages of civilian peacekeeping. This will be followed by a section in which I will consider three potential objections to civilian peacekeeping. These are that it (1) can rely on racism and is predicated on privilege (the "Privilege Objection"), (2) is impracticable on a larger scale because it relies on volunteer human shields (the "Supererogation Objection"), and (3) cannot achieve much (the "Inefficacy Objection"). I will go on to argue that, if civilian peacekeeping were upscaled, it could face several problems that would resemble some of the current problems facing military peacekeeping and humanitarian intervention. Nevertheless, I will argue that civilian peacekeeping *should* be upscaled and that, more broadly, military peacekeeping and humanitarian intervention should be undertaken when required. In the final section, I will consider some of the implications of the analysis for Just War Theory and pacifism. In particular, I will suggest that civilian peacekeeping is a plausible option of first resort and that the case for it should be separated from the case for pacifism.

WHAT IS CIVILIAN PEACEKEEPING?

Civilian peacekeeping is "the prevention of direct violence through influence or control of the behaviour of potential perpetrators by unarmed civilians who are deployed on the ground" (Schweitzer 2010, 9). The most frequently undertaken activities in civilian peacekeeping are international protective accompaniment and observing and reporting human rights abuses (Janzen 2014). As noted above, international protective accompaniment involves "unarmed bodyguards, often spending twenty-four hours a day with human rights workers, union leaders, peasant groups, and other popular organizations who face mortal danger from death squads and state forces" (Mahony 1997, 208). Other activities include inter-positioning between fighting forces, negotiation and dialogue with the relevant actors, relationship building, solidarity actions, rumor control, early warning, and training (Nonviolent Peaceforce 2014, 3; Schirch 2006, 31–40; Schweitzer 2010, 11–12).

Civilian peacekeeping differs *somewhat*, but not *altogether*, from UN peacekeeping and from the roles played by other non-state actors before, during, and after conflict, such as certain journalists, human rights advocacy groups, and humanitarian organizations. On the one hand, unlike many of the more well-known contemporary manifestations of UN peacekeeping, which have received a Chapter VII mandate from the UN Security Council to use coercive means to militarily ensure the protection of civilians, civilian peacekeeping is nonmilitary and comparatively non-coercive. It clearly differs, for instance, from the UN's "Intervention Brigade" in the Democratic Republic of Congo, which has a mandate to use force to coerce spoilers. However, although the UN's more coercive peace operations, such in the Democratic

Republic of Congo, attract much more attention, there are still several UN peace operations, such as the missions in the Western Sahara (MINURSO), the Israel-Syria border (UNDOF), and Cyprus (UNFICYP), which do not involve the direct use of military force. Similarly, several of the roles played by humanitarian organizations and human rights advocacy groups can resemble that of civilian peacekeeping. For instance, the presence of humanitarian aid workers in a refugee camp may help to deter attacks on the camp. These may be unintended but welcome effects of these organizations' main objectives or secondary, subsidiary ones. Unlike for civilian peacekeeping organizations, however, international protective accompaniment or similar roles are not their *primary* intention.

Thus far, civilian peacekeeping has been on a relatively small scale. As Randy Janzen (2014) documents, the exact number of civilian peacekeepers is very difficult to determine, but around fifty organizations have engaged in unarmed civilian peacekeeping since 1990, with a significant recent rise. Civilian peacekeeping is also largely new. It mostly developed in the 1980s, largely in Latin America with the work of Peace Brigades International, the best-known organization. Founded in 1981, Peace Brigades International focuses on nonpartisan protective accompaniment and it has served in Nicaragua (1983), Guatemala (1983–1999; 2003–present), El Salvador (1987–1992), Sri Lanka (1989–1998), North America (1992–1999), Haiti (1992–2001), Columbia (1994–present), Mexico (1995–present), Indonesia (2000–2011), Nepal (2005–present), Kenya (2013–present), and Honduras (2013–present).[1]

There are differences between civilian peacekeeping organizations, such as variations in the importance given to being nonpartisan, avoiding interfering in the situation, and obeying the law (Coy 2012). For instance, Christian Peacemaker Teams and International Solidarity Movement are much more partisan in their interventions: in addition to international protective accompaniment, they engage in solidarity activities, such as rebuilding destroyed homes, dismantling barricades and blockades, organizing demonstrations, and even engaging in civil disobedience (Coy 2012, 971). Note that I will focus on *international* civilian peacekeeping. Protective accompaniment may also be provided by local organizations (or have a local element to it), but my focus is on the international element.

Civilian peacekeeping has had some notable successes. For instance, Tim Wallis (2010, 30), the former Executive Director of Nonviolent Peaceforce and International Secretary of Peace Brigades International, documents the success of protective accompaniment in Nicaragua during the 1980s. The mission began when several US citizens went to border towns in Nicaragua to investigate the effects of the Reagan Administration's funding of the Contras. They found that, contrary to what they had expected, there were no attacks on civilians. The villagers told them that as long as "you're here they are not going to attack us." The Americans reportedly responded, "oh, if that's really the case, then we'll stay here and we'll get more people, and we'll stop them attacking you!" Subsequently, over the next seven years, Witness for Peace (a civilian peacekeeping organization) sent 7,000 US citizens to Nicaragua. The presence of these Americans meant that the Contras could not attack due to the risk of killing American citizens, given that they were being funded by the United States, so they stopped attacking the villages. More generally, many organizations have noted that there have been immediate shifts in the treatment of human rights activists once civilian peacekeepers have been deployed (Janzen 2014). Indeed, in 2004, Peace Brigades International reported that *no* human rights activist accompanied on a one-to-one basis by one of their civilian peacekeepers had been killed in the last two decades (Schirch 2006, 57).

How is civilian peacekeeping – and particularly international protective accompaniment – successful in the face of violence? As Christine Schweitzer, one of the founders of the International Balkan Peace Team, notes, "[m]any people find it hard to understand what an unarmed peacekeeper can achieve in a violent environment . . . [T]hey cannot shoot and kill attacking perpetrators . . . Unarmed peacekeepers do, however, have their own sources of power" (2010, 13). These include the moral authority that comes with using nonviolent methods in the face of violence. More precisely, protective accompaniment works by changing the perceived costs of using violence, since aggressors "typically see a higher political cost in using violence around foreigners" (Mahony 1997, 210). These costs include the reporting of international misdeeds globally, which can lead to direct or indirect repercussions, including pressure on the supporters of perpetrators (Schweitzer 2010, 13). It is important to highlight here that what matters is the *perception* of such costs: "[i]f they believe foreign witnesses will produce international political consequences, then any foreigners may play some protective role, whether or not they can really produce such consequences" (Mahony 1997, 212). Beyond affecting strategic calculations, international civilian peacekeeping can also help with long-term stability by emphasizing the potential role played by nonviolence, such as by developing cultures of peace (Janzen 2014).

More generally, nonviolent methods work – and contrary to much popular opinion – work *better* than violent ones. This has been documented recently in the influential work of Maria Stephan and Erica Chenoweth (e.g. 2008) on civil resistance movements, who find that major nonviolent campaigns are *six* times more likely to be successful than violent campaigns facing repression. The reasons they give include nonviolent movements' increased legitimacy and, in turn, participation rates, as well as the fact that regime violence against nonviolence can lead to higher costs for the regime, such as increasing solidarity with the resistance movement, defections, and external support for the opposition. This builds on the work of Gene Sharp (three-times nominated for the Nobel Peace Prize), who, in his three-volume *The Politics of Nonviolent Action*, catalogues 198 nonviolent measures, outlines how these can be used successfully, and defends the case for nonviolence.[2] A central notion is what he calls "political *jiu-jitsu*" (1973, 657–697). This concerns the process by which nonviolence deals with violence. Violence against nonviolent groups is much more likely to delegitimize the oppressors than if it were against violent groups, with third parties (including international ones) and members of the oppressor group more likely to dissent. At the same time, the victims' cause will be viewed more favorably and there will be increased support, as well as increased resistance from the oppressed group. Thus, "*[t]heir nonviolence helps the opponent's repression to throw him off balance politically. The nonviolent group is also able to gain far more support and power than if it had met violence with violence*" (Sharp 1973, 658; emphasis in original). As violent groups become aware of these effects, they may become less willing to use force in the first place, out of fear of repercussions.

THE PRIMA FACIE CASE FOR CIVILIAN PEACEKEEPING

To show the prima facie case for civilian peacekeeping, and particularly protective accompaniment, this section will outline how it appears to be comparatively advantageous to military peacekeeping and humanitarian intervention. To do this, I will first consider seven leading objections presented to military peacekeeping and humanitarian intervention in the literature on International Relations, civilian peacekeeping, pacifism, and Just War Theory (some of the objections are more applicable to humanitarian intervention or to military peacekeeping, and some apply equally to both). For instance, versions of the "Selectivity Problem," the "Motive Problem," the "Harm Problem," and the "Unrealistic Expectation Problem" are presented by Roland Paris (2014) as some of the "structural problems" of humanitarian intervention that, he claims, ultimately render the responsibility to protect doctrine as "fated to flounder." I will then consider five apparent advantages of civilian peacekeeping and, in particular, protective accompaniment.

(1) The Selectivity Problem: Humanitarian intervention (and, to a lesser extent, military peacekeeping) is alleged to be carried out selectively. It is claimed to occur only where the major powers – and particularly the major Western powers – have vested interests.
(2) The Motive Problem: As the Selectivity Problem alleges, humanitarian intervention is often claimed to be carried out for purely self-interested motives. In similar vein, it may be alleged that troop-contributing countries only contribute troops to UN peace operations for financial reasons. It may also be alleged that the particular soldiers involved agree to such operations only out of purely self-interested reasons, such as those related to financial incentives.
(3) The Capacity Problem: In recent times, the UN Security Council has authorized peace operations that the UN lacks the capacity to deliver.

This is in terms of both the number and the quality of troops available from troop-contributing countries and the in-house capacity of the Department for Peacekeeping Operations to run the missions.

(4) The Unrealistic Expectation Problem: Both military peacekeeping and humanitarian intervention can face unrealistic expectations about what can be achieved by the operation from those enduring the current crisis and from the international community more generally. Intervening forces are often expected to make significant, visible increases in civilian protection across vast areas, yet lack sufficient troop numbers or equipment to be able to achieve this. They are also often judged according to much more ambitious political goals, rather than whether they contribute to improving civilian protection. Moreover, situations can deteriorate further while intervening forces are in the field. Although such operations may still be effective, this is often only counterfactually – the situation would have been even worse without the intervening forces. Establishing their effectiveness can therefore be very difficult.

(5) The Harm Problem: Humanitarian intervention and military peacekeeping often harm innocents. This is sometimes through the direct use of force, such as through bombing campaigns that cause collateral damage, or through indirect effects that can arise with the presence of an intervening military force, such as prostitution rings, human trafficking, and dramatic changes to the local economy and cost of living. The worry in both cases is not simply a consequentialist one about the foreseeable problematic, unintended effects of humanitarian intervention and military peacekeeping. It is also deontological in that the intervening parties *do* harm. That is, even if they are effective all things considered, they still *do* harm. This is particularly important for those who hold that there is a significant and perhaps absolute moral difference between the *doing* and *allowing* of harm.

(6) The Risk Problem: Both humanitarian intervention and military peacekeeping can lead to casualties on behalf of the intervener or peacekeeping force. This may be reduced by significantly increasing force protection by, for instance, conducting only aerial bombing campaigns, but this can in turn exacerbate the Harm Problem.

(7) The Conscription Problem: Humanitarian intervention and peace operations, the argument runs, rely on soldiers who, even if not conscripts, have signed up to risk their lives only to provide national defense, not to protect the lives of those beyond the borders of the state (Cook 2000). Such operations are therefore a form of conscription in that they require soldiers to fight wars to which they have not agreed.

To be clear, I think that, despite these (real and alleged) problems, humanitarian intervention and peacekeeping operations *are* often justifiable and indeed morally required (see section V). Yet, civilian peacekeeping, at least as it is currently practiced, seems to avoid many of these problems. In fact, it has the following notable advantages.

(1) The Motive Advantage: Civilian peacekeepers are *more likely* to be motivated by altruistic reasons *in the overall balance of reasons* than regular soldiers. There may be exceptions where some regular soldiers may overall be better motivated (even by solely altruism) and there may be civilian peacekeepers who are motivated largely by self-interest. But even if both civilian peacekeepers and regular soldiers possess mixed motives, it seems that altruism is likely to be a weightier reason, in the overall balance of reasons, for civilian peacekeepers. For instance, members of Witness for Peace and Christian Peacemaker Teams have been reported to be motivated out of a spiritual desire to confront violence nonviolently, and other groups have cited their members' humanitarian motives and the desire to help people in need (Schirch 2006, 82). Similarly, Matthew Eddy's (2011) study of International Solidary Movement highlights the import of volunteers' construction of a cosmopolitan identity.

(2) The Effectiveness Advantage: The apparent success of international protective accompaniment can be more easily demonstrated. It depends, in part, on whether the specific individuals accompanied have been killed or subject to various abuses, which is easier to establish than showing that human rights abuses have been prevented across vast areas. To be sure, counterfactual assessments may be required to prove, in reality, that protective accompaniment was in fact successful, given that the protected individual may not have been killed. However, even if the counterfactual judgment is questioned, protective accompaniment is not simply about tackling *objective* threats to individuals and groups, but also about improving *subjective* perceptions of security. That is, civilian peacekeepers can reduce the subjective perceptions of insecurity of such individuals and groups that can lead to them being too fearful to engage in their human rights activism. As Liam Mahony (1997, 210) argues, international protective accompaniment provides encouragement to engage in activism, regardless of whether the accompaniment actually protects people from anything – it helps them overcome the long-term fear installed by statist terror.

(3) The Nonviolence Advantage: Given that it does not involve any violent methods, protective accompaniment seems to *do* no harm, or at least do no *direct* harm using military force. To the extent that the difference between doing and allowing has significant moral weight, this may be a major reason in favor of it.

(4) The Risk Advantage: Despite the appearance of significant risk, civilian peacekeepers have rarely been subject to attack. For instance, attacks on

the peacekeepers of Peace Brigades International have been remarkably few (although include the bombing of its offices and the knifing of its volunteers in Guatemala) (Coy 2012, 967–968). Indeed, Janzen (2014) finds that the fatality rate for UN peacekeeping mission staff is more than twelve times as much as than that of civilian peacekeepers. This may be because of the success of political *jiu-jitsu* or, instead, because civilian peacekeepers tend to operate in situations where they are less likely to be subject to attack. (To be sure, there are more attacks on civilian peacekeepers perceived to be partisan, such as members of International Solidarity Movement (see Coy 2012).)

(5) The Volunteer Advantage: All the members of civilian peacekeeping forces are volunteers (in the sense that they are not conscripted; some are paid) and often from states where they have several other reasonable options, rendering their consent sufficiently free.

It seems, therefore, that there is a strong prima facie case for protective accompaniment. It appears to have several potential, notable advantages over military peacekeeping and humanitarian intervention.

OBJECTIONS TO CIVILIAN PEACEKEEPING

Thus far, I have painted a very rosy picture of civilian peacekeeping. I will now consider three potential objections to it. Note that there are several other objections that could arise if protective accompaniment were used for unjust causes, used to protect military personnel or installations, used in clear contravention of the consent of those protected, and in contravention of a UN mandate. Although they raise several interesting issues, these objections are only hypothetical since civilian peacekeepers do not currently act in these circumstances and are very unlikely to be used in these ways in the future. I will focus instead on what I see as the three main current and prospective ethical issues.

The Privilege Objection

The first objection, which I will call the "Privilege Objection," is that protective accompaniment is premised upon, and reinforces, privilege, potentially including racism. The objection stems from the fact that "outsiders are often seen as more effective peacekeepers than insiders because of the power of their Western passports, their white skin, and/or their ability to be impartial" (Schirch 2006, 52). To that extent, Patrick Coy (2011) discusses the example of "George," a veteran of multiple Peace Brigades International teams, who responds to the question, "if there is violence all around, who is going to protect you?" Coy reports that "[w]ithout missing a beat he raised the bare underbelly of his forearm to the group, and with his other hand he pinched a gathering of the pale skin there to highlight it and said simply, 'My white skin'" (2011). The privileged status of civilian peacekeepers is also often influential in obtaining access in the first place (Boothe and Smithey 2007, 46). In addition, civilian peacekeeping may also be claimed to reinforce prejudice (which gives rise to privilege to the beneficiaries), and, in particular, racist attitudes by highlighting that white skin renders one as immune from attack and darker skin renders one more dispensable.

Given these sorts of concerns about relying upon and reinforcing prejudice (and in turn privilege), Coy (2011) notes that many members of Peace Brigades International felt extremely uncomfortable. The issue is not limited to Peace Brigades International, however; Coy (2011) suggests that this has been a problem for *all* international accompaniment organizations in the past and will be in the future. This is because such organizations "can never operate completely outside the prevailing dynamics of race and privilege that still permeate the social and political systems within which accompaniment is applied" (Coy 2011). That is, where there are white Westerners performing protective accompaniment, or simply even Western organizations employing civilian peacekeepers, the underlying dynamics of race are likely to be present, often through colonial legacies or the systemic privilege of the West.

Although the Privilege Objection is, of course, potentially very serious, it is not as worrisome as it may first seem. First, some of the reliance on racist attitudes and privilege more generally has been reduced (if not eliminated altogether for all organizations). This is because many organizations, including Peace Brigades International, are now much more ethnically diverse and use uniforms, rather than simply their white skin color, to demarcate themselves (Coy 2011). They also employ more local staff. For instance, Nonviolent Peaceforce (2014, 7) report that 41 percent of their staff are from the host state.[3] In addition to those who come from the host state (e.g. South Sudan), many of the internationals are from developing countries in Africa and Asia.

Second, as Coy (2011) documents, some members of Peace Brigades International argue (quite plausibly) that international protective accompaniment subverts status quo relations because white people become the escorts, rather than the stars of the show. This is particularly for nonpartisan groups such as Peace Brigades International, given that they do not direct any of the activism. It is often based on solidarity rather than usurpation (Boothe and Smithey 2007, 42).

Third, even if reliant on racist attitudes (or privilege more generally), international protective accompaniment may be morally justifiable on occasion if there are much greater benefits achieved overall. International protective accompaniment may not reinforce racism (or privilege) and may do much to undermine it in the long run, even if somewhat reliant on racist attitudes to do so in the first place. Indeed, protective accompaniment often attempts to protect human rights activists that defend moral equality and this may be much more important in challenging racism and other prejudices (see Schirch 2006, 57).

The Supererogation Objection

The second objection, the "Supererogation Objection," is that civilian peacekeeping – and in particular international protective accompaniment – cannot be defended as anything more than supererogatory. This is a worry because it may be wrong then to claim that this is a policy that *should* be put in place as an alternative or addition to other means of tackling human rights abuses. The objection, in brief, is as follows: (1) International protective accompaniment largely relies on, in effect, people willing to be human shields. (2) Individuals cannot be morally *required* to be human shields since this seems far too demanding. They are in the field without any weapons to defend themselves. (3) Protective accompaniment therefore relies on supererogatory action and, as a result, cannot be prescribed.

To be sure, prescriptions may still be made while there are sufficient volunteers. For instance, we can say that various actors in the international community should try to encourage and support the volunteers as far as possible. But, if protective accompaniment is to be expanded, it will need many more high-quality volunteers, which the organizations may find very difficult to obtain. The issue could be resolved by significantly incentivizing protective accompaniment. At the moment, some civilian peacekeepers are paid a wage; this could be significantly increased. Yet this risks protective accompaniment facing many of the problems that arise with the use of financially motivated private actors (e.g. private military and security companies) in a conflict zone, such as that of mercenary motive (see Pattison 2014).

Alternatively, civilian peacekeepers may be conscripted. On the face of it, this may seem abhorrent. Yet, it is widely thought (e.g. Rawls 1999) the conscription for wars of self-defense may be, on occasion, morally permissible. It also seems that it may be occasionally permissible to use conscription for humanitarian intervention (see Baker and Pattison 2012; Pattison 2013). If individuals can be conscripted permissibly to defend fellow nationals, it may also seem that they may, on occasion, be conscripted to defend those beyond their borders. Even when conscripted soldiers will be subject to notable risks, states and – more generally – third parties, may still be able to permissibly subject their soldiers to such risk. This is if they will be able to save a much greater number of innocent individuals, such as when using a conscripted army to halt a genocide. Suppose, for instance, that in 1994 François Mitterrand could have used France's conscript armed forces to intervene military much earlier and more effectively that it did in response to the Rwandan genocide (and suppose that the French conscripts would not have consented to the operation). Even if the humanitarian intervention would have been very costly for some of the soldiers (e.g. death was likely for some), Mitterrand still could have permissibly ordered the intervention (and perhaps was obliged to do so). In such cases, any fiduciary obligations owed by a leader to his or her soldiers are outweighed by the greater moral import of saving a large number of lives by using the conscript army.

Hence, the consent and interests of soldiers should not be given overwhelming weight in a leader's deliberations when they decide whether to order intervention. It may seem that similar arguments provide the case for conscription for protective accompaniment. That is, the consent and interests of potential civilian peacekeepers should not be given *overwhelming* weight in third parties' deliberations in the case for protective accompaniment.

Note, though, that the form of conscription differs. Conscription for civilian peacekeeping would not force individuals into becoming *combatants*. The civilian peacekeepers would still be civilians since they would not engage in combat. As such, the risks to them will not be likely anywhere near as high as they are for when individuals are conscripted to be soldiers. In other words, the potential conscription would not be *military* service, but rather would be compulsory *civilian* service, albeit international and somewhat risky. It also follows that, unlike regular soldiers, they would be conscripted without having any weapons to defend themselves when in the field.

There is an obvious worry with the case for conscription for civilian peacekeeping: the potential benefits of protective accompaniment seem to be of insufficient weight to render conscription permissible. There will not be enough vulnerable people protected to outweigh the wrongness of forcing individuals to be civilian peacekeepers, who are potentially at significant risk and, even if not, are forced to give up their own pursuits and take on significant hardships in the field.

Could instead the second premise of the Supererogation Objection be disputed? That is, could it be denied that being a civilian peacekeeper is only supererogatory? On the one hand, it may seem that being a civilian peacekeeper could, on occasion, be morally *required* if we hold that individuals are under an enforceable duty to protect vulnerable populations, when this can be done at relatively small cost. This may mean that they are required to even volunteer to be a human shield, if this is not too costly. (Note that by "human shield," I simply mean someone whose presence deters an attack on another. It is a further question whether the individual consents to being a human shield or whether they are used by state or non-state actors.) Consider the following case:

Human Shield: Alan is trying to kill Barbara. Christine can save Barbara by placing herself in front of Barbara, since she knows that Alan would be very unlikely to attack her. He has always had a crush on her and would not want to be violent in front of her.

One might think that Christine has a duty to act as a human shield, given that the risks to her are quite small. This might even be the case if there are *some*, albeit small, risks to Christine, such as if Alan has been drinking heavily and there is a small risk that he may become violent. To that extent, individuals may be morally required to be human shields on occasion.[4]

However, there are two countervailing problems with applying this to protective accompaniment. The first is that the costs to particular peacekeepers do seem likely to be often much greater than they can be reasonably required to bear. In addition to the risk of harm (even if, as in the Risk Advantage, this is not actually that high), there is significant bravery required, discomfort, and cost borne by civilian peacekeepers. For protective accompaniment to be effective, it is vital that peacekeepers maintain their presence in the face of danger – this is in order to show the inefficacy of intimidation or violence in halting civilian peacekeeping (Schirch 2006, 47). In addition to risks in the field, being a civilian peacekeeper can involve quite significant hardship. Coy (2011) reports that Peace Brigades International members had to pay their own travel expenses, and received only limited health care and a stipend of $50 per month; in return, they put themselves at physical risk while working in a stressful, demanding job, living together with foreign nationals in a building that also doubled up as an office. (That said, and as noted above, many civilian peacekeepers are now paid a wage.)

The second problem is that, even if there is a duty to be a civilian peacekeeper, this does not seem to be a duty that could be permissibly enforced, at least at the moment. This is because there are not currently the accompanying institutional structures to render this permissible. NGOs are not appropriate agents to force individuals to be peacekeepers. States, for various reasons, can sometimes legitimately use coercive measures, but do not tend to engage in civilian peacekeeping. Even if they did, they would be morally required to develop institutional structures to render conscription for civilian peacekeeping permissible (such as a lottery to determine who is required to be a peacekeeper) and to show that alternative measures to increase the number of civilian peacekeepers, such as those considered below, would not render the resort to the draft redundant.

Hence, it seems that the Supererogation Objection is largely valid and can, at best, only be ameliorated, at least for the foreseeable future. The following steps might be taken to ameliorate the problems. More volunteers could be encouraged by, for instance, publicizing civilian peacekeeping and the need for volunteers. More expenses could be paid to cover training and travel. It could also become more professionalized, increasingly being seen as a career option, even if it is not directly incentivized with very high wages or other similar benefits. Other costs to volunteers could also be reduced as far as possible, such as risks in the field and lengths of service in the field, so that volunteers are encouraged and, in time, civilian peacekeeping may become morally required of individuals.

As an aside, it is worth noting here that, even if conscripted, civilian peacekeepers would not be liable to attack. They would still clearly be noncombatants: they almost always protect only other noncombatants, rather than those engaged in hostilities. They therefore differ from other forms of human shield, who protect military personnel or military infrastructure. Even on a revisionist approach to Just War Theory (e.g. McMahan 2009), which famously takes a more permissive view of noncombatant immunity, civilian peacekeepers would almost always not be liable. They act in just causes and so therefore seem very unlikely to do anything to abrogate their right not to be killed. In theory, it may be permissible to harm them collaterally, but they enjoy at least the same protections as innocent civilians. In fact, they probably require greater protections, given their morally valuable protection work of others, such as human rights workers, which means that most attacks on them would be disproportionate. The issue of collaterally harming civilian peacekeepers is also unlikely to arise in practice, given that organizations do not tend to send their peacekeepers into places where they might be harmed. This brings us to the next objection.

The Inefficacy Objection

The third objection, which I will call the "Inefficacy Objection," is that civilian peacekeeping cannot achieve much. It is limited only to cases, first, when governments do not reject the presence of civilian peacekeeping. Access may often be revoked when, for instance, the state is repressive. Second, it is unlikely to work in situations of major conflict, where belligerents have few scruples about using force against international peacekeepers. In such situations, civilian peacekeepers may be killed indiscriminately, along with those whom they are trying to protect. Thus, Lisa Schirch (2006, 98–99) notes that there are no recent examples of effective civilian peacekeeping where there is high-intensity, widespread, decentralized fighting with massive numbers of troops and large-scale weaponry.

Is the Inefficacy Objection correct? On the one hand, these limitations clearly demonstrate that protective accompaniment may not always work and cannot fully replace more coercive options, most notably humanitarian intervention. As I will reiterate further below, even though civilian peacekeeping is desirable, humanitarian intervention and military peacekeeping may still sometimes be morally permissible (and required). On the other hand, such limitations should not be overstated; they may sometimes not apply.

First, civilian peacekeepers can work without the express consent of the government (even if civilian peacekeepers still seek it) and are often better placed to negotiate access. This is because governments may not perceive them to be a major threat, given that they are unarmed, and so find less reason to oppose them than a military presence by peacekeeping or intervening forces.

Second, although civilian peacekeeping may not work in areas where there is major, ongoing fighting, it may still work in areas where there is still conflict but at a lower level of intensity. For instance, Nonviolent Peaceforce has been operating in South Sudan, despite the ongoing, brutal civil war, with tens of thousands being estimated to have been killed. They report that they have provided international protective accompaniment for vulnerable civilians, such as women at risk of sexual violence and internally displaced persons, and stayed on even while many humanitarian organizations pulled out (and provided protection for them) (Easthom 2014, 11). They also report that they have protected 31,160 children, extracted thirty-three civilians from areas where mass atrocities were ongoing, saved the lives of "dozens of civilians" who were at imminent risk of being killed in an ethnically mounted attack, helped 60,000 internally displaced persons to avoid being raped, attacked, or killed (which apparently were common occurrences when they were not present), and even negotiated with gunmen to stop them shooting women and children (Easthom 2014, 11).[5] As the latter case shows, belligerents can, in certain cases, still be influenced by the various tactics of civilian peacekeepers.

THE UPSCALING ISSUE AND THE RELATION TO MILITARY PEACEKEEPING

A related problem to the Inefficacy Objection, as already alluded to, is that civilian peacekeeping is currently on a small-scale. But Rachel Julian and Christine Schweitzer (2015) suggest that Nonviolent Peaceforce and other civilian peacekeeping organizations set themselves the goal of deploying enough peacekeepers so as to be comparable to military peacekeeping. If civilian peacekeeping were to be used more widely, which seems attractive given the notable benefits outlined above, it may run into some notable problems of upscaling. These problems, I will now suggest, would mean that it could face some of the similar real and perceived problems of military peacekeeping and humanitarian intervention, although, like these two options, it would still sometimes be morally permissible and perhaps even morally required in the future.

If civilian peacekeeping organizations were to become larger, they may become much more dependent on funding from particular streams. This may mean that civilian peacekeeping organizations lose some of their independence, which is easier to maintain when a smaller organization. Decision-making may also become increasingly influenced by political concerns – even if ultimately for the greater good – and this could lead to accusations of improper motive and selectivity (the Motive Problem and the Selectivity Problem). In fact, according to Schirch (2006, 71–72), the latter is an issue that civilian peacekeepers already face. In addition, if there were more civilian peacekeepers in the field, occasional mistakes may be more likely. Mistakes could include shows of strong partisanship, which could make redundant a whole civilian peacekeeping mission that depends on nonpartisanship (e.g. by Peace Brigades International), as a government takes a different stance and views them as activists rather than simply protectors. In addition, if there were many more civilian peacekeepers in the field, this would raise the probability of peacekeepers *doing* harm, even if unintentional, such as by distorting local practices. For instance, as Mahony notes, there is already a worry that, "[w]ith accompaniment, activists might perceive their available space far exceeding the real space. That is, they may risk dangerous activities because of accompaniment's encouraging function" (1997, 211). A much larger presence could also mean that peacekeepers face the Unrealistic Expectation Problem, as various actors in the international community and those who are vulnerable think that civilian peacekeeping could achieve much more than it can. Civilian peacekeepers could also become expected – and relied upon – to do much more than they would have the ability to do, leading to a form of the Capacity Problem.

Do these potential issues mean that civilian peacekeeping should remain on a small scale? No, since some of these potential problems may be avoided or at least minimized by careful management of expansion. For instance, an increased professional ethos being taught could reduce the risks of occasional shows of partisanship and a repeated public reiteration of the limits of civilian peacekeeping may limit some of the risks of the Capacity Problem. And, even if they would apply, they would not necessarily preclude justifiable civilian peacekeeping. This is because many of the frequently noted problems listed above about humanitarian intervention and military peacekeeping are either (1) not really problems or (2), they are problems but they are not, all things considered, sufficiently weighty to render impermissible humanitarian intervention and military peacekeeping that will be highly effective at improving the enjoyment of basic human rights.

For instance, I have argued elsewhere (Pattison 2010) that the Motive Problem and the Selectivity Problem are unpersuasive objections to humanitarian intervention because the value of an intervener's having a humanitarian motive is likely to be overshadowed by other, more morally important factors and because selectivity only really repudiates the failure to act, rather than the actual intervention. Similarly, the Conscription Problem seems mistaken since (1) intervening soldiers often *do* seem to consent to peacekeeping operations and humanitarian interventions and (2) even if they do not (as suggested above), conscription may still sometimes be permissible, even if only rarely. In addition, the Unrealistic Expectation Problem is not a problem for interveners per se, but rather is a matter of managing expectations – this might be achieved with better communication.

The Harm and Risk Problems pose more valid moral concerns. Yet military peacekeeping or humanitarian intervention may still, on occasion, be morally permissible (and even required) because they are likely to make a significant improvement in tackling the mass violations of basic human rights, compared to doing nothing, and will be much better than any other option, including civilian peacekeeping. As already suggested, this seems particularly likely in situations where there is significant ongoing conflict. In doing so, despite some negative effects that they cause, such as risk to intervening soldiers, they will *sometimes* do a lot more good overall by tackling the mass violation of basic human rights. The efficacy of UN military peacekeeping is supported by a recent quantitative study by Lisa Hultman, Jacob Kathman, and Megan Shannon (2014), who find that UN peace operations lead to a 73 percent reduction in battlefield violence (where there is at least a 10,000 troop deployment).

The same replies would be open to defenders of civilian peacekeeping if it were to face these issues. Despite the more complex moral picture that may develop if civilian peacekeeping were upscaled significantly, it may still be morally permissible and even potentially a duty (if sufficient civilian peacekeepers could be recruited). Although it may face several further alleged problems, some of these may be only illusory and other problems may be outweighed by much greater improvements in the overall enjoyment of basic human rights that outweigh these problems.

CONCLUSION

In summary, rather than being overly critical of military peacekeeping or humanitarian intervention, civilian peacekeeping is best seen as an *additional* means to military peacekeeping or humanitarian intervention, rather than a full replacement. Given the Inefficacy Objection, in more conflict-laden situations military peacekeeping or humanitarian intervention may be the only suitable option.[6] In situations where there are mixed levels of conflict it may be appropriate to carry out both military peacekeeping or humanitarian intervention (in the more conflict-laden areas) *and* civilian peacekeeping (in the less conflict-laden areas). Although protective accompaniment may appear to be required to be undertaken in less conflict-laden situations *instead of* military peacekeeping or humanitarian intervention, given the Supererogatory Objection and the fact that civilian peacekeeping is currently only on a small scale, this cannot yet be prescribed. As such, in all levels of conflict, civilian peacekeeping cannot yet be seen as a replacement for military peacekeeping or humanitarian intervention, given the Supererogatory and Inefficacy Objections. If it were upscaled, civilian peacekeeping might be able to take on more cases where there is lower-level conflict, but military peacekeeping or humanitarian intervention would still be required where there is more intense conflict.

To finish, I want to highlight two points about my argument. The first is that, although civilian peacekeeping is often defended by pacifists, civilian peacekeeping can – and should – be endorsed (when appropriate) by both pacifists and those who reject pacifism, given the arguments above. Those who reject pacifism can accept the strong desirability of nonviolence, such as in the form of civilian peacekeeping, as a response to violent situations, even if violence may sometimes be required to tackle violence (Howes 2013). This is in similar vein to the "strategic," rather than "principled," view of nonviolence, such as taken by Gene Sharp (see Coy 2013). Another way of putting this is that nonviolence can be justified for consequentialist, and not simply deontological, reasons.

The second point is that civilian peacekeeping should be seen as a plausible and desirable option under the last resort principle of Just War Theory. There are various understandings of this principle in the literature (see Aloyo 2015). I think the most plausible is what I call "Presumptive Last Resort" (Pattison 2015). Presumptive Last Resort compares the various military and nonmilitary options, weighing the various goods and harms. Importantly, unlike accounts that reduce last resort simply to this weighing, and so are therefore the same as an *ad bellum* principle of necessity (e.g. Aloyo 2015), Presumptive Last Resort also holds that *doing* harm should *generally* (if not *always*) be avoided. From this basis, it requires that, when there is a choice of feasible options, (1) war should (generally) be the last feasible option and (2) the comparatively best nonviolent option(s) should be tried first. This second point goes beyond prevailing accounts of last resort to offer an account of first resort, second resort, and so on. It is in this context that civilian peacekeeping can be located. It will often be a desirable option to be pursued before war and other more coercive alternatives, such as economic sanctions, particularly since it appears often to be effective and to *do* less harm.

But, as we have also seen, sometimes military peacekeeping and humanitarian intervention are required. How should we understand this in terms of Presumptive Last Resort? First, Presumptive Last Resort is only a *presumption* against war, based on the foreseeable negative consequences of war; sometimes the risks of war or military intervention, and the fact that it involves *doing* harm, will still be worth taking, given that it may save many more lives. As such, the import of Presumptive Last Resort will be outweighed.

Second, as noted above, military peacekeeping and humanitarian intervention could be undertaken alongside civilian peacekeeping. Comparative Just War conditions such as Presumptive Last Resort should not be seen as always requiring *one* particular means; a combination of means may be required. That is to say, the comparative Just War conditions such as last resort should not involve considering whether war and intervention would be better than each of the various alternatives, but rather whether war and intervention, potentially *in combination* with other alternatives, would be better than particular alternatives or a combination of them (also see Lango 2014, 154–155). As such, civilian peacekeeping may be viewed as desirable *alongside* violent and nonviolent options.

Hence, civilian peacekeeping seems to be a desirable option of first resort and, even when other options have been undertaken, a desirable addition to the current central mechanisms of addressing human rights abuses.

ACKNOWLEDGMENTS

An earlier version of this chapter was presented at the University of Manchester in a workshop on the Ethics of Alternatives to War in April 2015 and at the EISA conference in Sicily in September 2015. I would like to thank the participants for their helpful comments; I would also like to thank Patrick Coy, Christopher Finlay, Jonathan Gilmore, Michael Gross, Randy Janzen, Rachel Julian, Tamar Meisels, Christine Schweitzer, and an anonymous reviewer for their very helpful written comments on an earlier draft of this chapter. This chapter was written while holding a research fellowship from the Arts and Humanities Research Council (AHRC) for the project, "The Ethics of the Alternatives to War" (AH/L003783/1). I would like to thank the AHRC for their support.

NOTES

1. Descriptions of the roles performed in these states are available at www.peacebrigades.org/about-pbi/pbi-history/.
2. An updated list of methods to include digital forms of nonviolent resistance has been compiled by Mary Joyce and Patrick Meier, available here: http://digital-activism.org/projects/cr20/.
3. The issue may still not be resolved though. Boothe and Smithey (2007, 51–52) claim that, despite some improvements, certain organizations pay insufficient attention to the role of privilege in their training of staff.
4. For a defense of (exceptional) permissibility of using human shields in war, see Fabre (2012, 256–267). Much of Fabre's case depends on the chances of the human shields living a minimally decent life being improved by this use. By contrast, my point here relies simply on human shields' duty to rescue. Also see Gross (2014) for a defense of the use of human shields.
5. Nonviolent Peaceforce has also recently received a grant from the EU to strengthen Syrian civil society's capacity to protect civilians from violence, with a view to providing protective accompaniment when "appropriate and safe" (Duncan 2015).
6. What is a suitable option will also depend on not simply the *intensity* of the conflict, but also its *other characteristics*, such as the degree to which the belligerents are concerned about harming foreign civilians.

10

How Subversive Are Human Rights? Civil Subversion and the Ethics of Unarmed Resistance

Christopher J. Finlay

Human rights define a set of *ends* whose special value is commonly held to mandate the coercive powers of those states that respect them and sometimes to justify remedial measures by external intervention or internal resistance against others that don't (Buchanan 2004; Doyle 2015; Finlay 2015). But in addition to specifying its ends directly, human rights can also legitimize political action by protecting a range of versatile civil liberties that may be employed as political *means*. In doing so, rights offer indirect protection (a political guarantee) for some other purposes that people might use them to pursue, purposes not inconsistent with human rights but not directly warranted by them either. I want to shed some light on this thought by exploring the possibility that some such rights could provide tools for a strategy to subvert the authority of a state. It is in this sense that I intend the question: How subversive are human rights? I argue that they could have considerable subversive potential if used as part of a method I will call Civil Subversion. Although it might be used to pursue other types of political objective, I will focus particularly on how Civil Subversion could exploit vulnerabilities even in legitimate states to pursue secessionist goals.

Civil Subversion combines three techniques: divestment from existing political institutions, the establishment of parallel institutions, and the use of civil liberties to ensure that, whereas everything the resisters do is protected by rights, many of the things the opposing state needs to do to defend against them would violate rights. It thereby places the state in a predicament where the actions it might need to take for the sake of its ability to rule in the contested territory would at the same time undermine its legitimacy and thereby diminish its power. By exploiting the political-normative salience of rights in this way as a means of constraining the state and compelling it to concede ends that they don't substantively entail, this strategy may be said to involve a form of normative coercion.

The potential for using human rights in this way is most clearly visible in a peculiar subset of confrontations between resisters and government that falls between the two types that receive most attention in the literature. On the one hand, analysis of the ethics of civil resistance and armed rebellion tends to focus on cases where the state fails to satisfy human rights, thus triggering a right to resist on the parts of its *opponents* (e.g. Finlay 2015). On the other hand, theorists of militant democracy are interested in cases where the threat to human rights is posed by illiberal opposition movements, triggering a right to resist on the part of the democratic *state* (e.g. Kirschner 2014; Macklem 2006). I am especially interested, by contrast, in intermediate cases where the prospects for human rights satisfaction are equal between (a) the secessionist state at which opponents of the state aim, (b) the original state minus the secession, and (c) the original state had there been no secession (cf. Caney 1997, 371). By focusing on these cases, it is possible to abstract away the more prominent issues triggered by human rights violations in order to reveal a feature of human rights that those issues overshadow. Clarifying this feature may in turn shed light on conceptual and tactical possibilities that could be exploited by a wider range of movements confronting regimes they have legitimate reasons to try to change.

The first two sections outline the key features of the technique by drawing on a historical example outlined by the Irish nationalist Arthur Griffith some time before the contemporary international human rights regime was created but in a context in which the legitimacy of the state nevertheless depended on claims about civil liberties. The final section then analyses its normative dimensions, focusing on how they might be worked out in the context of human rights.

THE METHODS OF CIVIL SUBVERSION

The methods of Civil Subversion were devised and put into action during the growing mobilization of secessionist nationalism in Ireland between 1904 and 1921. Later overshadowed as the proponents of armed force came to predominate after 1916, at the beginning of that period Arthur Griffith, the founder of Sinn Féin, drew on examples from Hungarian nationalist agitation in the nineteenth century to formulate a strategy built out of nonviolent techniques that, he thought, could undermine the power of the British state in Ireland while simultaneously founding an alternative. His ideas offered both a significant contribution to the tactical repertoire of Irish nationalism and beyond and an early articulation of the essential components of a model for civil resistance that has since become much more popular.

A self-consciously nonviolent strategy, the "Sinn Féin Policy," as it became, was formulated on the one hand as an alternative to armed struggle. But it was intended equally to rival participation in constitutionally mandated parliamentary politics (parliamentarism). Its aim was to generate a novel form of political power that was *neither* violent *nor* constitutionally authorized but that could exert force in contemporary politics sufficient to secure nationalist goals without the moral and political compromises of its rivals.

Parliamentarism in particular, Griffith argued, demanded a fatal trade-off, selling out the cause of Irish independence properly understood for the sake of political advantages that were mostly illusory in nature. The "evil fruits of Parliamentarism masquerading as constitutionalism," he wrote, could be seen in a fundamental disorientation of the Irish people, compromising instead of nourishing the culture and institutions that it should have been the nationalists' chief objective to promote and liberate (Griffith 1918, x). His analysis has a distinctly Schmittian flavor (*avant la lettre*) as he bemoans how by situating their representatives in the British legislature, "They grew to look upon this English party or class as a friend, and that English party or class as an enemy" and "ceased to recognize in all English parties and classes the same England in different garments" (Griffith 1918, xi). Griffith needed a strategy that could rival the leverage promised by parliamentarism but without the trade-off.

His idea combined two moments, one negative, one positive (Townshend 2013, 83; cf. Gandhi 2008, 164–184). Negatively, its central component was "abstentionism": The Irish people and its leaders must withdraw from the institutions of English rule. They must divest active support from the political institutions at Westminster and disengage from the political machinations of British politicians and their parties. But disengagement shouldn't stop at politics in the narrow sense: Irish subjects of British rule must not take legal disputes to English courts. Nor must they send their most talented educators and administrators to work in an English education system and civil service. Their diplomats must not serve in the embassies of Britain or contribute to the maintenance of foreign relations focused on London. And in 1919, nationalists added the important tactic of boycotting the Royal Irish Constabulary (the police force before independence), aiming to "render them harmless, and prevent them getting information," as Constance Markievicz put it (and also, she added, "to make them ashamed of themselves") (Townshend 2013, 84).

Positively, the Irish must build for themselves a set of rival institutions and reinvest their active support in them. They must create "A National Civil Service" to which those currently serving the English may defect (Griffith 1918, 155–156). Only through such a rival institution could Irish administrators serve a truly Irish education policy by means of measures designed specifically to deepen Irish culture and identity. No less important, Griffith argues, "are National Courts of Law" (156). In the nineteenth century, Hungary had "established Arbitration Courts, which superseded the courts which Austria sought to impose upon her." So must Ireland. At the center of it all, Irish delegates withdrawn from Westminster must attend instead a "de facto Irish Parliament in Dublin" (156). So far as foreign relations are concerned, instead of "orating" to the English in London, they ought to represent the Irish case as consuls in foreign states (151). As Townshend writes, "the counter state" was intended "to purloin the national administration from beneath the noses of the British authorities" (Townshend 2013, 84).

Following the example of Hungarian nationalists, the "policy [was to be one] of Passive Resistance – with occasional excursions into the domain of Active Resistance at strategic points" (Griffith 1918, 90). So far as its feasibility is concerned, Richard Davis writes that, "In 1905 Griffith's ideas seemed to many ludicrously far-fetched" but with "the establishment of Dail Eireann [the Irish parliament formed by separatists elected through the British general election] in 1919, it was to be a different story." The necessary component of a de facto power in the form of an "elective representation of Ireland" was achieved at that point once Sinn Féin demolished their parliamentarist opponents in the 1918 general election and then withdrew en bloc to form an independent Irish legislature (Davis 1976, 14). In fact, the Sinn Féin policy was so successful by 1920 in achieving Griffith's intermediate goals that the General Officer Commanding in Chief of British forces during the War of Independence, Sir Nevil Macready, claimed "to have bought a copy of [Griffith's] *The Resurrection of Hungary* and ticked off, item by item, each positive action of Dail Eireann" (34; on the unpromising early years of the policy, McGarry 2010, 27–29).

The precise salience that Civil Subversion had in the Irish independence movement is hard to measure due to the growth of a parallel and in some ways complementary armed force movement from 1916 onward. But it draws on techniques often cited as key parts of the repertoire of nonviolent resistance that have been employed with varying degrees of success in a number of important cases since the end of the Irish War of Independence in 1921 (notably in India, on which see Brown 2009; on Palestine and Kosovo, see Gross 2015, 242–244; on withdrawal of support, Sharp 2006, 67–68 and on parallel institutions, 70).[1] I turn now to the question of how Civil Subversion might be expected to work, exerting a peculiar kind of "force" in pursuit of nationalist aims.

CIVIL SUBVERSION, POWER, AND UNARMED "FORCE"

The term "Civil Subversion" captures, I think, the key features of Griffith's idea while flagging a contrast with other more famous examples of nonviolent resistance such as Martin Luther King's. On the one hand, like King's *civil* disobedience, it is scrupulously "non-military" in its pure form and pursues "goals [that] are 'civil' in the sense of being widely shared in a society" (Roberts 2009, 2). But whereas King sought to modify particular parts of the law in more or less radical ways while upholding the authority of the state as a whole, Civil Subversion attempts to negate entirely the existing source of legal authority and it may or may not seek in doing so to achieve any reform in the way the laws allocate and protect individual rights.[2] In order to get a clearer sense of how it might work, we need to give some attention to how the Civil Subversion strategy relates to *force* and to do this we need to start with its relationship with *power*.

For Hannah Arendt, power is not a question of domination, of "Who? Whom?" as Lenin encapsulated it. Nor, paradigmatically, does it "flow from the barrel of a gun" (Mao) and it isn't, therefore, a phenomenon intimately connected with the threat of violence. Rather, power arises where people act in concert, coming together and forming political relationships, identifying and committing to common political goals, and "empowering" leaders. States and governments that can rely on widespread, active support in this form have what Arendt calls *power*: they are, as it were, *empowered to act* by a population that supports them collectively. By the same token, if a government or state loses this sort of legitimacy, it suffers a commensurate loss of power (Arendt 1972, 143ff; also, Sharp 2006, 8–10 *et passim*). Revolution occurs, then, where a new power emerges through the concerted action of a populace that simultaneously divests power from the established government. Civil Subversion aims to achieve precisely this sort of political transformation: Just as it concentrates and deepens the commitments of a secessionist population to political, cultural, and economic independence, it dissolves the sinews of power – economic, intellectual, psychological, and institutional – by which "foreign" rule is maintained.

If a popular movement progressively shifted the balance of power in this way within the disputed territory, it would pose a critical dilemma for the regime. On the one hand, rulers could capitulate, conceding their opponents' demands. On the other, they might seek an alternative basis for ruling by supplementing their failing resources in popular support with the threat of violence, an option available only so long as the armed forces are prepared to carry out its orders. But resorting to coercion in this way poses a problem with three interrelated dimensions: First, violence is widely thought likely to prove a less reliable basis for government than power in Arendt's sense (Arendt 1972, 148–149; also Sharp 2006; Wolin 2004, 200). Second, the more use is made of violence, the more power is likely to leach away as violence itself further erodes support (Arendt 1972, 152–155). The third is a variant of the second, specific to contexts in which individuals can claim moral recognition and legal protection for civil rights (cf. Griffith 1918, 26–27 on the first two points and, on the third, 24, 92–93). If the practice of Civil Subversion is able to harness these rights, restricting its methods to those they protect, and if the legitimacy of the state depends on its commitment to civil liberties, then the state is confronted with a dilemma between [a] honoring rights at the cost of losing power and [b] challenging the opposing power at the expense of losing legitimacy. It is in creating this predicament that Civil Subversion may be said to generate a form of force: by "force," I mean that the secessionists succeed by structuring the alternatives available to the government in such a way as to coerce – "force" – it into making concessions. The force is, of course, unarmed since it need involve no credible threat of violence (it is not "kinetic" in the sense Cécile Fabre discusses (2012, chapter 3)). But Civil Subversion nevertheless mimics the coerciveness of threatening violent harm: whereas threats of violence usually take the form, "Do this or *I* harm *you*," Civil Subversion declares, "Do this or *you* will harm *yourself*."

CIVIL SUBVERSION AND HUMAN RIGHTS

The strategy of divestment combined with parallel institutions is likely to benefit in a very practical sense from some of the civic privileges now codified as human rights. Without at least an implicit permission to exercise them, creating the new loci of popular support that it requires would be much more difficult. But in contexts where these privileges are explicitly protected, it contributes in a further way to the forcefulness of Civil Subversion as a strategy. The final section analyzes this additional component by which the strategy could exploit their status as *human rights*.

Human Rights as Guarantees

First, let's return to the suggestion that individual (human) rights might *guarantee* further, collective ends, such as that of self-determination through secession. There are two ways in which they might be thought to do so. The first is *substantive*, i.e. where the ends specified by the right include or entail some further end as a corollary. The second I will call *political*.

As regards *substantive* guarantees, Jack Donnelly, for instance, writes that "there is substantial overlap [between collective self-determination and] well-established individual human rights":

> For example, the right of a people to determine its political status and path of development can be seen as a collective expression of the right to political participation ... Likewise, the right of a people to its natural wealth and resources can be seen as a guarantee that the material means to satisfy a wide range of rights will not be subject to continued plunder by foreign states or corporations.

Consequently, the chief demands arising from a right of self-determination are satisfied by "respecting all other human rights and, in particular, the rights to political participation and freedom of speech, press, assembly, and association" (Donnelly 2003, 222).

On this view, then, any state honoring fully the standard set of individual rights would *ipso facto* also find itself satisfying collective projects for self-determination. In many cases, presumably, these would be realized through policy and lawmaking in parliaments and so on. In some instances, the policies might further realize collective self-determination through constitutional changes that permit a degree of intra-state autonomy. And conceivably, it might even be possible for one part of the population to agree with the others, through its constitutionally appointed public representatives, that it will secede, founding a breakaway state.

What isn't clear, however, is that individual political rights would mandate unilateral secession even if it was strongly desired by those seeking it, i.e. an actionable (still less, enforceable) decision to secede in the face of opposition from (political representatives of) the other human rights–wielding citizens who would remain behind. Some theorists argue that whereas secession might be claimed unilaterally as a remedy for prior or threatened violations of *other* (human) rights or of intra-state autonomy agreements, for example, it cannot be claimed unilaterally as a *primary* right (Buchanan 2004, 331, 343, 351–359; Seymour 2007; for contrasting views, see Caney 1997; Moore 2015, 128–134, 231–234). What I want to draw attention to, however, is a second, distinct way in which individual rights could be said to *guarantee* collective ends, even (to a certain extent) such as unilateral, non-remedial secession.

Human rights can potentially offer a *political* guarantee insofar as any state honoring them might thereby be exposed to attempts by individual rights holders to force it into accepting radical changes to its boundaries or institutional arrangements. Stated formally, a *political* guarantee has the following components in its strongest (and pure) form:

> A set of rights x may be said to *guarantee* a further end z when [1] x equips its owners with means y; where [2] y is sufficient for an attempt with a reasonable chance of success at securing z; and where [3] z is neither included in, a corollary of, nor forbidden by the scheme of rights to which x belongs.

In the type of case we are considering, let x be the set of civil rights guaranteed by the major human rights conventions; z is the ambition of various members of a particular state to break away. Component y is utilized in the strategy of Civil Subversion. The degree to which x should be thought to guarantee z depends, of course, on the efficacy of y in any particular situation, which will vary. In any case, this specifies how a legal *right* might protect certain *means* ("forceful" in the sense indicated in the previous section), which, in turn, sometimes *guarantee* further *ends* (cf. Benjamin 2004, 237).

Turning to clause [3], human rights cannot be said without self-contradiction to guarantee ends that conflict with them substantively, such as the introduction of a system of laws prejudicial to the dignity of women or minorities. A state confronted with resisters bent on such ends could cite human rights to justify necessary and proportionate measures to defend against them (on the ethical complexities of this sort of case focused on democratic rights, see Kirschner 2014). On the other hand, although it is possible that the set of rights, x, might guarantee *politically* a set of ends that x also guarantees *substantively*, the focus here is on how it might do so for ends *not* guaranteed substantively, thereby offering political guarantee in its "pure" form. The focus is therefore on the way human rights politically guarantee ends that are neither directly required by human rights nor at odds with them.

Unilateral, non-remedial secession by a particular population would seem to be an end of this kind. Whereas the right to participate in a self-determining polity of *some* sort might either be a human right or a corollary of other human rights (per Donnelly's point, 2003, 222), to exercise it in a *particular* territorial-jurisdictional form arguably is not (per Buchanan 2004, chapter 8). Moreover, the metajurisdictional power-right to alter existing, otherwise legitimate constellations of populace, jurisdiction, and territorial sovereignty (Stilz 2009) is neither a human right nor the logical corollary of such either. However, it is also not true that pursuing such aims is necessarily prohibited by human rights.

Permissible as they may be, a successful pursuit of these aims could challenge the form and authority of an existing legitimate state. It raises the question: By what rights (if any) might the state seek to justify such actions as may be necessary to thwart the secessionists? The answer depends partly on how we interpret the powers conceded to the state by human rights conventions to curb the exercise of some rights in the interests of "national security" and "public order," which I discuss in the subsection after next. But first I ask which individual human rights specifically could be claimed as equipment for secessionists committed to a strategy of Civil Subversion.

Subversives versus the State

Since the strategies I am concerned with are based on extra-parliamentary means of resistance, we have to set aside the "political" rights of democratic participation (e.g. the Universal Declaration of Human Rights (UDHR), art. 21). Civil Subversion chiefly harnesses the sort of "civil" (human) rights that are generally characteristic of liberal-democratic states (cf. Gandhi 2008, 348–349). Indeed, Griffith's contemporaries could count on being permitted to exercise a similar array of abilities in the first quarter of the twentieth century in Britain.

The key civil rights include, first of all, the right to assemble and associate. The UDHR, art. 20, for instance, states that, "(1) Everyone has the right to freedom of peaceful assembly and association" and that "(2) No one may be compelled to belong to an association." Second, Civil Subversion harnesses the right to speak, write, and publish freely: UDHR, art. 19: "Everyone has the right to freedom of opinion and expression; this right includes freedom to hold opinions without interference and to seek, receive and impart information and ideas through any media and regardless of frontiers." Underpinning both sets of rights is the protection of rights of conscience and opinion (UDHR, art. 18).[3] Taken together and used in a concerted way, this cluster of civil rights alongside personal freedoms of movement (UDHR, art. 13), from violence (UDHR, art. 3), and from arbitrary arrest (UDHR, art. 9) provide the necessary minimum equipment that Civil Subversives would need.

Positively, rights of assembly and association would make it possible to establish a movement like Sinn Féin and protect its members' ability to meet and formulate views and plans. Moreover, further institutional arrangements arising from their discussions could also be protected, provided they didn't wrongfully infringe on the human rights of others (which would risk justifying suppression by the state). If courts of arbitration, for example, were offered as a non-compulsory alternative to de jure courts and if participants explicitly consented to abide by their judgments, then it is hard to see how they could be accused of entailing direct human rights violations. Similarly, a more ambitious move like the establishment of a rival representative political assembly could harness the rights of some (of assembly, association and speech) without directly violating those of others. Within such an assembly, then, the exercise of civil liberties would enable delegates to discuss political vision and policy.[4]

Hence, human rights could provide secessionists with the positive abilities needed to arbitrate in disputes between members of its population (and even, conceivably, between them and others if the others also agree to abide by decisions of the courts), outline and define policies, and legislate for the secessionist population. But whereas a legitimate state can enforce its laws and judgments issuing from its courts coercively, it is unlikely that secessionists could do so citing human rights alone. Trying to do so would risk offering a pretext for coercive measures against the subversives by a state citing as grounds that they are private parties committing serious violations of the rights of those under the state's protection. Subversives, however, might be able to develop some enforcement capabilities based on consent. If, for instance, a private club required its members to abide by certain rules, it could stipulate and the members might agree that persistent defaulters be subject to expulsion and, as an intermediate step before cutting ties, they might also agree on financial penalties (enforceable on pain of losing membership). Secessionist subversives might follow this model, permitting them to function collectively in a manner with some resemblance to a democratic state.

So the secessionists might have considerable scope within human rights to engage in the positive aspects of a subversion strategy, but what about the negative? Negatively, the strategy of Civil Subversion involves abstention from parliament, a practice unlikely to break any enforceable human rights–based rules. But more than this, in the Irish case it also required disengagement from the institutions of "foreign" rule more generally. Moves like withdrawing from the civil service might be unproblematic in a human rights perspective. Likewise, insofar as boycotting the police involves *not bringing problems to them for help*, it is less likely to be illegal than positive non-compliance with prima facie legitimate orders. On the other hand, failure to volunteer evidence concerning a serious crime might be a punishable offense (and punishment might be prima facie morally justifiable). But it is also covert, and one therefore that might go undetected. So, more passive methods are likely to avoid the kind of direct confrontation that will (appear to) permit the state to repress a secessionist opposition. By contrast, if the secessionist strategy demands more direct, *active* disobedience in the face of orders from the police or de jure courts, it is more likely to run into difficulties. There may be *moral* objections to face if their actions impose costs on innocent parties within the non-secessionist population, whether through the campaign to secede or the resulting secession, and these might give rise to political difficulties if the collateral costs in turn justify coercion of the subversives by the state.

Gandhi's policy of refusing to pay tax in the context of general civil disobedience in India throws the ethical complexity of the question of disobedience into sharp relief (Gandhi 2008, 348–349; cf. Griffith 1918 on the Hungarian policy). On the one hand, insofar as the state is able to claim that an obligation to pay tax on the parts of citizens arises from a duty to support institutions necessary to satisfy human rights, it might try to justify enforcement. On the other hand, as Gene Sharp writes, the "withdrawal of support" envisaged in Gandhi's practice of *satyagraha* was supposed to "be in proportion to 'their ability to preserve order in the social structure' without the assistance of the ruler" (Sharp 2006, 85). If Civil Subversion follows this principle and commits credibly to satisfying human rights for the secessionist population through its parallel institutions, then it brings into question the state's justification for taxing the same individuals. This is, of course, provided that the secessionists do not compromise the ability of the original state to maintain human rights protections among the residual population or violate other justice-based duties, for instance by withdrawing a much wealthier part of the state and leaving the remainder uncompensated and impoverished (cf. Caney 1997, 370–371; Moore 2015, 128–134). Where this is not the case (or where, per Moore's analysis, duties of reciprocity and distributive justice are satisfied by means of resource transfers (Moore 2015, 128–134)) and provided just institutions are probable in both the residual and the secessionist states, secessionists might justifiably levy funds through contributions from their "home" population in order to support their own ability to satisfy human rights requirements without providing the state with an obvious human rights–based pretext for action against them.

States versus Subversives

I am assuming that if secessionists mobilize enough people behind a strategy of Civil Subversion within a continuous territorial space, then it could effect a critical reduction in the power of the state within that zone and threaten to replace it with a new source of political authority were it not resisted by state forces of some kind. To defend against such an exigency, the state, we must then suppose, will have to use means that infringe upon the capacities that facilitate the strategy, capacities I have identified with key human rights. Whether involving armed force or not, such means will manifest themselves as a forceful curbing of the exercise of assembly and association rights and those of speech and expression along, perhaps, with some other freedoms such as those of movement. To do so without trading off legitimacy and wider support, the state will need a morally compelling justification. But in what terms can it be expressed?

One line of argument might draw on hints dropped in the major international human rights covenants. In the European Convention on Human Rights (ECHR), for instance, freedom of expression is subject to potential limitations:

The exercise of these freedoms, since it carries with it duties and responsibilities, may be subject to such formalities, conditions, restrictions or penalties as are prescribed by law and are necessary in a democratic society, in the interests of national security, territorial integrity or public safety, for the prevention of disorder or crime, for the protection of health or morals, for the protection of the reputation or rights of others, for preventing the disclosure of information received in confidence, or for maintaining the authority and impartiality of the judiciary.

Freedoms of assembly and association may also be limited by laws if "necessary in a democratic society in the interests of national security or public safety, for the prevention of disorder or crime, [...] and for the protection of the rights and freedoms of others." Further unspecified "lawful restrictions on the exercise of these rights by members of the armed forces, of the police or of the administration of the State" are likewise envisaged. Moreover, article 15 permits "derogation" from obligations defined by the ECHR "[i]n time of war or other public emergency threatening the life of the nation." The same is indicated in International Covenant on Civil and Political Rights (ICCPR), article 4, which permits derogation from rights to free expression (art. 19, para. 2), assembly (art. 21), and association (art. 22). All three may be curtailed by law insofar as doing so is necessary to "national security" and "public order" (arts. 19, 21, & 22) "in a democratic society" (arts. 21, 22). But these hints are perhaps nothing more than that. Cited by a state that faced Civil Subversives who didn't themselves violate human rights or prejudice the prospects for human rights protection, all would beg the question of what humanly significant value was being protected.

If "national security" and "public order" don't mean "human rights protection" or "capacity for protecting human rights," then an alternative grounding for argument is needed, in the absence of which the state would be left with a vital deficit when it comes to legitimizing actions necessary for preserving its territorial integrity. One other possibility is to argue from rights of collective self-determination. It might be claimed that laws and orders issuing from the state that fulfill its obligations vis-à-vis individual human rights (either directly or indirectly) generally mandate coercive enforcement. But among those human rights are included political rights of democratic participation and, whether considered as a collective or an individual right, self-determination. Both rights may be understood to undergird the authority of a democratic state to issue laws and orders that extend beyond human rights insofar as these reflect popular will. It might be argued on this basis that even laws that are indifferent from a human rights point of view in the abstract – that is, neither directly (substantively) entailed by them nor violating them – may realize human rights indirectly insofar as they reflect the will of a particular self-determining, democratic community. Human rights might therefore be cited as ends the protection of which justifies coercive measures necessary to enforce such laws.

The problem with such an argument, however, is that the stronger the subversive threat the secessionists pose, the weaker is the basis for any claim the state might make that it reflects popular self-determination in its present form. The strength of the threat increases, that is, with the strength of dissent concerning the validity of the claim that the state represents a single, legitimate self-determining community. More specifically, if we cash out the respective claims by the opposing agents to express legitimate rights of self-determination, the state can only accurately describe its claim as representing those members of the de jure community who remain once we subtract the dissidents, whether we consider them as an aggregate of individual rights-holders or as a collectivity (a "people"). And then it is hard to see why the rights of the individuals it *can* accurately claim to represent negate the dissidents' rights or can uphold a claim on their obedience or continued membership. The same problem, incidentally, would arise from arguments citing consent. Even if we supposed that states could commonly cite widespread consent as a basis for political legitimacy, the nature of Civil Subversion is such as to give the lie to the claim that consent mandates rule in the contested region and over the population asserting the secessionist claim.

Another argument to consider is that the risk that permitting one movement to effect secession through unresisted Civil Subversion could encourage other nationalist movements to imitate them. If there were enough such imitators, it might be claimed, it could give rise to widespread attempts at state-breaking and if human rights law did not permit actions necessary to prevent this, it could pose a wider danger to political order and, in turn, to human rights protection globally. This argument relies on the empirical assumptions that not only (a) are there many nationalist claims internationally that could in principle express themselves in a desire for secession but that (b) many of them could pose a real threat to their existing rulers by means of Civil Subversion and that (c) this would have disastrous effects on political stability.

Even if we granted (a) for the sake of argument, I presume that if (b) falls then so does (c). There are two reasons to doubt (b). First, for Civil Subversion to be effective to any extent, it requires widespread popular support and energetic mobilization, which I presume narrows the range of probable cases. The cases I am focusing on, moreover, are only those in which secession serves no remedial purposes because human rights compliance is already adequate (or optimal) in the existing state or at least no worse than is to be expected in a breakaway state. So there will be no motive to secede based on escaping human rights violations and injustices. Imitators will have to mobilize sufficient support based purely on the appeal of political independence as such and successful cases are therefore likely to be few and far between. Second, we are interested here only in cases where *neither* side has a human rights–based claim against the other; where either side *does* have such a claim, then it *substantively* guarantees ends that ground a claim against its adversary. A state facing a subversive movement that aimed to reduce human rights protection could justify repressive action against attempts at subversion directly or indirectly on human rights grounds and the secessionists therefore wouldn't be able to secure the shielding that Civil Subversion aims at.[5] This is another reason to think that the claim a state might make of setting a dangerous precedent as grounds to justify repressing a human rights–compliant secessionist opponent would be rather weak: Not many such cases where human rights expectations are equal between opponents are likely to arise that could lay claim to such a precedent. On the other hand, we should be at least equally worried about the example a state might set to others by forcefully suppressing a secessionist movement with strong support and a good record and prospect of human rights compliance.

If the arguments above fail, then the state might be forced as a last resort back onto an argument from territorial rights. But if the foregoing arguments have already been rendered moot, it would have to be a variant that is independent of claims about self-determination as well as individual human rights. For instance, Margaret Moore summarizes (and rejects) one sort of "property" based argument that could serve:

> On a property theory of territory, when we say that state S has territorial rights in land L, what we mean is that the relationship between the state and the land is analogous to the relationship between an individual property-owner and his or her property, and encompasses rights to make decisions about the land, to exclude people from it (control over immigration), and to exploit the resources on the land for the property-owner's instrumental benefit (right to resources). The central relationship is between the state and the land: the relationship of people to both these (the state and territory) is purely contingent. (Moore 2015, 16)

Other ways of trying to anchor the state's territorial claims might invoke historic ties of the residual (i.e. non-secessionist) people to the current extent of the territory as a whole, whether by invoking ancient texts, origin myths, national narratives, or merely a familiar image on the map (for the latter in Ireland, see Bowman 1989; in liberal nationalist political theory, see Meisels 2009; Miller 2007; and, as a critic, Moore 2015, 82–83). But arguments of this sort, I presume, will have relatively weak salience in a political atmosphere dominated by human rights.

POLITICAL CONSEQUENCES

The strategy of Civil Subversion as I envision it attempts to instantiate a peculiarly acute variant of what Alexander Kirschner calls "the paradox of militant democracy: the possibility that efforts to stem the challenges to self-government might themselves lead to the degradation of democratic politics" (Kirschner 2014, 2). The idea that democracies might need to adopt a militant stand in the face of hostile domestic movements arises in response to *anti*-democratic and *illiberal* movements such as those that brought down the Weimar Republic in 1933. In its pure form, however, Civil Subversion creates a similar dilemma by confronting a democratic state with forces that oppose *neither* human rights *nor* democracy, but only that state's specific territorial form and extent. As such, it confronts the general legitimacy claim a state can make on grounds of individual rights with something we might call a concrete particularity problem: whereas the state can claim legitimate authority to rule within *a* territorial unit of *some* shape, it cannot do so in a way that specifies its claim over the entirety of *this particular* territory (cf. Simmons 1979, 31–35; also Laudani 2013; Sitze 2013, xi).

The true potential for subversion that human rights offer is such that even a state that was *wholly* compliant with all possible human rights–based duties could conceivably be forced into retreat by Civil Subversives. Confronted by wholly human rights–compliant secessionists, it would face a dilemma between conceding power and territory, or defending its rule. But if defense requires force (especially *armed* force) it is likely not to be justified either directly or indirectly by human rights. Unless an alternative grounding for sovereign authority can be invoked whose persuasiveness equals that of a human rights–based claim, repressive actions are likely to delegitimize the ruling authority in the disputed territory. As one of Griffith's contemporaries, Robert Lynd, remarked in 1919, the method relies on "a paradoxical belief that [the state] cannot injure [the Subversives] without injuring itself." Even if they couldn't hope to defeat the military means that might be deployed against them, Civil Subversives might therefore "believe that they could defeat the *purpose* of those who make use of the armed force" (in Townshend 2013, 85, my emphasis).

NOTES

1. On the complexity of the varying relationship between civil resistance and armed force, see Roberts 2009, 13–20. Important studies that quantify the effectiveness of nonviolent resistance strategies are Chenoweth and Stephan (2011) and Bailey (2015).
2. Griffith, for instance, opposed strikes for workers' rights in Dublin during 1913, which he thought threatened the unity necessary for promoting his nationalist agenda.
3. See especially ICCPR Arts: 18, 19, 21, & 22. The public freedoms bestowed by these rights are clearly important but so too, arguably, are privacy rights.
4. For comparable claims in the Irish context, see Griffith (1918, 92): "even under the Coercion Act," he wrote, "there is no violation of the law committed by 300 gentlemen meeting in Dublin and recommending the adoption of measures to the Irish people calculated to improve their condition …."
5. Such cases are the focus of a good deal of scholarship in recent years. See, for instance, the work on "militant democracy" by Macklem (2006) and Kirschner (2014).

11

Bearers of Hope: On the Paradox of Nonviolent Action

Cheyney Ryan

> I believe that even amid today's motor bursts and whining bullets, there is still hope for a brighter tomorrow. I believe that wounded justice, lying prostrate on the blood-flowing streets of our nations, can be lifted from this dust of shame to reign supreme among the children of men.
>
> – Martin Luther King, Jr., "Nonviolence and Racial Justice" (1957)

After much deliberation, Martin Luther King, Jr. decided to get arrested. He was needed in the struggle against segregation in Birmingham, Alabama, that had begun in spring 1963. The movement had little money to pay his bail and no one knew what his sentence would be. But something dramatic was needed, so on April 12 he purposefully violated the city's anti-protest injunction and was placed in solitary confinement. It was there he composed a key text in the history of nonviolence, "Letter from a Birmingham Jail," prompted in part by the tepid response his movement was receiving from many of Birmingham's religious leaders.

While King was in jail, James Bevel, a twenty-seven-year-old veteran of civil rights struggles, had another idea. "Most adults felt that segregation was permanent, that it was just that way," Bevel would later say (Bevel 1985). Young people could see other possibilities; they were "bearers of hope." So he would organize Birmingham's children to act as the adults would not, to nonviolently disrupt the institutions of segregation with the aim of being arrested – and thus "fill the jails" in true Gandhian fashion. In his jailhouse epistle, King was writing that sometimes oppressive conditions required "creative tension," i.e. conflict, for a breakthrough. Bevel would do just that by what Newsweek Magazine later dubbed "The Children's Crusade."[1]

Bevel approached his crusade strategically. He started in his words with "the queens of the high schools, the basketball stars, the football stars," to get "the influence and power leaders involved. And then, they in turn got all the other students involved." He enlisted Birmingham's black radio station, WENN, which told students to arrive at the demonstration's meeting place with a toothbrush to be used in jail. Flyers said, "Fight for freedom first then go to school." One young participant, Larry Russell, reflected years later that the disk jockeys called it a "party": "On the broadcast they'd say, 'There's going to be a party Monday night at six at Sixteenth Street Baptist Church, and everybody's invited.' We good old Baptists knew there wasn't going to be any dance." Another, Audrey Faye Hendricks, remembered,

> We started from Sixteenth Street Church. We always sang when we left the church. The singing was like a jubilance. It was a release. And it also gave you calmness and reassurance. I was in jail seven days. We slept in little rooms with bunk beds. We called ourselves Freedom Fighters, Freedom Riders.

"When I told my mother that I wanted to go. She just said, 'Okay,'" Audrey notes. "I was in third grade" (Levine 2000).

Needless to say, some in the African American community were appalled, and there was deep division among movements leaders themselves about such tactics.

PROTEST AND/OR PROVOCATION

The Birmingham action is now seen as a major triumph, a turning point in the civil rights struggle. The tactics of nonviolent direct action were not developed by King and his organization, the Southern Christian Leadership Conference (SCLC). They were pioneered by African American college students, initially under the guidance of James Lawson, a devotee of Gandhi.[2] They were later appropriated by King's wing of the movement. As Clayborne Carson writes, King "had never led a massive campaign of civil disobedience before," on the contrary his previous action had failed. He found that "there were not enough adults prepared to be arrested. So the Children's Crusade turned the tide of the movement" (quoted in Joiner 2013). Birmingham led to the March on Washington later that year, the site of King's "I Have a Dream" speech. It played a central role in pressuring the federal government to pass the landmark 1964 Civil Rights Act; it was instrumental to King's winning the 1964 Nobel Peace Prize.

No one doubted the success of Birmingham. The violence provoked by the actions of demonstrators stirred the nation's conscience. The sight of children facing dogs and hoses provided dramatic images for the front pages of newspapers. Afterward, a surge of nonviolent protest swept the nation, 758 demonstrations in 186 cities in the South alone, with more than 20,000 arrests. Yet they remained controversial. The first day's march, over 1,000 strong, included some just starting elementary school. Seven-year-old Jennifer Fancher was attacked by a charging police dog; others were clubbed by police officers or hit by the flying bricks churned up by the fire hoses trained on them. Malcolm X complained, "Real men don't put their children on the firing line." Critics questioned if such a movement was truly "nonviolent" or just employed violence in a different way. Even sympathizers have termed it "the paradox of nonviolent direct action" (Colaiaco 1986). The problem was exacerbated by the role of children in the Birmingham case. Hence the *irony* of the name, "Children's Crusade" – as the first "Children's Crusade" constituted the manipulation and exploitation of children on a massive scale!

At the time, King himself was ambivalent. Informed of the plans when released from jail, he deferred to others, and for much of the first day's actions remained out of sight. But over time he came to regard Birmingham as a massive affirmation of what nonviolence was all about. Indeed, he chastised those who used it to raise questions about nonviolence itself. It is those questions I explore in this essay.

The Birmingham case was not unique. Others have been larger and more costly. The South African Soweto Uprising of June 1976 involved an estimated 20,000 young people and resulted in the killing of hundreds (some estimate up to 700). The Intifada actions involving young people also resulted in loss of human life. (No children were killed at Birmingham.) Yet Birmingham is more problematic in some respects. Soweto and the Intifada were rather spontaneous, at least compared to Birmingham where much decision and planning by political organizers went into placing young people in harm's way. And Birmingham, unlike these other cases, presented itself as an exercise in disciplined nonviolence, inspired by values like love.

For purposes of discussion, I shall distinguish two issues. One is the role that provoking violence plays in nonviolent politics, and its success. This is an issue for many nonviolent political actions and, as Michael Gross (2015, 252) notes, it is an especially "vexing" one. "Whether a nonviolent campaign may deliberately provoke violence sufficiently extreme to fundamentally transform an adversary's policies is a question that makes theorists uncomfortable." Perhaps this is why so little has been written about it, a surprising fact given its importance to many nonviolent actions. The second issue is enlisting children in such actions. This is an issue specific to the Birmingham case. King's ambivalence, and that of many others, pertains to this second issue, not the first. I address each in the section "The Dilemmas of Birmingham" in this chapter. But first in the next section I explore the political philosophy of King and that part of the civil rights movement he led. I call it "African American prophetic pacifism," to mark its multiple and – to me, at least – intriguing dimensions. It is a politics developed mainly, though not entirely, by African Americans from two sources: the Biblical prophetic tradition, and pacifism, influenced deeply but not solely by Gandhi.

In choosing the Birmingham case I do not mean to privilege American experiences over others. I focus on it for several reasons.

To begin with, I know a lot more about it and its political/philosophical context, in no small part because my own participation in the civil rights movement was what first brought me to the politics of social change, as it did so many of my generation. Individual acts of nonviolent protest have occurred for a long time and were a staple of African American resistance.[3] What was distinctive about King was that he, like Gandhi, perceived them as part of a larger *movement* and planned them accordingly. Not every politics construes itself as aspiring to create a "movement." Despite their importance to the politics of social change, political philosophy has rather little to say about political movements and the normative questions they raise (an exception is discussions of the feminist movement). This is further reason for focusing on King and the civil rights movement. Finally, I think that, for all the official celebrations of him, King has been ignored by the hegemonic academic culture of the Northeast United States. Martin Luther King, Jr., is the only major political figure in American history with a Ph.D. in philosophy, whose writings include discussions of Hegel, Marx, and other canonical political philosophers. (His FBI file takes special interest in his views on Hegelian dialectics!). Yet King the philosopher is invisible to mainstream political philosophy. Its discussion prefers to regard the civil rights era as primarily a story of Supreme Court decisions, made by enlightened privileged white federal judges. The remarkable and wholly unexpected political activism of young African Americans in the South is ignored. Part of the problem is that the civil rights movement and its leaders were deeply religious and saw that fact as central to their activities, while today's academic political philosophy is deeply skeptical of religion. Hence my attention, in what follows, to the role of religion in the most important progressive movement of twentieth-century America.[4]

AFRICAN AMERICAN PROPHETIC PACIFISM

The impact of Gandhi on the African American community is one of the more interesting stories of modern politics, and one of the least known (see Kapur 1992; Slate 2012). It culminates in King, but involves some of the giants of twentieth-century African American politics such as Howard Thurman (see Thurman 1981; 1996), Benjamin Mays (see Jelks 2012), Bayard Rustin (see Anderson 1997; D'Emilio 2004; Rustin 2003), and the aforementioned James Lawson. From the start, the African American community saw Gandhi's achievements as speaking to the conditions of their own community, which many construed as colonial oppression. They were attracted to how its nonviolent politics was attentive to local traditions, especially religious ones, and to how it offered a wide choice of tactics for confronting problems at hand. African American newspapers regularly reported on the Indian independence movement, and a significant number of black leaders journeyed to India to witness it firsthand (a major task in the days of steamships!). In 1935, Thurman, the twentieth century's most important African American theologian, made a "pilgrimage of friendship" to India to meet Gandhi, the upshot of which he said changed his life forever (see Chabot 2011; Dixie 2011; Scalmer 2011).

Gandhi urged Thurman to develop a new brand of American Christianity to stress social justice themes. He remarked, "[I]t may be through the

Negroes that the unadulterated message of nonviolence will be delivered to the world." Others that followed included Benjamin Mays, later president of Morehouse College, whose 1936 speech to students introduced a young Martin Luther King, Jr. to nonviolence, and later James Lawson, recently released from prison for draft resistance. The brand of American Christianity they developed would be deeply indebted to the prophetic books of the Hebrew Bible and the prophetic elements of the Christian Gospels. This marks the greatest difference between American nonviolence and that of Gandhi, or Moslem nonviolent figures like Bacha Khan (see Pashtun Times 2016), or Eastern figures like Thich Nhat Hanh (see Hanh 2005). Intellectually, it is evidenced in the powerful influence Martin Buber had on King's thinking, most clearly in his "Letter from a Birmingham Jail." Politically, it was evidenced in King's strong personal bond with Rabbi Abraham Joshua Heschel, whose masterpiece, *The Prophets*, King carried with him the day he was assassinated.

King spoke of his politics as "true pacifism," and his wing of the civil rights movement occupies a central place in the story of American pacifism and pacifism generally. Established pacifist figures had a major influence on King and his movement, especially in its formative years. Later, King championed pacifist views on international conflict in becoming, at the time he was assassinated, America's most prominent opponent of the Vietnam War. But King's "true pacifism" had its own unique inflection, best explored by relating it to the pacifist tradition more generally.

Personal Pacifism

> "Too long has our beloved Southland been bogged down in a tragic effort to live in monologue rather than dialogue."
>
> – Martin Luther King, Jr., "Letter from Birmingham Jail" (1963a)

Western pacifism has two main strands that can be distinguished both philosophically and historically (see Ryan 2013; 2014). They have often had little to do with each other despite being lumped under the same term. Both condemn violence, for reasons to be noted, but they have differed sharply on the question of *power*. A key to King's success is how he mixed together the two traditions of pacifism, leading to a novel conception of nonviolent power.

But first let me speak to the two types of pacifism (see Brock 1972; 1999; 1991; Cortright 2008).

One type of pacifism I call *personal* pacifism. It opposes killing as a personal act, hence it opposes any social practices involving that act, such as war, but also practices such as capital punishment. This pacifism arose with the first Christians; it acquired a shadowy existence after Augustine and Christian just war theory, then it reemerged with the Protestant Reformation in the so-called left wing of that movement with groups like the Mennonites and later the

Quakers. It is found in the work of Tolstoy, the most prominent late nineteenth-century pacifist. It almost always has a religious coloring.[5]

Before the twentieth century, proponents of this view called it "*nonresistance.*" ("Pacifism" is an early twentieth-century term that initially denoted opposition to war, only later did it acquire more specific connotations.) This pacifism is distinguished by its deep suspicion of power: its stigma on killing is a rejection of violence, but also a rejection of the Godlike power people are seen as claiming in the taking of human life – a power properly reserved for God alone. This same rejection of claims to Godlike power also informed personal pacifism's rejection of slavery. This suspicion of power led to a suspicion of the political realm generally, so that, with a few exceptions like the Quakers, the politics of personal pacifism has been a politics of personal withdrawal from the political realm, i.e. an anti-politics.

King rejected personal pacifism's anti-power, anti-political stance. But he was deeply influenced by some of its views, especially those grounded in the prophetic tradition.

One involved its privileging of *dialogue*, to the point of equating the dialogic with the peaceful, the monologic with the warlike. The religious story goes like this: speaking is the most Godly endeavor, and the most creative – as marked by God's speaking creation into being; human beings share in this through the power of the word. Dialogue is something further. On one reading of the story, humanity was not complete until God created a second being, Eve, which God did from the concern that Adam have someone to converse with – the worry was that, left by himself, Adam might delude himself that *he* was God (see Zornberg 2011). Dialogue, thus construed, is not just a creative collaboration, it has connotations of questioning, even challenging. As Buber writes, "The Thou confronts me": humans need another human, a Thou, "so that man will not imagine that he, like God, has no partner," in the words of Rashi. A key influence on King was the prophet Jeremiah, for whom the tension of dialogue and power was a focal concern. Power numbs us to the claims of other people: in placing ourselves above others, in refusing to face them as equals, we refuse all speaking with them, and, most importantly, refuse all answering to them. (As Thomas Merton [1971a] wrote, "The language of the war-maker is self-enclosed in finality.") Monologue is thus construed as a failure of responsiveness, hence a failure of responsibility. Little wonder, then, that the story of Cain and Abel identifies the first murder with the (non)-response: "Who, me?"

Another prophetic influence involved the construal of *justice*. The test of justice is the treatment of the powerless, symbolized in this tradition by "the widow, the orphan, the fugitive slave." It does not matter how wealthy society is or how well the average person does if those at the bottom are abused. Justice is the dialogue of welcoming the powerless into society, hence its strong associations with hospitality. "If a slave has taken refuge with you, do not hand them over to their master. Let them live among you wherever they like and in whatever town they choose" (Deuteronomy 23:15–16). The work of justice means speaking for the powerless, the voiceless, bringing their suffering, especially their grief, to public expression. Almost all these themes resonated throughout the words and deeds of the nineteenth-century Abolitionist movement, where talk of welcoming the fugitive slave could be taken literally. They speak to their place in King as well, but for some words on the other tradition of pacifism.

Political Pacifism

The other type of pacifism I call *political* pacifism. Its focus is not killing as an act but war as a social practice. Specifically, it opposes what the early political pacifist Charles Sumner called the "war system," by which is meant the practices of killing and destruction that characterize war making, and the practices of mobilizing human and material resources to those ends that characterize war building. Both personal pacifism and political pacifism oppose war unconditionally, but their logics differ. The personal pacifist is opposed to killing *per se*, and hence opposed to any endeavors involving it, such as war or capital punishment. By contrast, the political pacifist is like death penalty opponents who object to the *kind* of killing the practice involves: its social organization, accompanying rituals, etc. But just as such death penalty opponents may permit killing in other circumstances, political pacifists may permit it as well – in personal self-defense, say. So, personal pacifism's approach is from the bottom up while political pacifism's approach is from the top down. Historically, political pacifism's origins are more recent and secular. It first emerged in the Enlightenment, though it is anticipated by figures like Erasmus. It coalesced after the Napoleonic wars when the global nature of that conflict convinced people that war was not a product of personal whims or stupidity but possessed a structure all its own, and as such required a more systematic response.

I speak of the critique of war, but political pacifism as it arose in the United States was intimately connected with the critique of other oppressive systems, especially slavery. America's first important radical pacifist was also its first important white radical abolitionist, William Lloyd Garrison, for whom the "war system" and the "slave system" were part of the same problem. This remained a staple of antiracist thinking. The formal end of the American Civil War meant the end of war between regions but inaugurated the almost century of low-intensity warfare that constituted the era of segregation, whose centerpiece was the terrorist tactic of lynching.

Like personal pacifism, political pacifism privileges both violence and power, but with a structural emphasis. War is both a collective act of violence and a collective exercise of power. War's violence requires instruments of violence, so the story of war is one of changing technology, and its exercise of power requires agencies of power, to mobilize and deploy the human and material resources for war, so the story of war is also one of changing organizations. (In recent centuries, the principal agent of war has been the state, which is why political pacifism has often been associated with anarchism.) Slavery, too, is a system of both violence and power. Clausewitz claimed the aim of war was to break the will of the enemy, achieving dominance – absolute power over the other – through the infliction of violence. This describes war between states, but, with slight modification, domination through violence also describes the relation of masters and slaves. This suggests why, once the institution of slavery was questioned, it was just a matter of time until the institution of war was questioned as well.

War was critiqued on two grounds. One was its *injustice*: both war making, the act of war itself, and war building, the ongoing preparations for war, were taken to violate the rights of individuals and groups. A special focus in the nineteenth century was the institution of national conscription, which political pacifism identified as a type of enslavement at the heart of war. But another worry was captured in the term, *inhumanity*: war was seen as taking on a life of its own, detaching itself from all human agency in ways that rendered it indifferent to all limits on warfare. (Readers may note that Marx's critique of capitalism also contains both claims: capitalism is a system of injustice, insofar as one class exploits another, but also a system of inhumanity, insofar as economic relations acquire a life of their own that place everybody, regardless of class, at their mercy.)

Personal pacifism's focus is interpersonal; in the words of Buber "Justice begins with you and me." Political pacifism's focus is structural, but the problem of inhumanity resonates with prophetic concerns. The idea that the creations of human beings, in this case a social system, escape their control in ways that eventually dominate them evokes the prophetic critique of *idolatry*. (This is exactly the language Marx uses to characterize humanity's relation to capital, starting with money.) So too does the notion that all of this undermines humanity's capacity for responsibility, hence overthrowing it means reclaiming the very capacity for moral agency.

What Does Peacemaking Look Like?

Personal pacifism's answer is simple. Opposing war means not killing oneself, just as opposing slavery means not enslaving another oneself; in the conditions of the time, as I've noted, both meant detaching oneself from society. But things are more complicated for political pacifism, which doubts one can individually defect from the system, and anyway feels there is an imperative to transform the system. Abolitionism showed that people can hold the same judgment of a system but still disagree sharply on what to do about it. All abolitionists felt that slavery was absolutely immoral, but some felt that the solution lay in legislative action, others public education, others armed insurrection, etc. Similarly, political pacifists have all judged war absolutely immoral, but have had the same range of responses to ending it (except for armed insurrection, of course).

How Does One Absolutely Oppose a System, From Within?
I have noted King's stress on creating a political movement, and I think it can be understood as a response to this problem. In the words of Thomas Merton (1971b), "Nonviolence must be aimed above all at the transformation of the present state of the world. But this poses enormous problems – for if nonviolence is too political it becomes drawn into the power struggle and identified with one side or another in that struggle, while if it is totally apolitical it runs the risk of being ineffective or at best merely symbolic." A political movement does not just aim at radical transformation, for King the creation of a "Beloved Community" constituted by the mutuality of dialogue; it works to realize such a community within its own movement. In the words of Gandhi, it works to "Be the change."

But this just sharpens the problem posed by Birmingham: Was engaging children, as it did, truly realizing the kind of "Beloved Community" the nonviolent movement claimed to be?

Dialogic Power

Gandhi convinced King that power and nonviolence were compatible. Indeed, they required each other. "Power without love is reckless and abusive, and love without power is sentimental and anemic. Power at its best is love implementing the demands of justice, and justice at its best is power correcting everything that stands against love" (King 1967). Over time, King's stress on power increased due to the frustrations he encountered. "Lamentably, it is an historical fact that privileged groups seldom give up their privileges voluntarily," he wrote in "Letter from a Birmingham Jail." "We know through painful experience that freedom is never voluntarily given up by the oppressor; it must be demanded by the oppressed." The challenge was to fashion a *kind* of power truthful to nonviolence.

Nonviolence aims at transforming the opponent, not defeating them. King hewed to the religious notion that the real enemy is the sin, not the sinner, but he construed this in structural terms. The enemy is the social system of racism, or that system most exemplified by racism, which, in its inhumanity, victimizes all its members. The question, then, is our relation *to* that system. The relation of white people to it differed mainly by degrees. The racist policemen, like those encountered in Birmingham, were deeply implicated in it, but white liberals were also implicated in it insofar as they did nothing to challenge it but stood by silently. Transformation of the opponent, then, meant redefining their relation to that evil system.

Nonviolence aims to do this by what may be termed *dialogic* power. How should it be understood? Proponents of nonviolence conceive it as forceful, but not coercive. They mean by this that nonviolence aims to transform the opponent from the inside, as it were. The language of "awakening" is important here, as in "awakening" people to their conscience, to their better selves, etc., marking the fact that, like the Biblical prophet, nonviolence does not preach entirely new values so much as aims to call people back to those they already hold but fail to enact. The language of "creativity" is also important, but the picture of creativity is one of realizing possibilities already there, in the words of Buber, "calling forth" the "work" through acts that involve both "sacrifice" and "risk" (Buber 1958, 16). Talk of creatively awakening people to their better selves helps explain the connection drawn by this tradition between nonviolence and forgiveness, insofar as we may forgive another in the hope that, by forgiving them, we will inspire them to change themselves.

But nonviolent direct action has an element of forcefulness forgiveness lacks. All dialogue for the prophetic view involves confrontation, but nonviolence privileges this. This is most evident in the prominent role it accords to *shame.*

"The nonviolent resister must often express his protest through noncooperation or boycotts, but he realizes that these are not ends themselves; they are merely means to awaken a sense of moral shame in the opponent." King insisted the goal was not to defeat opponents or humiliate them but "to awaken a sense of shame within the oppressor and challenge his false sense of superiority." And the shame is not just a personal one, but a public one. Not all civil disobedience aims at public exposure. Henry David Thoreau's refusal to pay his taxes and going to jail in protest of slavery was a private act of conscience. And not all instances of nonviolent direct action make shaming prominent. Rosa Parks' refusal to take her place on a segregated bus eventually drew public attention to the shameful practice but it didn't seek to shame the immediate opponent. In Birmingham, by contrast, the whole *point* of involving children was eliciting shame, revealing the injustice of the system and how it was willing to treat even the weakest and most vulnerable.

A crucial distinction here is between shame and humiliation. It bears on the question of power. Humiliating others seems to involve an assertion of power over them, presuming and promoting a sense of superiority over another that King identifies with racism. The power differential means that most if not all systems of oppression are, among other things, constant exercises in humiliation. Shaming, at least as King understands it, aims at puncturing a false sense of superiority that comes with power, leveling the playing field to allow for true face-to-face encounters. Shame, at least as King understands it, aims to awaken people to their better selves, humiliation involves no such reference. It does not speak to the other's integrity so much as attack their dignity.

Did nonviolence succeed in this regard? There are a few instances, but not many, where it had this impact on its immediate opponents. There is little evidence in the Birmingham case that police officials experienced any transformation by the actions they encountered. But the "opponent" included all those implicated in the racist system, and here it succeeded. King rightly remarked that the civil rights movement did more to awaken white people to the shame of segregation than anything in the previous hundred years. Our concern is not with the success of such tactics, but with their ethics.

THE DILEMMAS OF BIRMINGHAM

No one expected the Birmingham campaign to be easy given the city's history of extraordinary racial violence. The city was nicknamed "Bombingham" for its incidents of white bombing of black houses and establishments. One neighborhood of more affluent African American homes was called "Dynamite Hill." Newspapers deemed it "The South's Johannesburg."

More than anywhere else, King's movement assumed that Birmingham would bring violence and almost certainly deaths.

The Birmingham action sputtered at the start in failing to mobilize significant numbers for direct action. News coverage diminished to the point the press was starting to leave town. This is what prompted King's symbolic act of going to jail. The day he did so, James Bevel arrived from Mississippi. From the start, Bevel saw young people as a resource for the movement. He named his action "D-Day." That morning, one thousand elementary school and high school students, briefly trained in dealing with police tactics, assembled in churches. Just after noon, they marched in disciplined waves to City Hall and the downtown business district. Six hundred were arrested. The next day, since jails were full, police chief Bull Connor decided to stop the marches forcibly rather than make arrests. As television cameras rolled, billy clubs, fire hoses, and dogs were unleashed on the marchers. Then, and in subsequent days, national and international media carried images of police clubbing black children and firemen hosing them with jets of water powerful enough to strip the bark off trees at one hundred feet. As the days passed, more than one thousand students were arrested while pressure increased on civic leaders to resolve the crisis. Eventually, an accord was reached calling for desegregation of lunch counters, restrooms, and drinking fountains and more economic opportunities for African Americans. Marian Wright Edelman, founder and president of the Children's Defense Fund, later wrote, "Pictures of the bravery and determination of the Birmingham children as they faced the brutal fire hoses and vicious police dogs were splashed on the front pages of newspapers all across America and helped turn the tide of public opinion in support of the civil rights movement's fight for justice" (Joiner 2013).

The Question of Provocation

I've noted Michael Gross's remark that the problem of provocation is especially vexing for nonviolence. He contrasts it with the guerrilla war strategy of employing innocent human shields to discourage a violent response. Such shielding, if successful, brings no violence, whereas "backfire," his term for nonviolent provocation, succeeds only if it brings such violence. "Herein lies the paradox and moral challenge of a campaign that professes nonviolence" (Gross 2015, 241). As Gross notes, much rests on the kind of provocation involved – this was clearly an issue with rock throwing in the Intifada. He also notes that there is a proportionality consideration, akin to just war principles: anticipating and inviting a violent response need not mean inviting a deadly one.

Here I focus on the Birmingham case. Others are quite different, though Birmingham shares much with the other canonical case of nonviolent protest inviting violence, Gandhi's "Salt March." Let me suggest some responses to the criticism of this tactic as conducted here.

The first point to stress is that, in the Birmingham case, the actions of demonstrators were perfectly *legal*. And not just legal, most were the sort of actions that in other circumstances would be innocuous, or certainly not cause for alarm. People might notice a silent march, but no one would pay special notice to people eating at a lunch counter, shopping at a clothing store, or registering to vote – the kind of actions deemed "provocations" by civil rights opponents and some white liberals. During the civil rights years, other groups sometimes did engage in actions that, while legal, were still alarming. The Black Panther Party first achieved prominence carrying firearms into the lobby of the California state capital. Their doing so was actually legal at the time (it did not remain so very long!), but it was also outrageous and meant to be so. In contrast, the actions of King and his allies were chosen for their normalcy. Their conception of nonviolence excluded things like rock throwing. So the issue here is not the abstract one, "Doing some action X that provokes some violent response Y," but "Doing a perfectly legal/normal action X etc."

Suppose I perform an act I have every right to do, but it leads someone – call them P – to commit violence against me. In what sense have I "provoked" it? Since the language of provocation is so often used in victim blaming, consider this parallel case:

> If a woman wears a dress she has every right to wear, and it leads P to rape her, has she "provoked" the rape?[6] This is a common excuse for rape. The very language serves to deny any agency to the aggressor, suggesting that, while the woman wore the dress as a matter of full volition, her attacker was somehow driven to do it by her actions – which is nonsense. Now suppose she had every right to wear the dress she did, but that dress violated what P took to be standards of propriety, and this led him to conclude she was inviting his actions. I assume this is the thought at work when someone says of a rape, "She was asking for it." So too, white racists might say of an attack on a peaceful law-abiding demonstration, "They were asking for it." The problem, of course, is that one person's "standards of propriety" ("Proper women don't dress that way," "Proper Negroes don't act that way") is another person's cultural oppression ("Stay in your place!"). I can imagine a friend of the woman suggesting it is *imprudent* to wear a dress that might lead men to respond this way, given sexist standards, just as some felt the civil rights demonstrators were imprudent in acting as they did, given racist standards. But anything more suggests an endorsement of the "standards of propriety" that, in the civil

rights case, demonstrators meant to challenge (and which the woman, in my example, might mean to challenge).

But what if someone knows not just that their actions could generate a harsh response, but takes them with the *aim* of generating such a response? This is the parallel to "backfire" strategies, in Gross's terms.

So consider another case, drawn from real life.

When I first started teaching, we had a ferocious sexist in the department named Frank. He was opposed to the whole idea of women in philosophy and made it clear that if the department ever hired one he would make her life miserable. Eventually, due to administrative pressure, the department hired its first woman. As things progressed, whenever she spoke up in department meetings, Frank responded with nasty sexist comments, sometimes subtle, sometimes not. Often, within her hearing, he would refer to her as "Little Bo Peep." He was a generally obnoxious man, and some of my colleagues dismissed his ugly abusive behavior as "That's just Frank!" But I remember feeling that dismissing his behavior as personal idiosyncrasy was mistaken. People say nasty things all the time in department meetings with no larger message. Frank's actions were not just obnoxious, they *did* send a message, and a political one: "You are not the type of person that belongs in this profession, or academia generally. I will keep reminding you of this in ways you can do nothing about, because most others agree with me or basically don't care."

The situation was intolerable, but there was no way to address it short of outside intervention. One day we learned the dean of the college would be attending the department meeting. It seemed that if he witnessed Frank's behavior he might do something to stop it, but it was also clear that Frank might act to restrain himself on this occasion, for fear of being found out.

I spoke with my woman colleague beforehand. I learned she intended to say precisely those things most likely to elicit Frank's sexist rants, with the aim of exposing him before the dean. She intended a "backfire" strategy, and it succeeded. (My sole contribution was to interrupt Frank at some point to say that I was more interested in hearing from my woman colleague.) Frank launched into one of his sexist tirades, stunning the dean at first, then leading him to take appropriate action. (Frank was later forced into retirement.)

Here, like Birmingham, the aim was to provoke a harsh response. It is crucial that what was provoked was not an isolated individual act but an instance of a larger pattern, itself expressing entrenched practices of domination/inequality (sexism, in the one case, racism, in the other). Also important is that the practices in question were sustained by an element of duplicity: Frank would engage in his sexist actions in some contexts but not others, just as white racists engaged in their actions in some contexts but not ones witnessed by the world at large. Not all systems of oppression have this duplicity, but those that do pose special challenges in confronting them. The duplicity is not just individual; it requires a larger context of support or at least passivity to be sustained. I learned afterward that the department head, Don, had counseled Frank to keep his temper when the dean came. He claimed not to be supportive of Frank's sexism, but rather wanted to keep it "in the department." Exactly the same logic inspired white moderates in the South to counsel more racist elements to "behave themselves" when outsiders were around. Finally, it's important that in both cases the protesters by protesting were exercising agency of a type that the system they confronted aimed to undermine.

Critics of the Birmingham actions alleged there was something paradoxical, at worst hypocritical, in opposing racist violence with actions aimed at provoking that violence. I don't see why. In my department case, my woman colleague opposed sexist practices generally, and Frank's sexism in particular. Her strategy for doing so was to provoke that very behavior. I don't see anything paradoxical or hypocritical about this. There might be questions if she'd done it by hurling sexist epithets at him, just as there might be questions if the Birmingham protesters had elicited violence by engaging in violence themselves. But this is precisely what neither did. To me, the point is sufficiently obvious that I can understand King's dismissive attitude to white liberal concerns. (After the department encounter, Don complained to me about all the "unpleasantness" provoked in the department meeting. I took this to signify his cluelessness about the larger problem.)

The cases are dissimilar in an important respect. In the department case, the sexist diatribes came from an ordinary faculty member, while in the Birmingham case the racist violence came from official figures who were not just reacting to perfectly legal actions, but in a manner *itself* illegal. This, too, sent a message – that African Americans could expect to be treated by figures of authority that ignored all the standard constraints on authority. It is as if my female colleague experienced sexist diatribes every time she went to the dean's office (when no one could hear it), and was subjected to the most arbitrary sanctions afterward. (I am sure this happened to many women, but not in this case.) The idea that someone bringing this to public light by provoking it would be acting paradoxically, or hypocritically, strikes me as absurd.

I've assumed that the actions of the protesters were perfectly legal, but complications could arise. Almost always, protesters were instructed by local police officers to desist. But this did not make their actions illegal; it only made them contrary to the wishes of the local police. More serious questions arose when demonstrators were faced with court-ordered injunctions against proceeding. This typically led to disagreement among activists, with some feeling they should be ignored, others feeling things should be kept in abeyance until such court orders could be legally challenged. Finally, complications arose from the United States' federal system, in which local courts/officials and federal courts/officials could disagree. This raises important issues about the logic of civil disobedience, but it's important not to focus on the actions of demonstrators alone. Whether or not protesters acted entirely legally, the white power structure clearly responded *illegally* – employing tactics, that is, that were inappropriate regardless of the legality of protesters' actions. This is precisely why officials did not want their responses to be seen. This likens things to the "She was asking for it" rape case. If a protester breaks the law, they can hardly blame the authorities for arresting them. But they can certainly blame the authorities for flouting the law in their response.

The Question of Children

But What of Engaging Children *in Such Protests?*

I don't agree with all aspects of this tactic, principally with the exceptional youth of some of the demonstrators. I also don't agree with some of the arguments James Bevel gave at the time. He noted that African Americans as young as 17 were being drafted to fight and die in Vietnam, "if a young person could go to Vietnam and engage in war, then a person certainly the same age and younger could engage in a nonviolent war at home" (Bevel 1985). This might show that someone is hypocritical who supports youngsters fighting in Vietnam but not for civil rights. But both may be exploitative of young people. Rather than justify it in full, let me suggest why engaging children seemed reasonable, despite the obvious worries, and in so doing say something about why civil rights leaders responded to white liberal criticism with annoyance.

Starting with the Supreme Court decision *Brown vs. Board of Education* (1954), judging segregated public education unconstitutional, children were at the center of desegregation struggles.[7] But that decision contained a crucial ambivalence. It outlawed segregation, but then ruled that desegregation in public schools should proceed "with all deliberate speed." History threatened to repeat itself: from the end of the Civil War, in matters of race, history showed that court decisions by themselves meant nothing. The so-called Civil War Amendments, abolishing slavery and granting former slaves rights like equal protection under the law, were ignored for a century. Telling the racist power structure to desegregate "with all deliberate speed" could mean another century of inaction. (If anyone thinks the achievement of civil rights for African Americans was inevitable, consider that Native Americans have yet to receive their full civil rights.) The civil rights movement was a response to this fact.

The white power structure responded to the Brown decision by immediately announcing its refusal to comply. In time, this was termed the policy of "Massive Resistance," which involved explicit statements that any attempts to force compliance would be met with armed resistance. White liberals immediately issued cautionary statements about not "provoking" violence. When actions were initiated to compel the University of Alabama to admit an African American student, Life Magazine branded it a "new provocation by an organization which inflames the Negroes' most bitter enemies," one that could only "alienate" their supporters. Leading liberal figures like Arthur Schlesinger, Jr. called for a two-year "moratorium" on any actions designed to implement the Brown decision (see Polsgrove 2001).

The "provocation" issue had long been central to the case for segregation. The Supreme Court decision legalizing segregation, *Plessy vs. Ferguson* (1896), which Brown overruled, argued that races must be separated since mixing them would provoke violence. After Brown, children were on the firing line. In September 1957, the governor of Arkansas blatantly defied a federal order to integrate Central High School in Little Rock, Arkansas. First, he called out the National Guard to prevent nine young African American students, one as young as fifteen, from entering the school, then he quickly withdrew the Guard, leaving them at the mercy of the angry mob he'd whipped up. The crisis was only resolved, if that is the right word, when President Eisenhower sent the 101st Airborne Infantry to occupy Little Rock and designated federal marshals to escort the children through the angry crowds.

Many northern liberals protested vehemently at placing children at risk. They included Hannah Arendt, one of the leading liberal intellectuals in America. "Under no circumstances would I expose my child to conditions which made it appear as though it wanted to push its way into a group it was not wanted," she wrote. She stated that doing so would only "strip the child" of "personal pride, essential for personal integrity." "If I were a Negro mother in the South, I would feel that Supreme Court ruling, unwillingly but unavoidably, has put my child into a more humiliating position than it had been in before." Such actions, she concluded, forced children to bear the brunt of adult political zeal.[8]

There is much nonsense in these remarks, commonly attributed now to Arendt's ignorance of American race relations. Suffering abuse from an angry white mob could not have been the most pleasant experience for African American children. But the idea that it would "strip" them of a personal pride they otherwise possessed, and humiliate them more than they were already humiliated, betrays an indifference to the impact of white racism. It also suggests a complete ignorance of the *Brown vs. Board of Education* decision. For the heart of that decision was a series of psychological studies showing that segregation in public education undermined an African American child's most basic sense of self-worth, in ways that could damage them the rest of their lives.

Arendt's views were not entirely without merit. The parents of those African American children reflected seriously on their actions, as evidenced in the fact that only some chose to put their children in that situation. So, there were prudential concerns here. But the problem with saying that African American children were somehow used in being sent to integrated schools, or that it was improper to send them there because of the violence it might provoke, is that *any* act of integration (in schools, and most other institutions) could provoke this response, so sparing children from it meant renouncing the goal of integration itself. This is different from the claim that young people are already being subjected to violence (though they were); it is not quite the claim that the violence provoked is "worth it." But I think it explains the impatience with white liberal critics, whose reasons for counseling "Go slow!" amounted to an argument to "Stop!"

A final note is that many of the young people involved in the Birmingham protests have since been interviewed, and none voice doubts about their actions. Quite the contrary, they all evidence pride. Legitimate questions can be raised about how accurate these studies are, e.g. how many views have been sampled, and were they chosen for their positive viewpoint. By contrast, for example, at least one of the children involved in the Little Rock incident, Elizabeth Eckford, voiced great ambivalence about it later on. While she did participate in anniversary celebrations later on, she struggled mightily with the personal impact of the experience, and said that while she was pleased to have done it once she wouldn't do it over again.

CODA: BIRMINGHAM SUNDAY

Birmingham was a turning point in the civil rights struggle. It may have succeeded partly because, as conducted, some of the most serious doubts that can be raised about nonviolent provocation could be met. But that is just to say that it may provide a model of what an ethically satisfactory action of this type should look like. Also, there was a degree of sheer luck, insofar as the violence provoked could have been much worse. The fire hoses trained on children could have caused permanent disability or death. The New York Times' chief war correspondent, R.W. Apple, later said that none of the war zones he covered upset or frightened him as much as Birmingham. (The night the crisis was resolved, an explosive went off near the *Gaston Motel* room where King and SCLC leaders had stayed, and the next day the home of King's brother Alfred Daniel King was bombed.) The response to the Birmingham actions might have been quite different if its human costs had been much higher.

And those costs got even higher. Four months after the Birmingham actions, and just weeks after King's "I Have a Dream," Ku Klux Klan members bombed the Sunday morning service at Birmingham's Sixteenth Street Baptist Church. Four young girls were murdered: Addie Mae Collins, Carol Denise McNair, Cynthia Diane Wesley, and Carole Robertson. Martin Luther King, Jr. delivered the eulogy at the joint funeral of three of the victims. Drawing on the text, "A little child shall lead them," he assured those gathered there that the girls had not died in vain:

> They are the martyred heroines of a holy crusade for freedom and human dignity. And so this afternoon in a real sense they have something to say to each of us in their death. They have something to say to every politician who has fed his constituents with the stale bread of hatred and the spoiled meat of racism. They have something to say to all those who have passively accepted the evil system of segregation and who have stood on the sidelines in a mighty struggle for justice.
>
> They say to each of us, black and white alike, that we must substitute courage for caution. They say to us that we must be concerned not merely about who murdered them, but about the system, the way of life, the philosophy which produced the

murderers. Their death says to us that we must work passionately and unrelentingly for the realization of the American dream. (King 1963b)

Apologists for the bombing said it would never have occurred without the provocation of the African American struggle for civil rights.

NOTES

I am indebted to the editors of this volume and an anonymous reviewer for comments and improvement. For a discussion of the ethical problems raised by other types of nonviolent action, see Ryan 1994.

1. Excellent discussions can be found in Branch (1999), Garrow (2004), Gilbreath (2013), Halberstam (2012), McWhorter (2013), and Rieder (2014).
2. See Carson (1995); Hogan (2009).
3. See the work of A. Philip Randolph, called, before King, the "American Gandhi" (Anderson 1973; Bynum 2010).
4. Excellent discussions of the role of religion in the civil rights movement are found in Chapel (2005), Marsh (2004; 2008), and Slessarev-Jamir (2011).
5. The leading American personal pacifists of our times are John Howard Yoder (see Yoder 1994) and Stanley Hauerwas (see Hauerwas 1991).
6. I am uncomfortable with the phrase, "leads P to rape her . . .," I can't think of a better way to put it.
7. There are excellent studies of Brown in Kluger (2004) and Patterson (2002).
8. Arendt's reactionary views on the civil rights movement are increasingly a topic of discussion. She rejected the Brown versus Board of Education decision, for example, on the grounds that education was part of the private sphere, like the family, thus outside the sphere of rights and freedoms appropriate to the public, political sphere. She was apparently unfamiliar with the institution of public education. See Gines (2014) and Hinze (2009).

HOSTAGE TAKING AND PRISONERS

12

A Cooperative Globalist Approach to the Hostage Dilemma

Ariel Colonomos

Since the early years of the twenty-first century, hostage taking has become an important concern, part of a worldwide confrontation between states and non-state actors. Although according to international humanitarian law (chapter 32, rule 96, Henckaerts and Donswald-Beck 2005: 334–336) hostage taking cannot be considered a legal or justifiable means of warfare, the responses to the phenomenon also pose several problems, which this chapter aims to address.

Hostage taking involves the use of force. In contemporary international politics, as I argue in this chapter, it is extremely disruptive and unduly threatens the lives of both civilians and soldiers. The practice also imposes dilemmas on those who are blackmailed or from whom a ransom is demanded. This chapter focuses on responses to hostage takers. It argues for a "cooperative" approach to the dilemmas arising from hostage taking: States should make compromises with hostage takers to the extent that this is possible, and should also cooperate with other members of the international society of states to which hostage taking poses a threat. Finally, if the use of force is an option, it should always be used only as a last resort and if it stands a good chance of saving hostages' lives.

This chapter thus rebuts the widespread normative claim that states whose citizens have been abducted are solely responsible for freeing them and are thereby authorized to decide how to react to hostage taking (the sovereignist approach). It also rejects the policy of refusing to negotiate with hostage takers that states usually claim their national interest demands (the realist approach).

As a preliminary, we must emphasize that global hostage taking differs from regular criminal kidnapping in several respects. Kidnapping does not necessarily have an international dimension and therefore should not necessarily trigger the same responses as global hostage taking. Furthermore, kidnapping does not usually have a political dimension. It is essentially motivated by economic factors, namely increasing the personal wealth of the kidnappers, and such increases do not translate into the financing of political action. Moreover, hostages are representatives of larger groups, usually the nation states that are the declared enemies of the hostage takers. Humiliating the hostages serves as a weapon with which the hostage takers seek to publicly harm their enemies.

It is therefore important to define what a "hostage" is. In the next section, I define a hostage as an "unbounded prisoner." Hostages are an anomaly in the international system and violate its norms. Hostages are thus a concern not only for the states of which they are citizens but also for the international system. This is one of the primary reasons why, in order to meet this challenge, the best policy is a global one – an inter-state cooperative policy – that favors negotiation but, as a last resort, can also include some measures that involve the use of force.

In the section "The Fallacies of the Realist and Sovereignist Arguments," I rebut the interest-based argument whereby hostage taking should be countered by a national policy that involves inaction and a refusal to negotiate. I challenge this argument with reference to both efficiency and rights.

In the section "Inter-Temporal Challenges," I show that one of the main challenges facing responses to hostage taking is intertemporality. I argue that a global and coordinated approach is necessary to solve this problem.

In conclusion, I offer some brief guidelines for a global institutional design that would face the challenges of hostage taking and avoid the fallacies of both the sovereignist and realist approaches.

HOSTAGES AS "UNBOUNDED PRISONERS"

The Historical Context

In Greek and Roman times, hostage taking was an activity that could hasten negotiations, ultimately leading to peace. In such a context, hostage taking itself might be viewed as a "soft war" tactic, and accorded some degree of legitimacy. The norms of warfare, however, reflect contextual, political, and historical factors. Clearly, contemporary hostage situations differ significantly from those of the ancient world.

Hostages taken by the Romans were traditionally the sons of foreign rulers. They served as intermediaries between Rome and its enemies who were destined to become its vassals. Although it may seem surprising in the current context, their function was to bring about peace between Rome and its adversaries (Allen 2011). Therefore, hostages were traditionally well-treated. They were usually young, received a Roman education, and in some cases became Roman citizens. Hostages were prisoners who warranted special attention and who performed an important political function. This practice whereby hostages were instruments of diplomacy and pacification persisted throughout the ages (Kosto 2012, 200–226). We even find some traces of it as recently as the nineteenth century, when Abraham Lincoln wrote in 1863 that "a hostage is a person accepted as a pledge for the fulfillment of an agreement concluded between belligerents" (Griffiths 2003, 13).

Commenting on Greek and Roman cases, Gentili and Grotius considered the practice to be acceptable so long as states treated their hostages well (Gentili 1933, 241–243; Grotius 2005, 1289, 1455, 1551–1590). However, they also expressed concern that some hostages would be abused and eventually sold into slavery. In such cases, hostages would be hard to trace, making it very difficult to free them and return them to their home countries. Moreover, Gentili doubted whether non-Christians (i.e. Muslims) could be trusted to treat their prisoners appropriately (Gentili 1933, 395–403). Grotius noted that pirates failed to abide by the laws of war (Grotius 2005, 1626–1632). He also feared that those with whom civilized nations had no commerce and who had different rules and values might sell the free men they captured into slavery (Grotius 2005, 1408–1409).

Concerns about slavery are hardly relevant to contemporary hostage crises, but several further issues that occupied just-war thinkers in previous eras remain as pertinent today as they were in the seventeenth century. What are the implications of hostage taking in an international society of states? What is the difference between a hostage and a prisoner of war, and is the former a subcategory of the latter?

Hostages versus Prisoners of War

Contemporary political hostage taking is usually employed during armed conflict, constituting a form of wartime imprisonment. From a purely functionalist perspective, there appears to be little difference between hostage taking and the legitimate internment of prisoners of war: both types of wartime imprisonment offer a strategic advantage to the detaining forces (Gross 2015, 102–126). From a normative perspective, however, I argue that they are fundamentally different. Prisoners of war (POWs) are kept in custody because their release would be too costly and would impair the strategy of the army that captured them. Hostages, by contrast, are a resource that facilitates their captors' strategy. Moreover, the hostage's life is conditional on the acceptance of his abductors' demands. Taking prisoners is a defensive measure, incapacitating other combatants, and is an alternative to killing them. Taking hostages, by contrast, is an offensive measure. It is seen as more profitable than using direct force against other combatants, whether because they are out of reach or because the payoff would be too small. Threatening to kill the hostages allows their captors to achieve their goals without endangering themselves.

Contemporary leading powers as a rule do not take hostages, and the practice is viewed as an unacceptable violation of international humanitarian law. However, there are exceptions. Since the mid-1980s Israel has abducted two enemy combatants, Sheikh Abdul-Karim Obeid and Mustafa Dirani, because they were seen either as a bargaining chip in the liberation of Ron

Arad, an Israeli Air Force officer captured in Lebanon in 1986, or as a source of information. Nevertheless, contemporary leading powers as a rule do not take hostages, and the practice is viewed as an unacceptable violation of international humanitarian law.

Modern states do take prisoners of war, who enjoy rights that have been established by the Geneva Conventions. Alternatively, states such as the United States and Israel treat captured insurgents as "unlawful combatants," denying them the full set of rights attached to POW status. Neither category neatly fits the definition of a hostage, whose release depends on the transfer of certain resources. If the captors' conditions are not met, the hostage's life may be forfeited.

Hostages can by no means be considered as an instrument of peace as they were, in some specific cases, during Roman times. In modern conflicts between states and non-state actors, hostages are a source of income for their abductors. They are also used as a means to humiliate the collective to which the hostages belong. Movements such as Da'ech (also known as ISIS) use images of their murder as a resource to mobilize their troops.

Most hostage situations occur within international conflicts characterized as "asymmetric," which are the focus of this chapter. Although the notion of "asymmetric warfare" is problematic (Colonomos 2016b), I refer here to those conflicts between states and non-state actors where the former command considerably more resources than the latter. In this context, the weaker parties – non-state actors – exercise power by taking hostages. When demanding ransom, groups such as Da'ech, Al-Qaeda and its affiliates, or Hamas count on the high value their enemies place on human life. For their part, these groups are prepared to suffer major losses in any retaliation against their abductions. Although ISIS, Al-Qaeda, Boko Haram, and Hamas have different strategic goals and in my opinion do not have the same political and moral status, they all share certain political and ideological positions that align them on the same side in the division in the international system between supporters and opponents of what is commonly referred to as "the West," "Western powers," and "Western values." Indeed, a great number of hostages abducted by Islamist movements are Westerners. Although Boko Haram is known for abducting African civilians, it also captures Westerners and is radically opposed to "the West." This antipathy is evident in the fact that the literal translation of its name is "Western education is forbidden."

I suggest that hostage taking is one of the latest forms of contesting the international order imposed by Western states and international organizations. Hostage taking is a violation of international law that can trigger or prolong wars. The phenomenon is a threat to the general structure of an "international society of states" as defined by Hedley Bull in the Grotian tradition, in that it jeopardizes the rules established by states whose goal is to limit the use of force and avoid its escalation (Bull 2002). Subsection 1.3 emphasizes the normative distinction between lawful wartime imprisonment and the taking of hostages, by identifying four significant differences between the two practices. Hostage taking, I argue, is characterized by a lack of boundaries, challenging international peace and order. I go on to argue that it should be treated as amounting to an international crisis, and appropriately addressed by international institutions.

Four Characteristics of Hostages as "Unbounded Prisoners"

Unlike prisoners of war, who are captured within a bounded institutionalized framework, hostages are seized in situations that fall outside the regular and legitimate inter-state conflict setting. Therefore, I refer to hostages as "unbounded prisoners." Hostages, I suggest, share four important features that are highly relevant in any discussion about their rights and the duties of the states that witness their capture.

Time Frame

- A hostage's release is not bounded by time. Unlike a criminal who is sentenced to prison for a set period of time or a prisoner of war who goes free at the end of hostilities, a hostage is held captive for an indefinite period of time. His fate depends exclusively upon the goodwill of his abductors and their negotiations with the agents responsible for the hostage's well-being. These are typically the representatives of the hostage's state or of the private company (e.g. a newspaper or an oil company) with which he is affiliated. States can occasionally decide to exchange prisoners as the war continues. However, the freeing of prisoners is an obligation once the conflict ends. It is also in states' mutual interest to release prisoners of war after the conflict, because at that point such prisoners might be an unnecessary burden. Being a prisoner of war is a temporary status, whereas there is no such certainty in the hostage condition. There is no law that obliges the different parties to make an agreement that, as a consequence, will result in the freeing of the hostage.

Location

- A hostage's location is not territorially bounded. The whereabouts of POWs are well known; they are usually held on enemy soil within well-defined state borders. This is not the case with hostages, who can be moved anywhere, including to other states that are not direct parties to the conflict between the abductors and the country to which the hostages belong. Hostages are in principle very mobile, as their abductors fear military or police intervention to release them. Hostage takers are sometimes members of transnational networks and can therefore benefit from their own connections when relocating their prisoners. This is a very important constraint on those who want to see the hostages freed. Operating in a transnational and regional space gives hostage takers a decisive strategic advantage vis-à-vis states or other entities with whom they want to engage in negotiation. Hostage takers, then, are out of the reach of their opponents, giving them important leverage in the negotiations they want to conduct with their adversaries.

Truth and Transparency

- Hostage taking, as an activity, is not bounded by the rules of truth. States that have POWs in their custody are obliged by international humanitarian law to grant them rights that include the right to visits from the International Committee of the Red Cross (chapter 37, rule 126, Henckaerts and Donswald-Beck, 2005: 448–449). POWs must also be granted the right to communicate with their families. These rights would be meaningless if truth did not prevail as a meta-norm regulating the relations between enemy states. Transparency is a requirement of the legitimate custody of prisoners, and, of course, access to prisoners retroactively leads to the reinforcement of transparency as a norm. This is extremely important because it supports reciprocity in the relations between the warring parties, and truth helps maintain a minimal level of trust in warfare. No such requirements obtain in the case of hostage taking. The secrecy of the whereabouts of hostages is an essential aspect of their condition. There is no reliable information about their medical state or about whether they are being treated decently.
- Nevertheless, credibility is a complicated issue for hostage takers.
  Abductors require channels of communication, so in some instances they must be trustworthy. On the one hand, deception is their main modus operandi; on the other hand, opening up and maintaining channels of negotiation requires them to supply evidence establishing that they hold the hostages in their custody and are attending to their welfare. Consequently, abductors habitually convey images of hostages showing them alive and often displaying a printed newspaper indicating the time when those pictures were taken. As for those attempting to free the hostages, the commitment to truth is also extremely limited. States whose citizens have been captured are not inclined to disclose information about the prisoners, because they consider discretion and secrecy important for the hostages' safety. Admittedly, in some cases, such as securing the release of the Israeli soldier Gilad Shalit in 2011, transparency is essential. Nevertheless, the security doctrine of secrecy is consistent with two political principles, *raison d'Etat* and *Kriegsraison*. *Raison d'Etat* imposes serious limits on transparency because it implies that the state has the right to make decisions that are not bounded by the same

rules that traditionally regulate political behavior. *Kriegsraison* would go even further, allowing states in times of war to violate international law and holding that international law should not be an impediment to achieving fundamental goals indispensable for winning the war (Jochnick and Normand 1994, 64). In the case of hostage taking, secrecy applies to the world of intelligence and detection. Hostage taking belongs to the underworld of warfare. It is also a criminal activity that detectives investigate and in which informants play an important role: hence the need to enforce strict rules of confidentiality.

Law

- Hostages fall into a gray area in international politics. Indeed, hostage taking breaks the rules of inter-state warfare as it includes non-state actors who refuse to abide by the traditional rules of warfare embodied in international humanitarian law and who act without regard for human rights. Non-state actors engage in conflicts that today can be easily internationalized, as other parties to the conflict usually rapidly enter the war zone. Hostages can be either victims of a domestic violation of the law (as in the case of the abduction of American contractors in Iraq after the post-Saddam Iraqi regime had been put in place) or victims of an international conflict (as when Da'ech takes hostages in Syria). It is sometimes difficult to find an appropriate comprehensive legal setting in which hostage takers can be held accountable for their crimes.

In all these ways, hostage taking as an "unbounded" practice is distinct from lawful wartime imprisonment. Section 2 considers the dilemma faced by states whose citizens are held captive by insurgent organizations and criticizes what the United States or other world powers such as, for example, the United Kingdom or Russia consider the most appropriate response to hostage taking, based as it is on the unilateral refusal to negotiate and compromise.

THE FALLACIES OF THE REALIST AND SOVEREIGNIST ARGUMENTS

Those states that refuse to negotiate with hostage takers justify this practice by arguing that it is rational and is dictated by the imperatives of national security. This rationale and this doctrine, I argue, rest on two pillars: realism and sovereignism.

Realism is the doctrine according to which states do and should pursue their national interest in international politics (Beitz 1979; Morgenthau 1948). In the case of hostage taking, both domestic and international security are what defines the national interest of the state whose citizens have been abducted.

If the state were to negotiate, it is argued, this would be interpreted as a sign of weakness by its adversaries, providing them as it does with both resources and incentives to continue pursuing the tactic of hostage taking. Realism is also implicitly based on the rule of sovereignty. Decisions about security pertain to the nation-state, and it comes as no surprise that, traditionally, realists distrust multilateral policy. At best, they consider it irrelevant and sometimes detrimental to states' interests and to the international system of states, which is based upon the rule of sovereignty.

In the case of hostage taking, two tactics are often invoked in order to promote the national interest: avoiding all contacts with the hostage takers, and, eventually, using force against them.

The Approximations of the Realist Calculus

States contending with a hostage crisis are confronted with the following dilemma: Should they enter into negotiations with the abductors, possibly conceding some or all of their demands, or would this undermine their national security? Expressed in this way, the dilemma reflects a "realist" vision of the world that seeks a resolution based on a realistic assessment of the foreseeable consequences. This approach is often adopted by states such as the United States and the United Kingdom and also by those who criticize what they view as excessive concessions by states to hostage takers. One such example is Israel's decision to free 1,027 Palestinian prisoners as the price of the return of Gilad Shalit.

The realist position emphasizes the empirical dimension of negotiations and their consequences. It also stresses the importance of adopting an objective viewpoint that distances itself from any emotional or moral reactions that might impair a judgment grounded in political rationality. Although refusing to negotiate with hostage takers can have serious consequences, some favor inaction on the grounds that negotiating and eventually accepting some of the abductors' demands empowers and legitimizes these criminal groups and may encourage further abductions. Indeed, the refusal to meet the abductors' demands is often seen as a wise choice.

Morally speaking, non-compliance with hostage takers' demands or, more radically, refusing to engage in any negotiations at all with hostage takers is consistent with a rule-consequentialist approach. Nevertheless, I argue that this moral position is untenable, because it relies unjustifiably on unreliable predictions of future events (Colonomos 2016a), a well-known problem for consequentialism generally.

The weakness of the utilitarian justification for the no-concession policy is glaring. Although some claim that the no-negotiation policy yields better results than attempts to make concessions to hostage takers (Brandt and Sandler 2009; Hayes 2002, 420; Weill 2014), the economics literature contains no consensus to this effect (Lapan and Sandler 1988). It is also difficult if not impossible to compare contemporary forms of hostage taking with aircraft hijackings or criminal kidnappings, which constitute the main data sources for these studies, since the motivations and the goals of the different groups involved as well as the international settings where they take place, differ dramatically. Moreover, there are no formal empirical studies of global hostage taking. Demonstrating that compliance with some of the hostage takers' demands explains an increase in hostage taking is very difficult. Even if such a study existed, it would not provide sufficient evidence to predict the future effects of compliance. Finally, the no-concession policy of the United Kingdom and the United States has yielded some results that seem, at best, inconclusive. Da'ech and Al-Qaeda have held, and continue to hold, hostages from those two countries, and are willing to make public displays of their beheadings, which, in itself, is a form of reward for these groups (although Al-Qaeda officially abandoned this practice in 2014). On the other hand, although Israel has made great concessions to hostage takers, few Israelis have been abducted since 2006.

When Israel releases a large number of Palestinian prisoners in exchange for one of its soldiers, many argue that a rule of parity should prevail whereby one or a few prisoners could be released in exchange for one living hostage. This claim is largely intuitive, but it violates the rule of rationality in which it pretends to be grounded. Indeed, numbers should not necessarily matter significantly (Munoz-Dardé, 2005; Taurek 1977). What matters is the value attributed to the person whose release is being sought. Interestingly, the critics who argue against the release of a large number of prisoners never envision the possibility of a high-ranking political dignitary falling into the hands of hostage takers.

The realist position is thus quite problematic. It has direct negative effects in the present and uncertain positive effects in the future. Indeed, it might never be possible to prove the positive long-term effects of the realist abstentionist approach and the doctrine it supports.

Fighting Unfairness

Realist thought encourages us to act in defense of one's state's interests. However, the concept of national interest is so loosely defined and so open to interpretation as to render this approach very unsatisfying. In the context of hostage taking, governing in the national interest is highly problematic as this sovereignist approach is unfair to those who are the victims of injustice.

Indeed, the fate of persons seems to be determined by the stamp on their passports whereas when they become hostages, they become part of a global context. Whether civilians or soldiers, they are citizens of the world. Indeed soldiers who are no longer fighting and who are not treated as POWs are no longer truly soldiers. When abducted, they are hostages and this category includes both civilians and those who have been captured when fighting within an army. Independently of his or her nationality, every hostage should be granted the same rights.

This is clear also when hostages are taken in states that pursue their national interest. Imagine such a country deciding for itself on the appropriate response to the crisis, as was the case in Algeria in January 2013 when workers of different nationalities in an oil plant were abducted. It is worth noting that military interventions to free hostages while putting their lives in danger are most likely to happen in countries that traditionally violate human rights, such as, for example, Algeria or Russia. This is another problem of the sovereignty approach, which asserts the state's claim to control over its territory. For both political and economic reasons, the primary goal of the country is essentially to deter further attacks on its soil and avoid protracted negotiations. Its main concern is to preserve its national security and its economic reputation. These considerations favor killing the abductors and harming their organization rather than ensuring the security of the hostages. It is regrettable and unfair that hostages have to pay the price of securing a country's economic reputation. In such cases, the sovereignty and the national interest of a third party decide the fate of citizens of different countries. A much fairer approach would be to consider the rights of hostages as a group and to view the attack on them as an international crime instead of treating it as a one-off threat to national security. Indeed in such cases, states whose citizens are taken hostages abroad try to use diplomacy in order to influence decisions that are taken by the host country in response to the hostage taking crisis or to bring assistance (which can imply the use of negotiators), as France did with Algeria. In those cases, states' reluctance to intervene or to extend aid abroad should be overcome.

The Sovereignist Decision to Use Force: The Hannibal Case

Risk is indeed an important variable, which those who feel responsible for the hostages' lives have to take into account. The risk factor is difficult to assess. However, we know that military operations place hostages' lives at considerable risk.

In this regard, the recent Israeli case of the "Hannibal procedure" is extremely interesting (Pfeffer 2014). Although the Israel Defense Forces (IDF) insists on saying the name was chosen randomly, this name is telling with regard to the purpose of this measure. During the Second Punic War fought between Carthage and Rome, Hannibal committed suicide to avoid capture by the Romans. Israel fears the abduction of its soldiers, who could become bargaining chips in negotiations with Hamas or Hezbollah, weakening Israel's position. This concern is particularly pertinent during an ongoing military operation. Under the Hannibal procedure that was implemented in the 2014 Gaza war, force may be used to prevent abduction even at the risk of the soldier's life. The procedure does not, of course, envisage the deliberate killing of the soldier in order to stop the kidnapping. However, it does allow for the possibility of the soldier being killed unintentionally during the military operation to rescue him or her. There are three possible scenarios. The most desirable scenario is, of course, the return of the living captive. There are two other possibilities: the massive use of force stops the abduction and kills the soldier; and the massive use of force does not stop the abduction and the captors flee with their hostage and are beyond the reach of the Israel Defense Forces (IDF). The Hannibal doctrine acknowledges that Israel is prepared to endanger the life of the soldier in order to stop the abduction. Moreover, it is well known that when massive force is used in such an operation, the hostage as well as any abductor or bystander might be killed. Therefore, we may infer that what the Hannibal procedure is designed to avoid is the abduction of the hostage in a location where he or she will be beyond the reach of the IDF and become a bargaining chip in a future negotiation between Israel and one of its enemies.

This procedure is extremely problematic (Colonomos 2014). It goes against the cultural, political, and military tradition according to which soldiers' lives are sacred and ransoms can be paid to save them from the enemy. The killing of the soldier is not intentional, but it is not unintentional either, because the very possibility of being killed by fellow soldiers is an accepted principle, and the central purpose of the operation is to block the abduction process. Such a killing also fails the test of the doctrine of double effect (DDE), which is widely cited in discussions about the legitimacy of the use of force in warfare when, as very frequently happens, force has both bad and good effects. The DDE comprises four criteria. In order to pass this test, the intention to use force must be good, and its negative effects, even if foreseen, should not be intended. The two other criteria are clearly problematic for the Hannibal procedure. One of them stipulates that the negative consequences of the use of force must not outweigh its benefit, i.e. the rule of proportionality should be observed. As the Hannibal procedure explicitly countenances the use of massive force, in current asymmetric warfare it is very likely that the decision will not be consistent with the norm of proportionality. Indeed, when civilians are present in the vicinity of the abduction, military action seriously jeopardizes their lives as well. This was the case when the IDF launched the Hannibal procedure to stop the abduction of Lt Hadar Goldin: Dozens of Palestinian civilians were killed. Finally, the negative consequences of the decision to use force ought not to furnish the means to reach a positive outcome. But if the soldier is killed in the military operation that is undertaken in response to his abduction, the operation will prevent him from becoming a bargaining chip in the negotiation between the hostage takers and Israel. Therefore, the death of the soldier, a negative consequence of the operation, enables those who make this decision to achieve one of their most desired outcomes, i.e. stopping the abduction and thus preventing the hostage takers from gaining the advantage they sought.

When confronted with hostage taking, a state should not necessarily be prohibited from using force. However, this should be a last resort if the chances of saving the hostage are good. The Hannibal procedure is quite different, as the decision to use force is taken immediately after the hostage is captured and without any negotiation with his or her abductors. It is also different in that massive force is used, thereby putting the life of the hostage at considerable risk. For all these reasons, the Hannibal doctrine is a very disputed norm. At the time this book goes to print, it has been revoked by the IDF (Harel 2016).

INTER-TEMPORAL CHALLENGES

The sovereignist and realist positions raise a major problem that current policies and reflections about hostage taking have hardly taken into account, let alone resolved: Responses to hostage taking imply a choice of temporal preferences.

The Value of Future Lives

As we have seen, every decision in the face of abduction entails risks. These risks are difficult to assess and compare. Choices are further complicated by the fact that we are confronted with two different levels of risk, short-term and long-term.

What is the value of a future life compared with a present life? Philosophers have long argued about this difficult question (Broome 2001; Parfit 1984, 351–379). Future discounting is a common practice in our daily lives. Especially in the case of the environment (although this view is very controversial; Caney 2009), we might consider that discounting the future is normatively acceptable, given that our obligations to the living in the present are stronger than our obligations to hypothetical future beings. Indeed, while we know which lives are imperiled in the very short term, we do not know which lives, if any, could be saved if we shifted our preferences from the present to the future.

Surprisingly, as the policies of the United States and the United Kingdom indicate, a preference for the future over the present seems to prevail when states face hostage crises. There are various reasons for this choice. One of them lies in the very definition of the "national interest" or "state interest." State leaders usually believe the state acts, and ought to act, in accordance with the national interest. Political scientists in the realist tradition have promoted this notion, which is both theoretical and practical, although they have always had difficulty defining it. The notion itself is future-oriented. From a normative perspective, the Weberian notion of an ethic of responsibility (Weber 1994) is consistent with realism, and realists believe they have a duty to prolong the life of the national community (Smith 1986). Among the components of the national interest we find the preservation of political autonomy and national integrity.

If one assumes that realism inspires security policies, it does not come as a surprise that making concessions to those who challenge the authority of the state and potentially make its decisions dependent upon threats and blackmail is difficult if not impossible. According to realist theory, if security concerns are not too strong, states adopt a long-term perspective and refuse to discount the future. They have a short-term approach and discount the future only in the face of massive security threats that require an immediate response (Brooks 1997). The notion that negotiation threatens the national interest in the long term is consistent with a realist approach. Indeed, it prescribes that we ought not to discount the future as the killing of the hostage is not a massive security threat, whereas, in the long run, agreeing to negotiate will harm the reputation of the state and thus the national interest.

To what extent can a non-discounting policy be justified? One may argue that the loss of a few lives is acceptable in order to ensure the survival of one's political community. But it is very difficult to make such a claim in the case of hostage taking. One may even argue that a political community that does not come to the rescue of its members undermines its political foundations and the values it is built upon, such as solidarity. If hostage taking is a crime, accepting the deaths of hostages killed following a refusal to negotiate with their abductors is problematic. This would be to remain passive in the face of injustice when a major offense is about to be committed, i.e. the killing of the hostage. Moreover, favoring a cooperative approach – i.e. a focus on negotiations – would also reinforce relations between states at the international level while invoking the value of humanity as a bond between nation-states.

Whose Futures?

The sovereignist approach is unpersuasive for a further reason. The freeing of hostages is a problem of great concern for future generations, and not only those residing within the state. Let us assume, as do those who argue against any negotiation with hostages' abductors, that hostage takers' demands can have an effect on future lives. In this case, hostage takers would understand that abduction is a tactic that works, and be empowered by the ransom they received. However, this argument is set in a sovereignist framework: it assumes that those future generations are fellow nationals. This assumption amounts to a strategic and normative claim that is incorrect. It is indeed not possible to know the national identities of those future lives that might be put at risk as a consequence of the empowerment of hostage takers (that is, if hostage takers are more harmful as a result of their activities that have enriched them). Indeed, hostage takers might change the location of their activities and therefore harm people other than those whose security is now threatened. New alliances could be forged with other combatants in other parts of the world. The case of Israel might serve as a counterexample, as Hamas is arguably a future threat that could harm only Israeli civilians. However, even this is questionable, because, as in the case of Gilad Shalit, some Israeli citizens are bi-nationals.

If the decision is not to discount the future, as with the sovereignist and realist position, the debate has to include states other than the one that is immediately concerned with the abduction, because in the long run they too may be affected by the phenomenon and the consequences of the initial decision on negotiating with hostage takers. If future lives matter more than present ones, states other than the one whose citizens are abducted should be involved in decisions about negotiations. We can see here that linking the no-concession policy with sovereignty for the sake of preserving future lives lacks robustness.

Allowing individual states to refuse to negotiate might also have global implications. Unilateral refusal to negotiate could encourage terrorist organizations to relocate their activities and their associated harm to other societies. A monopoly on decisions on security matters is consistent with the principle of sovereignty. However, the security of other states might be harmed by such decisions, so affecting their sovereignty in the long run. Countries that allow states confronting the abductions of their citizens to make decisions on their own might find themselves in a state of moral dissonance. They have abstained from participating in decisions about negotiating with hostages and in the formulation and implementation of the norms involved in these activities. If their nationals become victims of hostage taking, they will regret the unfairness of the sovereignty game, since if the abductors relocate their activities to other countries, the citizens of those countries will become the abductors' primary targets.

A PLEA FOR A POST-SOVEREIGNIST MULTILATERAL POLICY

Unless it is proven that by acting alone the state whose nationals have been abducted has generally a much better chance of freeing them alone than if other states aided its efforts, multilateralism is a better approach to resolving the dilemmas of hostage taking. Even in such cases, given the consequences that the abduction of one person has for the security of those from other countries, the state whose citizen has been kidnapped has the obligation to warn other states about the emergence of this threat. Given that other states could suffer from the consequences of any one state's responses to hostage takers, we need to engage in a debate over the best solution to the crisis and the best norms and doctrines to guide policy decisions. Moreover, this debate must also address the more general political and social problems that generate hostage taking.

Multilateralism is essentially a corrective to some of the main fallacies of the sovereignist approach. Institutional design is not the focus of this chapter. But I support the creation of a multilateral institution whose task would be to negotiate with hostage takers and seek the capture of the criminals who engage in this activity. International cooperation, whether through existing international organizations or, more efficiently, through ad hoc international coalitions, enables the sharing of information. In this case, the intelligence of the many is likely to be more efficient than the intelligence of the few. States use *raison d'Etat* to justify their refusal to cooperate on such matters. However, this situation could change if a persuasive case could be made for the advantages of a cooperative mode of crisis resolution. International cooperation should imply the inclusion of non-state actors such as NGOs and advocacy groups that would bring information from the ground and share their experience.

Inter-state cooperation would foster the emergence of an "epistemic community" composed of specialists in hostage taking who would share their experiences from different perspectives, such as security, law, economics, and psychology, to improve future decision-making.

Studies have revealed a correlation between economic development and security on the micro level (Abrahamsen and Williams 2015). Therefore, international cooperation could also be a form of economic aid to populations that might be accomplices to hostage takers, providing incentives not to support such activities.

We are unaware of the alternatives to the decisions taken by states in the face of hostage taking. We are also unaware of the criteria according to which those decisions were made. In the pragmatist and democratic tradition, deliberation has both an epistemic and a moral function in that it improves the quality of political decisions. This approach should be applied to the decision-making process over hostage taking as well because it requires expertise and knowledge that is spread across various countries and social sectors.

Multilateral institutions should not dictate terms to states that are directly concerned with hostage crises, since this would discourage them from joining international coalitions. Instead, such institutions would provide resources, in the form of security and logistics, knowledge and financial aid. Multilateral bodies would define guidelines upon which states could agree. They would take on the responsibility of rescuing hostages and mobilize all the resources needed to achieve this goal. The state whose citizens have been taken hostage would act as the negotiator with the hostage takers. However, observers from other countries would be present during these negotiations and offer advice.

A multinational task force should not reproduce the inequality of power that structures international politics. It would be composed of experts from different countries, which would also help neutralize national biases. Overcoming the divide between states and non-state actors that specialize in norm building and have experience in fieldwork is also important. It would foster both the efficiency and the legitimacy of their decision-making.

Such a multinational organization is the best protection against the charge that the no-concession response to hostage taking is an expression of Western dominance in international politics and reflects asymmetrical warfare between civilization and barbarity.

CONCLUDING REMARKS

In this chapter, I have argued in favor of multilateral cooperation between states that should accept some compromises in order to have one's hostages freed. I have shown that both normatively and strategically this appears to be a better solution more coherent and more effective than the sovereignist and non-cooperative approaches praised by some policy makers.

Countries that are known for making concessions have not altered their policy. On the contrary, we are witnessing today a softening of hostage policy both in Israel and in the United States. As for the former, the Hannibal directive has been revoked. As for the latter, President Obama announced in June 2015 that families who decided to pay ransom will not face criminal prosecution (The White House 2015). This new policy also implies that the United States communicates with hostage takers and that it will stand closer to the hostages' families (Carroll 2015).

However, multilateral cooperation is still lacking in the face of hostage taking and there is no official coordination of states' initiatives. This is regrettable as, especially in the context of an accrue willingness to compromise, cooperation would be extremely beneficial. This would maximize the operational and logistical resources used to bring the hostages back to their homes and it would also put some limits to the willingness to pay excessive ransoms.

Norms are sometimes highly contextual. Although the shift toward a multilateral approach looks today unlikely, norms evolve over time. In the near future, eventually, if, in the context of a single operation, groups such as Da'ech or Al-Qaeda were to seize a group of hostages of different nationalities all together, this could spark a multilateral initiative and eventually a multilateral doctrine.

13

Kidnapping and Extortion as Tactics of Soft War

Tamar Meisels

One relatively soft wartime measure, falling just below deadly kinetic force, is the capture and incarceration of enemy combatants. Armies take prisoners during wartime, and are required to offer quarter; states are entitled to make arrests and hold insurgents and criminals. At the same time, some sub-state organizations are widely condemned for responding in kind by apprehending enemy soldiers. As George Fletcher puts this, "Terrorists do not take prisoners. They take hostages whom they are prepared to mistreat for their own purposes" (Fletcher 2002, 55–56).[1]

Recent cases come to mind: In 2006, Hamas captured Israeli Corporal Gilad Shalit, releasing him five years later in exchange for 1027 Palestinian security prisoners serving sentences in Israel. In 2009, the Taliban captured and held one American soldier, until his release in 2014 in exchange for five Taliban members held by the United States.

Back in 1947, the *Irgun*, a Jewish underground group in mandatory Palestine, kidnapped two British sergeants, threatening to kill them if the death sentences passed on *Irgun* militants by British authorities were carried out. When the imprisoned *Irgun* members ultimately went to the British gallows, the organization hanged their British captives, declaring that: "we recognize no one-sided laws of war" (Bell 1977, 236).[2]

Why maintain the double standard? The answer is twofold and arises clearly from Fletcher's aforementioned comment about terrorists taking hostages: Its first prong concerns the status and identity of the captors; the second relates to the purpose of captivity. I address the first of these issues, concerning the status of the captors, in the following sections. The first section outlines the legal distinction between privileged and unprivileged combatants within international and non-international armed conflicts. This is then followed by a section defending the privileging of one set of belligerents over another, regardless of the cause for which they fight. The next section suggests that wartime capture and imprisonment may be an agent-dependent act, i.e. an action whose legitimacy depends on the status and identity of the performing agent and with reference to the goals of *jus in bello* as a whole. The specific practice of hostage taking versus the taking of prisoners of war is addressed in the remaining three sections.

LICENSE TO KILL, AND CAPTURE

International Armed Conflict

In the normal course of events, individuals are immune from attack and imprisonment by anyone. As Michael Walzer observes, "… the theoretical problem is not to explain how immunity is gained, but how it is lost. We are all immune to start with; our right not to be attacked is a feature of normal human relationships" (Walzer 1977, 144–145).

Wartime killing and imprisonment introduces an exception (Waldron 2010b, 109–110). The laws of international armed conflict license attacks on particular individuals, namely combatants, traditionally assumed to have lost their natural immunity from attack by virtue of the threat they pose to their adversaries (Walzer 1977, 144–145). More specifically, international law grants immunity from prosecution for violent crimes for attacking enemy combatants in the course of an armed conflict. This wartime immunity is granted selectively to a particular subset of direct participants who achieve the relevant legal status of "combatants" during armed conflict, and to no one else.

Traditionally, the rights and duties of war applied to state armies and their soldiers. The Hague and Geneva conventions extended these rights to militia and volunteer corps, stipulating the conditions under which they are entitled to the war rights of soldiers, specifically prisoner of war (POW) rights when captured. In order to achieve this status, along with the legal immunity from prosecution, combatants must wear "a fixed distinctive sign visible at a distance" and must "carry their arms openly" (Fletcher 2002, 106; Geneva Convention III 1949, Part I, Art. 4; Hague Regulations 1907, Section I, Chap. I, Art. 1; Walzer 1977, 182). Two further conditions are that combatants form part of a chain of command within an organization that obeys the customs and the laws of war (Walzer 1977, 182).

In the aftermath of WWII, the Third Geneva Convention explicitly includes members of "organized resistance movements" belonging to a party to the conflict, as potentially eligible for full combatant status under the law, provided such militias fulfill the aforementioned conditions, notably that of overt combat, and "that of conducting their operations in accordance with the laws and customs of war" (Geneva Convention III 1949, Art. 4.2).

More recently, Additional Protocol 1 (API 1977) partly, and controversially, waves the uniform requirement, but only in exceptional cases in which "an armed combatant cannot so distinguish himself" (API 1977, Art. 44 (3)). Even in these presumably rare instances in which distinctive dress is utterly impossible, the Protocol nonetheless requires that such combatants clearly separate themselves from noncombatants by carrying their arms openly at all times (API 1977). Only combatants who fulfill these requirements enjoy the privileges of lawful belligerency and are immune from prosecution when they kill and capture other combatants.

When captured by the enemy, "combatants" may refuse to answer any questions beyond name, rank, and serial number (Geneva Convention III 1949, Art. 17; Hague Regulations 1907, Sec. 1, Chapter II, Art. 9). Prisoners of war are also guaranteed basic levels of humane treatment (Geneva Convention III 1949, esp. Art. 13; Hague Regulations, Sec. I, Chap. 2, Art. 4). Qualified combatants must not be prosecuted for the mere fact of their belligerence, either during wartime or in its aftermath, provided they are not personally responsible for atrocities or any other violations of the laws of war. These special wartime immunities are vital because in their absence, most actions performed by soldiers would be prosecutable under various domestic laws.

In Israel, a series of Supreme Court rulings maintain that the relevant normative framework for considering counter terrorism measures is that of an international armed conflict (HCJ 2005, 769/02 par. 16). Subsequently, the court described the status of terrorists as "civilians who are unlawful combatants"(HCJ 2005, 769/02 Par. 27–31). On this understanding, a civilian who participates directly in hostilities loses the protections accorded to civilians in wartime, though he remains a civilian who does not acquire the war rights of soldiers (HCJ 2005, 769/02 esp. 31).

While no distinction between lawful and unlawful combatants is explicitly laid down within international law, the status of lawless combatants can be deduced negatively from the positive definition of combatants eligible for POW status under The Hague and Geneva Conventions. Combatants who bear no external insignia and carry their arms in secret fail to achieve a particular legal status – that of a soldier or lawful combatant – and are therefore ineligible for the specific protections that accompany this legal status (Fletcher 2002, 109). Vitally, these immunities include an unusual guarantee against prosecution by their enemies for killing combatants in wartime or restricting their freedom. Absent the immunities granted to lawful combatants within the ILOAC, civilians who function as "unlawful combatants," such as Hamas in Israel, are subject to domestic prosecution on charges of murder, assault, kidnapping, and hostage taking, whether they attack civilians or combatants.

Non-International Armed Conflicts

Most armed conflicts since 1945 have been non-international conflicts, or civil wars, and the overwhelming majority of wartime casualties following World

War II have occurred within them (Cassese 2008, 112; Fabre 2012, 130; Fearon and Laitin 2003, 75; Kalyvas 2000, 1–45; Lee 2012, 240–241). Moreover, when dealing with insurgencies and terrorism it is not always easy to distinguish clearly between international and non-international conflicts.

As opposed to the Israeli ruling on Hamas in Gaza, the United States Supreme Court has favored classifying its own anti-terrorist campaigns – its ongoing conflict with Al Qaeda and associate forces – as a *non-international* armed conflict, bringing a smaller part of humanitarian law into play (Blum and Heymann 2010, 157; Maxwell 2012, 40–41, 49–50). The laws that apply to non-international armed conflict – Article 3 common to the Geneva Conventions (1949) and Protocol II (APII 1977) – aim to uphold civilian immunity and the rights of the sick and wounded, as well as prohibiting torture and further excesses in wartime. They do not, however, apply the full set of laws *in bello* applicable within international armed conflicts to non-international strife.

Crucially, among the deficiencies in regulating non-international armed conflict is the lack of legally defined "combatant" status, along with any requirement that fighters wear uniforms or insignia distinguishable from afar. Article 4 of the Third Geneva Convention, stipulating these requirements, does not apply to non-international armed conflict so the conditions demanded there for recognizing members of militias as combatants entitled to POW status do not apply in these conflicts. Subsequently, the ICRC has suggested that in NIACs members of organized armed groups who have a continuous combat function may be targeted as though they were combatants in international armed conflict, namely, even when they present no imminent danger.[3] As far as their liability to direct harm is concerned, there is no demand that such fighters be recognizable by their dress in order to be identified as belligerents.

Combatant liability notwithstanding, the United States does not extend privileged combatant status to its adversaries in "The War on Terror," described as "unlawful combatants" (The United States Military Commissions Act of 2006). As such, the United States regards captives taken by their opponents as unlawfully apprehended, or kidnapped, and denies its adversaries POW rights when they are captured.

Regarding the rights of detainees, Common Article 3 and Protocol II accord similar provisions to those guaranteed in international conflicts, safeguarding the life, person, and dignity of all prisoners regardless of their status or that of their captors. They do not, however, specify whom among the belligerent parties are entitled to take prisoners to begin with, or under what conditions.

In his *Ethics of Insurgency*, Michael Gross argues for the right of just guerrilla organizations to take prisoners as part of their right to fight a just war. Throughout, Gross suggests that the laws of armed conflict ought to be adjusted more extensively, and interpreted more liberally, in order to accommodate just insurgents, enabling them to fight legally and take prisoners (Gross 2015, esp. 9–10, 118–126). As a matter of existing law, he cites Tuck, commenting that

> international law does not prohibit armed groups from taking prisoners and, in fact, implies their right to take captives. Otherwise, the provisions safeguarding detained or interned persons in Common Article 3 and APII articles 5 and 6 are "superfluous." (Gross 2015, 118; Tuck 2011, 765)

The right to take prisoners in wartime is undeniably linked to the right to fight, as Gross asserts (2015). It is not, however, a forgone conclusion that either of these rights can in fact be deduced from the absence of a legal prohibition, or from the humanitarian provisions of Common Article 3 and Protocol II. In the absence of a specific legal privilege to fight with impunity, there may be no need for an explicit prohibition on taking prisoners because outside the special war rights of soldiers one is not usually permitted to apprehend, nor does one remain immune from kidnapping charges if one chooses to do so.

More importantly, guaranteeing the basic human rights of all wartime prisoners – whether combatants or civilians – does not automatically imply the legality of their internment. The law is very clear on this – one cannot deduce the right to fight and take prisoners from humanitarian provisos. Mindful of the natural fear of governments of accepting a convention that might be construed as granting legitimacy to those rebelling against it by recognizing their war rights, Article 3 closes with the explicit assurance that "The application of these preceding provisions shall not affect the legal status of the Parties to the conflict" (Geneva Convention III 1949, Art. 3). Humanitarian provisions apply universally as human rights, declared and guaranteed by international law rather than granted, whether the detention in question is legal or not and regardless of any specific immunity or culpability of either the detainee or his jailors.

Nonetheless, Gross is right in observing that "the right to take prisoners follows from insurgents' right to fight. Indeed, taking prisoners is often necessary to prosecute a just war" (Gross 2015, 118). Where Guerrillas have a right to fight, they must also have a right to take captives, as a lesser harm, he argues (Gross 2015). While states are under no duty to grant fighters in non-international armed conflicts immunity from domestic prosecution, insurgents do not face international liability for killing or capturing combatants, which may imply their license to fight and capture.

Moreover, Gross raises a valid concern about regulating the restriction of liberty as a measure of contemporary warfare. In reality, many non-international armed conflicts, including "the war on terror," will involve the taking of prisoners by both state and non-state parties. In a world in which the majority of armed conflicts are non-international, it may be preferable to lay down new rules, in the hope that they create an incentive for some non-state groups to comply. If every form of wartime imprisonment performed by non-state actors is regarded as a war crime, insurgents will have no legal incentive to refrain from killing their prisoners.

In fact, "unlawful" identity is not in itself an offense under international law (Dinstein 2004, 208–211), nor does every action performed in this capacity constitute an international crime. In this sense, the status of non-state actors taking prisoners is similar to the status and liabilities of other "unlawful combatants," such as state spies on foreign soil. As Fletcher observes, the very notion of lawless combat invokes a legal status rather than a crime (Fletcher 2002, 109). Under international law, irregular combatants remain unprotected by the war rights of soldiers and are rightly subject to prosecution and punishment "but only on the basis of the national criminal legislation of the belligerent state against whose interests he acted" (Dinstein 2004, 211).

If insurgents mistreat their captives, then they also commit war crimes, and the domestic state then *must* try them and other jurisdictions may exercise their powers, too.[4] But if the non-state actors treat the prisoners in a dignified fashion they will not be subject to international criminal liability. At the same time, the state party may still prosecute the non-state actors under its domestic law, as they do not enjoy immunity from prosecution.

To sum up: When sub-state combatants take prisoners, they violate domestic law, though not necessarily international law – provided they comply with Common Article 3 or APII. They are "unprivileged belligerents" for purposes of domestic law, and may consequently stand trial in an enemy state, though they have committed no war crime and therefore would not be subject to international jurisdiction.

UNLAWFUL COMBATANTS

Legalities aside, some insurgents fight against "colonial domination, alien occupation or racist regimes" (API 1977, Preamble), while armies do not always pursue just causes or treat their prisoners in strict accordance with the law. Why maintain traditional regulations that deny un-uniformed guerrillas the full war rights of soldiers, regardless of cause?

Politically, the unprotected status of irregulars reflects the fact that international law is made by states, naturally reluctant to accord immunity to insurgents who rise up against their authority, as is well reflected in the closing paragraph of Common Article 3. Notwithstanding, the distinction between lawful and unlawful combatants also has significant normative justification, and its reasoning can be traced back to international agreement and practice (Fletcher 2002, 96–112, esp. 107; HCJ 2005, 769/02 par. 25; Nabulsi 1999, 32). Briefly stated, the unprivileged status of irregulars is based on two interrelated features of their identity and behavior: first, they place civilians at risk; second, lack of reciprocity – clandestine irregulars do not abide by the rules themselves, and are therefore ineligible for their protections (Scheipers 2010, 316–317).

As for the first, the obligation to wear uniforms and fight overtly is intrinsically tied to the protection of civilians, which forms the cornerstone of the morality and laws of war (Bugnion 2002, 16). Even Protocol I, generally regarded as a narrowing of the traditional rule on wearing of uniforms or recognizable insignia, states:

> In order to promote the protection of the civilian population from the effects of hostilities, combatants are obliged to distinguish themselves from the civilian population while they are engaged in an attack or in a military operation preparatory to an attack. (API 1977, Art. 44(3))

Walzer explains this, prior to the Protocol, back in *Just and Unjust Wars* (Walzer 1977, 176–186). Acknowledging straightaway that some incidences of covert warfare are morally justified in terms of their cause, and even worth the accompanying risks to the civilian population, he recalls the French resistance to Nazi occupation as an exemplar. Regardless of cause, guerrillas in civilian disguise generate a moral hazard by subverting the most fundamental rules of war, whose purpose is to protect the civilian population by specifying for each individual a single identity: either soldier or civilian. Fighting in civilian disguise, insurgents entice their enemy to attack them in the midst of civilians (Walzer 1977, 179–181; Walzer 2013, 436–437). "By refusing to accept a single identity, they seek to make it impossible for their enemies to accord to combatants and non-combatants their 'distinct privileges and disabilities'" (Walzer 1977, 180).

Disguised guerrillas or partisans fighting amidst their population (however justifiably) blur the distinction between soldier and civilian and threaten to draw their stronger adversary into a conflict that makes no such distinction. They specifically defy those rules that lie at the heart of humanitarian conventions and are vital to the well-being of civilians, above all to the welfare of the members of the weaker population whom they profess to represent.

However noble their cause, clandestine militants remain unprivileged by laws designed to protect civilians. Where covert resistance is morally justified in spite of the danger it poses to civilians, belligerents must assume the accompanying risks for themselves, just as they assume the dangers to their surrounding population (Walzer 1977, 178).[5] In the case of the noble partisan, we would be justified in applauding his behavior, without reproaching his opponent for denying him the rights of a regular soldier. Where occupying authorities attempt to restore "everyday peacefulness," Walzer tells us, they are entitled to regard insurgents as criminals, rather than treating them as prisoners of war if captured (Walzer 1977, 178; cf. Finlay 2015, 99). Criminals, needless to say, may not take prisoners of war.

As for reciprocity, irregulars do not abide by the basic laws of distinction, essential for maintaining the safety of civilians and are therefore un-entitled to the unique immunities granted by law. The reverse justifies the rights of uniformed combatants, regardless of cause, because their compliance serves to protect civilians and restrict the horrors of war. Maintaining civilian immunity by distinguishing oneself as a soldier carries a heavy price – it marks out combatants as legitimate targets, optimally drawing the fire toward them and away from civilians. Guerrillas in civilian clothes take no such risks and hazards involved in overt and identified warfare (Fletcher 2002, 108).

While insurgents are not always "terrorists" in the strictest sense of murdering civilians, they are not legally eligible for the special privileges and immunities granted to soldiers by international conventions, nor should they be (Fletcher 2002, 104–112; Walzer 1977, 181–182). Granting clandestine insurgents the right to kill and capture with impunity would considerably subvert the war convention and erode the protections accorded to civilians during wartime. This is obviously all the more so as far as actual terrorists are concerned.

DIGNITY AND AGENCY

The resulting legal and moral asymmetry between types of combatants strikes many insurgents, as well as some scholars, as morally incoherent. Agent-based differentiation means that seemingly identical acts – wartime capture and incarceration – are deemed legitimate only when they are performed by one type of agent rather than another, based on nothing but the agents' formal status.

The notion that right and wrong cannot always be determined independently of the status and identity of the agent is not, however, unfamiliar to legal theorists, nor is it peculiar to the law and morality of war. Arguing against privatization, Israeli legal scholar Alon Harel explains that some practices are simply "agent dependent," "namely, enterprises or practices whose success depends on the agent performing them" (Harel 2014, 51–106, 69). In such cases, determining who can perform a specific task does not turn on the quality of performance or the level of service provided, but rather on the status of the agent (Harel 2014, 51, 66–69).

State-inflicted punishment is a case in point (Harel 2014, 71). Private individuals within the state may not perform executions or carry out prison sentences, no matter how justifiably or humanely they inflict their "punishments," simply because they lack the relevant status required to do so (Harel 2014). It is not merely that acts of violence, killing, and incarceration are *legally* impermissible when performed by private individuals. Private acts of violence, however well-deserved or performed, are fundamentally different from acts of punishment inflicted by the criminal justice system. The very nature of the act of punishment (and not only its legality) hinges on the identity and status of the agent performing it. "It is false therefore to say that private individuals *ought not* to punish; they simply *cannot punish*, as their acts do not constitute punishment" (Harel 2014, 72, 81). This is not merely a formality. The key concept here is that securing certain goods, such as those resulting from a public criminal justice system, "are contingent upon the identity or status of the agent inflicting it" (Harel 2014, 72).

In the case in hand, a similar point may hold regarding wartime capture and incarceration. The overall good of maintaining a reciprocal prisoner of war regime, upholding distinction, limiting war, protecting non-combatants – civilians and prisoners alike – are goals that can only be served by identified combatants fighting overtly. It is perhaps no wonder that the majority of casualties in non-international armed conflicts, to which most rules do not apply, are in fact innocent civilians (Kalyvas 2000, 54).

Moreover, above and beyond distinction and the obligation of overt combat, the laws of international armed conflict also require that combatants be "commanded by a person responsible for his subordinates" and belong to organizations "conducting their operations in accordance with the laws and customs of war" (Geneva Convention 1949, Part I, Art. 4; Hague Regulations 1907, Sec.1, Art. 1). Both specifications point to a further moral reason for denying most insurgents the full war rights of soldiers. As Walzer points out, restraining combatants, preventing "extra" killings or ill-treatment outside the permission of the laws of war, e.g. murder or brutalizing prisoners, "is a crucial aspect of what is called 'command responsibility'" (Walzer 1977, 308). Armies are the type of organization capable of applying and enforcing *jus in bello*, though they do not always comply. Informal paramilitary organizations, on the other hand, may not even be able to impose military discipline.

Discussing the French in Algeria, Raphaelle Branche notes that as early as 1956, Algerian guerrilla organizations (ALN/FLN) issued guidelines requiring their fighters to take prisoners (rather than kill them), "[h]owever, the FLN did not have the power to enforce its view on the combatants" (Branche 2010, 183). While the criminal ill-treatment of Algerian prisoners by the French is notorious, the point remains that the sheer ability to secure certain goods may depend on the identity of the agents performing wartime tasks and the nature of their organization. Upholding humanitarian concerns – restricting warfare and maintaining the rights and dignity of soldiers and civilians – may only be achievable by organizations with a clear hierarchy, in which commanding officers have the oversight and resources to carry out their operations in accordance with the laws and customs of war, as well as to enforce compliance on their subordinates.

Regarding the laws and conventions that apply to prisoners of war specifically, Gross readily admits that "[g]iven their complexity and cost, … some of the rules are difficult for guerrilla organizations to fulfill" (Gross 2015, 119).

> Guerrillas lack medical and administrative personnel and the resources necessary to house prisoners. Guerrillas are often mobile so that infrastructures are often makeshift and transient. Most guerrilla movements lack the necessary oversight to assure that

prisoners of war are treated properly. Guerrilla bases, moreover, are often clandestine forcing captors to restrict or prohibit third party visits. (Gross 2015, 119)

Nevertheless, Gross worries about denying insurgents the right to capture and detain, arguing that this deprives sub-state militants of any legal incentive to abide by the laws and take prisoners alive (though his discussion of lopsided exchanges supplies ample practical incentive). In practice, he notes, guerrillas do take prisoners, and the concern is that they maintain their captives' basic human rights (Gross 2015). Some guerrillas, he admits, "do not meet the threshold for humane care and severely undermine their right to fight when they deny their prisoners their basic rights" (Gross 2015, 119).

In other cases, however, Gross is prepared to grant even covert insurgents the right to fight and take prisoners, so long as they meet some minimal standards of humane treatment reasonably adjusted to their limited abilities. And he points out that "the treatment of prisoners varies enormously among contemporary guerrilla armies, just as it does among the states they fight" (Gross 2015, 103, 114–117).

The point about agency, however, means that un-uniformed guerrillas cannot perform the task of taking prisoners, rather than kidnapping, regardless of the level of treatment they accord to their captives. States have, undeniably, mistreated prisoners of war, and are guilty of war crimes when they do so.[6] In the case of insurgents, however, the mistreatment of prisoners is neither here nor there in determining the nature of their act, though it pertains to the severity of their crime. This status-dependent liability is not based on an arbitrary rule, or state bias. Instead, wartime imprisonment is a typical "agent dependent" practice, whose success rests on the identity and status of the performing agents. Insurgents are rightly denied immunity from prosecution for committing acts of war, including the capture of combatants, because they cannot provide the goods that the LOAC strive to guarantee.

The prisoner of war regime is an enterprise nested within the framework of *jus in bello* as a whole, the overall purpose of which is to restrict warfare. Securing these goods and protecting noncombatants depends crucially on the status of the agents empowered to perform wartime tasks. Privileging insurgency would erode the prospect of limited warfare and endanger wartime civilians as well as prisoners. Moreover and in practice, when insurgents do take prisoners they usually perform an entirely different act altogether.

HOSTAGES

Armies capture soldiers in wartime in order to disable a threat, removing enemy combatants from the hostilities, thereby weakening their adversaries by measures short of killing. Insurgents are usually incapable of disabling a significant number of enemy soldiers, and can capture and hold only very few prisoners (Gross 2015, 119).[7] When insurgents succeed in capturing a soldier, they often do so in order to compel their enemy to comply with their demands; typically, they use their captives to bargain for the release of captured insurgents held by a stronger adversary.

According to the International Convention against the Taking of Hostages (June 3, 1983), Article 1:

Any person who seizes or detains and threatens to kill, to injure, or to continue to detain another person . . . in order to compel a third party . . . to do or to abstain from doing, any act as an explicit or implicit condition for the release of the hostage commits the offense of taking hostages ("hostage-taking") within the meaning of this convention.

Moreover, hostage taking is already unequivocally prohibited by the Geneva Conventions (IV) and its additional protocols, with no distinction between civilian and soldier (Dinstein 2004, 227; Geneva Convention (IV) 1949, Art. 34; API 1977, Art. 75(2)(c); Green 2008, 311, 328, 352). As Yoram Dinstein notes, "Article 34 of Geneva Convention (IV) declares that '[t]he taking of hostages is prohibited', subject to no qualifications or exceptions. No doubt, this is customary international law today"(API 1977, Art. 75(2)(c); Dinstein 2004, 227; Green, 2008, 352).

The rule against the taking of hostages is broader than an interdiction of their execution. It follows that . . . the taking of hostages can never be excused even if ultimately they are not killed . . . The taking of hostages constitutes a grave breach of Geneva Convention (IV). As such, it is specifically listed as a prosecutable . . . war crime (without any specific reference to civilians) in Article 8(2)(a)(viii) of the Rome Statute. Although in practice the victims of hostage-taking in wartime are usually civilians, there is no reason to regard them as the sole beneficiaries of the norm. No hostage can be taken, whether civilians, combatants (especially, prisoners of war), or even neutrals. (Dinstein, ibid; UN General Assembly 1998, Art. 8(2)(a)(viii))

Regarding soldiers specifically, Leslie Green points out, Protocol I extends the definition of "grave breaches" of the Geneva Conventions (notably the taking of hostages) in regard to anyone protected by the Protocol, i.e. including combatants and prisoners of war (Green 2008, 328).

Nevertheless, Gross dismisses the distinction between the acceptable wartime practice of capturing combatants and the prohibited offense of hostage taking, which is said to exploit the captive as a means. Relying on commentary to Article 34 of the Geneva Conventions (IV), he points out that the underlying rationale for the prohibition on hostage taking is: "the natural right of man not to be subjected to arbitrary treatment and not to be made responsible for acts he has not committed" (Gross 2015, 120). Imprisoned soldiers, Gross argues, do not suffer an "*arbitrary* deprivation of liberty": Capturing military personnel is not arbitrary. Both insurgents and armies alike take prisoners because they "are vying for a military advantage. Disabling one soldier *reduces* enemy capabilities while exchanging that one soldier for hundreds or thousands of guerrillas *increases* guerrilla capabilities" (Gross 2015, 120–121).

For Gross, the legitimacy of detaining combatants hinges exclusively on maintaining humane treatment, rather than on the identity of the captors or their motivation for imprisoning. "In principle, then," he argues, "guerrillas do not take military *hostages*. Rather they take prisoners who enjoy the fundamental right of humane treatment but whom guerrillas may hold or exchange as military conditions demand" (Gross 2015, 122).

No doubt both armies and guerrillas struggle to gain advantage. Nevertheless, gaining advantage by increasing military capabilities or freeing one's comrades is quite a different type of motivation than disabling a wartime threat. While various advantages may be pursued during wartime, not all motivations serve equally to justify capture and imprisonment.

Removing an ongoing threat is the traditional just war theory justification for killing soldiers during wartime, and hence also for disabling them by lesser means, namely capture. Combatants may be attacked in war because they pose a danger to other people (Walzer 1977, 144–145). Disabling threatening soldiers and removing them from hostilities is an immediate military advantage, whereas bargaining for the release of fellow insurgents is a longer term, and partly political, goal. From the fact that the former motivation – disabling a threat – justifies detention (in lieu of killing) it does not follow that the latter long-term political motives suffice to justify this practice as well. Furthermore, while humane treatment is a necessary condition of lawful imprisonment, it is insufficient to render the detention in itself legitimate, either morally or legally.

ARBITRARY TREATMENT

The notion of arbitrariness serves to explain how motivation matters, and why the prohibition on hostage taking in Article 34 applies to military captives as well as civilians. Morally, hostage taking, like terrorism, defies a most basic standard of liberal-humanist morality, which fundamentally forbids the use of human beings as means only, and commands their treatment as ends in themselves (Kant [1785] 1964, 96; Rawls [1971] 1989, 179). This prohibition serves to further formulate the basic imperative to "act only on that maxim through which you can at the same time will that it should become a universal law" (Kant [1785] 1964, 88). Treating each other as ends, never as means only, requires us to treat our adversaries in ways that would be minimally acceptable to us, were we in their shoes, and that are therefore reasonably explicable to them from a neutral and objective standpoint, regardless of our own subjective (or arbitrary) point of view or political goals.

When the laws and customs of war that cover the treatment of POWs are complied with, captors can, and do, will that their maxims become universal law. The prisoner of war regime satisfies the Kantian requirements because it is reciprocal in nature and intended for everyone's advantage. Lawful wartime imprisonment is a temporary tactical restriction of liberty that facilitates disabling a military threat for the duration, by measures short of maiming or killing. Such immobilization is legally limited to the end of the conflict, and both sides are duty bound to ensure that everyone goes home when the war is over.

Within this reciprocal system, an imprisoned soldier can easily understand and accept the justification for restricting his freedom. When the laws of war are roughly adhered to, prisoners of war are treated in ways to which they could rationally consent, and which benefit them along with others. In this sense, the deprivation of liberty is non-arbitrary, because it is justifiable from an impartial standpoint to any rational agent, including the detainee himself.

Moreover, while imprisoning a soldier is a means of disabling his military capabilities, the POW himself also shares the benefits of an international regime that accords him extensive rights. He is not merely a tool toward gaining military advantage, but also treated as an end in himself, an independent agent whose interests are accounted for. A prisoner of war shares the goals of the reciprocal system – namely, maintaining civilized warfare and restricting the horrors of war – and is a rights holder within this regime. Though his detention is subjectively unpleasant, the POWs dignity and agency are not offended because he can be offered an objective explanation for the legitimacy of his predicament as well as its benefits. He can also reasonably predict and look forward to the end of his imprisonment. He has rights within the regime under which he is held and shares its ends with his captors.

By stark contrast, a soldier who is held incommunicado at the mercy of a clandestine organization cannot be offered a similar justification and therefore could not have consented to his predicament. The reasons for his unlawful detention can be explained – they are not irrational, random, or illogical – and in this sense his captivity is admittedly non-arbitrary. Such explanations, however, can only describe the insurgents' motivation, rather than supplying a neutral justification acceptable to soldiers on the opposing side.

Moreover, hostage taking is not limited by the end of the conflict, and its termination also depends on the subjective will of the captors. A hostage situation may carry on endlessly, depending on the negotiations and the "price-tag" attached to the hostage.

At these points, reference to insurgents' "just cause" and symmetrical inferiority will raise its head, offering *just* guerrillas an objective justification for kidnapping combatants. Contra traditional just war theory and international law, many contemporary theorists of the just war deny that moral permissibility/impermissibility in warfare can, and should, be determined neutrally and impartially, irrespective of the justice of the war itself. Recall that Gross's argument is designed to extend the war rights of soldiers (notably including the right to capture) to *just* insurgents, enabling them to contend with their strategic weakness and advance their struggle against injustice.

Similarly, revisionist just war theorists might argue that a *bona fide* resistance movement can justify hostage taking with reference to the status of their cause together with the military asymmetry of the conflict.[8] In such a case, the justification offered to their captive need not proceed solely from the insurgent's subjective motivations, relying instead on objective justice, combined with empirical comparison of military capability.

Appeals to higher causes, however, cannot yield practical rules of just conduct in war because they form the very crux of disagreement between the warring parties, nor can they justify instrumentalizing individuals. Whatever the deep moral truth about the conflict (just/unjust) as viewed from a god's-eye perspective, this cannot supply us with action-guiding rules of conduct in war, let alone internationally accepted laws for restricting the horrors of warfare. Absent divine revelation, the rules of war, moral as well as legal, must proceed independently of just cause by ruling out practices that offend agency and dignity in familiar ways – torture, terrorism, and hostage taking are all cases in point. Moreover, even if justice of cause were discernible, this would not justify treating others in any way imaginable.

When insurgents capture a soldier and employ him as a bargaining chip, their victim is exploited indefinitely as an instrument of his captors' ends. Even if the prisoner sympathizes with his captors' goal, he is still no party to their scheme and holds no rights within it (as distinct from his innate human rights), nor any guarantee of its resolution. Such captivity is arbitrary because no justification could be acceptable to even the most reasonable of hostages, any more than one could justify torture or terrorism in the name of just cause. "See here, we are sacrificing your liberty indefinitely as a means towards attaining our just political goals" is not a justification that passes the Kantian test. It is like saying to a bus load of civilians under terror attack: "we are blowing you up in order to liberate our nation," or informing a victim of torture that his interrogators will gauge out his eyes in order to obtain useful information that may save many lives.

In all these cases, an individual's basic rights are sacrificed for controversial "greater goods" or "just causes," in ways to which the victim could not have consented. None of the victim's preferences are accounted for, nor can any justification for misusing a human being as mere currency for transaction be offered to her as a distinctly independent individual. Instead, the hostage is employed as a prop in his captors' project, in a way that is appropriate for the use of things rather than individuals.[9] This is precisely what an arbitrary deprivation of rights amount to, or what it means to exploit another human being as a means only.

MERELY AS A MEANS

I have argued that the act of hostage taking is fundamentally different from taking prisoners in wartime, and that the use of captives as mere means toward political ends is quite rightly prohibited by law. Might there, nonetheless, be cases in which hostage taking, particularly of soldiers, is morally permissible? While Kant's requirements allow for no exceptions, others may be less categorical.

Derek Parfit denies that harming someone as a means always amounts to treating that person *merely* as a means, or even that treating an individual merely as a means is always impermissible (Parfit 2011, 212–232). We might harm an attacker as a means of self-defense, Parfit argues, without thereby treating our assailant *himself* as a means, let alone merely as a means. Thus, in *Self Defense*:

> [W]hen Brown attacks me with a knife, trying to kill me, I save myself by kicking brown in a way that predictably breaks his leg. (Parfit 2011, 221)

"[w]e do not *use* the people who attack us when we protect ourselves from their attack" (Parfit 2011, 222). Clearly, culpable aggressors may be attacked in our defense against their unwarranted assault without violating any moral imperatives. Are there parallel cases in which it is permissible to take culpably threatening agents hostage, and would such permission apply to kidnapping soldiers?

This question cannot be answered without reference to just cause, as well as the individual responsibility of soldiers, to determine who is a culpable aggressor. It is therefore unhelpful in forging practical POW rules, legal or moral, that can be internationally agreed on in advance of armed conflict and adhered to throughout, regardless of deep wartime disagreements about justice.

Moreover, above and beyond the indeterminacies surrounding just cause, there remains a key difference between self-defense against aggression on the one hand (whether individually or in war), and hostage taking on the other. When I break Brown's leg in order to thwart his attack in *Self-Defense*, Parfit points out, "my aims would be more easily achieved if Brown wasn't even there. If I was using Brown, I *would* want him to be there" (Parfit 2011, 222). Defense against aggression implies we do not want our attacker to be present, and therefore cannot be accused of using him (Parfit 2011). Soldiers kill, maim, and capture in order to defuse an undesirable threat. Kidnappers want their opponent to be there.

This point of disanalogy brings us full circle in distinguishing soldiers who take prisoners in war from terroristic hostage taking. Once again, removing a threat in battle is the traditional justification for soldiers' immunity from prosecution for killing and capturing. Kidnappers, by contrast, desire and require the presence of their hostage as a means of achieving their ends.

Admittedly, kidnappers might prefer that their enemy did not exist to begin with. That is an aspiration regarding international relations and world politics. Hamas, for example, wishes that Israel did not exist at all. When they capture an Israeli soldier, however, they cannot claim they would prefer he were not in Gaza, when they clearly require his presence for their purposes. Hostage taking uses the captive *himself as* a means, and therefore cannot claim analogy with self-defense against aggression, which would most easily be achieved if the attacker were entirely absent.

Notwithstanding this observation, my argument does not necessarily imply that kidnapping – either of soldiers or civilians – can never be morally justified, or at least excused, in exceptional circumstances. We might defend some kidnappers along the lines that Walzer defends World War II partisans, in spite of moral reasons for prohibiting covert combat and hostage taking, and without granting the offenders the war rights of soldiers. We might construct a hypothetical in support of a lesser evil argument: What if the Resistance had captured German soldiers, using them merely as means to negotiate the release of concentration camp inmates? Or imagine some fanciful extreme emergency: What if the only way of stopping the gas chambers was to kidnap one of the Goebbels children?

I am neither capable, nor interested, in resolving these difficulties. (To paraphrase a familiar idea, quite possibly, "Nazi cases make bad law.") Extreme cases that arouse sympathy are poor bases for general rules. I do not deny the possibility of rare exceptions to the ban on kidnapping and hostage taking, arguing only that these prohibitions are morally justified as a rule. There is no inconsistent double standard involved in upholding a POW regime for state armies, while at the same time unequivocally prohibiting and denouncing the kidnapping of soldiers. Kidnapping and hostage taking bear little resemblance to the lawful regime of wartime imprisonment, or to any action sincerely undertaken in self-defense. Instead, hostage taking is a reprehensible form of instrumentalization, appropriate for the treatment of objects rather than human beings, whether soldiers or civilians.

CONCLUDING REMARKS

Outside the qualifications of lawful belligerency, individuals are normally prohibited from capturing and incarcerating anyone at all. The exceptional wartime license to kill and imprison with impunity is not, and ought not to be, extended to covert guerrillas. Legitimizing clandestine combat, sanctioning hybrid identities of civilian-combatants, would erode the purposes of the war convention. Distinguishing starkly between soldiers and civilians is part and parcel of upholding noncombatant immunity, which forms the very cornerstone of the laws of war.

Moreover, insurgents habitually take hostages whom they use to vie for the release of their comrades. Hostage taking is unequivocally prohibited by international law because it is an arbitrary use of human beings. Contra POWs, a hostage is not a rights holder or a recipient of benefits within the regime that restricts his liberty and dignity. Instead, he is merely a pawn, or mere means, toward achieving the ends designed by his captors.

Kidnapping and hostage taking, just like torture, hijacking, and terrorism, are arbitrary assaults on individuals because no impartial justification can be offered to the victim for the depravation of his most basic rights. This is true regardless of whether the kidnapping is performed by states and their lawful soldiers or by clandestine groups, just or unjust.[10] Analogies with self-defense are implausible, because defense is most easily achieved by removing an aggressor, whereas kidnappers desire the presence of their hostage as a means. In the case of the kidnapped soldier, with which we set out, price tagging and bargaining techniques are flagrantly inconsistent with the attribution of intrinsic value to human beings, civilians, and soldiers alike.

NOTES

This research was supported by the Israel Science Foundation (Grant no. 45/12).

1. I assume that capturing civilians is always illegitimate, even in wartime. For the view that some civilians may be liable to attack, see McMahan 2009, 108, 221–235; McMahan 2008, 22. Gross 2015, 64–71 (on liability), 115–116 (regarding potentially legitimate targets for capture).
2. Other historical accounts suggest that the sergeants suffocated as a result of the difficult underground conditions in which they were held, and their bodies were subsequently hanged after their death. See Zeev Tzahor, *We Were the Revival* (2015), 17–18.
3. I am grateful to David Kretzmer for these points on the status of combatants in NIAC vs. IAC, and for many other helpful comments.
4. I am grateful to Gabby Blum for clarifying this point with precision.
5. For an opposing view, see Fabre (2012, 159–160).
6. For many historical cases of mistreatment of POWs, see Scheipers (2010, esp. chapters 4–9).
7. E.g. Hamas, Hezbollah, the Taliban, and IRA, etc.
8. I am grateful to Cécile Fabre for posing this objection.
9. On Kant's formula of humanity, see O'Neill (1989, esp. 110–114, 111, 114, and 138).
10. In 1989, Israel abducted Sheikh Abdul-Karim Obeid from his home in Lebanon. Obeid was thought by Israel to be a useful bargaining chip toward gaining the release of its missing airman Captain Ron Arad. In 1994, Israel kidnapped Muslim Guerrilla leader Mustafa Dirani, whom Israel believed could point them toward Arad's location. While Obeid was viewed primarily as a bargaining chip, Dirani was viewed more as a source of information. Moreover, on revisionist just war theory, Dirani might be construed as a liable target – as he had been partly responsible for the capture, disappearance, and inhumane treatment reportedly suffered by Arad. Regardless of cause, however, I doubt anyone would argue for the legality of these abductions. Neither attempt proved successful. See Hundley 1994.

CONCLUSION

14

Proportionate Self-Defense in Unarmed Conflict

Michael L. Gross

When states or guerrilla organizations face unarmed force – cyber-attacks, sanctions, nonviolent resistance, or a well-oiled propaganda machine – how might they legitimately respond? May the victim of a cyber-attack respond with one of equal or greater measure or do circumstances permit a kinetic missile attack against switches and servers? Does recurrent propaganda justify electronic jamming or the physical destruction of broadcast facilities? How should states confront nonviolent resistors or contain a potentially explosive hunger strike? As the chapters in this volume attest, unarmed force may pose a significant security threat. What measures may states or non-states take to protect themselves from unarmed force?

When states face armed force, the legal principle of military necessity allows states to secure legitimate military objectives by means permitted by international humanitarian law (Commentary to API Article 35, paragraph 1389). This gives states a wide berth to wage war while protecting noncombatants from direct harm and disproportionate collateral harm. During unarmed conflict, these restrictions do not readily apply. First, soft war often targets noncombatants directly. This is true of cyber warfare, information operations, and economic sanctions. Each may harm noncombatants significantly. Second, the principle of proportionality governing armed conflict is not obviously suitable for soft war. The law of armed conflict permits an armed response that adequately meets security needs but also incurs significant collateral costs. But other interpretations of proportionality, common to trade disputes and sometimes applied to cyber warfare, economic sanctions, and nonviolent resistance, permit only an *equivalent* response that is no more severe that the original affront. Its purpose is to enforce compliance with law and impose sufficient costs so that offenders do not profit from violating the law. Proportionality as equivalence is generally absent from armed conflict: States need not respond to an armed attack with one of equivalent force and destruction. But what of an unarmed attack?

To answer this question, this concluding chapter addresses two themes: First, how expansive a right to self-defense does a state or guerilla organization enjoy against unarmed force? The law of armed conflict is just that; it says little or nothing about how a state may respond during *unarmed* conflict. Unarmed force, however, may rise to the level of armed force if significant casualties and destruction ensue. In these cases, the rule of military necessity applies. But even when unarmed attacks remain relatively restrained, states should, I will argue, enjoy more latitude than equivalent countermeasures permit. Second, what does proportionate self-defense look like? In armed conflict, proportionate self-defense permits reasonable collateral harm but forbids direct, intentional harm. To make room for attacking civilians directly, soft war looks to the principle of participatory liability. Although noncombatants enjoy legal immunity from direct harm, participatory liability imposes moral liability when civilians provide war-sustaining aid. And while participating civilians remain protected from deliberate death and injury, they are not immune to lesser harms that unarmed force may cause. Attacking these civilians directly is a significant component of self-defense in soft war.

THE RIGHT TO PROPORTIONATE SELF-DEFENSE

International law allows states to utilize force in several circumstances. Facing an *armed* attack, states and non-states may defend themselves with armed force. Means and consequences define "armed attack." The means are usually kinetic – bombs and bullets – while the consequences include "territorial intrusions, human casualties or considerable destruction of property" (Dinstein 2005, 193). When a non-kinetic attack causes similarly catastrophic consequences, it rises to the level of an armed attack and permits an armed response. Consequences are definitive.

As the essays in this book demonstrate, soft war does not usually pose such dire threats. As such, international law permits states to employ "countermeasures" in response to unlawful actions. Countermeasures are acts of "self-help" that usually include temporary, and sometimes unlawful, coercive measures to force compliance with international law following treaty violations, environmental damage, human rights violations, or aggression against third parties. Countermeasures include "non-forcible" measures or a response in-kind but preclude the "threat or use of force as embodied in the Charter of the United Nations" (Draft Articles of Responsibility of States, 2001; Article 22.1; Article 50.3). In 1991, for example, Czechoslovakia unilaterally dammed the Danube River after the Hungarian government pulled out of an agreement to develop a joint water project (ICJ 1997). Countermeasures are the equivalent of *unarmed* reprisals. Their purpose is to compel a lawbreaker to comply with the law by exacting an equal measure of harm. Reprisals are guided by the magnitude of the initial infraction, not the more expansive goal of military victory that might easily demand far harsher measures than an equivalent response to a breach of law. This reinforces the one-shot nature of reprisals. Justified by an unlawful act of war, but unlawful acts themselves, reprisals cannot exceed the illegality or the harm of the initial infraction (Kalshoven 1971; Leiser 1975). To do otherwise only creates grounds for counter-reprisals. With similar caveats in mind, The Tallinn Manual on the International Law Applicable to Cyber Warfare (Schmitt 2013), for example, endorses counter-cyber measures in the wake of a cyber-attack but do not permit armed force (below).

Each of these legal categories helps us assess permissible responses in soft war. Self-defense permits an armed response following an armed attack. Soft war, by definition, comprises unarmed attacks so that armed responses are generally impermissible. As such, paradigms of armed self-defense only play out at the margins. But the margins are very important. Cyber-attacks may disrupt or destroy critical infrastructures bringing death or injury when trains derail, planes crash, or dams burst. Economic sanctions may cause grave humanitarian crises and propaganda machines may incite genocide and ethnic cleansing. In these cases, the consequences are sufficiently severe to permit an armed response (Gross 2015, 184–212). Nevertheless, there are reasonable fears of escalation when unarmed force, however destructive, is met with kinetic force (Libicki 2017). Such fears factor into a reasonable assessment of effectiveness. If the chances of escalation are sufficiently high, then the costs of a kinetic response may outweigh its benefits.

When unarmed force does not rise to the level of an armed attack, countermeasures are on the table. And while countermeasures are an effective self-help measure, they "counter" an unlawful act with the goal of restoring the status quo with equivalent force. None of these characteristics, however, necessarily applies to soft war. Unlike the acts that trigger countermeasures, many acts of soft war are lawful. Some economic sanctions are imposed lawfully or, like conditional sales (Fabre, this volume), reflect permissible commercial or political decisions. Short of prohibiting incitement or "war propaganda" there are no legal constraints on media warfare or information operations. Nonviolent resisters (Ryan, this volume) or unarmed defenders (Pattison, this volume) are usually beyond moral reproach. Yet each of these unarmed actions poses a threat that a state or guerrilla organization may answer. Some cyber-attacks, for instance, seek information, while others disable networks to cripple cyber capabilities and/or terrorize the civilian population (Lucas, this volume). Economic sanctions hope to wring military, political, and/or economic concessions from an adversary, while information operations or lawfare mobilize public support to force similar concessions. Unarmed actions may strive for symbolic victories (through nonviolent resistance or boycotts) or military victories (by using blockades). These are not isolated transgressions, but well-planned and concerted military and political strategies. There is no compelling moral reason that self-defensive measures cannot look beyond restoration of the legally sanctioned status quo to further disable or weaken an adversary.

As a result, proportionate countermeasures in soft war expand in two ways. First, proportionality moves beyond equivalent responses to one closer to that embraced by armed conflict. Legally enshrined in Additional Protocol I (API 51.5) *in bello* proportionality prohibits "an attack which may be expected to cause incidental loss of civilian life, injury to civilians, damage to civilian objects ... which would be excessive in relation to the concrete and direct military advantage anticipated." *In bello* proportionality dictates a vague ratio between two incommensurate variables: civilian harm and military advantage. Neither easily admits of a common denominator. The common solution is to translate military advantage into human lives (while largely ignoring the effects of an attack on military capabilities, morale, or deterrence) and simply compare enemy civilian lives lost with compatriot civilian lives saved (Gross 2008). When the former is somehow excessive compared to the latter, an attack is disproportionate. This is hardly the *equivalent* ratio of harm that countermeasures or reprisals usually demand (Cannizzaro 2001; Franck 2008). Rather, anticipated enemy civilian casualties must far outstrip the number of compatriots one expects to save before an attack becomes *in bello* disproportionate. As such, *in bello* proportionality permits far more harm than countermeasures allow and, when necessary in the pursuit of a legitimate military goal, should guide soft war as well hard.

Second, and also unlike countermeasures, self-defensive measures in soft war allow states or non-states to defend themselves against unjust threats rather than merely unlawful acts. An unjust threat, aggression for example, is any that imposes a cost on its victims to which they are not legally or morally liable. When the justice of an act remains a matter of legitimate legal or moral debate (even if legally sanctioned), states and non-states enjoy the right of self-defense. Examples might include Cuba's right to counter US sanctions or Kosovo's right to circumvent the UN arms embargoes in 1998 (Bromley 2007). In each instance, there is room to argue that sanctions, although legal, unjustly infringe on the victim's moral and/or legal rights. Kosovo will argue the moral justice of its fight against Serbia, while Cuba, with the backing of almost the entire United Nations, will condemn the United States for undermining Cuba's legal right to free trade and navigation (UN 2013). Under such circumstances, the right to take unarmed self-defensive measures is as robust as the right of armed self-defense and guided by principles of military necessity and humanity.

MILITARY NECESSITY IN SOFT WAR

To evaluate soft war, it is useful to define military necessity as the means necessary to secure a legitimate military target. A legitimate military target is any asset that facilitates an unlawful or unjust threat. Necessary means are those that effectively secure the same military advantage at less cost and attendant harm than any other means. While, perhaps, a straightforward utility calculation, the benefits and costs of soft war are much different from those of hard. The goals of soft war are exceptionally varied, ranging from a symbolic show of force (a well-attended demonstration) to modest gains (successfully prosecuting a war criminal or refuting fabricated media stories) to transformative events (disarming a nation of nuclear capabilities). The costs are equally varied. If, in conventional kinetic war, costs are measured by injury, loss of life, and infrastructural devastation, the costs of soft war are often more restrained. These include limited material losses (e.g. data, communications infrastructures, economic output), nonphysical human costs (e.g. psychological suffering and hardship), reputational harm, as well as risks of retaliation and escalation.

Keeping these costs in line requires the appropriate measure. One advantage of unarmed force is the wide range of possible responses it offers. Armed force only admits of violence, but unarmed force runs the gamut. In some cases, a like-kind response may be the least costly and most advantageous response. Countering boycotts with boycotts or information operations with information operations may prove less risky and more effective than responding to sanctions with cyber-attacks or lawfare with media warfare. Although disparate responses are not necessarily disproportionate, they may excite countermeasures or condemnation because they cause qualitatively different sorts of harm that one may construe as unsuitable. Or they may not. Unlike the occasional breach of law that prompts countermeasures, soft war is an ongoing activity comprising an arsenal of weapons that opponents use simultaneously. There are currently no empirical data to evaluate the effectiveness self-defensive measures in soft war. Should they prove equally effective, there is no inherent reason to prefer a like-kind to a dissimilar response. Cyber operations may target cyber facilities but may also target lawyers who practice unjust warfare or media facilities that disseminate propaganda. Disparate responses do not violate an obvious right of the aggressor unless they violate the prescriptions of humanitarianism.

HUMANITARIANISM IN SOFT WAR

Direct attacks on civilians are the most serious deviation from international humanitarian law in soft war. Cyber warfare undermines civilian networks, information operations sabotage the flow of information, and economic warfare squeezes the civilian population. And although lawfare usually prosecutes combatants (rightly or wrongly), unjust lawfare tries to generate prosecutable enemy offenses by deliberately endangering the civilian population (below). As adversaries weigh a response to these threats, they too must ask whether they may harm noncombatants directly. If self-defensive measures track the self-help logic of reprisals, then the answer is probably yes, particularly since they bring no severe pain and suffering. But if self-defensive measures track armed conflict, then the answer is no because noncombatants are not liable to direct harm.

One way to help resolve this question is to invoke "participatory" liability (Gross 2015, 68–72). This is not legal liability; civilians performing anything but war-fighting duties are immune from any form of direct harm. But as they contribute to an unjust threat, participating civilians who provide "war-sustaining" aid – logistical, legal, financial, telecommunications, transportation, diplomatic, or security support – incur moral liability. War-sustaining aid corresponds to *indirect* participation in armed conflict. In contrast to direct participation or a war-fighting role, war-sustaining aid provides the means to wage war but does not pose a direct threat to life and limb. Among guerrilla organizations and states, providers of war-sustaining aid include individuals working for a group's "political" wing or state bureaucracies, respectively. Moral liability to disabling harm is commensurate with these persons' contribution to the war effort. As their contribution intensifies, so does the level of direct, permissible force that states or non-states can use against them. When their contributions reach the equivalent of armed support, noncombatants are liable to lethal force and defensive killing. But long before they reach this level, they remain subject to varying degrees of *nonlethal* force and the losses that may come, for example, from sanctions that target their assets (smart sanctions) or cyber-attacks that cripple war-sustaining infrastructure (banks, security apparatuses, transportation networks, internet etc.). In these cases, noncombatants may suffer disparate but proportionate harm: financial loss, insecurity, fear, collapse of social networks, and loss of virtual communities. Thus unarmed, self-defensive measures may take direct aim at civilian institutions that are protected from kinetic force.

Still, one may ask: Can unarmed force target *innocent* (i.e. nonparticipating) noncombatants directly in the spirit of reprisals? Reprisals, remember, do not demand liability. Here, I think, the answer is "sometimes" but subject to two conditions. First, targeting noncombatants with unarmed force must be a last resort and exhaust all the legitimate civilian targets connected with war-sustaining operations. Given the availability of liable civilian targets, such instances will be rare. Nevertheless, one can still imagine calls for unarmed retaliation: lawfare to combat lawfare, propaganda to rebut propaganda, and in-kind cyber retaliation. The targets may easily be noncombatants. Armed reprisals fail because they target noncombatants with unacceptable harm – death and injury – to which they are not liable. Are they liable to much lesser harms? It seems not. Yet the harm an unarmed attack causes civilians might be overridden by the benefits it brings. This assumes that unarmed reprisals are effective (i.e. the target government cares enough about its citizens or their commercial interests to comply) and that the interim costs to noncombatants are relatively minor and transient. Because noncombatants lack liability, argues Uniacke (2011), they enjoy a "right against harmful interference." This is true, but I take this to mean irreversible and severe harm. Otherwise the right is not absolute and would permit moderate harms when necessary to achieve significant benefits on balance.

The preceding discussion describes when self-defense measures may target liable and non-liable civilians. Broad military advantage in pursuit of self-defense, not law enforcement narrowly defined, is the aim of soft war. While this permits defenders to exercise necessary force, the key is to modulate force commensurate with the limits imposed by liability. Not all shows of force and resulting harms are permissible; participatory liability varies with each person's contribution of war-sustaining aid.

Three case studies illustrate the reach of proportionate self-defense soft war: cyber operations, economic sanctions, and lawfare. These are the same topics Jessica Wolfendale discussed at the head of this volume as she worked through definitions of war. Here, they exemplify dilemmas of self-defense. Each is an exercise of unarmed force but differs with regard to consequences and legality. Cyber-attacks are generally unlawful but currently pose no threat of catastrophic harm. Economic sanctions may be lawful but often threaten penury, hardship, and humanitarian crises. Lawfare, in contrast to cyber and economic measures, is usually lawful (though sometimes unjust) and, by its nature, nonlethal. Each of these parameters affects the exercise of proportionate self-defense.

PROPORTIONATE SELF-DEFENSE: CYBER WARFARE, CYBER TERRORISM

The Tallinn Manual (Schmitt 2013) discusses proportionate self-defense at length (Rule 9). Cyber operations that rise to the level of an armed attack warrant an armed attack in response, but unlawful cyber-attacks that target government, private, or commercial sites to steal financial assets, corrupt data, or reveal proprietary data only warrant an equivalent response. Cyber-attacks that disable or abuse email, internet, or social networks to undermine confidence in the government or economy or spread false information (Schmitt 2013, §36.3; §11.3) deserve hardly a mention because they do not cause significant harm. They are, on this interpretation, neither unlawful acts of terrorism nor an armed attack.

In each case, proportionality and humanitarianism constrain a self-defensive response. When a cyber-attack rises to the level of an armed attack by causing widespread injury, loss of life, and destruction of infrastructure, *in bello* proportionality governs proportionate self-defense, allowing governments or guerrillas to respond with proportionate and discriminating kinetic force. Although cyber-attacks have yet to cause widespread destruction, emerging cyber security strategies envision kinetic counter-attacks against cyber warfare facilities (as well as those civilian structures that support cyber warfare), cyber command posts and servers, cables, switches etc. (Farrell and Glaser 2016; Libicki 2009, 40, 71; US Department of Defense 2015). The goal is not only to destroy cyber capabilities but also to weaken military capabilities more generally and defeat or deter an armed adversary. In this case, as in all armed attacks, proportionality weighs military advantage against civilian harm. Calculating the effectiveness and advantage of a kinetic cyber-attack is sure to be taxing. One might draw a cautionary lesson from attempts to defeat TV and radio broadcasts with kinetic force. These rarely work and, when they do, the effects are very short-lived. US, NATO, and Israeli attacks against broadcast facilities in Iraq, Serbia, Libya, and Lebanon in recent years were entirely unsuccessful (Gross 2015, 234–239). As a result, civilian casualties cannot be justifiable collateral harm but are, instead, inexcusable unnecessary harm. It remains to be seen whether kinetic counter-attacks against cyber facilities are any more effective.

When cyber-attacks do not constitute armed attacks, then countermeasures are up for consideration. Countermeasures would permit an equivalent response against a cyber-attack. In most cases, cyber counter measures would enforce the legal regime governing cyber activities and restore the status quo that prohibits hacking, computer fraud, espionage, and destruction or damage of data (see, for example, the US Computer Fraud and Abuse Act, 18 U.S.C. 1030). Nevertheless, countermeasures against guerrilla organizations or non-states may strive for significant military advantages if not military victory. Some countermeasures are passive and include firewalls to prevent malware penetration or decoys that channel hackers to fabricated files and false information. Others, however, are active computer defenses (ACD) that include potentially unlawful "hack backs" that reach beyond an offending network to breach the networks, programs, data, and servers of hostile agents to destroy malware and the threatening servers (Lachow 2013). Alternatively, the victim of a cyber-attack may respond with an *equally* debilitating cyber-attack. The purpose of the attack is not to regain lost data or destroy offensive malware but to cause an equal measure of harm and compel compliance with the law. Such attacks need not target the original perpetrator or constitute an attack strictly in kind. In response to "a cyber operation by State B against an electrical generating facility at a dam in State A to coerce A into increasing the flow of water into a river running through States A and B," writes the Tallinn Manual (Schmitt, 2013, 40), "State A may lawfully respond with proportionate countermeasures, such as cyber operations against State B's irrigation control system."

In this account, cyber countermeasures hope to restore the status quo and deter future cyber-attacks. The incentive to comply is economic: State A exacts a price from State B by forcing B to either compensate farmers whose crops were ruined and/or provide alternative sources of water. State A inflicts proportionate harm because the costs State A imposes neatly offset whatever benefits State B gains by increasing the flow of water to its territory. Such retaliatory cyber-attacks to enforce the law conform to the self-help logic of reprisals but can be intensely problematic if the target does not provide war-sustaining support. If, in the above operation, the targets are equivalent it is only because each is a water facility. But there is no necessary equivalence of aims, harm, or liability to attack. The attempt to divert the headwaters of a common river may be part of a longstanding feud over hydroelectric power, while the irrigation systems of State B only serves the livelihood of farmers. The moral basis for the countermeasures is weak unless the target has some war-sustaining value. Alternatively, a lesser evil argument may prevail if some tangible military or political advantage comes from destroying the irrigation system that overrides the economic and other harms farmers suffer from unarmed force *and* noncombatants do not suffer serious injury or loss of life.

As states pursue proportionate self-defense, they enjoy the right to utilize armed or unarmed force and exact harm in excess of equivalence. In response to cyber aggression, states may reasonably turn to active defense measures or cyber retaliation, practices generally unavailable to individuals and businesses by law (Denning 2014). Because the private sector does not command the same self-defense prerogative as states or national movements they must turn to the state when they suffer cyber-attacks. State defense of private and commercial interests is a pressing concern because civilians, i.e. noncombatants, are a soft and easy target for hostile governments or terrorist groups. Arguing that "the internet is not indispensable to the survival of the civilian population (§81.5)," the Tallinn Manual shakes off cyber operations that block email or internet services (§30.12) involving, "mere economic coercion" (§11.2) or intending solely to undermine confidence in a government or economy (§11.3). Such acts are inconvenient but not terrorism.

The view of the Tallinn Manual experts is dangerously naïve. Terrorism works by undermining daily life, not by killing large numbers of people. Terrorism breeds fear, anxiety, political extremism, dysfunction, and lack of confidence in government institutions. Targeting civilians no less directly than kinetic terrorism, cyber terrorism imposes similar costs on civilians. Publicizing proprietary information, robbing people of financial assets, data, identities, and/or disrupting social networks and internet communications undermine human security, imperil civil liberties, and erode public confidence in many ways that are similar to mass casualty attacks (Gross, Canetti and Vashdi 2016, 2017). Thus, a limited, equivalent response to a cyber-attack may not account for the sweeping damage even nonlethal cyber-attacks can cause. Proportionate, defensive counter measures, however, must consider these costs when balancing the costs and benefits of collaterally or directly harming noncombatants. Thus, and in contrast to Tallinn's legal opinion, a hostile government or guerrilla organization that tweets to cause panic by "falsely indicating that a highly contagious and deadly disease is spreading through the population" (§36.3), or pursues cyber psychological operations to undermine confidence in a government or economy bears substantial liability.

Disabling these perpetrators should permit a measure of harm to participating enemy civilians and that may exceed an equivalent response in kind.

Cyber defense emphasizes the need to marshal the resources of state to meet the growing threat of cyber theft, espionage and terrorism. Under these circumstances, a state's (or non-state's) right to self-defense emerges as the reigning paradigm of proportionate self-defense. In the absence of armed attacks, nonlethal countermeasures subject to the broad constraints of *in bello* proportionality guide retaliatory response. Targets may be military but proportionate self-defense in soft war also permits direct attacks on civilian targets subject to the conditions of participatory liability.

PROPORTIONATE SELF-DEFENSE: ECONOMIC SANCTIONS

While many cyber-attacks are unlawful, this is not true of economic sanctions. And here, the law founders. Sanctions imposed on Iraq in 1990 to force Saddam Hussein to withdraw from Kuwait and, later, to disarm were lawful. As such, Iraq enjoyed no right to respond with countermeasures of its own. Yet, when faced with an invasion by Coalition forces in 1990 and US forces in 2013, Iraq enjoyed the right to self-defense. More precisely, Saddam Hussein, guilty of aggression, possessed no *ad bellum* right to wage war but his soldiers enjoyed the *in bello* legal and moral right to defend themselves by force of arms. There is something about an armed attack that allows soldiers to defend themselves independent of the lawfulness of their government's decision to go to war. Revisionist theorists object to this "independence thesis" but whatever one thinks about its role in armed conflict, the thesis does not seemingly pertain to unarmed force. Faced with the just exercise of unarmed force, a nation or national group enjoys no right of self-defense. Two explanations may account for this. First, the revisionists may be right and the independence thesis wrong. In which case, there are no moral grounds to permit any response to the just exercise of armed *or* unarmed force. Second, the pragmatic reasons some revisionists cite for granting *in bello* equality are absent from unarmed conflict. Denying equality to unjust adversaries undermines their motivation to obey the law and weakens the reciprocal nature of law of armed conflict. Branding unjust combatants as outlaws drives them from law abiding behavior and leaves international law unable to mitigate the devastation of war. But sanctions are not so devastating. If Saddam Hussein cannot respond to sanctions with *legal* sanctions of his own, then so what? He may of course respond with a round of unlawful countermeasures but there is nothing to be gained from allowing him the legal or moral right to do so.

Recourse to fight sanctions with sanctions or other soft war measures gains traction when the moral or legal status of economic sanctions, boycotts, or blockades is suspect. Impermissible economic measures are those imposed upon an aggressor but which precipitate disproportionate harm (e.g. a humanitarian crisis) or those measures that are not rightfully imposed. Consider first, disproportionate sanctions. Norms of international conduct say little about economic warfare except to prohibit humanitarian crises by demanding that sanctioning parties ensure food security, potable water, medical care, utilities, and shelter (Cohen 2009; Reinisch 2001). The law of armed conflict is quiet because sanctions do not constitute armed force. Just war theorists, on the other hand, take a harsher and more restrictive view (Gordon this volume). Most sanctions target noncombatants collectively. Such measures are morally impermissible unless noncombatants are liable to harm because they provide war-sustaining aid *or* the benefits of collective sanctions outweigh reasonable costs. Just war theory, therefore, places a greater burden on sanctioning states than the law does.

Nevertheless, sanctioning states do not always bear responsibility for deleterious outcomes. When sanctions fail to fulfill basic human needs and cause substantial suffering, the cause may lie with the sanctioning or the sanctioned state. The sanctioning state may fail to permit transfer of the necessary resources to forestall a humanitarian crisis. Or, the government of the sanctioned state may divert available resources to state or military purposes and exacerbate a humanitarian crisis. When fault lies with the sanctioning state, severe outcomes on par with a humanitarian crisis rise to the level of an armed attack and permit the use of proportionate and discriminate armed force in response. Iraq between 1990 and 2003 as well as Gaza 2006–2010 may offer pertinent examples of this permission. "May offer" because some details remain unclear. If international sanctions proved egregiously disproportionate, then Iraq could claim recourse to armed, self-defensive measures. If, on the other hand, the Iraqi government exacerbated sanctions by denying essential resources to the civilian population, then Iraq loses any right of proportionate self-defense. In Gaza, sanctions were debilitating but generally avoided a humanitarian crisis because smugglers and international relief organizations boosted the economy and provided aid. Had they not, and Israel continued to impose sanctions to the intense distress of the civilian population, proportionate self-defensive measures would be appropriate.

Unjust or indeterminately unjust sanctions also permit proportionate self-defensive measures. Sanctions in response to armed aggression are morally and legally permissible, but sanctions to force a nation to relinquish weapons it never possessed are not. In such cases, the right to self-defense reasserts itself. Ambiguous moral cases – US-imposed sanctions on Cuba, arms embargoes against national liberation movements in N. Ireland or Kosovo, or Palestinian-led boycotts of Israel, for example – also offer grounds to provide target states or non-states with the right of proportionate self-defense. Proportionality varies in each case. Israeli responses to the boycott, divestment, and sanction movement (BDS) take the form of counter boycotts and public diplomacy (Lim 2012). Cuba's responses to the US embargo did not confront the United States directly but sought support from the UN and EU to end the embargo while Cuba looked to compensate for economic losses though close relationships with the USSR, Venezuela, and other allies. While national liberation movements usually lack the wherewithal to mount counter embargoes, they may choose boycotts (like BDS), kinetic attacks against economic targets, or blockade runs. Consistent with earlier arguments, these attacks must target liable military or war-sustaining facilities, cause proportionate collateral harm, or inflict direct but nonlethal harm on the civilian population. Subject to these conditions, effective "smart" sanctions that aim at high-level government officials, terrorists, or guerrilla operatives or less discriminating collective sanctions that aim at large civilian populations are permissible soft war tactics.

Kinetic attacks, such as the IRA's bombing campaign against commercial centers in the mid-1990s and blockade runs such as the well-publicized attempt by Palestinians to break the Gaza blockade in 2010 (the Marmara incident) point to the complexities of using armed force in response to economic sanctions (UN Secretary General 2011). When confined to commercial targets, as were the IRA bombings in Manchester in 1992 and 1996, or Basque bombing campaigns against Spanish tourist resorts in 2004 and 2008 (The Guardian 2004; Turbo News 2008), kinetic attacks need not bring loss of life and may, therefore, constitute a proportionate self-defensive response (Gross 2015, 190–196). The danger, of course, lies in collateral harm. Similarly, while Israel's right to establish a sea and land blockade of Gaza received considerable attention, few considered the Palestinians' right to run the blockade. Assuming that the Israeli blockade was either unjust (because it brought a humanitarian crisis) or morally ambiguous (depending upon how one views Palestinian self-determination), the blockade of Gaza leaves room for a legitimate self-defensive response. A peaceful, nonviolent blockade run, while perhaps unlawful is nevertheless proportionate and morally permissible but not, as events later proved, particularly effective. Armed force, on the other hand, proved remarkably effective and turned the Marmara incident into a transformative event that compelled Israel to relax its land embargo significantly. But the costs were high when nine activists died. Given that the Palestinians pursued a military target, and sought (and gained) a significant military and political advantage, these deaths (which may or may not have been noncombatants) did not necessarily render the blockade run disproportionate. The deaths do, however, implicate the organizers who failed to take proper precautions to protect activists. Provoking a violent response from state authorities to publicize a political cause is a common tactic of nonviolent resistance but fraught with moral dilemmas as demonstrators are often placed at considerable risk without their consent (Gross 2015, 240–270).

In summary, each type of economic warfare – collective sanctions, smart sanctions, blockades, and boycotts – merits proportionate self-defense when morally unjust. Permissible self-defensive responses run the gamut from public diplomacy to counter boycotts to blockade running and kinetic attacks against economic targets. The defining condition of unjust economic warfare does not necessarily turn on illegality. Many of the sanctions described above were legally imposed by states or international organizations. Rather, injustice turns on unjust consequences (e.g. a humanitarian crisis), a violation of the target's rights (e.g. the right of self-determination), or a violation of the antecedent conditions of just unarmed conflict (e.g. effectiveness). There is a large body of literature that documents the ineffectiveness of economic sanctions (e.g. Gordon 2011; Hufbauer, Schott, Elliott, and Oegg 2007; Lopez 2012; Pape 1997). Ineffective tactics cannot be just; their costs are unnecessary and their victims, therefore, enjoy the right of self-defense. Once awarded the right of proportionate self-defense, the first targets to attack are those liable. Depending upon the sanctioned state's or organization's capabilities, proportionate self-defense may utilize armed or unarmed force. In either case, there is room for collateral harm subject to expected military advantages.

PROPORTIONATE SELF-DEFENSE: LAWFARE

Just as it is possible to distinguish between just and unjust economic or cyber warfare, one can distinguish between just and unjust uses of the law. Janina Dill (this volume) reserves "lawfare" for the latter alone but there is no agreement on this score. Instead, lawfare may be just or unjust. Just lawfare, as I use it in this chapter, refers to what Dill characterizes as appeals to the law to "halt the use of a specific weapon or tactic, to shame the adversary, [or] to gain the attention of the ICC Prosecutor's office (p. 242)." Unjust warfare (or what Dill refers to as simply "lawfare") reflects appeals to the law to exploit "a rule's indeterminacy to justify breaches of the rule that defy its own object and purpose." Defining torture as "exceptional interrogation techniques" to circumvent the prohibition against torture and ill-treatment illustrates Dill's point. Unjust lawfare also uses the law against its purpose. To feign civilian status (by masquerading as aid workers for example) and exploit the immunity it affords to attack a law-compliant adversary is one such example. Positioning offensive weapons close enough to civilians to provoke a disproportionate counter-attack is another. In the first case, belligerents abuse the principle of distinction to gain a military advantage. In the second case, belligerents abuse the requirement to take feasible steps to protect civilians from harm. Their purpose is to elicit an unlawful response and then pursue their adversary in the court of law or the court of public opinion. How may states or non-states respond to just and unjust lawfare? What constitutes proportionate self-defense?

Consider, first, just lawfare. Just lawfare embraces appeals to the UN, ICC, or states with universal jurisdiction to bring war criminals to justice and/or deter others from violating international humanitarian law. But if lawfare is just, then states have no legitimate response beyond what the law affords them. Unfortunately, the question of justness is not decided until the judges speak.

That is, the intent to use the law to rectify a breach of law is not determinative of justice. Lawfare, unlike sanctions or countermeasures, is not a self-help provision but an appeal to a third party for adjudication. As such, the process is justice-neutral until a decision is rendered. This leaves a target state or non-state with only two options. It may either engage the legal process and defend itself, or refuse to cooperate and risk punitive measures and international condemnation.

Unjust lawfare, in contrast, immediately raises the right of self-defense. There are two liable targets. One might be unjust lawyers or religious leaders who tender dubious legal decisions to cover for acts such as torture, the execution of POWs, or terrorism. The others are combatants who commit torture and murder or draw an adversary into violating the law to provide grounds for legal action. Reprobate jurists and theologians and the institutions they work for have no immunity from disabling force. This is the principle of participatory liability. The legal personnel of states and guerrilla organizations, like that of the diplomatic corps, telecommunications facilities, or financial institutions, provide varying degrees of war-sustaining aid. And lawfare can be among the most effective shows of unarmed force, affecting a belligerent's behavior on and off the battlefield (Crane 2010; Dunlap 2009; Scheffer 2010; Werner 2010). When lawfare induces compliance with humanitarian law, its effects are morally laudatory. But when lawfare unjustly interferes with the exercise of self-defense, its effects are morally condemnable. In the face of unjust lawfare, then, the force permitted to disable lawfare-related facilities (e.g. justice ministries or offices of paid consultants) will vary with the level of the unjust threat. Moderate threats (e.g. spurious or libelous charges) might merit the detention of legal and support personnel, censorship, or the destruction of infrastructure with unarmed force (e.g. cyber-attacks). Major threats that provide the legal cover to commit genocide or ethnic cleansing, on the other hand, may warrant lethal force.

Combatants who violate the law to draw their adversaries into unlawful acts present a vexing problem. When Hezbollah positioned missile launchers in front of a UN refugee camp near Qana, Lebanon, in 1996, guerrillas made a counter-attack exceedingly risky. And, when the Israeli response went awry, killing more than a hundred civilians, Israel had no choice but to curtail and soon cease military operations. Such shielding offers a win-win outcome for guerrillas: either civilian shields prevent a counter-attack or civilians suffer devastating injuries and hand guerrillas a public relations and legal coup. Whether Qana qualifies as unjust lawfare remains an open question. The UN (1996) only contested Israel's claim that a technical failure led shells to fall in the UN compound. Amnesty International (1996, 16–17), on the other hand, also condemned Hezbollah for "a clear breach of the laws of war's prohibitions on using the civilian population as a shield," before concluding, "Hezbollah's action in no way justifies the IDF attack on the compound." Here, of course, is the rub. The world community may certainly prosecute Israel for the attack on Qana and, if this was Hezbollah's intent, their missile operations were both a violation of the law and unjust lawfare.

Under these circumstances, it is difficult to separate liability for unjust lawfare from liability for unjust warfare. Perfidious actions as well at those that unlawfully put noncombatants at risk are punishable by law. When feasible, there is every reason to arrest perpetrators as any other war criminal. But once the same perpetrators ply their trade and wage war, whether under the cover of aid workers or civilians, their adversaries may permissibly respond with effective, discriminate, and proportionate *armed* force.

CONCLUSION

The cases above illustrate how proportionate self-defense plays out in unarmed conflict. From a moral and legal perspective, unarmed conflict is unique. It neither fits the *in bello* framework of armed conflict nor the self-help paradigm that permits states to take equivalent countermeasures to fight another state's unlawful activity. Nevertheless, the underlying logic of threat and liability inform defense during soft war. Unarmed conflict poses a threat of varying degrees perpetrated by agents of varying complicity. When the threat violates the rights of a nation or legitimate national liberation organizations, the victim enjoys the right of self-defense. Rights violations may be unlawful or ostensibly legal but morally dubious, while complicity depends upon the contribution of the perpetrator to the violation of the victim's rights. In response, proportionate self-defense may entail in-kind or disparate equivalent measures or more expansive measures consistent with *in bello* proportionality. The latter may include unarmed or armed force as dictated by military necessity. Humanitarianism constrains all responses. When armed force is on the table, humanitarianism tracks the dictates of IHL and protects noncombatants from unnecessary, excessive, or direct harm. When unarmed force is on the table, humanitarian protections are more subtle. They do not always protect noncombatants from direct attack and may not spare them the insecurity and anxiety of cyber warfare, the hardships of sanctions and boycotts, or harassing lawfare.

Participatory liability is the key to justifying harm to noncombatants during unarmed conflict. Although participatory liability narrows the scope of noncombatant immunity in a way similar to that which Valerie Morkevičius describes in her chapter about classical just war theory, the underlying justifications are different. For classical just war theorists, inflicting *nonlethal* harm on noncombatants is acceptable when necessary and proportionate. Underlying this reasoning is the assumption that property destruction is so less severe than loss of life or severe injury that it forms an entirely different category of harm where liability is irrelevant. Contemporary war, on the other hand, recognizes a myriad of significant, nonlethal harms – psychological suffering, displacement, disruption of essential services, media incitement, and material losses – that might only be inflicted on civilians if they somehow participate in armed or unarmed conflict.

These guidelines also establish the parameters of proportionate self-defense for the other forms of unarmed force described in this volume. States will ask how to proportionately respond to nonviolent resistance. Hunger strikes, for example, leave states with three options – force feeding, acquiescence, or compromise – all of which are often unpalatable but all permissible depending upon circumstances (Gross 2013). Faced with adversaries who shade the truth, manipulate the media, and stage events, parties to an unarmed conflict will ask whether they can only respond in kind or take more severe steps to fight media wars. Media wars, by their very nature, target civilians directly as parties to a conflict struggle to shape the opinions of compatriots, enemies, and third parties worldwide (Blank, Kaempf, this volume). Similarly, states will contemplate hostage taking of their own or, failing that, utilize substantial armed force, when confronting adversaries who kidnap soldiers or civilians (Meisels, Colonomos, this volume). In all these cases, and probably more, soft war poses an abiding challenge for just war theory.

NOTE

My thanks to Tami Meisels, Janina Dill, James Pattison, George Lucas, and Cécile Fabre for their thoughtful and incisive comments on earlier drafts of this chapter.

References

Abrahamsen, Rita and Michael C. Williams. 2015. "The Corporate-Security-Development Nexus. Assembling Security in the Post-Political Age." Sciences Po, March 21.

Ackerman, Andrew. 2015. "Obama Expresses Sympathy for New Greek Government." *The Wall Street Journal*, February 1. www.wsj.com/articles/obama-expresses-sympathy-for-new-greek-government-1422830309.

Air Force 2025. Maxwell AFB, AL: Air University, August 1996.

Allen, Joel. 2011. *Hostages and Hostage Taking in the Roman Empire*. Cambridge: Cambridge University Press.

Aloyo, Eamon. 2015. "Just War Theory and the Last of Last Resort." *Ethics & International Affairs* 29(2): 187–201.

Altman, Andrew. 2014. "Targeted Killing as an Alternative to War: The Problem of the Fair Distribution of Risk." ELAC Annual workshop.

Amnesty International. 1996. *Israel/Lebanon: Operation Grapes of Wrath*, July. AI Index: MDE 15/42/96.

Anderson, Jervis. 1973. *A. Philip Randolph*. New York: Harcourt Brace Jovanovich.

1997. *Bayard Rustin: Troubles I've Seen: A Biography*. New York: Harper Collins.

Ansah, Tawia. 2010. "'Lawfare': A Rhetorical Analysis." *Case Western Reserve Journal of International Law* 43: 87–120.

Anscombe, G.E.M. 1961. "War and Murder." In *Nuclear Weapons: A Catholic Response*, edited by Walter Stein, 45–62. New York: Sheed and Ward.

API. 1977. Protocol Additional to the Geneva Conventions of 12 August 1949, and relating to the Protection of Victims of International Armed Conflicts (Protocol I), 8 June 1977.

APII. 1977. Protocol Additional to the Geneva Conventions of 12 August 1949 and relating to the Protection of Victims of Non-International Armed Conflicts (Protocol II), 8 June 1977.

Aquinas, Thomas. 2002. "Summa Theologiae." In *Aquinas: Political Writings*, edited by R.W. Dyson, 239–278. Cambridge: Cambridge University Press.

Arendt, Hannah. 1972. "On Violence." In *Crises of the Republic*, by Hannah Arendt 103–198. New York: Harcourt Brace.

Aristotle. 2010. *Rhetoric*, edited by W.D. Ross. Munich: Cosimo Inc.

Arquilla, John. 1999. "Ethics and Information Warfare." In *Strategic Appraisal: The Changing Role of Information Warfare*, edited by Zalmay M. Khalizad and John P. White, 379–402. Washington, DC: RAND.

Arya, Neil and Sheila Zurbrigg. 2003. "Operation Infinite Justice: Impact of Sanctions and Prospective War on the People of Iraq." *Canadian Journal of Public Health* 94 (1) 9–12.

Attorney General of the State of Israel. Directive No. 9.1002, last updated April 2015. Accessed July 23. http://index.justice.gov.il/En/Units/AttorneyGeneral/Documents /AGDirectiveMilitaryAdvocateGeneral.pdf.

Augustine of Hippo. 1984. *City of God*. New York: Penguin Books.

1994. "Letter to Boniface." In *Augustine: Political Writings*, edited by Ernest L. Fortin, Roland Gunn, and Douglas Kries, 219–220. Indianapolis, IN: Hackett Publishing Company, Inc.

2006. "Questions on the Heptateuch." In *The Ethics of War: Classic and Contemporary Readings*, edited by Gregory Reichberg, Henrik Syse, and Endre Begby, 70–90. Malden, MA: Blackwell.

Austin, John. (1832) 1995. *The Province of Jurisprudence Determined*, edited by W. Rumble. Cambridge: Cambridge University Press.

1879. *Lectures on Jurisprudence or The Philosophy of Positive Law*, edited by R. Campbell. London: John Murray.

Bailey, David. 2015. "Resistance Is Futile? The Impact of Disruptive Protest in the 'Silver Age of Permanent Austerity.'" *Socio-Economic Review* 13(1): 5–32.

Baker, Deane-Peter and James Pattison. 2012. "The Principled Case for Employing Private Military and Security Companies in Interventions for Human Rights Purposes." *Journal of Applied Philosophy* 29(1): 1–18.

Baldwin, David A. 1985. *Economic Statecraft*. Princeton, NJ: Princeton University Press.

Barber, James. 1979. "Economic Sanctions as a Policy Instrument." *International Affairs* 55(3): 367.

Barnes, Rudolph C. Jr. 2009. "The Rule of Law and Civil Affairs in the Battle for Legitimacy." *Military Legitimacy and Leadership Journal*.

Bayles, William J. 2001. "The Ethics of Computer Network Attack." *Parameters* 31 (1): 44–58.

BBC News. 2015. "Greece Debt Crisis: German MPs Vote 'Yes' to Bailout Talks." www.bbc.com/news/world-europe-33560366.

Beard, Jack. 2009. "Law and War in the Virtual Era." *American Journal of International Law* 103: 409–445.

Beckhusen, Robert. 2013. "How Mexico's Drug Cartels Recruit Child Soldiers as Young as 11." *Wired*, March 28. www.wired.com/2013/03/mexico-child-soldiers/.

Beitz, Charles. 1979. *Political Theory and International Relations*. Princeton: Princeton University Press.

Bell, John Bowyer. 1977. *Terror out Of Zion – The Fight for Israeli Independence*. New York: St. Martin's Press.

Bellflower, John W. 2010. "The Influence of Law on Command of Space." *Air Force Law Review* 65: 107–144.

Bender, Jeremy and Armin Rosen. 2014. "Mexico's Drug War Is Entering a Dark Phase." *Business Insider*, October 24. www.businessinsider.com/mexicos -drugwar-is-entering-a-dangerousphase-2014-10.

Benjamin, Walter. 2004. "Critique of Violence." In *Walter Benjamin: Selected Writings Volume 1: 1913–1926*, edited by Marcus Bullock and Michael W. Jennings, 236–252. Cambridge, MA: Belknap Press, Harvard.

Berger, J.M. 2014. "How ISIS Games Twitter" *The Atlantic*, June 16. Accessed July 29, 2015. www.theatlantic.com/international/archive/2014/06/isis-iraq-twitter-social-media-strategy/372856.

Bertram, Anton. 1931. "The Economic Weapon as a Form of Peaceful Pressure." *Proceedings of the Grotius Society* 17: 139–174.

Bevel, James. 1985. Interview by Blackside, Inc., November 13, for *Eyes on the Prize: America's Civil Rights Years (1954–1965)*. Washington University Libraries, Film and Media Archive, Henry Hampton Collection. http://digital.wustl.edu/e/eop/eopweb/bev0015.0491.010jamesbevel.html.

Biddle, Tami Davis. 2014. "Strategic Bombardment: Expectation, Theory, and Practice in the Early Twentieth Century." In *The American Way of Bombing: Changing Ethical and Legal Norms, From Flying Fortresses to Drones*, edited by Matthew Evangelista and Henry Shue, 27–46. Ithaca, NY: Cornell University Press.

Blank, Laurie R. 2010. "Finding Facts but Missing the Law; the Goldstone Report, Gaza and Lawfare." *Case Western Reserve Journal of International Law* 43: 279–306.

2011. "A New Twist on an Old Story: Lawfare and the Mixing of Proportionalities." *Case Western Reserve Journal of International Law* 43: 707–738.

2012. "Protecting Civilians or Using Them as Pawns: The Israel-Hamas Conflict." *JURIST*.

Blum, Gabriella and Philip Heymann. 2010. "Law and Policy of Targeted Killing." *Harvard National Security Journal* 1.

Bonhoeffer, Dietrich. 1997. *Letters and Papers from Prison*. New York: Touchstone.

Bonzio, Alessandro. 2014. "ISIS' Use of Social Media Is Not Surprising; Its Sophisticated Digital Strategy Is." *The Huffington Post*, September 15. Accessed July 29, 2015. www.huffingtonpost.co.uk/alessandro-bonzio/isis-use-of-social-media-_b_5818720.html.

Boothe, Ivan and Lee A. Smithey. 2007. "Privilege, Empowerment, and Nonviolent Intervention." *Peace & Change* 32(1): 39–61.

Bowman, John. 1989. *De Valera and the Ulster Question, 1917–73*. Oxford: Oxford University Press.

Branch, Taylor. 1999. *Pillar of Fire: America in the King Years 1963–65*. New York: Simon and Schuster.

Branche, Raphaelle. 2010. "The French in Algeria: Can There Be Prisoners of War in a 'Domestic' operation?" In *Prisoners in War*, edited by Sybille Scheipers, 174–186. Oxford: Oxford University Press.

Brandt, Patrick T. and Todd Sandler. 2009. "Hostage Taking: Understanding Terrorism Event Dynamics." *Journal of Policy Modeling* 31: 758–778.

Breaking the Silence. 2015. *This Is How We Fought in Gaza*. Jerusalem (no publishing house given).

Brenner, Joel. 2011. *America the Vulnerable: Inside the New Threat Matrix of Digital Espionage, Crime, and Warfare*. New York: Penguin Press.

Brock, Peter. 1972. *Pacifism in Europe to 1914*. Princeton, NJ: Princeton University Press.

1991. *Freedom from War: Nonsectarian Pacifism, 1814–1914*. Toronto: University of Toronto Press.

1999. *Challenge to Mars: Pacifism from 1918 to 1945*. Toronto: University of Toronto Press.
Bromley, Mark. 2007. *United Nations Arms Embargoes, Their Impact on Arms Flows and Target Behavior Case study: Federal Republic of Yugoslavia, 1998–2001*. Stockholm: Stockholm International Peace Research Institute. http://books.sipri.org/files/misc/UNAE/SIPRI07UNAEFRY.pdf.
Brooks, Stephen G. 1997. "Dueling Realisms." *International Organization* 51(3): 445–477.
Broome, John. 2001. *Weighing Lives*. Oxford: Oxford University Press.
Brown, Davis. 2006. "A Proposal for an International Convention to Regulate the Use of Information Systems in Armed Conflict." *Harvard International Law Journal* 47: 179–222.
Brown, Judith M. 2009. "Gandhi and Civil Resistance in India, 1917–47: Key Issues." In *Civil Resistance and Power Politics: the Experience of Non-Violent Action from Gandhi to the Present*, edited by Adam Roberts and Timothy Garton Ash, 43–57. Oxford: Oxford University Press.
Brownlie, Ian. 1963. *International Law and the Use of Force by States*. Oxford: Clarendon Press.
Brunnée, Jutta and Stephen J. Toope. 2010. *Legitimacy and Legality in International Law. An Interactional Account*. Cambridge: Cambridge University Press.
Brunstetter, Daniel and Megan Braun. 2013. "From *Jus ad Bellum* to *Jus ad Vim*: Recalibrating Our Understanding of the Moral Use of Force." *Ethics & International Affairs* 27(1): 87–106.
Brzoska, Michael. 2001. "A Brief Background on the 'Bonn-Berlin Process'." In *Smart Sanctions: The Next Steps*, edited by Michael Brzoska, 9–17. Baden-Baden: Nomos Verlagsgesellschaft.
2002. "Putting More Teeth in UN Arms Embargoes." In *Smart Sanctions: Targeting Economic Statecraft*, edited by David Cortright and George A. Lopez, 125–144. Boulder, CO: Rowman & Littlefield.
Buber, Martin. 1958. *I and Thou*. New York: Charles Scribner's Sons.
Buchanan, Allen. 2004. *Justice, Legitimacy and Self-Determination: Moral Foundations for International Law*. Oxford: Oxford University Press.
Buffard, Isabelle and Karl Zemanek. 1998. "The 'Object and Purpose' of a Treaty: An Enigma?" *Australia Review of International Law and European Law* 3: 311–343.
Bugnion, Francois. 2002. "Just War, Wars of Aggression and International Humanitarian Law." *The International Review of the Red Cross* 84(847): 523–546 (French original). English Version: www.icrc.org/eng/assets/files/other/irrc-847–2002-bugnion-ang.pdf 1–26.
Buley, Ben. 2008. *The New American Way of War: American Culture and the Political Utility of Force*. London: Routledge.
Bull, Hedley. 1995. *The Anarchical Society*. New York: Columbia University Press.
(1977) 2002. *The Anarchical Society*. Basingstoke: Palgrave.
Burr, Ty. 2014. "Dopey and Gory, 'The Interview' Was Bound to Disappoint." *Boston Globe*, December 25. Accessed February 18, 2016. www.Bostonglobe.Com/Arts/Movies/2014/12/25/Dopey-And-Gory-The-Interview-Was-Bound-Disappoint/3pcttjiy1mu1aqrdbmzvpm/Story.Html.
Butler, Michael. 2012. *Selling a Just War: Framing, Legitimacy, and US Military Intervention*. New York: Palgrave Macmillan.

Bynum, Cornelius L. A. 2010. *Philip Randolph and the Struggle for Civil Rights.* Urbana, IL: University of Illinois Press.
Calhoun, Craig, ed. 1992. *Habermas and the Public Sphere.* Cambridge, MA: MIT Press.
Campbell, A. C., trans. 1990. *Hugo Grotius, The Rights of War and Peace.* Westport, CT: Hyperion.
Canada, Reservations and Statements of Understanding made upon Ratification of AP I, 20 November 1990, § 7. (1990) 2005. In *Customary International Humanitarian Law* Volume II, edited by Jean-Marie Henckaerts and Louise Doswald-Beck, 332. Cambridge: Cambridge University Press.
Caney, Simon. 1997. "Self-Government and Secession: The Case of Nations." *Journal of Political Philosophy* 5(4): 351–372.
2009. "Climate Change and the Future: Discounting for Time, Wealth and Risk." *Journal of Social Philosophy* 40(2): 163–186.
Cannizzaro, Enzo. 2001. "The Role of Proportionality in the Law of International Countermeasures." *European Journal of International Law* 12(5): 889–916.
Carisch, Enrico and Loraine Rickard-Martin. 2013. *Sanctions and the Effort to Globalize Natural Resources Governance.* New York: Friederich-Ebert-Stiftung.
Carlson, John and Neville Yeomans. 1975. "Whither Goeth the Law – Humanity and Barbarity." In *The Way Out – Radical Alternatives in Australia*, edited by M. Smith and D. Crossley, 155–162. Melbourne: Lansdowne Press.
Carr, Edward Hallet. 1946. *The Twenty Years' Crisis, 1919–1939: An Introduction to the Study of International Relations.* London: MacMillan.
Carriere, Rolf. 2010. "The World Needs 'Another Peacekeeping'." In *Civilian Peacekeeping: A Barely Tapped Resource*, edited by Christine Schweitzer, 17–24. IFGK Working Paper No. 23. Belm-Vehrte, Germany: Sozio Publishing.
Carroll, Rory 2015. "The Ransom Dilemma: Why the US Is Softening Policy on Cash for Hostages." *The Guardian.* 24 June.
Carruthers, Susan. 2011. *The Media at War.* London: Palgrave Macmillan.
Carson, Clayborne. 1995. *In Struggle: SNCC and the Black Awakening of the 1960s.* Cambridge, MA: Harvard University Press.
Cassese, Antonio. 2008. *The Human Dimension of International Law.* New York: Oxford University Press.
Chabot, Sean. 2011. *Transnational Roots of the Civil Rights Movement: African American Explorations of the Gandhian Repertoire.* Lanham, MD: Lexington Books.
Chapel, David. 2005. *A Stone of Hope: Prophetic Religion and the Death of Jim Crow.* Chapel Hill, NC: University of North Carolina Press.
Channel 4. 2014. "Unmasked: The Man Behind Top Islamic State Twitter Account." December 11. Accessed July 27, 2015. www.channel4.com/news/unmasked-the-man-behind-top-islamic-state-twitter-account-shami-witness-mehdi.
Chenoweth, Erica and Stephan, Maria. 2011. *Why Civil Resistance Works: The Strategic Logic of Nonviolent Conflict.* New York: Columbia University Press.
Christiansen, Drew and Gerard F. Powers. 1995. "Economic Sanctions and Just War Doctrine." In *Economic Sanctions: Panacea or Peacebuilding?*, edited by David Cortright and George A. Lopez, 97–120. Oxford: Westview Press.
Cilluffo, Frank J. and Curt H. Gergely. 1997. "Information Warfare and Strategic Terrorism." *Terrorism and Political Violence* 9(1): 84–94.

Clark, Kathleen and Julie Mertens. 2004. "Torturing the Law: The Justice Department's Legal Contortions on Interrogation." *Washington Post*, June 20.

Clarke, Richard A. and Robert K. Kanke. 2010. *Cyber War: The Next Threat to National Security and What to Do about It*. New York: HarperCollins.

CNN. 2009. "US Military: Taliban Killings Prompted Airstrikes." May 6. http://edition.cnn.com/2009/WORLD/asiapcf/05/06/afghan.us.airstrike/index.html?iref=24hours.

Cohen, Amichai. 2009. "Economic Sanctions in IHL: Suggested Principles." *Israel Law Review* 42: 117–149.

Coker, Christopher. 2001. *Humane Warfare*. London: Routledge.

2002. *Waging War without Warriors? The Changing Culture of Military Conflict*. London: Lynne Rienner.

Colaiaco, James A. 1986. "Martin Luther King, Jr. and the Paradox of Nonviolent Direct Action." *Phylon* 47(1): 16–28.

Colonomos, Ariel. 2014. "Hostage Dilemmas: Learning from Hamas to Use against ISIS." *Haaretz*, September 10.

2016a. *Selling the Future: The Perils of Global Predictions*. London and New York: Hurst and Oxford University Press.

2016b. "Precision Warfare and the Case for Symmetry: Hostage Taking and Targeted Killings." In *The Transformation of Contemporary Warfare*, edited by David Jacobson and John Torpey, 134–152. Philadelphia: Temple University Press.

Conetta, Carl. 2003a. *The Wages of War*. Accessed October 28, 2014. www.comw.org/pda/fulltext/0310rm8exsum.pdf.

2003b. *Catastrophic Interdiction: Air Power and the Collapse of the Iraqi Field Army in the 2003 War*. September 26. Accessed September 2, 2014. http://www.comw.org/pda/fulltext/0309bm30.pdf.

2004. "Disappearing the Dead: Iraq, Afghanistan, and the Idea of a 'New Warfare'." *Project on Defense Alternatives*, February 9.

Conroy, Richard. 2002. "The UN Experience with Travel Sanctions: Selected Cases and Conclusions." In *Smart Sanctions: Targeting Economic Statecraft*, edited by David Cortright and George A. Lopez, 145–170. Boulder, CO: Rowman & Littlefield.

Cook, Martin L. 2000. "'Immaculate War': Constraints on Humanitarian Intervention." *Ethics & International Affairs* 14: 55–65.

Corn, Geoffrey S., Laurie R. Blank, Eric Talbot Jensen, and Christopher Jenks. 2013. "Belligerent Targeting and the Invalidity of a Least Harmful Means Rule." *International Law Studies* 89: 536–626.

Corn, Geoffrey S. 2009. "Back to the Future: De Facto Hostilities, Transnational Terrorism, and the Purpose of the Law of Armed Conflict." *University of Pennsylvania Journal of International Law* 30: 1345–1354.

2015. "War, Law and the Oft Overlooked Value of Process as a Precautionary Measure." *Pepperdine Law Review* 42: 419–466.

Cortright, David. 2008. *Peace: A History of Movements and Ideas*. Cambridge: Cambridge University Press.

Cortright, David and George A. Lopez, eds. 2000. *The Sanctions Decade: Assessing UN Strategies in the 1990s*. Boulder, CO: Lynne Rienner.

Cortright, David and George A. Lopez. 2002. "Introduction." In *Smart Sanctions: Targeting Economic Statecraft*, edited by David Cortright and George A. Lopez, 1–22. Boulder, CO: Rowman & Littlefield.

Cotterrell, Roger. 2003. *The Politics of Jurisprudence: A Critical Introduction to Legal Philosophy*. London: LexisNexis.

Coy, Patrick G. 2011. "The Privilege Problematic in International Nonviolent Accompaniment's Early Decades: Peace Brigades International Confronts the Use of Racism." *Journal of Religion, Conflict and Peace* 4(2). www.religionconflictpeace.org/.

2012. "Nonpartisanship, Interventionism and Legality in Accompaniment: Comparative Analyses of Peace Brigades International, Christian Peacemaker Teams, and the International Solidarity Movement." *International Journal of Human Rights* 16(7): 963–981.

2013. "Whither Nonviolent Studies?" *Peace Review: A Journal of Social Justice* 25: 257–265.

Crane, David M. 2010. "The Take Down: Case Studies regarding Lawfare in International Criminal Justice: The West African Experience." *Case Western Reserve Journal of International Law* 43: 201–214.

Crawford, Neta C. 2013. *Accountability for Killing: Moral Accountability for Collateral Damage in America's post-9/11 Wars*. Oxford: Oxford University Press.

Crompton, Paul. 2014. "Grand Theft Auto: ISIS? Militants Reveal Video Game." *Al Arabiya News*, September 20. Accessed August 1, 2015. http://english.alarabiya.net/en/variety/2014/09/20/Grand-Theft-Auto-ISIS-Militants-reveal-video-game.html.

Damrosch, Lori Fisler. 1993. "The Civilian Impact of Economic Sanctions." In *Enforcing Restraint: Collective Intervention in Internal Conflicts*, edited by Lori Fisler Damrosch, 274–315. New York: Council on Foreign Relations Press.

Davis, Richard. 1976. *Arthur Griffith*. Irish History Series, No. 10. Dundalk: Dundalgan Press.

De Oliviera, Nythamar Fernandes. 2000. "The Critique of Public Reason Revisited: Kant as Arbiter between Rawls and Habermas." *Veritas* 45 (4): 583–606.

de Vitoria, Francisco. 2003. "On the Law of War." In *Vitoria: Political Writings*, edited by Anthony Padgen and Jeremy Lawrence, 293–329. Cambridge: Cambridge University Press.

D'Emilio, John. 2004. *Lost Prophet: The Life and Times of Bayard Rustin*. Chicago, IL: University Of Chicago Press.

Denning, Dorothy E. 2014. "Framework and Principles for Active Cyber Defense." *Computers & Security* 40: 108–113.

Department of the Army. 2006. *Counterinsurgency*. Field Manual 3–24. Washington, DC: Headquarters, Department of the Army.

Der Derian, James. 2001. *Virtuous War: Mapping the Military-Industrial-Media-Entertainment Network*. Oxford: Westview Press.

Deutsch, Karl W. and Dieter Senghaas. 1971. "A Framework for a Theory of War and Peace." In *The Search for World Order: Studies by Students and Colleagues of Quincy Wright*, edited by Albert Lepawsky, Edward H. Buehrig, and Harold D. Lasswell, 24–46. New York: Appleton Century-Crofts.

DeVries, Anthonius W. 2002. "European Union Sanctions against the Federal Republic of Yugoslavia from 1998 to 2000: A Special Exercise in Targeting." In *Smart Sanctions: Targeting Economic Statecraft*, edited by David Cortright and George A. Lopez, 87–108. Boulder, CO: Rowman & Littlefield.

Dill, Janina. 2015a. *Legitimate Targets? Social Construction, International Law and US Bombing*. Cambridge: Cambridge University Press.
2015b. "The 21st Century Belligerent's Trilemma." *European Journal of International Law* 26: 83–108.
Dinniss, Heather Harrison. 2012. *Cyber Warfare and the Laws of War*. Cambridge: Cambridge University Press.
Dinstein, Yoram. 2004. *The Conduct of Hostilities under the Law of International Armed Conflict*. Cambridge: Cambridge University Press.
2005. *War, Aggression and Self Defense*. 4th edn. Cambridge: Cambridge University Press.
Dixie, Quinton. 2011. *Visions of a Better World: Howard Thurman's Pilgrimage to India and the Origins of African American Nonviolence*. Boston: Beacon Press.
DOJ (US Department of Justice). 2014. "US Charges Five Chinese Military Hackers for Cyber Espionage Against US Corporations and a Labor Organization for Commercial Advantage." May 19. www.justice.gov/opa/pr/us-charges-five-chinese-military-hackers-cyber-espionage-against-us-corporations-and-labor.
Donnelly, Jack. 2003. *Universal Human Rights in Theory and Practice*, 2nd ed. Ithaca, NY: Cornell University Press.
Doyle, Michael. 2015. *The Question of Intervention: John Stuart Mill and the Responsibility to Protect*. New Haven, CT: Yale University Press.
Draft articles on Responsibility of States for Internationally Wrongful Acts, with commentaries. 2001. http://legal.un.org/ilc/texts/instruments/english/commentaries/9_6_2001.pdf.
Drezner, Daniel W. 2011. "Sanctions Sometimes Smart: Targeted Sanctions in Theory and Practice." *International Studies Review* 13: 96–108.
Duncan, Mel. 2015. "Nonviolent Peaceforce Receives Grant to Start Syria Project." *Nonviolent Peaceforce*, January 15. www.nonviolentpeaceforce.org/np-news/2014–06-26–17-22–51/378-nonviolent-peaceforce-receives-grant-to-start-syria-project.
Dunlap, Charles J., Jr. 2001. *Law and Military Interventions: Preserving Humanitarian Values in 21st Century Conflicts*, http://people.duke.edu/~pfeaver/dunlap.pdf.
2008. "Lawfare Today." *Yale Journal of International Affairs* 3: 146–154.
2009. "Lawfare: A Decisive Element of 21st Century Conflicts?" *Joint Forces Quarterly* 54: 34–39.
2010. "Does Lawfare Need and Apologia?" *Case Western Reserve Journal of International Law* 43: 121–144.
2011. "Lawfare Today . . . and Tomorrow." *International Law Studies* 87: 315–325.
2014a. "Will Lawfare Define the Palestinian-Israeli Conflict?" *Al-Monitor*, July 30. www.al-monitor.com/pulse/originals/2014/07/lawfare-palestine-israel-gaza-conflict-dunlap.html#ixzz3fZP1AXaI.
2014b. "Has Hamas Overplayed Its Lawfare Strategy?" *Just Security*, August 5. http://justsecurity.org/13781/charles-dunlap-lawfare-hamas-gaza/.
Eagleton, Clyde. 1932–33. "The Attempt to Define War." *International Conciliation* 15: 237–287.
Easthom, Tiffany. 2014. "As a New Civil War Gripped the Nation, NP Scaled Up to Become the Largest Protection Agency in South Sudan." *Nonviolent Peaceforce, Progress Report, January 2013-June 2014*. www.nonviolentpeaceforce.org/np-news/2014–06-26–17-22–51/334-the-2013–2014-progress-report-is-out-now.

Eddy, Matthew P. 2011. "Freedom Summer Abroad: Biographical Pathways and Cosmopolitanism among International Human Rights Workers." *Research in Social Movements, Conflicts, and Change* 31: 209–258.

Elliott, Kimberly Ann. 1995. "Factors Affecting the Success of Sanctions." In *Economic Sanctions: Panacea or Peacebuilding in a Post-Cold War World?*, edited by David Cortright and George A. Lopez, 51–60. Boulder, CO: Westview.

Ellis, Elizabeth A. 2015. "The Ethics of Economic Sanctions." In *Internet Encyclopedia of Philosophy*.

Ellyatt, Holly. 2015. "Strings Attached to German Vote on Greek Bailout?" *CNBC*, August 17. www.cnbc.com/2015/08/17/greek-bailout-vote-in-germany-lies-ahead .html.

Fabre, Cécile. 2009. "Guns, Food, and Liability to Attack in War." *Ethics* 120: 36–63.

2012. *Cosmopolitan War*. Oxford: Oxford University Press.

Farnsworth, Allan E. 1995. "Duties of Good Faith and Fair Dealins under the UNIDROIT Principles, Relevant International Conventions and National Laws." *Tulane Journal of International and Comparative Law* 3: 47.

Farrell, Henry and Glaser, Charles L. 2016. "An Effects-Based Approach to Escalation and Deterrence in Cyberspace." A paper presented at the Stanford Cyber Policy Program Workshop on Strategic Uses of Offensive Cyber Operations, March 3–4, 2016.

Farrell, Stephen and Richard A. Oppel. 2009. "NATO Strike Magnifies Divide." *New York Times*, September 4.

Fassbender, Bardo. 2006. "Target Sanctions and Due Process." United Nations Office of Legal Affairs. www.un.org/law/counsel/Fassbender_study.pdf.

Fearon, James D. and David D. Laitin. 2003. "Ethnicity, Insurgency, and Civil War." *American Political Science Review* 97(1): 75–90.

Feinberg, Joel. 1986. *Harm to Self – The Moral Limits of the Criminal Law*. Vol. 3. Oxford: Oxford University Press.

1988. *Harmless Wrongdoing- The Moral Limits of the Criminal Law*. Vol. 4. Oxford: Oxford University Press.

Finkelstein, Clair, Jens David Ohlin, and Andrew Altman. 2012. *Targeted Killings: Law and Morality in an Asymmetrical World*. Oxford: Oxford University Press.

Finlay, Christopher J. 2015. *Terrorism and the Right to Resist: A Theory of Just Revolutionary War*. Cambridge: Cambridge University Press.

Fletcher, George. 2002. *Romantics at War – Glory and Guilt in the Age of Terrorism*. Princeton & Oxford: Princeton University Press.

Foley, Hamilton. 1923. *Woodrow Wilson's Case for the League of Nations*. Princeton, NJ: Princeton University Press.

Ford, Shannon Brandt. 2013. "*Jus Ad Vim* and the Just Use of Lethal Force-Short-of-War." In *Routledge Handbook of Ethics and War: Just War Theory in the 21st Century*, edited by Fritz Allhoff, Nicholas Evans, and Adam Henschke, 63–75.

Foucault, Michel. 1995. *Discipline and Punish: The Birth of the Prison*. New York: Vintage Books.

Franck, Thomas. 1995. *Fairness in International Law and Instructions*. Oxford: Oxford University Press.

Franck, Thomas M. 2008. "On Proportionality of Countermeasures in International Law." *American Journal of International Law*: 715–767.

Frowe, Helen. 2016. "On the Redundancy of *Jus ad Vim*: A Response to Meghan Braun and Daniel Brunstetter." *Ethics and International Affairs* 30: 117–129.

Fruchart, Damien, Paul Holtom et al. 2007. *United Nations Arms Embargoes: Their Impact on Arms Flows and Target Behaviour*. Stockholm: Stockholm International Peace Research Institute.

Frum, David. 2008. "Misinformation Warfare." *National Post*, February 2.

Gandhi, Mahatma. 2008. *The Essential Writings*, edited by Judith M. Brown. Oxford: Oxford University Press.

Gardam, Judith. 1999. "Necessity and Proportionality in *Jus Ad Bellum* and *Jus in Bello*." In *International Law, the International Court of Justice and Nuclear Weapons*, edited by Laurence Boisson de Chazournes and Philippe Sands, 275–292. Cambridge: Cambridge University Press.

Garrow, David. 2004. *Bearing the Cross: Martin Luther King, Jr., and the Southern Christian Leadership Conference*. New York: William Morrow.

Garstka, John. 2004. Interview by Sebastian Kaempf, December 18. Washington, DC.

Geneva Convention III. 1949. *Convention Relative to the Treatment of Prisoners of War*. Geneva, August 12.

Geneva Convention IV. 1949. *Convention Relative to the Protection of Civilian Persons In Time Of War*. Geneva, August 12.

Gentili, Alberico. (1598) 1933. *De Jure Belli Libri Tres*. Oxford: Clarendon Press.

Gilbreath, Edward. 2013. *Birmingham Revolution: Martin Luther King Jr.'s Epic Challenge to the Church*. Downers Grove, IL: IVP Books.

Gillmor, Dan. 2010. *Mediaactive*. California: Creative Commons Attribution. http://mediactive.com.

Gilpin, Robert. 1981. *War and Change in World Politics*. Cambridge: Cambridge University Press.

Gines, Kathryn. 2014. *Hannah Arendt and the Negro Question*. Bloomington, IN: Indiana University Press.

Goldsmith, Jack L. and Eric A. Posner. 2005. *The Limits of International Law*. New York: Oxford University Press.

Goodman, Ryan. 2013. "The Power to Kill or Capture Enemy Combatants." *European Journal of International Law* 24(3): 819–853.

Gordon, Joy. 2004. "When Economic Sanctions Become Weapons of Mass Destruction." *Contemporary Conflict*, March 26.

2010. *Invisible War: The United States and the Iraq Sanctions*. Cambridge, MA: Harvard University Press.

2011. "Smart sanctions revisited." *Ethics & International Affairs* 25: 315–335.

2014–2015. "Economic sanctions, just war doctrine, and the 'fearful spectacle of the civilian dead'." *CrossCurrents*, December 5. www.crosscurrents.org/gordon.htm.

Green, Leslie C. 2008. *The Contemporary Law of Armed Conflict*. 3rd edn. Manchester: Juris Publishing, Manchester University Press.

Greenberg, Andy. 2012. *This Machine Kills Secrets*. London: Penguin.

Grieco, Joseph M. 1988. "Realist Theory and the Problem of International Cooperation." *Journal of Politics* 50: 600.

Griffith, Arthur. 1918. *The Resurrection of Hungary: A Parallel for Ireland with Apendices on Pitt's Policy and Sinn Féin*, 3rd edn. Dublin: Whelan & Son.

Griffiths, John. 2003. *Hostages: The History Facts and Reasoning behind Hostage Taking*. London: André Deutsch.

Gross, Michael, L. 2008. "The Second Lebanon War: The Question of Proportionality and the Prospect of Non-Lethal Warfare." *Journal of Military Ethics* 7(1), 1–22.

2005/2006. "Killing Civilians Intentionally." *Political Science Quarterly* 120(4): 555–579.

2013. "Force-Feeding, Autonomy, and the Public Interest." *New England Journal of Medicine* 369:103–105.

2014. "The Paradox of Using Human Shields in War." *Ethics & International Affairs blog*, October 6. www.ethicsandinternationalaffairs.org/2014/the-paradox-of-using-human-shields-in-war/.

2015. *The Ethics of Insurgency: A Critical Guide to Just Guerrilla Warfare.* Cambridge: Cambridge University Press.

Gross, Michael L., Daphna Canetti and Dana R. Vashdi. 2016. "The Psychological Effects of Cyber Terrorism," *Bulletin of Atomic Scientists*, 72(5), 284–291.

Gross, Michael L., Daphna Canetti and Dana R. Vashdi. 2017. "Cyber Terrorism: Its Effects on Psychological Well Being, Public Confidence and Political Attitudes." *Journal of Cyber Security* 3(1), 1–10. 2017

Grove, Thomas. 2012. "Russia Condemns America's Human Rights Record." *Huffington Post*, October 22. www.huffingtonpost.com/2012/10/22/russia-america-human-rights-record_n_2002427.html.

Grotius, Hugo. (1625) 2005. *The Rights of War and Peace.* Indianapolis, Liberty Fund.

Gutman, Roy. 1992. "Serbian Atrocities, Fierce Winter Put Bosnia in Peril. Butchery at Camp Leaves 1,000 Dead, Eyewitnesses Say." *Newsday*, October 20.

Haass, Richard. 1997. "Sanctioning Madness." *Foreign Affairs* 76(6):74–85.

2002. "Sanctioning Madness." In *21 Debated Issues in World Politics*, edited by Gregory M. Scott, Randall J. Jones, Jr., and Louis Furmanski, 82–103. New York: Pearson.

Habermas, Jürgen. 1991. *The Structural Transformation of the Public Sphere.* Trans. Thomas Burger. Cambridge, MA: MIT Press.

Hague Regulations. 1907. *Regulations Concerning the Laws and Customs of War on Land.* October 18. Accessed March 30, 2015. www.icrc.org/ihl.nsf/385ec082b509e76c41256739003e636d/1d1726425f6955aec125641e0038bfd6.

Halberstam, David. 2012. *The Children.* New York: Open Road Media.

Hanh, Thich Nhat. 2005. *Being Peace.* Berkeley, CA: Parallax Press.

Hanseman, Robert G. 1997. "The Realities and Legalities of Information Warfare." *A.F.L. Rev.* 42: 173.

Harb, Zahera. 2011. *Channels of Resistance in Lebanon: Liberation Propaganda, Hezbollah and the Media.* London: Tauris.

Harel, Alon. 2014. *Why Law Matters.* Oxford: Oxford University Press.

Harel, Amos. 2016. "Israel's Military Chief Orders to Revoke Controversial 'Hannibal' Directive", *Haaretz.* June 28.

Harris, Shane. 2014. *@War: The Rise of the Military-Internet Complex.* New York: Houghton Mifflin Harcourt.

Hart, H. L. A. and A. M. Honoré. 1959. *Causation in the Law.* Oxford: Clarendon Press.

Hartmann, Florence. 2011. "Bosnia." *Crimes of War.* www.crimesofwar.org/a-z-guide/bosnia/.

Hashem, Ali. 2014. "The Islamic State's Media Warfare." *Al Monitor*, October 22. Accessed August 2, 2015. www.al-monitor.com/pulse/originals/2014/10/islamic-state-media-strategy-propaganda-iraq-syria.html?utm_source=Al-Monitor+Newsletter+%

255BEnglish%255D&utm_campaign=4f1f3db316-October_23_2014&utm_medium=email&utm_term=0_28264b27a0-4f1f3db316-93098885%23%23ixzz3VAaqGfPm#.

Hauerwas, Stanley. 1991. *The Peaceable Kingdom: A Primer in Christian Ethics*. Notre Dame, IN: University of Notre Dame Press.

Hayes, Richard E. 2002. "Negotiations with Terrorists." In *Negotiations with Terrorists: Analysis, Approaches*, Issues, edited by Victor Kremenyuk, 364–376. San Francisco: Wiley.

HCJ (High Court of Justice). 2005. *HCJ 769/02 Public Committee Against Torture in Israel v. Government of Israel (Targeted Killings Case)*. http://elyon1.court.gov.il/Files_ENG/02/690/007/a34/02007690.a34.pdf.

Hegghammer, Thomas. 2006. "Global Jihadism after the Iraq War." *Middle East Journal* 60(1): 11–32.

Henckaerts, Jean-Marie and Doswald-Beck, Louise, eds. 2005. *Customary International Humanitarian Law* Volume II. Cambridge: Cambridge University Press.

Herberg, Will, ed. 1966. *The Writings of Martin Buber*. The World Publishing Company.

Himes, Kenneth R. 1997. "War By Other Means: Criteria for the Use of Economic Sanctions." *Commonweal* 124(4): 13–15.

Hinze, Christine Firer. 2009. "Reconsidering Little Rock: Hannah Arendt, Martin Luther King Jr., and Catholic Social Thought on Children and Families in the Struggle for Justice." *Journal of the Society of Christian Ethics* 29 (1).

Hobbes, Thomas. 1996. *Leviathan*. Cambridge: Cambridge University Press.

Hogan, Wesley. 2009. *Many Minds, One Heart: SNCC's Dream for a New America*. Chapel Hill, NC: University of North Carolina Press.

Holland, Joseph. 2004. "Military Objective and Collateral Damage: Their Relationship and Dynamics." *Yearbook of International Humanitarian Law* 7: 35–78.

Holmes, Oliver Wendell. 1998. "The Path to Law." *Boston University Law Review* 78: 699.

Horton, Scott. 2007. "A Kinder, Gentler Lawfare." *Harpers*, November 30. http://harpers.org/blog/2007/11/a-kinder-gentler-lawfare/.

2010. "The Dangers of Lawfare." *Case Western Reserve Journal of International Law* 43: 163–180.

Hoskins, Andrew and Ben O'Loughlin. 2010. *War and Media*. Cambridge: Polity Press.

Howes, Dustin Ells. 2013. "The Failure of Pacifism and the Success of Nonviolence." *Perspectives on Politics* 11(2): 427–446.

Hufbauer, Gary Clyde, Jeffrey J. Schott, and Kimberly Ann Elliott. 1991. *Economic Sanctions Reconsidered – History and Current Policy*. 2nd edn. Washington, DC: Institute for International Economics.

Hufbauer, Gary Clyde, Jeffrey J. Schott, Kimberly Ann Elliott, and Barbara Oegg. 2007. *Economic Sanctions Reconsidered*. 3rd edn. Washington: Peterson Institute for International Economics.

Hultman, Lisa, Jacob Kathman, and Megan Shannon. 2014. "Beyond Epping Peace: United Nations Effectiveness in the Midst of Fighting." *American Political Science Review* 108(4): 737–753.

Human Rights Watch. 2014. "Israel/Palestine: Unlawful Israeli Airstrikes Kill Civilians Bombings of Civilian Structures Suggest Illegal Policy." Accessed July 22. www.hrw.org/news/2014/07/15/israel/palestine-unlawful-israeli-airstrikes-kill-civilians.

Hundley, Tom. 1994. "*Lebanese Guerilla Abducted by Israel.*" *Chicago Tribune*, May 22. http://articles.chicagotribune.com/1994-05-22/news/9405220356_1_ron-arad-mustafa-dirani-israel-army-radio.

ICJ (International Court of Justice). 1988. "*The Border and Transborder Armed Action Case (Nicaragua v. Honduras).*" *ICJ Reports* 1988: 5.

1996. "*Legality of the Threat or Use of Nuclear Weapons, Advisory Opinion.*" *ICJ Reports* 1996: 226.

1997. *Case concerning Gabcikovo-Nagymaros Project (Hungary/Slovakia), Summary of the Judgment of 25 September 1997*. www.icj-cij.org/docket/index.php?sum=483&code=hs&p1=3&p2=3&case=+92&k=8d&p3=5.

1986. *Military and Paramilitary Activities in and Against Nicaragua (Nicar. v. US)*.

ICRC (International Committee of the Red Cross). 2010. "The Geneva Conventions of 1949 and Their Additional Protocols: 29-10-2010 Overview." October 29. www.icrc.org/eng/war-and-law/treaties-customary-law/geneva-conventions/overview-geneva-conventions.htm.

Ignatieff, Michael. 2000. *Virtual War: Kosovo and Beyond*. London: Chatto and Windus.

2003. *Empire Light: Nation-Building in Bosnia, Kosovo and Afghanistan*. London: Vintage.

ILA (International Law Association). 2010. *The Hague Conference (2010): Use of Force: Final Report on the Meaning of Armed Conflict in International Law*. www.ila-hq.org/en/committees/index.cfm/cid/1022.

International Campaign for Human Rights in Iran. 2013. *A Growing Crisis: The Impact of Sanctions and Regime Policies on Iranians' Economic and Social Rights*. www.iranhumanrights.org/wp-content/uploads/A-Growing-Crisis.pdf.

International Civil Society Action Network. 2012. "What the Women Say: Killing Them Softly: The Stark Impact of Sanctions on the Lives of Ordinary Americans." *Brief 3*. www.icanpeacework.org/wp-content/uploads/2013/04/WWS-Iran-Killing-Them-Softly-2013-Edit.pdf.

Ipsen, Knut. 2004. *Völkerrecht*. München: C.H. Beck.

Islamic Emirate of Afghanistan. 2015. "The Main Cause of the Civilian Losses is the Use of Heavy Artillery." Accessed July 23. http://shahamat-english.com/the-main-cause-of-the-civilian-losses-is-the-use-of-heavy-artillery/.

Israel Defense Forces. 2014. "How Is the IDF Minimizing Harm to Civilians in Gaza?" *IDF Blog*, July 16. www.idfblog.com/blog/2014/07/16/idf-done-minimize-harm-civilians-gaza/.

Janzen, Randy. 2014. "Shifting Practices of Peace: What Is the Current State of Non-Civilian Peacekeeping?" *Peace Studies Journal* 7(3). http://peaceconsortium.org/peace-studies-journal-vol-7-issue-3–2014.

Jelks, Randal Maurice. 2012. *Benjamin Elijah Mays, Schoolmaster of the Movement: A Biography*. Chapel Hill, NC: University of North Carolina Press.

Jensen, Eric Talbot. 2007. "The ICJ's 'Uganda Wall': A Barrier to the Principle of Distinction and an Entry Point for Lawfare." *Denver Journal of International Law and Policy* 35: 241–270.

Jochnick, Chrisaf and Roger Normand. 1994. "The Legitimation of Violence: A Critical History of the Laws of War." *Harvard International Law Journal* 35(1): 49–95.

Joiner, Lottie L. 2013. "How the Children of Birmingham Changed the Civil-Rights Movement." *The Daily Beast*, May 2. www.thedailybeast.com/articles/2013/05/02/how-the-children-of-birmingham-changed-the-civil-rights-movement.html.

Jonas, David S. and Thomas N. Saunders. 2010. "The Object and Purpose of a Treaty: Three Interpretive Methods." *Vanderbilt Journal of Transnational Law* 43: 565.

Joseph, Sarah. 2012. "Protracted Lawfare: The Tale of Chevron Texaco in the Amazon." *Journal of Human Rights and the Environment* 3: 70–91.

Julian, Rachel and Christine Schweitzer. 2015. "The Origins and Development of Unarmed Civilian Peacekeeping." *Peace Review* 27(1): 1–8.

Kaempf, Sebastian. 2009. "Double Standards in US Warfare: Exploring the Historical Legacy of Civilian Protection and the Complex Nature of the Moral-Legal Nexus." *Review of International Studies* 35: 651–674.

2013. "The Mediatisation of War in a Transforming Global Media Landscape." *Australian Journal of International Affairs* 67(5): 586–604.

2014. "Postheroic US Warfare and the Moral Justification for Killing in War." In *The Future of Just War: New Critical Essays*, edited by Caron E. Gentry and Amy E. Eckert, 79–97. Athens, GA: Georgia University Press.

Kahn, Paul W. 2002. "The Paradox of Riskless Warfare." *Philosophy and Public Policy Quarterly* 22(3): 2–9.

Kalb, Marvin and Carol Saivetz. 2007. "The Israeli-Hezbollah War of 2006: The Media as a Weapon in Asymmetrical Conflict." Paper presented at the US-Islamic World Forum, Doha, Qatar, February 18. www.brookings.edu/~/media/events/2007/2/17islamic-world/2007islamforum_israel-hezb-war.pdf.

Kalshoven, Frits. 1971. *Belligerent Reprisals*. Vol. 1. Leiden, Netherlands: A.W. Sijthoff.

Kalyvas, Stathis N. 2000. "The Logic of Violence in Civil War: Theory and Preliminary Results." *Estudio*/Working Paper 2000/151, 1–45. www.march.es/ceacs/publicaciones/working/archivos/2000_151.pdf.

Kamm, F.M. 2004. "Failures of Just War Theory: Terror, Harm, and Justice." *Ethics*. 114: 650–692.

Kant, Immanuel. (1785) 1964. *Groundwork of the Metaphysic of Morals*. Translated and analyzed by H.J. Paton. New York: Harper Torchbooks/The Academy Library, Harper & Row, Publishers.

Kapur, Sudarshan. 1992. *Raising Up A Prophet: The African-American Encounter with Gandhi*. Boston: Beacon Press.

Kathib, Lina. 2015. "The Islamic State's Strategy: Lasting and Expanding." *The Carnegie Middle East Center*, June 29. Accessed August 2, 2015. http://carnegie-mec.org/2015/06/29/islamic-state-s-strategy-lasting-and-expanding/ib5x.

Kelner, Simon. 2014. "The Interview: Is This Greatest Publicity Stunt in the History of the Movies?" *Belfast Telegraph*, December 26. Accessed February 18, 2016. www.belfasttelegraph.co.uk/opinion/news-analysis/the-interview-is-this-greatest-publicity-stunt-in-the-history-of-the-movies-30861398.html.

Kennedy, David. 2006. *Of Law and War*. Princeton NJ: Princeton University Press.

2012. "Lawfare and Warfare." In *The Cambridge Companion to International Law*, edited by James Crawford and Martti Koskenniemi, 158–183. Cambridge: Cambridge University Press.

Kilcullen, David. 2015. *Quarterly Essay 58: Blood Year: Terror and the Islamic State*. Carlton, Australia: Black Inc.Books.

2006. "Twenty-Eight Articles: Fundamentals of Company-Level Counterinsurgency." *IOSphere*. (Summer): http://navsci.berkeley.edu/ma154/C10%20MAGTF%20PrePos%20Expeditionary%20Ops/InstAid%20III-6-B%20-%20kilcullen_28_articles.pdf.

King, Martin Luther, Jr. 1957. "Nonviolence and Racial Justice," February 6. https://swap.stanford.edu/20141218225500/http://mlk-kpp01.stanford.edu/primarydocuments/Vol4/6-Feb-1957_NonviolenceAndRacialJustice.pdf.

1963a. "Letter from Birmingham Jail," April 16. http://kingencyclopedia.stanford.edu/kingweb/popular_requests/frequentdocs/birmingham.pdf.

1963b. "Eulogy for Martyred Children," September 18. http://kingencyclopedia.stanford.edu/encyclopedia/documentsentry/doc_eulogy_for_the_martyred_children/.

1967. "Where Do We Go from Here?" Annual Report Delivered at the 11th Convention of the Southern Christian Leadership Conference, Atlanta, GA, August 16. www-personal.umich.edu/~gmarkus/MLK_WhereDoWeGo.pdf.

Kirschner, Alexander S. 2014. *A Theory of Militant Democracy: The Ethics of Combating Political Extremism*. New Haven, CT: Yale University Press.

Kluger, Richard. 2004. *Simple Justice: The History of Brown v. Board of Education and Black America's Struggle for Equality*. New York: Vintage.

Knappenberger, Brian. 2012. *We Are Legion: The Story of the Hacktivists. DVD film*. Accessed February 17, 2016. http://wearelegionthedocumentary.com/.

Kosto, Adam. 2012. *Hostages in the Middle Ages*. Oxford: Oxford University Press.

Krasner, Stephen D. 1999. *Organized Hypocrisy*. Princeton, NJ: Princeton University Press.

Kutz, C. 2000. *Complicity: Ethics and Law for a Collective Age*. New York: Cambridge University Press.

Lachow, Irving. 2013. *Active Cyber Defense: A Framework for Policymakers*. Center for a New American Security.

Laffan, Michael. 1999. *The Resurrection of Ireland: the Sinn Féin Party, 1916–23*. Cambridge: Cambridge University Press.

Lamloum, Olfa. 2009. "Hezbollah's Media: Political History in outline." *Global Media and Communication* 5(3): 353–367.

Lango, John. 2014. *The Ethics of Armed Conflict: A Cosmopolitan Just War Theory*. Edinburgh: Edinburgh University Press.

Lapan, Harvey E. and Todd Sandler. 1988. "To Bargain or Not to Bargain: That Is the Question." *The American Economic Review* 78(2): 16–21.

Laudani, Raffaele. 2013. *Disobedience in Western Political Thought*. New York: Cambridge University Press.

Lazar, Seth. 2014. "Necessity and Non-Combatant Immunity." *Review of International Studies* 40(1): 53–76.

Lebowitz, Michael J. 2010–2011. "The Value of Claiming Torture: An Analysis of Al-Qaeda's Tactical Lawfare Strategy and Efforts to Fight Back." *Case Western Reserve Journal of International Law* 43: 357–392.

Lee, Stephen P. 2012. *Ethics and War an Introduction*. Cambridge: Cambridge University Press.

Leiser, Burton M. 1975. "The Morality of Reprisals." *Ethics* 85(2): 159–163.

Leventhal, Todd. 1999. *Iraqi Propaganda and Disinformation During the Gulf War: Lessons from the Future*. Abu Dhabi: The Emirates Center for Strategic Studies and Research. http://www.ecssr.com/ECSSR/appmanager/portal/ecssr_nfpb=true&_nfls=false&_pageLabel=PublicationsPage&publicationId=%2FPublications%2FSeries%

2FEmiratesOccasionalPapers%2FPublications0371.xml&_event=viewDetails&lang=en.
Levine, Ellen S., ed. 2000. *Freedom's Children: Young Civil Rights Activists Tell Their Own Stories*. New York: Puffin Books.
Leyton-Brown, David. 1987. "Extraterritoriality in United States Trade Sanctions." In *The Utility of International Economic Sanctions*, edited by David Leyton-Brown, 255–267. London: Croom Helm.
Liang, Quao and Wang Xiangsu. 1999. *Unrestricted Warfare: Warfare without Boundaries (超限战,)*. Eng. Trans. Los Angeles, CA: Pan American Publishing Co., 2002.
Libicki, Martin C. 2009. *Cyberdeterrence and Cyberwar*. Arlington, VA: The RAND Corporation.
"From the Tallinn Manual to Las Vegas rules." In *Cyberspace in Peace and War*, 324–331. Annapolis MD: Naval Institute Press, 2016.
Lieber, Francis. 1863. "War Department, Instructions for the Government of Armies of the United States In the Field," art. 14.
Lim, Audrea, ed. 2012. *The Case for Sanctions against Israel*. London: Verso.
Lo, Ping Ching. 2012. "The Art of War Corpus and Chinese Just War Ethics Past and Present." *Journal of Religious Ethics* 40(3): 404–446.
Lopez, George A. 2012. "In Defense of Smart Sanctions: A Response to Joy Gordon." *Ethics & International Affairs* 26(1): 135–146.
2013. Interview by Joy Gordon, March 5.
Lough, John. 2011. Russia's Energy Diplomacy. *Chatham House Briefing Paper*. Accessed 2011.
Louw, Eric. 2010. *The Media and Political Process*. London: Save.
Lu, Catherine. 2002. "Justice and Moral Regeneration: Lessons from the Treaty of Versailles." *International Studies Review* 4(3): 3–25.
Luban, David. 2002. "The War on Terrorism and the End of Human Rights." *Philosophy & Public Policy Quarterly* 22: 9–14.
2005a. "Liberalism, Torture, and the Ticking Bomb." *Virginia Law Review* 91: 1425.
2005b. "Selling Indulgences. The Unmistakable Parallel Between Lynne Stewart and the President's Torture Lawyers." *Slate*, February 4.
2007. "The Defense of Torture." *The New York Review of Books*, March 15.
2010. "Carl Schmitt and the Critique of Lawfare." *Case Western Reserve Journal of International Law* 43: 457–472.
2013 "Military Necessity and the Cultures of Military Law." *Leiden Journal of International Law* 26: 315–349.
Lucas, George. 2014. "Automated Warfare." *Stanford Law and Policy Review* 25 (June): 317–354.
2015. *Military Ethics: What Everyone Needs to Know*. New York: Oxford University Press.
2016. *Ethics & Cyber Conflict: The Quest for Responsible Security in the Age of Digital Warfare*. Oxford: Oxford University Press.
Luther, Martin. 1974. "Dr. Martin Luther's Warning to His Dear German People." In *Luther: Selected Political Writings*, edited by J. M. Porter, 133–148. Philadelphia, PA: Fortress Press.
Macklem, Patrick. 2006. "Military Democracy, Legal Pluralism, and the Paradox of Self-Determination." *International Journal of Constitutional Law* 4: 488–515.
Mahony, Liam. 1997. "On Armed Bodyguards." *Peace Review: A Journal of Social Justice* 9(2): 207–213.

Marans, Daniel. 2015. "U.S. at Odds with Germany Over Greek Debt Crisis." *Huffington Post*, July 6. www.huffingtonpost.com/2015/07/06/us-germany-greek-debt-crisis_n_7739422.html.

Marsh, Charles. 2004. *The Beloved Community: How Faith Shapes Social Justice, from the Civil Rights Movement to Today*. New York: Basic Books.

2008. *God's Long Summer: Stories of Faith and Civil Rights*. Princeton, NJ: Princeton University Press.

Martins, Brig. Gen. Mark J. 2011. "Rule of Law in Iraq and Afghanistan." Speech given at the Dean's Distinguished Lecture Series at Harvard Law School, Cambridge, MA, April 18. http://harvardnsj.org/wp-content/uploads/2011/04/Forum_Martins_.pdf.

Maxwell, Mark. 2012. "Rebutting the Civilian Presumption: Playing Whack-A-Mole without a Mallet?" In *Targeted Killing – Law and Morality in an Asymmetrical World*, edited by Claire Finkelstein, Jens David Ohlin, and Andrew Altman, 30–59 Oxford: Oxford University Press.

McConville, James E. 1997. "US Army Information Operations: Concept and Execution." http://fas.org/irp/agency/army/mipb/1997-1/mcconvl.htm.

McChrystal, Lt. Gen. Stanley A. Statement. 2009. *Hearing to Consider the Nominations of Admiral James G. Stavridis, USN for Reappointment to the Grade of Admiral and to be Commander, US European Command and Supreme Allied Commander, Europe; Lieutenant General Douglas M. Fraser, USAF to be General and Commander, US Southern Command; and Lieutenant General Stanley A. McChrystal, USA to be General and Commander, International Security Assistance Force and Commander, US Forces, Afghanistan Before S. Comm. on Armed Services*, 111th Cong. 11. http://fas.org/irp/congress/2009_hr/nominate.html.

McGarry, Fearghal. 2010. *The Rising: Ireland: Easter 1916*. Oxford: Oxford University Press.

McMahan, Jeff. 2006. "On the Moral Equality of Combatants." *The Journal of Political Philosophy* 14: 377–393.

2008. "The Morality of War and the Law of War." In *Just and Unjust Warriors*, edited by David Rodin and Henry Shue, 19–43. New York: Oxford University Press.

2009. *Killing in War*. Oxford: Oxford University Press.

2011. "Proportionality in the Afghanistan War." *Ethics and International Affairs* 25 (2): 143–154.

McWhorter, Diane. 2013. *Carry Me Home: Birmingham, Alabama: The Climactic Battle of the Civil Rights Revolution*. New York: Simon and Schuster.

Meisels, Tamar. 2009. *Territorial Rights*. 2nd edn. Dordrecht: Springer.

2011. "Economic Warfare – The Case of Gaza." *Journal of Military Ethics* 10(2): 94–109.

Merton, Thomas. 1971a. "War and the Crisis of Language." In *The Nonviolent Alternative*, by Thomas Merton. New York: Farrar, Straus and Giroux.

1971b. "Blessed Are the Meek: The Christian Roots of Nonviolence." In *The Nonviolent Alternative*, by Thomas Merton. New York: Farrar, Straus and Giroux.

Miller, David. 2007. *National Responsibility and Global Justice*. Oxford: Oxford University Press.

Moore, Margaret. 2015. *A Political Theory of Territory*. New York: Oxford University Press.

Morgenthau, Hans J. 1946. *Scientific Man vs. Power Politics*. Chicago, IL: The University of Chicago Press.

1948. *Politics Among Nations. The Struggle for Power and Peace*. Columbus, OH: McGraw Hill.
1958. *Dilemmas of Politics*. Chicago, IL: University of Chicago Press.
Morkevičius, Valerie. 2013. "Why We Need a Just Rebellion Theory." *Ethics and International Affairs* 27(4): 401–411.
Munoz-Dardé, Véronique. 2005. "The Distribution of Numbers and the Comprehensiveness of Reasons." *Proceedings of the Aristotelian Society* 105(1): 191–217.
Murphy, Dennis M. 2008. *Fighting Back: New Media and Military Operations*. Carlisle, PA: Center for Strategic Leadership, United States Army War College. http://www.carlisle.army.mil/dime/documents/FightingBack.pdf.
Nabulsi, Karma. 1999. *Traditions of War*. Oxford: Oxford University Press.
Nacos, Brigitte. 1994. *Terrorism and the Media*. New York: Columbia University Press.
Nardin, Terry. 2008. "Theorizing the International Rule of Law." *Review of International Studies* 34: 385–401.
National Iranian American Council. 2010. "Obama Administration Officials' Statements on Iran Sanctions," January 27. www.niacouncil.org/obama-administration-officials-statements-on-iran-sanctions/.
Neumaier, Joe. 2014. "The Interview: Film Review." *NY Daily News*, December 24. Accessed February 17, 2016. www.nydailynews.com/entertainment/movies/interview-movie-review-article-1.2049042.
Nonviolent Peaceforce. 2014. *Progress Report, January 2013-June 2014*. www.nonviolentpeaceforce.org/np-news/2014–06-26–17-22–51/334-the-2013–2014-progress-report-is-out-now.
Noone, Gregory, P. 2010. "Lawfare or Strategic Communications?" *Case Western Reserve Journal of International Law* 43: 73–86.
NPR (National Public Radio). 2016. "As Sanctions on Iran Are Lifted, many US Business Restrictions Remain," January 26.
Nye, Joseph. 2004. *Soft Power: The Means to Success in World Politics*. New York: Public Affairs Press.
O'Donovan, Oliver. 2003. *The Just War Revisited*. Cambridge: Cambridge University Press.
O'Neill, Onora. 1986. "The Public Use of Reason." *Political Theory* 14(4): 523–551.
1989.*Constructions of Reason*. Cambridge: Cambridge University Press.
Owen, Taylor. 2015. *Disruptive Power: The Crisis of the State in the Digital Age*. Oxford: Oxford University Press.
Pape, Robert A. 1997. "Why Economic Sanctions Do Not Work." *International Security* 22(2): 90–136.
Parfit, Derek. 1984. *Reasons and Persons*. Oxford: Oxford University Press.
2011. *On What Matters*. New York: Oxford University Press, Vol. 1.
Paris, Roland. 2014. "The 'Responsibility to Protect' and the Structural Problems of Preventative Humanitarian Intervention." *International Peacekeeping* 21(3): 569–603.
Pashtun Times. 2016. "Bacha Khan: Waging Non-violence," January 14. http://thepashtuntimes.com/bacha-khan-waging-non-violence.
Patterson, James T. 2002. *Brown v. Board of Education: A Civil Rights Milestone and Its Troubled Legacy*. Oxford: Oxford University Press.

Pattison, James. 2010. *Humanitarian Intervention and the Responsibility to Protect: Who Should Intervene?* Oxford: Oxford University Press.

2013. "Is There a Duty to Intervene? Intervention and the Responsibility to Protect." *Philosophy Compass* 8(6): 570–579.

2014. *The Morality of Private War: The Challenge of Private Military and Security Companies*. Oxford: Oxford University Press.

2015. "The Ethics of Diplomatic Criticism: The Responsibility to Protect, Just War Theory, and Presumptive Last Resort." *European Journal of International Relations* 21(4): 935–957.

Payne, Kenneth. 2005. *The Media as an Instrument of War*. Carlisle, PA: Strategic Studies Institute, United States Army War College. http://strategicstudiesinstitute.army.mil/pubs/parameters/Articles/05spring/payne.pdf.

Peters, John Durham. 2001. "Witnessing." *Media, Culture and Society* 23(6): 707–723.

Pfeffer, Anshel. 2014. "The Hannibal Directive: Why Israel risks the life of the soldier being rescued." *Haaretz*, August 3.

Pierce, A. 1996. "Just War Principles and Economic Sanctions." *Ethics and International Affairs* 10(1): 99–113.

Polsgrove, Carol. 2001. *Divided Minds: Intellectuals and the Civil Rights Movement*. New York: W. W. Norton & Company.

Pomerantsev, Peter. 2014. "Russia and the Menace of Unreality." *The Atlantic*, September 9.

Popescu, Ionut C. 2010. "War and Military Operations in the 21st Century: Civil-Military Implications." *Conference Summary*, p. 1. http://tiss-nc.org/wp-content/uploads/2015/01/BRIEF.WarMilOps2010.pdf.

Porch, Douglas. 2002. "'No Bad Stories': The American Media-Military Relationship." *Naval War College Review* 55(1): 85–107.

Posner, Eric. 2011. "Dockets of War." *The National Interest* 112: 25–32.

Posner, Eric and Adrian Vermeule. 2004. "A 'Torture' Memo and Its Torturous Critics." *Wall Street Journal*, July 6.

Rawls, John. (1971) 1989. *A Theory of Justice*. 9th edn. Cambridge, MA: The Belknap Press of Harvard University Press.

1999. *A Theory of Justice*, Revised Edition. Oxford: Oxford University Press.

Reeve, Andrew, ed. 1987. *Modern Theories of Exploitation*. London: Sage.

Reichberg, Gregory M., Heinrik Syse, and Endre Begby, eds. 2006. *The Ethics of War: Classic and Contemporary Readings*. Malden, MA: Blackwell Publishing.

Reinisch, August. 2001. "Developing Human Rights and Humanitarian Law Accountability of the Security Council for the Imposition of Economic Sanctions." *American Journal of International Law* 95(4): 851–872.

Richarz, Allan. 2010. "To Win the War in Afghanistan, the US Military Has to Beat the Taliban at the Propaganda Game: With Effective PR, the US Military Could Win the War in Afghanistan." *Christian Science Monitor*, March 15.

Ricks, Thomas E. 2002. "Target Approval Delays Cost Air Force Key Hits." *Journal of Military Ethics* 1: 109–112.

Rid, Thomas. 2013. *Cyber War Will Not Take Place*. London: C Hurst & Amp Co. Publishers Ltd.

Rid, Thomas and Marc Hecker. 2009. *War 2.0: Irregular Warfare in the Information Age*. Westport: Praeger.

Rieder, Jonathan. 2014. *Gospel of Freedom: Martin Luther King, Jr.'s Letter from Birmingham Jail and the Struggle That Changed a Nation*. New York: Bloomsbury Press.

Rivkin, David B. Jr. and Lee A. Casey. 2005. "Rule of Law: Friend or Foe?" *Wall Street Journal*, April 11.

Rivkin, David B. Jr., Lee A. Casey, and Mark Wendell Delaquil. 2004. "Not Your Father's Red Cross. Just Another Advocacy NGO?" *National Review Online*, December 20.

Roberts, Adam. 2009. "Introduction." In *Civil Resistance and Power Politics: The Experience of Non-Violent Action from Gandhi to the Present*, edited by Adam Roberts and Timothy Garton Ash, 1–24. Oxford: Oxford University Press.

Rumsfeld, Donald. 2006. Quoted in "Rumsfeld: We Need to Learn from al-Qaeda," by Daniel Trotta. *The Sydney Morning Herald*, February 19. Accessed June 3, 2010. www.smh.com.au/articles/2006/02/18/1140151849128.html?from=rss.

Rustin, Bayard. 2003. *Time on Two Crosses: The Collected Writings of Bayard Rustin*. San Francisco, CA: Cleis Press.

Ryan, Cheyney. 1994. "The One Who Burns Herself for Peace." *Hypatia* 9(2): 21–39.

2014. "Pacifism(s)." *The Philosophical Forum*.

2013. "Pacifism, Just War, and Self-Defense." *PHILOSOPHIA, Philosophical Quarterly of Israel* 41 (4).

Samson, Elizabeth. 2009. "Warfare through Misuse of International Law." *Viewpoint* 5770: 61.

Scalmer, Sean. 2011. *Gandhi in the West: The Mahatma and the Rise of Radical Protest*. Cambridge: Cambridge University Press.

Schachter, Oscar. 1986 "In Defense of International Rules on the Use of Force." *University of Chicago Law Review* 53(1): 113–146.

Scharf, Michael and Elizabeth Andersen. 2010–2011. "Is Lawfare Worth Defining? Report of the Cleveland Experts Meeting September 11, 2010." *Case Western Reserve Journal of International Law* 43: 11–28.

Scheffer, David. 2010. "Whose Lawfare Is It, Anyway." *Case Western Reserve Journal of International Law* 43: 215–229.

Scheipers, Sybille. Editor. 2010. *Prisoners in War*. Oxford: Oxford University Press.

Schirch, Lisa. 2006. *Civilian Peacekeeping: Preventing Violence and Making Space with Democracy*. Uppsala: Life & Peace Institute.

Schmitt, Michael N. 2006. "Fault Lines in the Law of Attack." In *Testing the Boundaries of International Humanitarian Law*, edited by Susan Breau and Agnieszka Jachec-Neale, 175–205. London: British Institute of International and Comparative Law.

2008. "'Change Direction' 2006: Israeli Operations in Lebanon and the International Law of Self-Defense." *University of Michigan Law Review* 29: 127–164.

2010. "Military Necessity and Humanity in International Humanitarian Law: Preserving the Delicate Balance." *Vanderbilt Journal of International Law* 50: 795.

ed. 2013. *Tallinn Manual on the International Law Applicable to Cyber Warfare*. New York: Cambridge University Press.

Schmitt, Michael N. and John Merriam. 2015. "The Tyranny of Context: Israeli Targeting Practices in Legal Perspective." *University of Pennsylvania Journal of International Law* 37: 53–189.

Schweitzer, Christine. 2010. "Introduction: Civilian Peacekeeping – A Barely Tapped Resource." In *Civilian Peacekeeping: A Barely Tapped Resource*, edited by

Christine Schweitzer, 7–16. IFGK Working Paper No. 23. Belm-Vehrte, Germany: Sozio Publishing.
Seymour, Michel. 2007. "Secession as a Remedial Right." *Inquiry* 50(4): 395–423.
Sharp, Gene. 1973. *The Politics of Nonviolent Action: Part Two: The Methods of Nonviolent Action*. Boston, MA: Porter Sargent Publishers.
2006. *The Politics of Nonviolent Action, Part One: Power and Struggle*. Boston, MA: Porter Sargent Publishers, Inc.
2010. *From Dictatorship to Democracy: A Conceptual Framework for Liberation*. East Boston, MA: The Albert Einstein Institution.
Shaw, Martin. 2005. *The New Western Way of War*. Cambridge: Polity Press.
Shue, Henry. 1980. *Basic Rights: Subsistence, Affluence, and US Foreign Policy*. Princeton, NJ: Princeton University Press.
2016. *Fighting Hurt*. Oxford, UK: Oxford University Press.
Simmons, A. John. 1979. *Moral Principles and Political Obligations*. Princeton, NJ: Princeton University Press.
Singer, J. David, and Mel Small. 1972. *The Wages of War, 1816–1965: A Statistical Handbook*. Wiley: New York
Sitze, Adam. 2013. "Foreword." In *Disobedience in Western Political Thought*, by Raffaele Laudani. New York: Cambridge University Press.
Sjoberg, Laura. 2014. "Just War without Civilians." In *The Future of Just War*, edited by Caron E. Gentry and Amy E. Eckert. Athens, GA: The University of Georgia Press: 148–165.
Slate, Nico. 2012. *Colored Cosmopolitanism: The Shared Struggle for Freedom in the United States and India*. Cambridge, MA: Harvard University Press.
Slessarev-Jamir, Helene. 2011. *Prophetic Activism: Progressive Religious Justice Movements in Contemporary America*. New York: New York University Press.
Slim, Hugo. 2003. "Why Protect Civilians? Innocence, Immunity, and Enmity in War." *International Affairs* 79(3): 481–501.
Smith, Michael Joseph. 1986. *Realist Thought from Max Weber to Henry Kissinger*. Baton Rouge: Louisiana State University Press.
Smyczek, Peter J. 2005. "Regulating the Battlefield of the Future: The Legal Limitations on the Conduct of Psychological Operations (PSYOP) under Public International Law." *Air Force Law Review* 57: 209–240.
Spens, Christiana. 2014. "Shock and Awe: Performativity, Machismo, and ISIS." *E-International Relations*, November 2. www.e-ir.info/2014/11/02/shock-and-awe-performativity-machismo-and-isis.
Stahl, Roger. 2010. *Militainment, Inc: War, Media and Popular Culture*. London: Routledge.
State of Israel. 2015. "The Gaza Conflict: 7 July – 26 August 2014. Factual and Legal Aspects." Accessed July 23, 2015. http://mfa.gov.il/ProtectiveEdge/Documents/IDFConduct.pdf.
Stephan, Maria J. and Erica Chenoweth. 2008. "Why Civil Resistance Works: The Strategic Logic of Nonviolent Conflict." *International Security* 33(1): 7–44.
Stern, Jessica and J. M. Berger. 2015. "ISIS and the Foreign Fighter Phenomenon." *The Atlantic*, March 8. www.theatlantic.com/international/archive/2015/03/isis-and-the-foreign-fighter-problem/387166.
Stilz, Anna. 2009. "Why Do States Have Territorial Rights?" *International Theory* 1: 185–213.

Sueddeutsche Zeitung. 2014. "Die Radikalisierung in Sozialen Medien: Die Social Media Strategie des Islamischen Staats." Accessed March 23, 2015. www.sueddeutsche.de/digital/radikalisierung-in-sozialen-medien-die-social-media-strategie-des-islamischen-staats-1.2400586.

Sulmasy, Glenn and John Yoo. 2007. "Challenges to Civilian Control of the Military: A Rational Choice Approach to the War on Terror." *UCLA Law Review* 54: 1815–1845.

Summers, Robert S. 1968. "'Good Faith' in General Contract Law and the Sales Provisions of the Uniform Commercial Code." *Virginia Law Review* 54: 195–208.

Syse, Henrik. 2007. "Augustine and Just War: Between Virtues and Duties." In *Ethics, Nationalsm, and Just War*, edited by Henrik Syse and Gregeory M. Reichberg, 36–50. Washington, DC: Catholic University Press.

Tagesschau. 2015. "Voelkermord Islamischer Staat." Accessed March 22, 2015. www.tagesschau.de/ausland/voelkermord-islamischer-staat-101.html.

Taurek, John. 1977. "Should the Numbers Count?" *Philosophy & Public Affairs* 6(4): 293–316.

Tertullian. 1955. "The Chaplet." In *Tertullian: Disciplinary, Moral and Ascetical Works*, translated by Rudolph Arbesmann, Sister Emily Joseph Daly, and Edwin A. Quain. New York: Fathers of the Church, Inc.

The Guardian. 2004. "Two Hurt as Eta Bombs Resorts." August 13. www.theguardian.com/world/2004/aug/13/spain.travelnews.

The United States Military Commissions Act of 2006, Pub. L. No. 109–366, 120 Stat. 2600 (Oct. 17, 2006), enacting Chapter 47A of title 10 of the US Code, Act of Congress (Senate Bill 3930) signed by President George.W. Bush on October 17 2006. Sec. 948a&b. http://frwebgate.access.gpo.gov/cgi-bin/getdoc.cgi?dbname=109_cong_bills&docid=f:s3930enr.txt.pdf.

The White House (Office of the Press Release). 2015. "Statement by the President on the U.S. Government's Hostage Policy Review." June 24. www.whitehouse.gov/the-press-office/2015/06/24/statement-president-us-governments-hostage-policy-review.

Thomas, Ward. 2001. *The Ethics of Destruction: Norms and Force in International Relations*. London: Cornell University Press.

Thompson, Alexander. 2012. "Coercive Enforcement in International Law." In *Interdisciplinary Perspectives on International Law and International Relations: The State of the Art*, edited by Jeffrey L. Dunnoff and Mark A. Pollack, 502–523. Cambridge: Cambridge University Press.

Thurman, Howard. 1981. *With Head and Heart: The Autobiography of Howard Thurman*. New York: Mariner Books.

1996. *Jesus and the Disinherited*. Boston: Beacon Press.

Tiefenbrun, Susan W. 2010. "Semiotic Definition of 'Lawfare'." *Case Western Reserve Journal of International Law* 43: 29–60.

Tiffin, Frederick. 2015. "There's No Chance That the Rohingya People Will End Up in the Gambia." *Vice News*. https://news.vice.com/article/theres-no-chance-that-the-rohingya-people-will-end-up-in-the-gambia.

Torres Soriano, Manuel R. 2008. "Terrorism and Mass Media after Al Qaeda." *Athena Intelligence Journal* 3(1): 1–20.

Tostensen, Arnie and Beate Bull. 2002. "Are Smart Sanctions Feasible?" *World Politics* 54(3): 373–403.

Townshend, Charles. 2013. *The Republic: The Fight for Irish Independence*. London: Allen Lane.

Tuck, David. 2011. "Detention by Armed Groups: Overcoming Challenges to Humanitarian Action." *International Review of the Red Cross* 93(883): 759–782.

Tuck, Richard, trans. 2005. *Hugo Grotius, The Rights of War and Peace*. Indianapolis: Liberty Fund.

Turbo News. 2008. "Basque Separatists Bomb Spanish Tourist Resorts: Police." July 20. www.eturbonews.com/3809/basque-separatists-bomb-spanish-tourist-resorts-police.

Tzahor, Zeev. 2015. *We Were the Revival (Hebrew)*, Bnei Barak, Israel: Hakibutz Hameuchad Press.

Uniacke, Suzanne. 2011. "Proportionality and Self-Defense." *Law and Philosophy* 30 (3): 253–272.

UN (United Nations). 1945. *Charter of the United Nations*, October 24.

1996. "Letter dated 7 May 1996 from the Secretary General addressed to the President of the Security Council." *United Nations Security Council, Document 337, S/1996/337*. www.un.org/ga/search/view_doc.asp?symbol=S/1996/337.

2013. *Necessity of Ending the Economic, Commercial and Financial Embargo Imposed by the United States of America against Cuba*. Sixty-eighth session Resolution adopted by the General Assembly on 29 October 2013 [without reference to a Main Committee (A/68/L.6)] 68/8.

UN General Assembly. 1998. *Rome Statute of the International Criminal Court*. July 17. Accessed April 1, 2015. www.icc-cpi.int/nr/rdonlyres/ea9aeff7-5752-4f84-be94-0a655eb30e16/0/rome_statute_english.pdf.

UN Human Rights Council. 2015. *Report of the Detailed Findings of the Independent Commission of Inquiry Established Pursuant to Human Rights Council resolution* S-21/1. A_HRC_CPR_4.

UN OCHA (Office for the Coordination of Humanitarian Affairs). 2015. *United Nations Humanitarian Civil-Military Coordination Field Handbook, v1.0*.

UN Secretary General. 2011. *Report of the Secretary-General's Panel of Inquiry on the 31 May 2010 Flotilla Incident*. New York: United Nations. www.un.org/News/dh/infocus/middle_east/Gaza_Flotilla_Panel_Report.pdf.

US DoD (United States Department of Defense). 1974. Department of Defense Law of War Programme, Directive 5100.77.

2005. The National defense Strategy of the United States. Accessed July 23, 2015. www.defense.gov/news/Mar2005/d20050318nds1.pdf.

2010. *Joint Publication 1–02 Department of Defense Dictionary*, November.

2012. *Joint Publication 3–13 Information Operations*, November.

Van Creveld, Martin. 1996. "War." In *The Osprey Companion to Military History*, edited by Robert Cowley and Geoffrey Parker, 497–499. London: Osprey.

van der Dennen, Johann. 1980. "On War: Concepts, Definitions, Research Data – A Short Literature Review and Bibliography." *UNESCO Yearbook on Peace and Conflict Studies*. Westport, CT: 128–189.

Virally, Michel. 1983. "Review Essay: Good Faith in Public International Law." *The American Journal of International Law* 77: 130–134.

Virilio, Paul. 1989. *War and Cinema: The Logistics of Perception*. London: Verso.

von Clausewitz, Carl. (1830) 1976. *On War*. Edited/translated by Michael Howard and Peter Paret. Princeton, NJ: Princeton University Press.

1984. *On War*. Princeton, NJ: Princeton University Press.
2008. *On War*. Translated by Colonel James J. Graham. Radford, VA: Wilder Publications.
Waldron, Jeremy. 2010a. "Cruel, Inhuman, and Degrading Treatment: The Words Themselves." *Canadian Journal of Law and Jurisprudence* 23: 269–286.
2010b. *Torture, Terror and Tradeoffs – Philosophy for the White House*. Oxford: Oxford University Press.
Wallensteen, Peter. 1968. "Characteristics of Economic Sanctions." *Journal of Peace Research* 5(3): 248–267.
Wallensteen, Peter, Carina Staibano, and Mikael Eriksson. 2003. *Making Targeted Sanctions Effective: Guidelines for the Implementation of UN Policy Options*. Uppsala: Uppsala University Department of Peace and Conflict Research.
Wallis, Tim. 2010. "Best Practices for Unarmed Civilian Peacekeeping." In *Civilian Peacekeeping: A Barely Tapped Resource*, edited by Christine Schweitzer, 25–34. IFGK Working Paper No. 23. Belm-Vehrte, Germany: Sozio Publishing.
Waltz, Kenneth. 1979. *Theory of International Politics*. Columbus, OH: McGraw-Hill.
Walzer, Michael. 1977. *Just and Unjust Wars*. New York: Basic Books.
2000. *Just and Unjust Wars*. New York, NY: Basic Books.
2002. "The Triumph of Just War Theory (and the Dangers of Success)." *Social Research* 69(4): 925–944.
2004. *Arguing about War*. New Haven, CT: Yale University.
2006. *Just and Unjust Wars: A Moral Argument with Historical Illustrations*. 4th edn. New York: Basic Books.
2013. "Coda: Can the Good Guys Win?" *European Journal of International Law* 24 (1): 433–444.
Weber, Max. 1994. "The Profession and Vocation of Politics." In *Max Weber: Political Writing*, 309–369. Cambridge: Cambridge University Press.
Wedgwood, Ruth and James R. Wolsey. 2004. "Law and Torture." *Wall Street Journal*, June 28.
Weill, Rivka. 2014. "Exodus: Structuring Redemption of Captives." *Cardozo Law Review* 36: 177–239.
Wenzel, Maraike and Sami Faltas. 2009. "Tightening the Screws in West African Arms Embargoes." In *Putting Teeth in the Tiger: Improving the Effectiveness of Arms Embargoes*, edited by Michael Brzoska and George A. Lopez, 101–136. Bingley, England: Emerald Publishing.
Werner, Wouter G. 2010. "The Curious Career of Lawfare." *Case Western Reserve Journal of International Law* 43: 61–72.
Wertheimer, Alan. 1987. *Coercion*. Princeton, NJ: Princeton University Press.
1996. *Exploitation*. Princeton, NJ: Princeton University Press.
Whitaker, Richard M. 1996. "Civilian Protection Law in Military Operations: An Essay." *Army Lawyer*, November. www.loc.gov/rr/frd/Military_Law/pdf/11-1996.pdf.
Williams, Paul R. 2010. "Lawfare: A War Worth Fighting." *Case Western Reserve Journal of International Law* 43: 145–152.
Wolin, Sheldon. 2004. *Politics and Vision: Continuity and Innovation in Western Political Thought*, revised edition. Princeton, NJ: Princeton University Press.
Yoder, John Howard. 1994. *The Politics of Jesus*. Grand Rapids, MI: Eerdmans.

Zehfuss, Maja. 2010. "Targeting: Precision and the Production of Ethics." *European Journal of International Relations* 17(3): 543–566.

Zimmerman, Michael J. 1985. "Intervening Agents and Moral Responsibility." *The Philosophical Quarterly* 35(141): 347–358.

Zoller, Elizabeth. 1977. *La Bonne Foi en Droit International Public*. Paris: Editions A. Pedone.

Zornberg, Avivah Gottlieb. 2011. *The Beginning of Desire: Reflections on Genesis*. New York: Schocken.

Index

abolitionism, 172–173
Additional Protocol I (1977), 38, 43, 95, 101, 201, 206, 220
Additional Protocol II (1977), 203, 204
Afghanistan, 97–98
African-American prophetic pacifism, 168, *See also* Birmingham action; King, Martin Luther Jr.; nonviolence and nonviolent resistance
  dialogic power and, 174
  dialogue and, 171
  forgiveness and, 175
  Gandhi and, 168–170
  justice and, 171
  personal pacifism of King and, 170–172
  political pacifism and, 172–173
  shaming and, 175–176
Algeria, 193, 208
Al-Qaeda, 107, 187, 199, 203
  hostage taking by, 192
Angola, 58
Aquinas, Thomas, 19, 25, 36, 44
  on killing innocents, 37
  on property damage in war, 38
  on self-defense, 39–40
Arad, Ron, 187
Arendt, Hannah, 156, 181
armed conflict
  ILA definition of, 19
arms embargoes, 56–57, 59
Arquilla, John, 38
asymmetric warfare, 187
Augustine, 19, 35, 36, 44
  on property damage in war, 38
  on self-defense, 39–40
aviation bans, 58, 60

Bevel, James, 166, 176, 180
Birmingham action, 9, *See also* African-American prophetic pacifism; King, Martin Luther, Jr.; nonviolence and nonviolent resistance
  as part of larger movement, 168–169
  as turning point in civil rights struggle, 182
  bombing of Sixteenth Street Baptist Church after, 182–183
  children in, 9, 167–168, 174, 175, 176, 180–183
  legality of, 177, 179
  Martin Luther King, Jr. and, 166–167, 168–169, 176
  provocation and, 167–168, 176–179, 182–183
  shame as tactic in, 175–176
Boko Haram, 187
boycotts, 2
Branche, Raphaelle, 208
Brown vs. Board of Education (1954), 180, 181
Buber, Martin, 170, 171, 173, 175
Bull, Hedley, 187

canonical just war tradition, 33, *See also* just war theory
  civilian property and, 38
  permissibility of coercion for creating order, 35–37

Cebrowski, Charles, 108
Chevron, 26–28
children, 9, 147
  child soldiers, 9, 24, 115
  deaths of due to economic sanctions, 29
  in Birmingham action, 9, 167–168, 174, 175, 176, 180–183
chlorine gas, 45
civil rights movement, 169, *See also* African-American prophetic pacifism; Birmingham action; King, Martin Luther Jr.; nonviolence and nonviolent resistance
civil subversion, 8, 69–70
  collective self-determination and, 162–163
  human rights as guarantees and, 157–158
  in Irish independence movement, 153–155
  negative aspects of, 160
  political consequences of, 164–165
  power and unarmed force and, 155–156
  right to assemble and associate and, 159–160
  state's curbing of rights of assembly and association and, 161–162
  state's repression of, 163
  state's territorial rights and, 164
civilian immunity, 6, 7, 15, 201, 202, 203
  economic sanctions and, 7
  in traditional just war theory, 38
civilian peacekeeping, 134
  as additional means to military peacekeeping or humanitarian intervention, 149, 150
  capacity problem in, 138, 139, 148
  conscription problem in, 139, 148
  defined, 8, 135
  differences between organizations of, 136
  effectiveness advantage in, 140
  harm problem in, 139, 148
  in Nicaragua, 136–137
  inefficacy objection to, 146–147, 149
  international protective accompaniment and, 8
  motive advantage in, 140
  motive problem in, 138, 148
  nonviolence advantage in, 140
  presumptive last resort and, 134, 150
  privilege objection to, 141–143
  risk advantage in, 140
  risk problem in, 139, 148
  scale of, 135
  selectivity problem in, 138, 148
  success of, 136–138
  supererogation objection to, 143–146
  unrealistic expectation problem in, 139, 148
  upscaling issue and, 147–149
  volunteer advantage in, 141
  vs. UN peacekeeping, 135
civilian property, 6, 33, 34, 47, 48
  civilian banking, 47
  in canonical just war tradition, 38
  likely permissible targets, 46–47
  necessity as principle in permissible targeting of, 39–40
  off limit targets of, 41–45
  order as principle in limiting targeting of, 40
  possibly permissible targets, 45–46
civilians. *See also* noncombatants
  civilian banking, 47
  exploitation of civilian casualties by insurgent groups, 98–99
  in context of unarmed conflicts, 5
  in just war theory, 6
  justifiable non-lethal attacks on, 6, 222, 226
  proportionality in media coverage of civilian casualties and, 94–95
  protection of in soft war, 4
  uniformed combatants as protection of, 205
coercion
  permissibility of for creating order, 35–37
  permissible and impermissible, 34
collateral damage, 18, 28, 39, 87, 93, 97, 131, 132, 139
  media coverage of, 108, 111
  proportionality and, 94–95
  targeted sanctions and, 60
combatants
  codification of status in IHL, 12
  in context of unarmed conflicts, 5
  legal distinction between privileged and unprivileged in international armed conflict, 201–202
  legal distinction between privileged and unprivileged in non-international armed conflict, 202–205
  liability and, 6
  uniformed combatants, 14, 21, 201, 203, 205, 206
command responsibility, 208
communications infrastructures, 46
comprehensive sanctions, 7, *See also* sanctions
conditional aid, 66, 76
conditional sale, 2, 7, 219
  as response to justified grievance, 67–70
  conditional aid and, 66
  defined, 7
  distributive justice and, 64

conditional sale (cont.)
illustration of with fictional political actors (Affluenza and Barrenia), 63–64
in absence of justified grievance, 70–74
permissibility of, 7, 64–65, 66, 76
private business and, 74–76
Russia and, 63, 72–73
vs. economic sanctions, 66, 76
Connor, Bull, 176
countermeasures, 14, 218, 220
against cyber attacks, 224
Coy, Patrick, 141–142
cultural property, protection of, 43
cyber warfare, 2, 5, *See also* hacktivism; state-sponsored hacktivism
background review of malevolent activities in cyberspace, 78–80
impermissible targets of, 42, 43, 46
lack of international law on, 84–86
need for soft law for, 86–87
permissible tactics of, 46, 47
proportionate self-defense and, 223–226
state-sponsored cyber attacks as war, 30–31
US DoD model of defense against, 226
vs. state-sponsored hacktivism, 83
Cyber Warriors of Izz ad-din Al-Qassam, 10, 30

Daesh. *See* ISIS
defensive ontology, 119
Democratic Republic of Congo (DRC), 59
dialogic power, 174
Dinstein, Yoram, 210
Dirani, Mustafa, 186
distinction, principle of, 3, 38, 53, 130–131, 132, 215
appropriate use of in soft war, 4
in law of armed conflict (LOAC), 90, 205–208, 210
ISIS's violation of, 114–115
distributive justice
conditional sale and, 64
doctrine of double effect (DDE), 37, 40, 45, 116, 194
four criterion of, 194
Donnelly, Jack, 157

Eckford, Elizabeth, 182
economic sanctions. *See* sanctions
Ecuador, 26–28
Edelman, Marian Wright, 176
Ethics of Insurgency (Gross), 203
European Convention concerning Cybercrime, 10
European Convention on Human Rights
freedom of expression in, 161
extortion, 3

Fancher, Jennifer, 167
Fletcher, George, 200
foreign policy, 5, 74, *See also* conditional sale
Franck, Thomas, 119

Gandhi, 161, 168–170, 174
Geneva Conventions, 187, 201, 203, *See also* Additional Protocol I (1977); Additional Protocol II (1977)
combatants eligible for POW status under, 202
prohibitions against hostage taking in, 210
Gentili, Alberico, 186
Gordon, Joy, 28
Green, Leslie, 210
Griffith, Arthur, 153–155
Gross, Michael L., 27, 38, 168, 203–204, 208–209, 210–211
on provocation, 176
Grotius, Hugo, 19, 25, 186
Guantanamo Bay, 13
Gulf War (1991), 6, 108

hacktivism. *See also* cyber warfare; state-sponsored hacktivism
defined, 78
transparency, whistle-blowing, and vigilantism in, 79–80
Hague Convention, 201
combatants eligible for POW status under, 202
Haiti, 58
Hamas, 4, 83, 93, 94, 101, 187, 197, 200, 202, 214
Hannibal procedure, 193–195
hard war, 1–3, 14
vs. soft war, 2, 87
Hendricks, Audrey Faye, 167
Heschel, Rabbi Abraham Joshua, 170
Hezbollah, 4, 94
hostage negotiations, 13, 14, 185, 189
need for multinational cooperation in, 196, 197–199
no-concession policy vs. compliance in realist theory of, 191–192
nondiscounting future policy and, 195–197

unfairness of sovereignist approach to, 192–193, 197
hostage taking, 4, 13, 232
as arbitrary treatment of human beings, 211–213, 215
as contestation of Western states and international organizations, 187
asymmetric warfare context of, 187
by non-state actors, 187
historical context of, 185–186
hostage's location and, 188
hostages as unbounded prisoner and, 185, 188, 190
human rights and, 13, 14
in Algeria, 193
in Geneva Conventions, 210
International Convention against the Taking of Hostages and, 210
international humanitarian law on, 184, 190
need for multinational cooperation in, 184, 185, 196, 197–199
no-concession policy *vs.* compliance in realist theory of, 191–192
nondiscounting future policy and, 195–197
removal of ongoing threat justification of, 211
rights of uniformed vs. irregular combatants, 14
self-defense and, 213–215, 216
time frame of release and, 188
truth and transparency and, 189–190
unfairness of sovereignist approach to, 192–193, 197
unprivileged status of unlawful combatants and, 205–207, 215
use of force and Hannibal procedure, 193–195
vs. kidnapping, 184
vs. POWs, 186–187, 209–215
hostility, intensity of in definition of war, 21–22
human rights, 8, *See also* civilian peacekeeping; civil subversion
arms embargoes and, 56
belligerents and, 16
civil subversion and, 69–70, 157–158
conditional sale and, 7, 65, 69–70
countermeasures against violations of, 218
hostage taking and, 13, 14, 190, 193
in just war theory, 38, 48
in law of armed conflict, 34
perception of violations of in media, 97
POWs and, 204, 209
sanctions and, 50, 53, 55
targeted trade sanctions and, 58, 59
human shields, 4, 11, 12, 83, 84, 85, 99, 101, 132, 135, 143, 144, 146, 176
humanitarianism, 221–223, 231
humanitarian consequences of sanctions, 49, 50, 53–54, 58, 59–60
hunger strikes, 232

information warfare, 88, *See also* media warfare
by Russia, 44
defined, 89
impermissible tactics of, 43, 44
lying and, 44
propaganda and, 89–90
psychological operations (PSYOPS) defined, 89
International Convention against the Taking of Hostages, 210
International Court of Justice (ICJ), 4
International Humanitarian Law (IHL), 12, 109, 120, 231, *See also* law of armed conflict (LOAC); Additional Protocol I (1977); Additional Protocol II (1977)
armed force and, 217
civilian property and, 38
hostage taking and, 184, 190
identifying breaches against the object and purpose of, 130–131
ISIS violation of, 113
lawfare and, 4
lawfare typology table, 129
POW's and, 12
reputational costs of violations of, 131–132
US compliance with, 111
use vs. abuse of, 122–127
international law. *See also* International Humanitarian Law (IHL); law of armed conflict (LOAC)
as substitute for armed force in international relations, 119–121
countermeasures in response to unlawful actions and, 218
lack of on soft war and cyber warfare, 84–86
legal distinction between privileged and unprivileged combatants in international armed conflict, 201–202
legal distinction between privileged and unprivileged combatants in non-international armed conflict, 202–205

international law (cont.)
media warfare and, 10
on POWs, 12
permissible responses to soft war and, 218–219
state's use of force in, 218
targeted sanctions and, 59
unprivileged status of unlawful combatants in, 205–207, 215
war's special status in, 16
International Law Association (ILA)
definition of armed conflict by, 19
definitions of intensity and, 21
on organized armed groups, 20, 21
IRA (Irish Republican Army), 228
Iran, 30
cyber-attack on, 4
indiscriminate sanctions against by United States, 4, 54–56, 60
Iraq
economic sanctions as war against, 29–30, 45, 50, 53, 55
economic sanctions on, 4, 6, 59, 226
Iraq war (2003), 108
Irgun (Jewish underground group), 200
Irish independence movement, civil subversion in, 153–155
ISIS, 21, 199
hostage taking by, 187, 192
mediatization of war by, 11, 111–116
Israel, 4, 13, 93, 101, 120
Hannibal procedure for hostage taking, 193–195
hostage taking by, 186
POWs as unlawful combatants in, 187
prisoner exchange by, 191, 192
status of terrorists in, 202

jus ad bellum, 3–4, 6, 16, 19
civilian property and, 48
Iraq wars and, 226
legitimacy and, 92
proportionality in, 91
UN Charter and, 91
jus ad vim (just use of force short of war), 3
as alternative to war, 3
kinetic force and, 3
jus in bello, xi, 16, 33–34, 35, 42
agent based differentiation in POW rights and, 207–209, 215
command responsibility and organizations enforcing, 208
discrimination and, 38
hostage taking and, 201
morally permissible targets and, 41
necessity and order and, 39
non-international armed conflict and, 203
proportionality and, 3, 39, 41, 48, 220, 223, 226, 231
proportionate self-defense and, 223, 226, 231
Just and Unjust Wars (Walzer), 2, 3, 206
just use of force short of war. *See jus ad vim*
just war theory, 1, 5, 6, *See also jus ad bellum*; *jus ad vim*; jus in bello; soft war; war
Aquinas and Augustine and, 19, 25, 35–37, 170
challenges of soft war tactics for, 232
civilian immunity in, 6, 38
civilian property and, 48
conditional sale and, 63
cyber warfare and, 9
definitions of just war, 5, 19, 20
economic sanctions and, 29, 53, 61
guerrillas rights in, 203–204, 212–213
historical just war tradition, 34
hostage taking and POWs and, 12, 203–204, 211, 212–213
human rights in, 38, 48
inevitability of war in, 33, 42
information warfare and, 43–45
juridical definitions of war, 19
last resort criterion of, 2, 8, 134, 150
media warfare and, 11
mediatization of war and, 104, 106, 116–118
moral purpose of, 116
necessity in, 39
necessity, order and proportionality principles in, 34, 39
neglect of soft war in, 2, 15
nonlethal harm on noncombatants in, 231
order in, 40
pacifism and, 170
permissible use of force in, 37
presumptive last resort and, 150
proportionality in, 41
removal of ongoing threat and, 211
sieges and, 7
United Nations Charter and, 91
Walzer and, 2

kidnapping, 3, 4
self-defense and, 213–215, 216
vs. hostage taking, 184
vs. POWs, 209–215

kinetic force, 3, 41, 47, 77, 80, 84, 200, 219, 222
  cyber warfare and, 223
  economic sanctions and, 29
  media warfare and, 224
King, Martin Luther, Jr., 9, 155
  Birmingham action and, 166–167, 176
  Buber and, 170, 171, 175
  creating of political movement and, 169, 174
  eulogy of victims of bombing of Sixteenth Street Baptist Church, 182–183
  Gandhi and, 174
  Letter from a Birmingham Jail of, 170, 174
  neglect of in hegemonic academic culture, 169
  personal pacifism and, 170–172
  shaming in nonviolence and, 175–176
  true pacifism of, 170
Kirschner, Alexander, 164
Kosovo, 92
Kriegsraison, 190

last resort, 2, 4, 8, 36, 134, 164, 222
  hostage taking and, 184–185, 195
  presumptive last resort, 134, 150
law of armed conflict (LOAC). *See also* International Humanitarian Law (IHL); international law
  denial of immunity for insurgents in, 202, 209
  distinction and, 90, 205–208, 210
  exploitation of civilian casualties by insurgent groups and, 98–99, 103
  human rights and, 34
  impact of media warfare on precautions of, 100–101
  in unarmed conflicts, 25
  legal status of belligerents in, 17–18, 23–24
  legitimacy and, 91–92, 103
  mediatization of war and, 109
  need to accommodate just insurgents in, 203
  precautions in, 90
  proportionality in, 90
  use of lethal force and, 90
lawfare, 4, 5, 11, 83
  abuse of, 11, 12, 121–122, 125–127, 132
  as form of war, 26
  as substitute for armed force in international relations, 119–121
  Chevron and, 26–28
  critique of critique of, 122–125
  good faith and bad faith, 125–127
  indeterminacy based lawfare, 128–130
  just and unjust, 121–122, 229
  legitimacy and, 4, 26, 132
  liability and, 231
  perfidy based lawfare, 130–131
  proportionate self-defense and, 221–223, 229–231
  reasons for popularity of as term, 121
  reputation destroying lawfare, 12, 131–132
  reputation preserving lawfare, 12, 132
  typology table, 129
Lawson, James, 169
legitimacy
  Afghanistan and, 98
  coercive power of international law and, 120, 123, 125
  direct nonlethal attacks on civilians and, 7
  economic sanctions and, 50–51, 53
  hostage taking and, 185, 198, 201, 211, 212
  human rights violations and, 8
  jus ad bellum (justice of resorting to war) and, 92
  law of armed conflict (LOAC) and, 91–92, 103
  lawfare and, 4, 26, 132
  media warfare and, 10, 88, 92–93
  mediatization of war and, 110
  of nonviolent movements, 137
  of states based on adherence to civil rights, 152–153, 156, 161, 163, 165
  propaganda and, 89
Letter from a Birmingham Jail (King), 170, 174
liability. *See also* participatory liability
  appropriate use of in soft war, 4
  combatants and, 6
  in cyber warfare, 225
  lawfare and, 231
  media reports on civilian casualties and, 98, 102
  of insurgents for killing or capturing combatants, 204–205, 209
  participatory liability, 15, 27, 218, 222–223, 226, 230, 231
Liberia, 57, 58
Libya, 58
Lincoln, Abraham, 185
Lucas, Jr., George R., 30
lying, as impermissible in war, 43, 44, 45
Lynd, Robert, 165

MacIntyre, Alasdair, 86
Martins, Brigadier General Mark, 92

media technology. *See also* media warfare
as soft power weapon, 11, 104–105, 106, 109, 111–112, 118
media coverage of war as essential, 103
media warfare, 4, 10, 88, 232
Afghanistan and, 97–98
erosion of necessity through, 100
exploitation of civilian casualties by insurgent groups and, 98–99
impact on LOAC precautions, 100–101
international law and, 10
just war theory and, 11, 116–118
lack of legal restraints on, 219
legitimacy and, 92–93
media coverage of war as essential, 103
morphing and, 94
propaganda and, 89–90
proportionality and, 102
proportionality in media coverage of civilian casualties and, 94–95
mediatization of war, 11
by ISIS, 11, 111–116
by United States, 11, 107–111, 116
during Vietnam War, 109–111
heteropolar global mediascape as leveling playing-field, 104–106
just war theory and, 116–118
medical equipment and information
as impermissible targets, 43
Merton, Thomas, 174
Mexican drug cartels, 23–24
military necessity. *See* necessity
Mitterand, François, 143
morphing, 94

necessity, 4, 34, 150
armed force and, 217, 218, 231
cyber attacks on civilian infrastructure and, 43, 47
defined, 220
erosion of through media warfare, 100
in law of armed conflict (LOAC), 90, 91
in permissible targeting of civilian property, 39–40
in soft war, 48, 220–221
International Humanitarian Law (IHL) and, 130
sanctions and, 42
self-defense and, 220
soft law and, 87
Nicaragua, 136–137
noncombatants, 12, *See also* civilians; civilian immunity; civilian property
agent based differentiation of combatants and, 209
as targets of soft war, 217, 225
civilian peacekeeping and, 146
combatants requirement to distinguish themselves from, 202, 215
exploitation of civilian casualties by insurgent groups, 98–99
International Humanitarian Law (IHL) and, 231
justifiable non-lethal attacks on, 222
noncombatant immunity, 14, 15, 48, 215
participatory liability and, 15, 27, 218, 222, 227, 231
sanctions and, 7, 227
targeting of in reprisals, 222
non-international armed conflict
international law on, 203
lack of legally defined combatant status in, 203
privileged and unprivileged combatants rights to take POWs and, 202–205
non-kinetic tactics, 1, 2, *See also* soft war
classification of as warfare, 2, 31
nonparticipating civilians, 37
nonviolence and nonviolent resistance, 174, 219, *See also* civilian peacekeeping; civil subversion
American vs. Eastern, 170
conditional sale and, 7
dialogic power and, 174
forgiveness and, 175
legitimacy of, 137
power and, 174
provocation and, 9, 176–179
shaming and, 175–176
transforming the opponent in, 174
Nonviolent Peaceforce, 8, 134, 136, 142, 147
North Korea, 9, 57, 80

order
as limiting targeting of civilian property, 40
permissibility of coercion for creating order, 35–37
organized armed groups, 20

pacifism, 149
personal pacifism, 170–172

political pacifism, 172–173
true pacifism of King, 170
Palestinian Authority, 4
Panama invasion, 108
Parfit, Derek, 214
participatory liability, 15, 27, 218, 222–223, 226, 230, 231
Peace Brigades International, 8, 134, 137
perfidy, 12
perfidy based lawfare, 130–131
Plessy vs. Ferguson (1896), 180
political pacifism, 172–173
Posner, Eric, 119, 122
post conflict reconciliation, 6
power
Arendt on, 156
civil subversion and, 155–156
coercive power of international law, 120, 121, 132
coercive power of state adhering to human rights, 152
dialogic power, 174
hostage taking by non-state actors and, 187
in nonviolent resistance, 174, 175
in political pacifism, 172
media technology as soft power weapon, 104–105, 106, 109, 111–112, 118
nonviolent power in pacifism of King, 170–171
of civilian peacekeepers, 137, 138, 141
of media coverage of war, 94, 95, 100, 102
political power of secessionists, 153, 155, 161
soft power, 1, 2, 35, 77, 82, 83, 97
white power structure in Brown decision, 179–180
precautions
in law of armed conflict (LOAC), 90, 100–101
prisoners of war (POW), 12
agent based differentiation and *jus in bello* goals, 207–209, 215
legal requirements for attaining rights of, 12
legality of taking for unprivileged combatants, 203–205
removal of ongoing threat justification of, 211
status of unlawful combatants in United States and, 203
vs. hostage taking, 186–187, 209–215
propaganda, 10, 89–90, *See also* media warfare
as soft war tactic, 1–2, 4, 10, 35
by ISIS, 113–114
defined, 89
erosion of law of armed conflict by, 94–95, 96, 98–100, 101
legitimacy and, 92–93
permissible responses to, 217, 219, 221, 222
proportionality, 3
appropriate use of in soft war, 4
as equivalence, 217–218
economic sanctions and, 45, 53, 61
in *jus ad bellum*, 91
in *jus in bello*, 220
in law of armed conflict (LOAC), 90
media coverage of civilian casualties and, 94–95
media warfare and, 102
morally permissible targeting and, 41
permissibility of economic sanctions and, 45
proportionate self-defense, 14, 91, 218–220, 231–232
cyber warfare and, 223–226
economic sanctions and, 221–223, 226–229
in Tallinn Manual, 223
just and unjust lawfare and, 221–223, 229–231
unarmed conflict and, 217–218
provocation
in Birmingham action, 167–168, 176–179, 182–183
in nonviolent resistance, 9
in segregation, 180–181
psychological operations (PSYOPS)
defined, 89

Raison d'Etat, 189
reprisals, 218–220
Rhodesia, 50, 56
Rights of War and Peace (Grotius), 19
Rumsfeld, Donald, 107
Russell, Larry, 167
Russia, 87
conditional sale and, 63, 72–73
cyber attacks from Russian Business Network, 80, 82
hostage taking and, 190, 193
information warfare of, 44
Rwandan genocide, 143

sanctions, 1, 2, 5, 6, *See also* conditional sale; targeted sanctions; UN Security Council
anti-sanctions activist groups and, 50
as a paradox, 52
as comparable to siege warfare, 50

sanctions (cont.)
as substitute for war, 51
as war, 28–30
as war against Iraq, 29–30, 45, 50, 53, 55
civilian immunity and, 7
comprehensive sanctions, 7
counterdiscriminate sanctions, 56
defined, 65
future of, 59–60
history of during WW I and II, 51–52
history of post-WWII, 52–53
humanitarian consequences of, 49, 50, 53–54, 58, 59–60
impact on vulnerable populations, 29, 55, 56
impermissible tactics of, 42
indiscriminate sanctions, 54–56, 60
just war theory and, 29, 53, 61
lack of moral scrutiny for, 29
lawfulness of, 219
moral legitimacy and, 50–51, 53
on Iran, 4, 54–56, 60
on Iraq, 4, 6, 59, 226
on Rhodesia, 56
on South Africa, 50, 56
permissibility of, 45, 46
proportionality and, 61
proportionate self-defense and, 221–223, 226–229
purpose of, 49–51, 60
rise of black market and, 56
sanctions decade, 53
United States as primary advocate for, 52
vs. conditional sale, 66, 76
Schweitzer, Christine, 137, 147
self-defense, 3, 14, 15, 65, 93, 100, *See also* proportionate self-defense
Aquinas and Augustine on, 39–40
belligerents use of in international law and, 125
countermeasures and, 14
hostage taking and kidnapping and, 213–215, 216
personal pacifism and, 172
right to proportionate, 218–220
UN Charter and, 14
self-determination
human rights and civil subversion and, 157–158
Shalit, Gilad, 189, 191, 197, 200
sieges, 7, 51
Singer, J. David, 19, 21
Small, Melvin, 19, 21
smart sanctions. *See* sanctions; targeted sanctions
soft law
need for soft war, 86–87
soft power, 1, 2, 35, 77, 82, 83, 97
media technology as soft power weapon, 104–105, 106, 109, 111–112, 118
soft war
advantages of for nations engaging in, 83
appropriate rules of engagement in, 4
as adjunct to hard war & as stand-alone set of strategies, 2
as form of warfare, 5, 16–17, 31, 35
as political action, 35
as positive alternative to hard war, 87
as unrestricted warfare, 77, 83–84
humanitarianism in, 221–223
lack of international law on, 84–86
lawful acts in, 34, 219
media technology as weapon in, 11
necessity in, 48, 220–221
need for caution in use of, 48
need for soft law for, 86–87
neglect of in just war theory, 15
noncombatants as targets of, 217
permissible responses to, 218–219
tactics of, 1, 2, 35, 48
unjust threats and, 220
vs. hard war, 2, 221
Sony Pictures, 9, 30, 80
South Africa
economic sanctions against, 50, 56
Soweto Uprising of June 1976, 168
South Sudan, 147
state-sponsored hacktivism, 9, 10, 77, *See also* cyber warfare; hacktivism
damage and harm inflicted by, 82
lack of international law on, 84–86
need for soft law for, 86–87
North Korean on Sony Pictures, 80
on U.S. financial institutions, 10, 81
rise of, 80
Russian Business Network on Republic of Georgia, 80
vs. cyber warfare, 83
Stuxnet virus, 4, 10, 47

Taliban, 107, 200
Tallinn Manual, 10, 219, 224, 225,
proportionate self-defense in, 223

targeted sanctions, 7, 53–54, *See also* sanctions
arbitrariness of implementation of, 54
arms embargoes and, 56–57, 59
as permissible, 45
aviation bans, 58, 60
collateral damage of, 60
commodity sanctions, 58–59, 60
counterdiscriminate sanctions, 56
efficacy of, 56–59
future of, 59–60
humanitarian consequences of, 53–54, 58, 59–60
indiscriminate sanctions, 54–56, 60
just war theory and, 53
lack of moral scrutiny for, 51, 54, 60
of Liberia, 58
on Angola, 58
on Haiti, 58
on Libya, 58
on Rhodesia, 50
structural effects of, 59
targeted trade sanctions, 58–59
unresolved problems with, 49
visa bans and, 57
terrorism, 122, 225
as arbitrary assaults on individuals rights, 211, 213, 215
distinguishing of in international vs. non-international conflicts, 202–203
hostage taking and negotiations and, 13, 14, 197
legitimacy as goal in, 89
status of terrorists in Israel, 202
targeted sanctions and, 59, 65
terrorists as unlawful combatants in U.S. law, 203
unjust lawfare and, 230
vs. cyber attacks, 223, 225–226
Thurman, Howard, 169
torture
indeterminacy based lawfare and, 128–130
truth and reconciliation commissions, 43

UN peacekeeping, 135
UN Security Council, 50, 60, 138
arbitrariness of sanctions of, 54
sanctions against Iraq by, 6, 29, 50
sanctions against Liberia by, 58
sanctions against Libya by, 58
sanctions against Rhodesia by, 50, 56
sanctions against South Africa by, 28, 50, 56
sanctions during WW I and II and, 51–52
sanctions post-WWII, 52–53
unarmed conflicts, 2, *See also* soft war
as war, 5, 16–17, 25, 31
determining combatant status in, 27–28
economic sanctions and, 226–229
law of armed conflict (LOAC) in, 25
liability and, 5
noncombatant immunity and, 14
proportionate self-defense and, 217–218, 231–232
United Kingdom
no-concession policy towards hostage taking of, 191–192
United Nations Charter, 91, 126, 218
sanctions and, 50, 52, 53
self-defense and, 14
United States, 120
as primary advocate for sanctions, 52
cyber attacks on U.S. financial institutions, 10, 81
mediatization of war by, 11, 107–111
no-concession policy towards hostage taking of, 191–192
POWs as unlawful combatants in, 187
terrorists as unlawful combatants in, 203
unlawful combatants, 202, 203
unprivileged status of in international law, 205–207, 215

Versailles peace process, 43
Vietnam War, 107, 109–111, 180
visa bans, 57
Vitoria, Francisco, 37–38, 41
von Clausewitz, Carl, 19

Wallis, Tim, 136
Walzer, Michael, 2–3, 19, 38, 40, 41
nonparticipating civilians and, 37
on command responsibility, 208
on immunity, 201
war, 1–3, 14, *See also* cyber warfare; just war theory; media warfare; mediatization of war; soft war; prisoners of war (POW)
coercive power of international law in, 120, 121, 132
conditions stipulating, 5, 16
definitions of, 18
economic sanctions as, 28–30

war (cont.)
  ILA definition of, 19
  in international law, 16
  intensity of hostilities in definition of, 21–22, 31
  juridical definitions of war, 19
  lawfare as form of, 26, 122–125
  liability for unjust warfare, 231
  no adjudicating authority in definition of, 22–23
  noncombatant immunity and, 215
  non-kinetic tactics as warfare, 31
  normative and legal significance of defining, 17–19
  omission of aims of belligerents in definition of, 23–25
  organized armed groups in definition of, 20
  pacifist critique of, 170–174
  participatory liability and, 202, 231
  political definitions of, 19
  presumptive last resort and, 150
  sociological definitions, 19
  soft war and unarmed conflict as possible form of, 5, 16–17, 31
  state-sponsored cyber attacks as, 30–31
  uniformed combatants and, 201, 205, 206,
  vs. soft war, 2, 221
WikiLeaks, 79
Witness for Peace and Christian Peacemaker Teams, 140